SCIENTIFIC VALUES
AND CIVIC VIRTUES

SCIENTIFIC VALUES
AND CIVIC VIRTUES

Edited by

Noretta Koertge

OXFORD
UNIVERSITY PRESS
2005

OXFORD
UNIVERSITY PRESS

Oxford University Press, Inc., publishes works that further
Oxford University's objective of excellence
in research, scholarship, and education.

Oxford   New York
Auckland   Cape Town   Dar es Salaam   Hong Kong   Karachi
Kuala Lumpur   Madrid   Melbourne   Mexico City   Nairobi
New Delhi   Shanghai   Taipei   Toronto

With offices in
Argentina   Austria   Brazil   Chile   Czech Republic   France   Greece
Guatemala   Hungary   Italy   Japan   Poland   Portugal   Singapore
South Korea   Switzerland   Thailand   Turkey   Ukraine   Vietnam

Published by Oxford University Press, Inc.
198 Madison Avenue, New York, New York 10016

www.oup.com

Oxford is a registered trademark of Oxford University Press

Library of Congress Cataloging-in-Publication Data
Scientific values and civic virtues / edited by Noretta Koertge.
    p.   cm.
Includes bibliographical references and index.
ISBN-13 978-0-19-517225-6; 978-0-19-517224-9 (pbk.)
ISBN 0-19-517225-6; 0-19-517224-8 (pbk.)
1. Political science.   2. Civil society.   3. Democracy.
4. Science—Political aspects. I. Koertge, Noretta.
JA80.S37 2005
300—dc22   2004058133

1 3 5 7 9 8 6 4 2

Printed in the United States of America
on acid-free paper

Acknowledgments

This project arose out of Tuesday lunch conversations around the *Stammtisch* at a local pizzeria. Most of the regulars are retired historians and philosophers of science, but sometimes a biologist, an economist, a professor of Near East Studies, or a twelve-year-old drops by to liven up our "seminar." We are a pretty diverse lot—there's a practicing Catholic, an old union organizer, a closet Republican (so I suspect), a Red Sox fan—and our debates can get pretty heated. Would the discovery of life on Mars have a big cultural impact? How will the gay marriage controversy play out? What are the real roots of terrorism? Sometimes the disagreement gets so intense that the twelve-year-old calls "Time out!" and tries to turn our attention to less controversial issues, such as questions about the literal meaning of the Latin spells in the Harry Potter books. But on one topic we could all easily agree: the quality of public debate in contemporary society is seriously deficient. And we feared that some of our university colleagues were part of the problem. What could be done?

We didn't want to just write another book protecting science from postmodernism. Many powerful books have shown how the pictures of science advocated by sociologists of knowledge and postmodernist critics are internally incoherent and factually mistaken. Instead, we wanted to provide a positive message. Though not perfect by any means, the way that scientists solve problems and resolve conflicts is probably the best example of rational discourse that we have today. And so with the ongoing support of the "lunch bunch" (thanks, folks!), I set out to assemble essays that would show how the values that are so salient in science could serve as a resource for the fostering of a respect for reason and integrity in public life.

I also want to acknowledge the hard work and enthusiasm of the contributors. They not only prepared their own essays in a timely fashion but also commented on each other's articles. Deborah Rush deciphered my glosses, formatted the manuscript, and helped prepare the index. Thanks to my department and Indiana University for providing office space and support for emeriti faculty.

I want to recognize the direct contributions that my parents, though both long dead, have made to this volume. My father called himself a "modern farmer" because he was one of the first in our community to use hybrid seed corn and fertilizer. I admired his habit of constantly looking for ways to reduce toil—and his most important resource was science. He was pleased when I began my studies in chemistry. My mother's great intellectual loves were poetry and political science. I successfully resisted the first, but did please her by entering Elks Club essay contests—the topics were always along the lines of "What America Means to Me." In this book, the two human endeavors that were so important to my parents are linked together—science and democracy.

Contents

Contributors

FREDERICK B. CHURCHILL is Professor Emeritus of History and Philosophy of Science at Indiana University. His books include *Huxley's Problems of Relative Growth* (ed.) and *Selected Letters and Documents of August Weismann* (ed.).

STEVEN M. DeLUE is Professor of Political Science at Miami University and Senior Associate Dean in the College of Arts and Science. His research and scholarship focuses in the area of political theory, with a special interest in modern and contemporary thinking. His books include *Political Obligation in a Liberal State* and *Political Thinking, Political Theory and Civil Society*.

BARBARA FORREST is Professor of History and Political Science at Southeastern Louisiana University. She is coauthor of *Creationism's Trojan Horse: The Wedge of Intelligent Design* (OUP, 2004).

ALLAN FRANKLIN is Professor of Physics at the University of Colorado. His recent works include *Are There Really Neutrinos? An Evidential History and Selectivity* and *Discord: Two Problems of Experiment*.

EDWARD GRANT is Distinguished Professor Emeritus of History and Philosophy of Science at Indiana University. His recent books include *God and Reason in the Middle Ages* and *The Foundations of Modern Science in the Middle Ages*.

PAUL R. GROSS is University Professor Emeritus at the University of Virginia. The author of many papers in molecular biology, he is also coauthor of a provocative and influential book *Higher Superstition: The Academic Left and Its Quarrels with Science*.

GERALD HOLTON is Mallinckrodt Professor of Physics and Professor of the History of Science, Emeritus, at Harvard University. His recent books include *Ivory Bridges: Connecting Science and Society* and *The Advancement of Science and Its Burdens.*

PERVEZ HOODBHOY is Professor of Physics at Quaid-e-Azam University in Islamabad, Pakistan. He is author of *Islam and Science: Religious Orthodoxy and the Battle for Rationality* and the editor of *Education and the State: Fifty Years of Pakistan.*

NORETTA KOERTGE is Professor Emeritus of History and Philosophy of Science at Indiana University and Editor-in-Chief of *The New Dictionary of Scientific Biography.* Her recent books include *A House Built on Sand: Exposing Postmodernist Myths about Science* (ed.) and *Professing Feminism: Education and Indoctrination in Women's Studies.*

JOHN C. MOORE is Professor Emeritus of History at Hofstra University. His publications include *Pope Innocent III (1160/61–1216): To Root up and to Plant* and *Love in Twelfth-Century France.*

MEERA NANDA is a fellow of the American Council of Learned Societies at Columbia University, New York. She is the author of *Prophets Facing Backward: Postmodern Critiques of Science and Hindu Nationalism in India* and *Planting the Future: A Resource Guide to Sustainable Agriculture in the Third World.*

KEITH PARSONS is Professor of Philosophy at the University of Houston–Clear Lake. He is author of *Drawing Out Leviathan: Dinosaurs and the Science Wars* and editor of the anthology *The Science Wars: Debating Scientific Knowledge and Technology.*

MICHAEL RUSE is Lucyle T. Werkmeister Professor of Philosophy at Florida State University. His recent books include *Evolution and Its Values: Is Science a Social Construct?* and *Darwin and Design: Does Evolution Have a Purpose?*

ROSE-MARY SARGENT is Professor of Philosophy at Merrimack College. Her recent books include *The Diffident Naturalist: Robert Boyle and the Philosophy of Experiment* and *Selected Philosophical Works of Bacon* (ed.).

PHILIP A. SULLIVAN is Professor of Aerospace Engineering at the University of Toronto's Institute for Aerospace Studies. His research interests include hypersonic flow, air cushion vehicle dynamics, and biological fluid flows.

SCIENTIFIC VALUES
AND CIVIC VIRTUES

What Science Can Offer
Contemporary Democracy

Noretta Koertge

This volume explores the positive relationship that exists between science and a liberal democracy. It is a response to widespread concern about the declining quality of deliberations intended to promote the common good. There are steadily expanding opportunities for collecting cogent information and communicating arguments, yet we seem to have an increasing use of slash-and-burn tactics in political debates. There is also a growing cynicism about corruption and the influence of special interest groups. Political scientists have responded to this crisis by emphasizing the importance of civil society, the traditions that form a link between institutions and the intentions of individual citizens. In this volume, we argue that the value system of science is an important resource for restoring a tradition of respect for public reason.

It is an axiom of political philosophy that democracy of any flavor requires not only certain kinds of institutions (e.g., a constitution) but also an educated populace. Citizens need to be well informed; it is equally important for them to have internalized civic virtues (e.g., tolerance for the viewpoints of others).

Science has traditionally been viewed as an important component of education for citizenship. Basic knowledge about how our world works is obviously important in an age of technology. It can also help dispel the myths and superstitions that lead to the harming of those who are unlike ourselves.

Yet in many parts of the university today, science, or technoscience as it is sometimes called, is viewed as a Golem, an enemy of civil society. This intellectual animus toward science has many roots and takes many guises. The philosophical stance called postmodernism posits an epistemic equivalence between the "sciences" of every culture: folk beliefs about cosmology or the causes of disease and disaster are declared to be just as adequate as those of contemporary science. At the same time, playing on understandable fears about the biosphere and weapons of war, postmodernism declares science to be morally inferior to folk beliefs about nature. There is also a concern that traditional cultures will lose their authenticity in the face of Western culture. Perhaps as a tacit recognition of the centrality of science today, postcolonialists make an especially strong effort to prevent the assimilation and appreciation of scientific ideas in countries outside of North America and Europe.

Partisans of the world's major religions, Christianity, Islam, and Hinduism, also find modern science a threat to their vision of a moral community. There is anxiety that the expanding success of science and its underlying naturalistic philosophy will leave no room for an active God. There are also objections to the use of stem cells and other specific lines of research. These fears of science can lead to undemocratic attempts to place restrictions on what students learn and what scientists can study.

This volume argues instead that a better knowledge and appreciation of the values embedded in scientific inquiry are essential for a liberal civil society. We do not rehearse here the importance of having a populace that understands the basic content and empirical methods of science. Rather, we describe the basic value system of organized science—its devices for encouraging systematic public criticism, its commitment to seeking out problems and solving them, its communitarian tradition of sharing its findings freely and openly—and show how these can serve as a resource to reinvigorate our dedication to public reason.

It is noncontroversial (or at least it used to be!) to view science as incorporating a variety of intellectual virtues, such as honesty and precision of language. Less well explored is the possibility that other aspects of the scientific value system that are only indirectly connected with truth-seeking might also prove useful. For example, the scientific community is truly international, and although there can at times be national styles and rivalries operating in science, it is nevertheless our best example of a well-functioning global enterprise. Science also provides a striking example of an activity dedicated to the production of a public good—scientific knowledge is, for the most part, free to everyone.

It was the philosopher Karl Popper who best described the commonalities between scientific inquiry and what he called the "open society." Both require traditions that foster an arena where people can voice disagreements and scrutinize conflicting views. If dissent is the soul of democracy, so is criticism the motor of scientific research. But in order that disagreement not generate disrespect, protagonists are enjoined to speak clearly and listen attentively before putting forward contrary arguments.

James Buchanan's characterization of democracy as "government by discussion" and Amartya Sen's analysis of the "ideal of public reasoning" could equally well be descriptions of the scientific community. Scientific debates are sometimes easier to resolve than are debates over public policy, but the same principles of intellectual integrity and openness to new evidence are crucial in each arena. The hope of this volume is that a clearer understanding of how science works might be helpful in improving public reasoning.

Although our project presupposes a positive take on the scientific enterprise, it in no way implies that scientists behave honorably at all times or that scientific institutions are in no need of improvement. Rather, what we will do is to look for examples of virtues in action when science is at its best. We also investigate the circumstances that tend to undermine good behavior. We then ask whether what we have discovered might perhaps serve both as inspiration and as a practical resource for improving our habits of discourse in civic society.

Part I

The Nexus between Scientific Values and Civic Virtues

Two things fill me with wonder: the starry sky above
and the moral law within.

—Immanuel Kant

Part I begins with two essays that lay out the two domains discussed in this volume. In chapter 1, Noretta Koertge reviews the attempts by sociologists and historians of science to characterize the norms that guide the scientific community. To those who have somehow formed a positivistic conception of science, some of the core values she presents may be surprising, such as the emphasis on heuristic power, conceptual simplicity, mathematical tractability, and explanatory depth. Following Popper's account of scientific research, she presents science as a problem-solving activity marked by both cooperation and critical debate. These aspects of scientific discourse serve as good reminders of the qualities that should be encouraged in public deliberations.

In chapter 2, Steven DeLue begins with Kant's discussion of intellectual autonomy, or the ability of individuals to think for themselves. A necessary ingredient for the formation of an autonomous, rational, thinking self is a communal setting that fosters a comparison of views and ideas so that the result is what Kant calls "enlarged thought," or a universal standpoint. Here, science again can serve as a paradigm. On the other hand, Kant's injunction to treat people as ends, not means, underscores the importance of preserving the autonomy of human subjects in scientific experiments. As Koertge points out

in chapter 1, the codification of ethical restrictions on the treatment of humans and animals is a fairly recent addition to the normative system of scientific inquiry.

Rawls's theory of political liberalism also stresses the importance of learning from debate and argument that is guided by the norms of public reason. But Rawls is less sanguine about the ability of pluralistic societies to maintain the values of a constitutional democracy when subgroups differ radically in their core views about religion and personal virtue. DeLue gives as examples the debates about prayer in schools and stem cell research. Science may not offer any solution to the controversy about prayer, but one can hope that a better popular understanding of embryonic development and the heuristic potential of therapeutic cloning might moderate some aspects of the second debate.

The nexus between science and civil society became explicit during the Enlightenment, but, as the next three chapters demonstrate, interactions between the value systems of natural philosophy and political theory predate the eighteenth century. In chapter 3, Edward Grant uses the example of Nicole Oresme, a natural philosopher who made important contributions to physics and economics, to illustrate the common elements in medieval conceptions of science and politics. Around 1370, King Charles

V commissioned Oresme to translate into French four Aristotelian works to be used by governmental officials. The reasons for his interest in books on ethics, politics, and economics are obvious. But he also requested Aristotle's *On the Heavens*, a treatise that Oresme described as the most beautiful and powerful book the world had ever seen. Yet Oresme included for the courtiers' delectation a long list of commentaries "opposing Aristotle."

At the end of chapter 3, Grant argues that the establishment of a scientific temperament—the habit of systematically organizing, analyzing, and disputing claims—began in the Latin West. He then contrasts the attitudes toward natural philosophy in medieval Islam. Although important classical works were translated into Arabic, for a variety of reasons that society never incorporated the critical methods of natural philosophy into their educational system and theology.

Whereas Grant focuses on the value system of natural philosophy, John Moore describes the evolution of ideas of civic virtue in prerevolutionary Europe. In chapter 4, he shows how Cicero's account of the duties of a citizen was revised and augmented as it was incorporated into a society ruled by princes and popes. For example, the influential collection known as the *Corpus Iuris Canonici* included stirring mottos such as "Let no one prefer custom to reason or truth." As the unit of society grew larger than the Greek *polis*, where citizens would have firsthand acquaintance of their rulers, new ways had to be developed to make rulers responsive to the body politic. In the thirteenth century, important new political concepts emerged. Reaffirming the Roman legal principle that "what touches all should be approved by all," the idea that people could elect representatives to advise or petition rulers on their behalf was slowly instantiated in both clerical and secular contexts.

Moore does not argue that any of these institutions were democracies in the modern sense—lessons about religious pluralism and equality before the law still had to be learned—but some of the key ingredients were now available. Moore ends chapter 4 with some cautionary considerations for those who posit too strong an overlap between the values of science and civic virtues. Whereas science begins by treating a hypothesis with "suspicion and hostility," as William James put it, modern civil society is based on a wholehearted *acceptance* of propositions about all people being created equal and having inalienable rights and a *conviction* that a government of, by, and for the people will not perish from this earth. On the face of it, the epistemological stance in science is quite different from the attitude of trust necessary for a functioning democracy.

In chapter 5, Rose-Mary Sargent discusses the birth of modern science, concentrating on Francis Bacon and the early Royal Society of London. Their enthusiasm for experimental knowledge and their conviction that it should be a cooperative undertaking sound quite familiar to the modern reader, but in other ways their image of science is interestingly different. Although Bacon often wrote of the power or utility of knowledge, he did not have a purely utilitarian goal in mind. He wrote that the true ends of knowledge are not profit, fame, or power. Neither is science for the "pleasure of the mind." Rather, natural philosophers should "cultivate truth in charity" and endow the human family with "new mercies."

Sargent describes how the gentlemen who began the scientific organization explicitly set out to include contributions from various social classes. The aristocrat Robert Boyle collaborated in the laboratory with laborers and ridiculed contemporaries who thought mechanical work was beneath them. Traditional enemies of England could also be included in the work of the scientific community—Charles II explicitly mandated that the Royal Society could "enjoy mutual intelligence and knowledge with all manner of strangers and foreigners." Thus, the *Transactions* were published in English to ensure a wide audience at home and in Latin in order to encourage an international exchange.

The early history of the interaction between the values required for naturalistic accounts of the world and those necessary for a decent society is a fascinating and inspiring story. And as Sargent remarks, it would be good for us to recapture some of the Baconian ideal of power tempered by intellectual modesty and charity.

I

A Bouquet of Scientific Values

Noretta Koertge

The project of this volume is to explore how scientific values might have a positive impact on the development of civic virtues within a society. Hence, our first order of business is to get a picture of what might fall under the rubric of scientific values. As is often the case, the word "science" in this chapter sometimes refers to the questions, claims, and arguments that scientists work with and at other times designates the institution dedicated to the production of that intellectual content. We will look at the norms that figure in both contexts.

My inquiry in this chapter differs from other topics that often come to the forefront when people hear the words "science" and "values" in close proximity. I want to look at the core values *within* science, not enter into a debate about the social value *of* science and technology. To ascribe a set of norms to the scientific community is not to assert that all scientists always act in accordance with them. However, it does imply that these values are generally evident in scientific practice.

A Brief Look at Sociological Accounts of Scientific Values

A good starting point is Talcott Parsons's list of four basic desiderata for scientific knowledge (Merton 1973, 270):

1. Logical clarity or precision
2. Logical consistency among claims
3. Generality of principles
4. Empirical validity

I suppose an Aquinas might remark that Parsons's norms could hardly be used to distinguish science from any other intellectually responsible bodies of knowledge. Systematic theology conforms to the first three desiderata and, by taking into consideration religious experience, makes a nod in the direction of the fourth. More needs to be said in order to capture the distinctive value ethos of science.

One aspect of science that is ignored in Parsons's list is the communal nature of scientific research. Bacon's dream of a new science included not only a new methodology but also a community dedicated to the task. His *New Atlantis* stressed the benefits of organized inquiry. In 1942 Robert Merton set out to describe the norms governing scientific institutions. He listed the following:

1. "Universalism" (scientific contributions should not be judged on the basis of the race, religion, national origin, etc., of the scientist)
2. Disinterestedness (science should not serve a particular social/political agenda)
3. Communality (scientific results should be freely shared)
4. Organized skepticism (Merton 1973, 267–278)

Merton does a better job than Parsons of demarcating science societies from many other communities. Theologians value faith more than skepticism. Although individuals may go through a process of doubt, trying to orchestrate a critical scrutiny of basic tenets in accordance with Merton's fourth norm would certainly not have a high priority in most religious communities. The openness of the scientific community regarding both who may join (second norm) and who may share the findings (norm three) is very unusual. Nation states set up barriers for citizenship, and the complex apparatus for copyrights and patents runs directly contrary to the scientific imperative to publish results for all to share.

Most controversial is whether science actually exemplifies Merton's second norm, *disinterestedness*, which echoes Max Weber's call in 1904 for a *wertfrei* social science. Weber himself spoke of the "endless . . . [and] almost incredibly wrong-headed misunderstanding[s]" that arose from his claim that it was possible and desirable that scientists not import "value-judgments" about the behavior of the humans he was studying into his scientific findings (Boyd, Gasper, and Trout 1991, 719). I return later to recent challenges to this norm, but suffice it to say that the successful separation of inquiry from a political agenda would sharply differentiate science from many other "information-generating" communities, such as "think tanks."

An astute student of history of science, Merton fully realized that his four norms did not fully capture the ethos of science. He wrote of the influence of the Puritan work ethic (Merton 1973, 229) and the norm of humility, quoting Newton's famous remarks about "standing on the shoulders of giants" and comparing himself to a boy playing with pretty pebbles on a beach "whilst the great ocean of truth lay all discovered before me" (303). Yet this same, purportedly humble, Newton engaged in all sorts of priority disputes, the most vicious being the battle with Leibniz over who should get credit for the discovery of the calculus. Merton soon collected dozens of examples of conflicts over whose name should be attached to a particularly important discovery. It was clear that his Edenic picture of disinterested scientists striving for truth that would be freely shared with everyone would not be complete without a discussion of the high value scientists placed on not only being the first to make some discovery but also being *recognized* as the person who got there first.

Scientists were ambivalent about this feature of their community. On the one hand, it was surely just a matter of common decency to be duly recognized. As

Robert Frost put it, "Of all crimes the worst is the theft of glory / Even more accursed than to rob the grave" (quoted in Merton 1973, 342). But on the other hand, science is a communal effort—everyone builds on the common body of knowledge. And given the fact that there are so many cases of simultaneous discoveries, was it not petty to spend so much energy on the analysis of photo finishes to see whose nose first crossed the line? Merton noted that this kind of scientific reward system played a useful function because it encouraged originality, but he also recognized that it encouraged a good deal of unproductive wrangling.

A fuller analysis of the premium placed on priority is found in David Hull's comprehensive study, *Science as a Process* (1988). Hull identifies three factors crucial to the scientific process: curiosity, credit, and checking (520). (We will learn more about both the nature of scientific curiosity and the requirements for severe testing when we look at Popper's account of science as problem solving.) In his account of scientific inquiry, Hull shifts the emphasis away from priority disputes per se and focuses instead on the practices of gaining recognition for oneself and giving credit to others.

The imperative to get credit for one's research findings pushes one to make those findings public and thereby take responsibility for any errors or sloppy methods they contain. Since more credit accrues to papers that make significant contributions to the field, scientists are motivated to work on important problems. Contrary to the opinions of some tenure committees, the sheer number of one's publications is not a very good measure of one's stature in the field, thus the interest in citation indexes, which rate a paper by looking at how often it is cited. Less formal evaluations, such as peer review, play a crucial role in the scientist's quest for external sources of funding. So credit not only satisfies scientists' egos but also animates the processes of problem solving, criticism, and dissemination that lie at the heart of modern science (Koertge 1990).

This description of the reward system in science may sound very familiar to us today. But it is worth pointing out that inquiries into nature have not always worked this way. In the so-called occult sciences, findings were either kept secret or attributed to some authority of mythic stature, such as Hermes Trismegistus. Furthermore, the process of gaining scientific recognition has certain distinctive elements not found in other fields. In science, results that turn out to be empirically inadequate quickly disappear from the active literature; this is one of the similarities with natural selection that Hull highlights. Unlike the situation in philosophy or literary criticism, there is no market for yet another critique of the phlogiston or caloric theories. One cannot garner fame simply by being outrageous and incomprehensible. (Recall Parsons's norm of clarity.)

The discussion of priority disputes and the pursuit of credit reveals the competitive side of science, but cooperation is also a crucial aspect of science. The requirement of publication ensures that each scientist can profit from the work of others. Through the mechanism of refereeing and peer review, scientists cooperate in keeping the corpus of findings of high quality. In this era of "big science," the teamwork aspects of science are more visible. (For a discussion of the general problem of coordinating scientific research, see the chapter titled "The Organization of Cognitive Labor" in Kitcher [1993].)

Philosophical Accounts of Intellectual Values in Science

The above accounts of scientific values grew out of an interest in the norms that are salient in scientific institutions. In the ideal situation, institutional norms reinforce the aims of the organization. As Hull put it, the hope in science is that one can do well by doing good! But what does it mean to do good science? Philosophers of science do not always agree on the details, but for our purposes here we will look for the broad similarities in the general pictures they provide. We will begin our discussion of the values intrinsic to science with a brief look at Popper's account of scientific inquiry.

Popper portrays science as a problem-solving activity. He not only agrees with Dewey in acknowledging the continuity between science and everyday life; he even draws parallels between the trial-and-error methods of an amoeba and Einstein (Popper 1972, 24)! But here we will focus on the distinctive elements in the way scientists approach problems. I follow Popper's overall account (see, e.g., Popper 1963, ch. 10), but some of the examples are my own.

The Nature of Scientific Problems

No inquiry begins in a vacuum. *Violated expectations* are one source of scientific problems. A central challenge for early astronomers was what Plato called the problem of the planets: in general, celestial bodies, such as the sun, moon, and stars, move across the sky in smooth arcs. However, it was discovered that the planets wander around the sky irregularly. Can one describe precisely how the planets move and explain why they move differently from the other heavenly bodies? Ptolemy, Copernicus, and Kepler each offered a different solution to this problem.

Here is another example of a scientific problem caused by violated expectations: in 1896, Becquerel was studying fluorescence. In a typical experiment, he would expose a chunk of a mineral to the sun. When it was placed on a photographic plate wrapped in black paper, an image would form on the plate. Becquerel assumed that the mineral had absorbed energy from the sun that was then emitted in the form of X-rays. Late in February, it was too cloudy to expect good results, so Becquerel laid the rock and the plate aside. When he developed the plate a few days later, he discovered to his amazement that the image was clearer and stronger than ever before. Somehow the mineral (which was potassium uranyl sulfate) was emitting radiation without the help of the sun! And it was thus that he detected what we know to be radioactivity. Madame Curie later studied which atoms were responsible for the radiation and showed that the rock also contained radium as a decay product.

Problems also arise out of a *quest for deep explanations*. Even if a scientist is lucky enough to discover a generalization that seems to have no exceptions, he or she is still faced with questions: What causes the regularity? Why do things happen just that way? For example, early astronomers asked why the sun rose every day in the east. Some said it was because the sun moved in a circle around the earth. Later this geocentric theory was replaced with a heliocentric theory. In either case, a further question arose: what caused the sun (or the earth) to move? According to Aristotle, there was a Prime Mover. Other natural philosophers suggested a law of circular inertia, saying a wheel would move forever if there were no friction. Newton explained the regular motion in terms of linear inertia and the force of gravity.

There are many other cases in which the problem is to explain a regularity. By the end of the eighteenth century, after the work of Boyle and Charles, everyone knew that gases expanded on heating. But why? Caloric theorists said that heat was an ethereal substance that flowed into gases; as a result of this inflow of heat the gases took up more room. Kinetic theorists said that heat was kinetic energy; hot gases expanded because their molecules moved faster. Both sides agreed on the regularity to be explained, but they offered competing explanations of it. Mendeleev and other chemists of the late nineteenth century wondered why the elements should arrange themselves so nicely into a Periodic Table. Bohr wondered why the wavelengths of the spectral lines of hydrogen should fit the simple mathematical formula discovered by Balmer.

As a science develops, a new sort of problem often arises: can one find a unified theory that covers two or more domains that have previously been treated separately? Scientists view it as problematic when their best scientific accounts *lack unity*. For example, traditionally organic chemistry (which deals primarily with covalent compounds) and inorganic chemistry (which is mainly concerned with ionic compounds) were considered to be quite distinct fields. At the time, people believed that naturally occurring organic compounds, such as urea, could not be synthesized in the laboratory because they contained a vital life force. However, today's theories of chemical bonding apply equally well to inorganic and organic materials.

Before Galileo, it was held that terrestrial bodies and celestial bodies obeyed different laws. Galileo (and later Newton) gave a unified account of the motions of all bodies. A pressing problem in physics today is the search for a unified field theory—a theory that would successfully combine relatively theory and quantum mechanics. And psychologists are looking for a general theory of learning. Behaviorists can account for some kinds of learning; cognitive psychology provides explanations for other types of learning. But one would like to find a single theory that provides a comprehensive account.

Problems can also arise when a *conflict between theories* is discovered. Often, the task of finding a unifying explanation becomes more pressing because of inconsistencies between the component theories. Contradictions can also arise between theories that appear to cover quite different domains. For example, the biggest objection to Copernicus's astronomical theory was its conflict with Aristotelian physics, according to which nothing could continue to move without a mover. And a strong contemporary objection to Darwin's theory of biological evolution was its inconsistency with Kelvin's geophysical calculation of the age of the earth. (It turned out later that Kelvin's thermal estimates were wrong because they did not include the heat generated by radioactive decay.)

Each of the four types of scientific problems discussed above arises out of a rich background of information and expectations. New scientific theories are invented when scientists are faced with questions: Why did my old theory or set of unconscious expectations fail? What causes this regularity that I have observed? Can I unify these two branches of science? Or can I resolve the inconsistencies between them?

It is noteworthy that although the popular image of a scientist is someone who is curious about everything, the question of how many leaves are on the tree in my front yard is not a scientific problem *unless* we supply a context in which the answer might clash with or supplement our general understanding of trees. The Newton quote about playing with pebbles on a beach is misleading if we take it to mean that scientists collect facts indiscriminately.

Some of the four problem types described above are not unique to science. Many of our practical problems of existence arise because the commonsense generalizations we make about the world, including other people, are violated. And myth makers are looking for what they deem to be deep, unifying explanations. As I describe below, however, the sorts of explanations that scientists value are quite different from myths.

In a well-developed scientific field, problems arise within a body of knowledge that is generally more extensive, more detailed, and better systematized than that of other domains. Furthermore, the scientific community for the most part actively rewards people who expose contradictions or gaps within the body of science. Folklore and religious systems, by contrast, are often embedded within conservative institutions that discourage criticism or revision of the traditional beliefs. Because scientific knowledge is so well articulated, it is relatively easy to discover flaws in it, and the norms of science encourage us to take such problems very seriously.

The Evaluation of Solutions to Scientific Problems

Popper is well known for his requirement that scientific theories should be *falsifiable*, namely that they should be formulated in such a manner that *if* they are incorrect, it should be possible in principle to discover their falsity through empirical testing. He uses the term "theory" to include all sorts of conjectural solutions to scientific problems. We could also speak of tentative solutions or hypotheses.

Because of the structure of a scientific problem, any proposed solution to it must have certain characteristics if it is to be taken seriously. Consider the first type of problem: to explain why our expectations are violated, we need a tentative solution that would account for both the exceptions and the normal states of affairs we had expected. For example, a good answer to the problem of the planets' irregular motions must also explain the sun's regular motion.

When the problem is to give a deep explanation of a regularity (such as the Balmer formula for hydrogen spectral lines), a proposed solution will typically have many other consequences as well (e.g., a formula for the spectral lines of sodium). In the case of the search for unification, obviously any proposed unifying theory must have more content than either of the separate fields. And generally such a theory will have lots of new consequences as well. (For example, the unified theory of chemical bonding covered not only traditional organic and inorganic compounds, but also a whole new domain of organometallic compounds, such as hemoglobin.)

So even before they are subjected to direct testing, tentative solutions to scientific problems must satisfy many constraints. When I was editor of a scholarly journal, I fairly frequently received papers from laypeople proposing esoteric new theories of space, time, the cosmos, what have you. The authors sometimes find it difficult to understand that their theories are not even starters because as nonscientists they had failed to understand the *structure* of the scientific problems they are trying to address. It can happen that a problem can be solved only by challenging the presuppositions underlying the way the problem is conceived. But a Galileo or an Einstein justifies the problem shift while putting forward the proposed solution.

Scientists test conjectures by comparing them with experimental results and observations. But not all tests have the same epistemic value. Collecting data in such a way that it would be impossible to uncover counterexamples to the conjecture has no probative value. Bacon gives an early example of what we might call "no-risk" data collecting in his *Novum Organon*:

> It was a good answer that was made by one who, when they showed him hanging in a temple a picture of those who had paid their vows as having escaped shipwreck, and would have him say whether he did not now acknowledge the power of the gods— "Aye," asked he again, "but where are they painted that were drowned after their vows?" And such is the way of all superstition." (bk. I, aphorism LXVI; Bacon 1960)

By looking only for examples of survivors who prayed, one would never happen upon a refuting example, namely, a beleaguered sailor who made a vow but nevertheless drowned at sea.

Popper adds to Bacon's point by stressing that good scientific tests should be severe ones, that is, they should be deliberately designed, using our general background knowledge, to probe the conjecture at its weakest point—that is, to find a refutation if one does in fact exist. A severe test is one that tests the least plausible claims of a theory.

For example, when Lawrence Kohlberg put forward a theory about the development of moral reasoning in children, he was well advised to test it on children from Turkey and Taiwan. We might expect a theory developed on the basis of experience with kids in Boston to fail when applied to children from quite different cultures and religions. (As it turned out, the Kohlberg theory passed this severe test. However, he did not include girls in his test population, and one of his students, Carol Gilligan, believes that his account does not work well for young women.)

Similarly, theories about the universality of the oedipal complex should be tested on aborigines, not just members of the Viennese middle class, and theories about language learning should apply to deaf and blind children. Conjectures about geological change and biological evolution should be tested, where possible, by data from other planets. Physicists know that theories often fail under conditions of high energy or high velocity, and often processes at the micro level violate generalizations that work well with medium-sized objects. For this reason, physicists want to build ever bigger accelerators for smaller and smaller particles and new kinds of telescopes to probe deeper into space.

There are ongoing debates among philosophers of science about the precise characteristics of scientific testing and about the exact epistemological status of theories that have passed severe tests. All that I have attempted to do here is illustrate the special kinds of evaluations that scientists bring to bear on both the problems they undertake to solve and the sorts of solutions they find scientifically acceptable.

Assessments of Research Programs

Popper's account of scientific problem solving highlights the critical methods that scientists employ in their research. Inconsistencies between a theory and experiment or among theories pose pressing problems that cry out solutions. Popper also emphasizes scientists' preference for deep explanatory theories. (When I attended his famous seminar at the London School of Economics in the 1960s, Popper often referred to a little German rhyme to the effect that it was nice to know that $2 + 2 = 4$, but what we wanted were more interesting truths.) In the search for theories that give accurate, detailed predictions about a wide variety of phenomena, scientists are often guided by views of the nature of things that cannot be directly tested but that can nevertheless be evaluated.

Gerald Holton describes the influence of ideals that he calls "themata," and his book *Thematic Origins of Scientific Thought: Kepler to Einstein* (1988) gives many examples of how they operate. For Newton, conceptual simplicity played an important role. His first rule of philosophy read, "Nature is pleased with simplicity, and affects not the pomp of superfluous causes" (quoted in Holton 1998, xxxii). Einstein considered symmetry and unification to be more than aesthetic desiderata; they provided powerful heuristic aids to the development of more satisfactory theories. Themata cannot be criticized directly through experiment, but they can be evaluated in terms of their fruitfulness.

A somewhat related kind of evaluation occurs in Lakatos's (1978) account of the history of science in terms of what he called "research programs." An example of how research programs are evaluated is provided by the dispute between corpuscular and wave conceptions of light in the early nineteenth century. Both Descartes and Newton conceived of light as behaving like tiny corpuscles. This approach fit in nicely with an atomistic worldview that hoped to explain all phenomena in terms of the interactions of particles. The wave theory, on the other hand, saw light as a propagating disturbance in an invisible medium (later called the ether). Neither account could be subjected to direct experimental test. Each account had positive successes: the simplest explanation of reflection (and the one that beginning students use today) was in terms of rebounding corpuscles. The wave account gave a more straightforward explanation of Young's two-slit experiment but could not specify the properties of the elastic medium it had to postulate. (For a detailed account of this episode, see Worrall [1976].)

In a dispute such as this, Lakatos (1978) says that scientific theories are evaluated not simply in terms of their empirical record but also in terms of the *fruitfulness* and *heuristic power* of the research programs in which they are embedded. In the early history of optics, it was much easier to work out models of optical phenomena by postulating corpuscles that obeyed the familiar laws of mechanics. Eventually, scientists developed more facility in dealing with modeling optical phenomena using waves. In this case, there was not a moment of instant refutation of the corpuscular theory. Rather, it became a situation where the corpuscular heuristic was running out of steam and the tools of wave theory were starting to predict novel phenomena.

In an essay written well after the publication of his famous account of the development of science as paradigm change, Kuhn (1977) argues that certain special kinds of value judgments figure importantly in the evaluation of scientific theories, and for this reason scientists may in good faith disagree. An example might arise if one scientist placed a higher value on fruitfulness and generality while another placed more emphasis on accuracy. Kuhn emphasizes that the differing values he has in mind are such things as accuracy, consistency, scope, simplicity, and fruitfulness (322). He is not talking about the values of either an engineer or an ideologue. I would simply add that, as time progresses, it is often the case that a theory is improved in such a way that it ranks high on all five of Kuhn's desiderata so hard choices are no longer necessary.

Feasibility Considerations

I have described the value scientists place on the explanatory power of a theory: its empirical adequacy, precision, generality, and depth, its conceptual economy, and its ability to provide a deep unification of previously disparate fields. In addition, scientists prefer research programs that have heuristic power. I should now briefly mention the more practical desiderata that play a role in the direction that scientific inquiry takes. Other things being equal, scientists certainly prefer projects that are feasible with today's conceptual, mathematical, and experimental resources. The last point is obvious: stellar parallax could not be detected with the telescopes available in Galileo's time, and this meant that the appraisal of Copernican theory had to be less direct than people would have liked. Some cosmological theories today are distant from readily available observations. It is a definite mark against a theory if it is impractical to test it. Hence, the great emphasis on the development of new instruments.

The mathematical or computational tractability of a theory is also extremely important. Often the scientists themselves invent the needed mathematics—familiar examples are Newton/Leibniz and the calculus, and the development of statistical tools by Galton and Pearson.

A related consideration is the availability of what Ron Giere (1988) calls "cognitive resources." Cutting-edge research often requires people who have various kinds of specialized expertise, be it in theory construction, software development, or the design of laboratory apparatus. Putting together a good team may be difficult, either because of local constraints when one is working far from major research centers or because certain skills are rare in the scientific community as a whole. This is one reason that it sometimes takes time to cultivate active scientific programs in developing countries even when money is readily available.

And it goes without saying that one important dimension of feasibility assessments is the availability of sources of funding. From early times, scientific research has been subsidized by wealthy patrons or powerful institutions. The motivations of these sponsors are mixed: Prince Cosimo was pleased to have Galileo name the planets of Jupiter after him, but he also saw the military and commercial potential of the telescope. (To scope out the enemy before he can identify you is obviously an advantage; it was also a boon to merchants who could first see arriving cargo ships.) I now look at how the prospect of practical applications figures into the array of scientific values.

The Value of Experimenta Fructus

Bacon described two aspects of scientific activity: first, there were *experimenta luxus*, experiments of light, which were designed to reveal the underlying workings of nature. These would lead to *experimenta fructus*, fruitful experiments, which would produce all sorts of new processes that would relieve the pain and drudgery of human experience. From the days of the Royal Society of London, people outside of science have traditionally placed a very high value on the new medications and technologies that result from science. In this chapter, I have placed less emphasis on the scientific goal of improving the human condition for several reasons. First of all, there is a tendency to conflate the explanatory and the ameliorative aspects of science. Slogans such as the old DuPont advertisement, "Better things for better living through chemistry," can easily lead us to focus too much on the applied side of science.

This conflation is encouraged by scientists themselves in their attempts to secure funding. Academics in every discipline may overplay the anticipated utility of their research efforts. (A philosopher friend once told me of his success in convincing the Office of Naval Research that his inquiries into nonstandard logic would help admirals make better decisions. And a colleague in history of medieval science was once encouraged by a National Science Foundation program officer to put the anachronistic word "energy" in his title simply because Congress was vetting projects for "relevance.") Scientists who would never dream of slanting their data are under tremendous pressure to present a rosy, imaginative picture of the utilitarian value of their project. And, of course, there is some historical justification for such optimism: seemingly esoteric projects, such as providing a satisfactory theoretical model for black body radiation, can have unforeseen important practical applications, such as the photoelectric cell.

But if we wish to understand the value system of scientists themselves, I would argue that the goal of understanding nature is ascendant. The kinds of problems that excite theoretical scientists can be quite different from those that drive inventors and engineers. Experimentalists probably fall somewhere in between. We should not overlook the fact, however, that many great scientists contribute in both areas. Galileo improved the telescope and invented devices for measuring pulse rate and the temperature of the atmosphere. Lavoisier investigated the efficacy of various chemical fertilizers. Fermi's legacy includes not only theoretical work on neutrinos and the statistical properties of particles known as fermions but also the production of the first controlled nuclear chain reaction, under the stands of the

University of Chicago stadium. The popular image of scientists as Dr. Frankensteins obsessed with obtaining power and control over the universe may be a fair description of ancient alchemists who were looking for the Philosopher's Stone, but it is a gross distortion of scientists today. In fact, the more we learn about the complexity and interconnectedness of the universe, the greater our sense of humility.

The order proposed by Bacon wherein experiments of light precede practical applications is not a terribly useful description of the history of innovations—we find instead a complicated zigzag path. But it is indeed true that a thorough scientific understanding of a class of phenomena provides an excellent basis for action. If we wish to prevent a disease, and we know the necessary conditions for its occurrence, perhaps we can find a method of removing one of those crucial factors. If we know sufficient conditions for a desirable sort of phenomenon, then maybe we can find practical ways of instantiating those precipitating factors. The high value that scientists place on explanatory knowledge has the indirect consequence of providing the basis for discovering practical innovations and interventions.

What about the Weeds?

As the word "bouquet" in the title of this chapter indicates, my account of the values that are normative within the scientific community suggests both that these "values" are indeed positive ones and that they are evident in the practice of scientists. However, each of these implications has been vehemently denied. It would not be practical here to survey all such critiques, but I will give an indication of the general lines of argument.

The worry that science will disenchant the world was eloquently articulated in 1903 by the gloomy late Victorian writer George Gissing:

> I hate and fear science because of my conviction that, for long to come if not for ever, it will be the remorseless enemy of mankind. I see it destroying all simplicity and gentleness of life, all the beauty of the world; I see it restoring barbarism under the mask of civilization: I see it darkening men's minds and hardening their hearts. (quoted in Mencken 1942)

The concerns about science intimated in this passage are threefold: that a scientific account of nature will destroy our aesthetic appreciation of it, that the use of the methods of science is detrimental to the mental health and moral character of the individual scientist, and that the products of scientific advance will endanger civilization. Each of these three fears still operates today. I will make a few comments on each of them.

The argument about whether analysis inhibits or enhances aesthetic appreciation can perhaps never be resolved. Does the knowledge that Seurat paintings are composed of little colored dots erode our ability to appreciate their beauty? Does knowing why the sky is blue in mid-morning and red at dusk and how the Grand Canyon was formed detract from the joy of a camping trip? I sincerely hope not. I would like to think that once people really understand the so-called reductionistic, objectifying explanations of natural phenomena that science provides, they will find that scientific accounts leave lots of room for personal experience while at the same time enriching our understanding. However, I am prepared to grant that there may be a kind of mystical union with nature that is threatened by science. But this is not a good reason for opposing the opportunity for other people to extend their appreciation of the world we live in.

The charge that science is dehumanizing to its practitioners is potentially much more damaging to the contention of this volume that the values of science can bolster civic virtue. Feminists have produced the most colorful negative descriptions of the science temperament. Sandra Harding says that in Bacon's influential writings "both nature and inquiry appear conceptualized in ways modeled on rape and torture" (Harding 1986, 116). Science, with its emphasis on analysis, abstraction, and quantification, is described by Mary Daly as a paradigm case of patriarchal, phallocratic necrophilia! On a more sober note, adherents of so-called object relations theory argue that one of the reasons women have traditionally not found science a congenial profession is that men find it easier to distance themselves from what they study; women are less eager to dissect and control. (For a discussion of these claims, see Koertge 1998, 259–265.)

Feminist accounts of scientific methods and values have been very widely and effectively criticized (see, for example, the critiques of so-called feminist epistemology in Pinnick et al. 2003). More worthy of discussion, in my opinion, are concerns about the treatment of human and animal subjects in scientific research. The argument here is that scientists are so concerned with the intellectual excitement and practical benefits of scientific problem solving that they pay little attention to the harm they inflict on their experimental subjects. There is no doubt that there have been in the past (including the recent past!) many very distressing episodes where scientists treated people and animals in an inhumane way. Whether that treatment was crueler that what went in society at large is quite a different matter (see Guerrini 2003).

But ever since Nuremburg, scientific societies have systematically adopted codes of ethics. And there is now an elaborate apparatus of governmental regulations and institutional review boards that vet scientific experiments before they are carried out. Although scientists are sometimes frustrated by the hassles that inevitably accompany bureaucratic oversight, there is wide acceptance of the need to include ethical considerations into scientific practice. Today, science education at the university level often includes formal instruction in research ethics. Students might discuss how the values of respect, beneficence, and justice can be instantiated in research with human subjects or learn about the practical aspects of getting informed consent.

More controversial are the policies concerning the ethical treatment of animal subjects. There is broad acceptance among scientists of the 3R program, which calls for a *refinement* of the experimental techniques used so as to minimize suffering, reduction of the overall number of animals used in experiments, and the *replacement* of animal experiments by the use of in vitro methods and computer modeling (Brody 2001, 134). But many disputes are unresolved. Animal rights activists want more protections for animals; philosophers have not been very successful in providing a reasoned basis for figuring out how to balance animal suffering against benefits to humans; scientists in fields such as ethology are sometimes much more concerned about animal welfare than, say, physiologists. But everyone agrees that there must be some sort of ethical constraints on animal research.

Seemingly irreconcilable differences arise, however, about the ethics of research with live human cells, especially ones where issues connected to reproduction are involved. Scientists have virtuously unanimously condemned any attempt to clone human beings but have also insisted that research on human embryonic stem cells should go forward. Part of the opposition to such research is connected with political debates about abortion. More interesting for our purposes of describing the value system of science, however, are objections to stem cell research (or previous research on reproductive technologies) that appeal to concepts of human dignity or the "wisdom of repugnance," to use the phrase coined by Leon Kass (see President's Council on Bioethics 2002). Some might argue that values such as human dignity play no operative role in science. I think they would be seriously mistaken. The goal of understanding our universe, including the nature of mankind, is surely among the noblest of human aspirations. There is no dignity to be attached to ignorance.

Scientists are also wise to place little weight on mere feelings of repugnance. There is the trivial fact that the study of things that other people find "yucky," be it slime molds, leprosy, or sexual perversions, enriches our understanding of the world. More important are the examples from the history of science where phenomena that were thought to be morally repugnant, such as people with Tourette's syndrome, test tube babies, or transgendered personalities, are reevaluated in the light of scientific knowledge. There may be good reasons for not pursuing certain lines of research, but they must be articulated and argued for.

We have noted concerns that scientific knowledge disenchants nature and that the practice of science is dehumanizing. The most serious worry about scientific values, however, stems from fears about the negative impact of technology. Some see science as a juggernaut fueled by an insatiable curiosity and lust for understanding and manipulated by commercial greed and the determination to build ever more destructive weapons. It is true that, given their social role as producers of knowledge, scientists will be attracted by the sheer intellectual challenge of a controversial line of research. But that same insider perspective also enables them to serve as sentinels for society at large. The *Bulletin of the Atomic Scientists* has been addressing issues of nuclear safety ever since its famous Doomsday Clock first appeared in 1947; the most informed concerns about global warming and ecological crises come from scientists; the Union of Concerned Scientists is a political action group that monitors technological dangers; and despite its boosterish sounding name, the American Association for the Advancement of Science has divisions that scrutinize science policy.

Karl Popper (1994) describes the special responsibility of the scientist to warn and inform the public as the principle of *sagesse oblige*:

Formerly, the pure scientist had only one responsibility beyond those which everyone else has: to search for truth ... Since the natural scientist has become inextricably involved in the application of science, he should consider it one of his special responsibilities to foresee as far as possible the unintended consequences of his work and to draw attention from the very beginning, to those which we should strive to avoid. (121, 129)

This principle applies equally to people with any kind of special expertise. The trick is to be able to communicate these expert opinions in an understandable fashion so that they don't have to be taken simply on faith.

Given the general low level of scientific literacy in many societies, this communication is a very difficult task, and it must be admitted that scientists can sometimes quite summarily reject qualms of laypeople that they have good reason to believe are ill founded. I well remember the disgust evinced by a nuclear science teacher of mine back in the 1950s when he described the public hysteria over using radiation as a means of increasing the shelf life of food—folks were worried that it would make their meat or fresh vegetables radioactive. When he compared for us the energy used in food processing with the energy required to induce the transformation of nuclei into radioactive isotopes, it was obvious that the public's concerns were totally implausible. It became equally obvious that it would be very difficult to convey this understanding, and in fact rules allowing the irradiation of meat were only passed in February 2002!

Scientists are cognizant of the problems of conflict of interest that arise when research projects are funded by groups that strongly prefer that the results turn out a certain way. Classic commercial examples are studies of the effects of smoking and asbestos; some journals require authors to declare that their contracts did not require the researcher to run their results past the funding company before publication. Government pipers also sometimes try to call the tune. For example, it is difficult for scientists to argue against the practicality of a Star Wars defense system or a manned expedition to Mars when governmental agencies are throwing money at the project, especially when the scientific reasons for thinking the initiative is ill conceived are theoretical or difficult to communicate. But the major problem here is not a lack of candor on the part of scientists. Rather, it is the lack of strong institutions dedicated to technology assessment and science policy discussions.

Conclusions

The dream of the Enlightenment was to transplant the habits of rationality and objectivity so characteristic of science into society at large. Today we realize that every part of that project is more complex than the *philosophes* could have imagined. And it is science itself that has complicated the picture. An adequate concept of rationality must now include statistics and game theory; cognitive psychologists have revealed the many-layered methods of approximation and schematization that operate when we try to be objective; and it is only within the last century that we have developed anything approaching a scientific understanding of the nature of society.

The norms of science have also evolved. Science has always been a cooperative (as well as a competitive) enterprise, but the advent of so-called Big Science has necessitated a level of role differentiation and teamwork way beyond what Bacon envisaged in his *New Atlantis*. Science has always valued reliable instruments that increased the scope and accuracy of observation, but the complicated structure of experimental equipment today has introduced all sorts of complications into the processes of calibrating and interpreting observational results. Scientists have always guarded their autonomy from pushy patrons, but as it costs more and more to do research today, it is less easy for scientists to undertake the projects that they believe are most fundamental. It is more difficult to be a virtuous scientist today. Yet I believe that a higher awareness of their many obligations can result in a more realistic value paradigm for the rest of society.

References

Bacon, Francis. *The New Organon and Related Writings*. Englewood Cliffs, NJ: Prentice Hall, 1960.

Boyd, Richard, Philip Gasper, and J. D. Trout. *The Philosophy of Science*. Cambridge, MA: MIT Press, 1991.

Brody, Baruch A. "Defending Animal Research: An International Perspective." *Why Animal Experimentation Matters,* edited by Ellen Frankel Paul and Jeffrey Paul. New Brunswick, NJ: Transaction Publishers, 2001.

Giere, Ronald N. *Explaining Science: A Cognitive Approach*. Chicago: University of Chicago Press, 1988.

Guerrini, Anita. *Experimenting with Humans and Animals: From Galen to Animal Rights*. Baltimore, MD: The John Hopkins University Press, 2003.

Harding, Sandra. *The Science Question in Feminism*. Ithaca, NY: Cornell University Press, 1986.

Holton, Gerald. *Thematic Origins of Scientific Thought: Kepler to Einstein*. Cambridge, MA: Harvard University Press, 1988.

————. *The Advancement of Science, and Its Burdens*. Cambridge, MA: Harvard University Press, 1998.

Hull, David L. *Science as a Process: An Evolutionary Account of the Social and Conceptual Development of Science*. Chicago: University of Chicago Press, 1988.

Kitcher, Philip. *The Advancement of Science: Science without Legend, Objectivity without Illusions*. New York: Oxford University Press, 1993.

Koertge, Noretta. "The Function of Credit in Hull's Evolutionary Model of Science." *Philosophy of Science* 2 (1990): 237–244.

————. "Postmodernisms and the Problem of Scientific Literacy." *A House Built on Sand*, edited by Noretta Koertge. New York: Oxford University Press, 1998.

Kuhn, Thomas S. "Objectivity, Value Judgment, and Theory Choice." *The Essential Tension*. Chicago: University of Chicago Press, 1977.

Lakatos, Imre. *The Methodology of Scientific Research Programmes: Philosophical Papers Volume 1*. London: Cambridge University Press, 1978.

Mencken, H. L., ed. *A New Dictionary of Quotations*. New York: Knopf, 1942.

Merton, Robert K. *The Sociology of Science: Theoretical and Empirical Investigations*. Chicago: University of Chicago Press, 1973.

Pinnick, Cassandra L., Noretta Koertge, and Robert F. Almeder, eds. *Scrutinizing Feminist Epistemology: An Examination of Gender in Science*. New Brunswick, NJ: Rutgers University Press, 2003.

Popper, Karl R. *Conjectures and Refutations: The Growth of Scientific Knowledge*. London: Routledge, 1963.

————. *Objective Knowledge: An Evolutionary Approach*. New York: Oxford University Press, 1972.

————. "The Moral Responsibility of the Scientist." *The Myth of the Framework*. New York: Routledge, 1994.

President's Council on Bioethics. *Human Cloning and Human Dignity: An Ethical Inquiry.* Washington, DC: U.S. Government Printing Office, 2002.

Worrall, John. "Thomas Young and the 'Refutation' of Newtonian Optics: A Case-Study in the Interaction of Philosophy of Science and History of Science." *Method and Appraisal in the Physical Sciences,* edited by Colin Howson. London: Cambridge University Press, 1976.

2

Public Reason and Democracy

The Place of Science in Maintaining Civic Friendship

Steven M. DeLue

The Public Realm, Civic Virtue, and Science

Western political philosophy is a tradition of thought that is concerned with defining the nature of, as well as the means to, realizing a decent society. Writers across the various periods of Western political philosophy hold that, in a decent society, people should be provided far more than just the goods necessary for mere existence, such as safety, health, food, and shelter. In addition, people must have goods—such as knowledge, justice, civic morality (or virtue), community, religion, science, and art—that when present in proper proportion are the foundation of worthwhile, prospering, and contented lives. Now, there are many challenges associated with achieving a decent society. One challenge involves identifying the proper relationship between civic virtue and scientific values. To frame my discussion of this challenge, it is first necessary to discuss civic virtue and science in the context of both the social and public realms.

The *social realm* includes a variety of activities, each of which is specific to the development and the distribution of the goods that contribute to human flourishing. I refer to each of the separate settings in which these activities occur as a "domain." Each domain consists of values and practices that both orient and enable people to achieve the purposes of the domain in question. For instance, within the social realm, the domain of the family life provides a context of values and practices to nurture children, whereas the domains that provide opportunities for a wide variety of associational affiliations outside the family enable people to pursue core interests that families by themselves do not satisfy. The economic domain refers both to the way work is organized to produce all the goods deemed necessary for a decent society and to the way these goods are distributed across society. Further, the domains of art and religion are the settings for aesthetic and religious perspectives and ways of life. And, in the scientific domain, people engage in reasoned inquiry to produce systematic knowledge that can be used to attain a variety of human purposes.

The *public realm* is the setting in which common issues—such as education, the rule of law, and protection from foreign powers—that cut across all the domains of the social realm are addressed. The main instrument of the public realm for addressing common issues is a government, whose major purpose is to make and enforce laws and policies that lead to a decent society. In some cases, the government promotes the public commitment to achieve a decent society by directing the social realm to support specified policies and laws, and in other instances the public realm serves the cause of achieving a decent society best when it stands at a distance to the social realm, allowing it to shape its own affairs without interference. Further, the public realm fosters a public culture consisting of important values that each of the citizens should uphold in their lives. Chief among these public values are what are referred to as "civic virtues." The latter can be understood in two ways. First, there are what William Galston (1991, 221) refers to as "general virtues," which are common to all societies and which include obligations to obey the law, to respect the principles upon which one's country is based, and to accept the call to sacrifice for one's country during times of war. And, second, there are civic virtues specific to particular regimes. For instance, in a theocracy, citizens have an obligation to uphold the beliefs of a particular religion, whereas in a liberal democracy religious diversity is encouraged and citizens are obligated by law and civic morality to tolerate multiple religious beliefs.

In this chapter, I address the relationship between science and civic virtue in a liberal democratic regime. To accomplish this purpose, I first discuss, through my treatment of Immanuel Kant, the main concerns of the eighteenth-century Enlightenment. In doing so, my intention is to demonstrate the way in which science supports a public culture that preferences critical reasoning, freedom, and intellectual pluralism, which permits people to consider diverse ideas and points of view during the course of developing their own judgments. These dimensions are the foundation of a public culture that is integral to a liberal democracy, which, in addition to securing basic rights (such as freedom of thought and conscience) within a representative, majority-rule form of constitutional government, is built upon the civic virtue of toleration. Moreover, the public culture of a liberal democracy shapes the societal discourse and deliberation on a host of issues of critical importance to civic life, including those involving science. My discussion of John Rawls in the last section of this chapter addresses the character of the civic discourse—guided by the commitments to critical reasoning, freedom, intellectual pluralism, and toleration—in a contemporary liberal democracy.

Kant: Modernity and Enlightenment

The eighteenth-century Enlightenment embodied the hope of establishing governments that freed people from superstition and tradition, so that people could use reason and science to generate knowledge useful in improving society (Masters 1964, 3–7; Beck 1980, xiv–xv). Kant manifested this perspective when he made intellectual autonomy (hereafter referred to as autonomy) the central element of the public culture of an enlightened world. Autonomy is made possible when individuals use their own reasoning capacity—as opposed to opinions superimposed on people by the state or by a church—to form judgments about all important issues, including science, politics, and morality. To explain how autonomous thinking arises, Kant discusses the structure of the rational mind—including its basic concepts and ideas—that enables people to make reasoned judgments.

I first discuss the structure of the rational mind by demonstrating its importance in developing the bases for science and morality. Then, I discuss Kant's approach to protecting the rational, autonomous mind through the creation of a public culture that fosters freedom of the will, intellectual pluralism, and toleration. For Kant, these major dimensions of the public culture are best preserved in a liberal democracy.

Kant's discussion of autonomy begins with his demonstration of how science is possible (Tinder 2004, 161). In his *Critique of Pure Reason*, Kant (1966, 1–18; Kant 1964, 13–14, 56, 118–119; Tinder 2004, 237–239) sought to show how science achieves systematic knowledge by describing the structure of the autonomous, rational mind that organizes our perceptions of objects in a way that allows us to comprehend their basic substance. The rational mind is described in terms of the concepts that organize the perceptions (what he calls "sensuous ideas") arising from experience of the natural world in terms of basic categories such as time and space, and cause and effect (Kant 1966, 23–26, 82–84; Tinder 2004, 238). Indeed, the rational mind, for Kant (1964), places with its concepts, the *"sensuous ideas under rules . . .* [in order] to unite them in one consciousness" (120; italics in original). Without the order imposed on our perceptions by the concepts arising from rational intelligence, the natural world would appear in our minds as it if were a chaotic and random mix of events (Tinder 2004, 238). However, when people approach understanding and experience of the natural world from the perspective of the ordering concepts of the rational mind, people acquire the capacity to replace randomness with systematic knowledge produced by science. Indeed, the ordering concepts of the rational mind enable science to obtain systematic knowledge of the natural world through techniques of observation that are used to validate, empirically, theories designed to depict various laws of nature that explain reality.

The rational mind, which provides the concepts needed to obtain systematic knowledge of nature, also makes clear the imperatives of morality. In this view of the rational mind, reason is the origin of moral obligations, which arise in the mind when individuals seek norms that all rational individuals would uphold (Kant 1964, 82–84, 98, 120). The chief moral obligation to arise from this process is Kant's "single categorical imperative," which requires us to *"act only on that maxim through which you can at the same time will that it should become a universal law"* (Kant 1964, 88; italics in original). This moral law shapes the moral perspective that governs how people should act toward others and toward themselves. Indeed, the chief moral principle, or maxim, to embody the categorical imperative, and thus to make clear how people should conduct their lives, is the requirement to treat all persons, others as well as oneself, as ends and not solely as means to purposes charted by others (Kant 1964, 95). A society governed by this principle would expect people to assess actions and proposed policies from the perspective of their contribution to a "kingdom of ends," a social setting in which the idea of respect for persons as ends is the primary motivation for conduct (Kant 1964, 100–101).

To make the moral law the basis for conduct, it is necessary to overcome a central dilemma that results from Kant's view of the structure of the rational mind. The solution to the dilemma, discussed in the next several paragraphs, makes freedom of the will, intellectual pluralism, and the civic virtue of toleration essential elements of Kant's conception of a public culture that supports his kingdom of ends.

Kant's (1964, 44–45, 123–124) discussion of the structure of concepts and ideas of the rational mind suggests that two contradictory viewpoints about the character of human life permeate human intelligence. From the standpoint of the concepts that make possible systematic knowledge of human life, our motivations for conduct are determined by laws of nature, which explain human behavior in terms of pre-dictable reactions—manifested in various desires and inclinations—to our experience. In large part, this means that people can be expected to respond to experience with a series of desires and inclinations that, when taken together, emphasize the predominance of human sensibilities that orient us to the pursuit of what we perceive as solely our own interests. Indeed, Kant (1980b) speaks of our "natural capacities" as "propelled by vainglory, lust for power, and avarice" (15). However, the rational mind is also the source of moral principles by which all should live, in particular, the commitment to treat all persons as ends. When seen from this perspective, human motivations are formulated by reason, which can establish moral motivations independent of the largely self-serving orientations predicted by the laws of nature for human life. As people follow the dictates of reason, human actions are determined not by self-interest oriented desires but by the "freedom of will" that itself is grounded in the view "that reason is independent of purely subjective determination by causes which collectively make up all that belongs to sensation and comes under the general name of sensibility" (Kant 1964, 44–45, 125). To act in a manner consistent with reason requires that people, through their own rational and autonomous will, make the moral law the primary motivating factor in their decisions. In the process, as Susan Nieman (2002) says for Kant, "the categorical imperative can be viewed as a constraint on our self-interested and sensual drives, but it's also a chance to escape our own limits anytime we feel brought low by them" (77).

Kant (1964, 124) says that it is a matter of great importance to "get rid" of this contradiction "in a convincing fashion." He (1964, 41–42, 125, 127) approaches this objective by making the presumption that individuals are free and, as such, can overcome any dependency upon factors described by laws of nature for human motivation, which turn people into nothing more than creatures following their desires. Indeed, Kant (1964) says that "to be independent of determination by causes [such as desires] in the sensible world . . . is to be free" (120). But reliance on freedom as the basis for overcoming the contradiction between these viewpoints is problematic because there is no definitive argument, located in either experience or in philosophy, demonstrating that a rational person is actually free (Kant 1964, 42, 127). Indeed, Kant (1964) says that "we shall never be able to comprehend how freedom is possible" (124):

> Freedom . . . is a mere Idea: its objective validity can in no way be exhibited by reference to laws of nature and consequently cannot be exhibited in any possible experience.

Thus, the Idea of freedom can never admit of full comprehension, or indeed of insight, since it can never by any analogy have an example falling under it. It holds only as a necessary presumption of reason in a being who believes himself to be conscious of a will—that is, of a power distinct from mere appetition (a power, viz., of determining himself to act as intelligence and consequently to act in accordance with the laws for reason independently of natural instincts). (Kant 1964, 27)

Given both the importance of freedom and the impossibility of establishing a definitive argument for it, Kant seeks to provide as good a defense of freedom as can be made against those who allege its impossibility (1964, 42, 48). Kant's defense strategy is to demonstrate that freedom is a reasonable belief, or what Kant (1964) calls a "presumption of reason" (127). Now, a belief is reasonable because it points to ends that rational people would support and because the belief in question comports with other beliefs also deemed indispensable by people who make reason the foundation of their lives. For instance, as just described, the rational mind is structured in a manner that not only makes science and the knowledge it produces possible but also demonstrates the moral purposes for which science-produced knowledge should be used. In consequence, a reasonable belief that emanates from Kant's notion of the rational mind is that people can—through science—produce knowledge and that knowledge should be used on behalf of achieving morally acceptable ends. This belief is consistent with the belief in freedom, since without freedom people might live in thrall to their own inclinations and desires that threaten the intellectual autonomy needed both for science and for formulating the moral predicates that suggest the right way to use science-created knowledge.

Moreover, this view of science suggests that moral progress for humankind is possible in society and across history. To be sure, the human situation appears to be chaotic and thus filled with circumstances suggesting the very opposite of progress. But the same was said about the external world of nature, until, as Kant says (1980b, 12), Kepler emerged to demonstrate that the "eccentric paths of the planets" actually conform to "definite laws." Newton deepened this understanding when he "explained these laws by a universal natural cause." Similarly, for Kant the human world, when viewed from the perspective of the many follies and the "idiotic course of things human," appears to be without a rational purpose (12). Still, despite this perception, it is acceptable for a philosopher to "see if he can discover a natural [or rational] purpose" in this chaotic mixture of forces (12). To fulfill this goal, a person must base one's thinking on a belief that, if one searches diligently, one can see a basis for rational order, even when on the surface such an order appears to be nonexistent. Here, for Kant, the human world would be organized by a "guiding thread" to become "a moral whole" (12, 15). When the world is viewed in this way, for Kant the "history of mankind" can be described as containing a "secret plan" to bring into existence societies in which mankind's "capacities" are "fully developed" (21). And this prospect for human life is reasonable because belief in moral progress is compatible with Kant's highest moral idea, the hope of achieving a kingdom of ends, which itself is only possible when there is freedom.

Kant's strategy for defending the freedom of the will is extended in his discussion of politics when he makes the idea of *equal freedom*—what in the next section I refer to as *civic equality*—central to a thriving public culture. For Kant (1999), society should be based on the "universal principle of justice," which says that "every action is just [right] that in itself or in its maxim is such that the freedom of the will of each can coexist together with the freedom of everyone in accordance with a universal law" (30). This major political principle is supported by his view of a liberal democratic form of government, based on the idea of shared powers among the legislative, executive, and judicial branches of government—an arrangement designed to ensure that no one branch of government accumulates so much power that it can violate the principle of equal freedom (Kant 1999, 118–123, 146–150; DeLue 2002, 184). Moreover, since people will often be motivated by "selfish animal impulses" and not by a morally grounded will—a fact that could destroy freedom—Kant (1980b, 17–18) argues that people need a "master" to "force" them to uphold the principle of equal freedom. Ideally, the best master would be a just leader, but the fact is that because men are like "crooked wood" from which "nothing perfectly straight can be built," such leaders are impossible to find. The best that citizens can do in this circumstance for Kant (1980b) is to be governed by people with appropriate experience and by good laws constituted under a "correct conception of a possible constitution" that the citizens freely accept, because doing so is the basis for embodying the principle of equal freedom into law (18).

Of course, given that humankind is like "crooked wood" that cannot be made straight, even this circumstance will be difficult to bring about. Nonetheless, Kant preferred a constitutional republic—what is today called a liberal democracy—as the best hope to attaining equal freedom and in so doing strongly opposed paternalistic forms of government. Kant (1997) thought that a paternalistic government, which presumes that the "head of state"—and not the citizens themselves—is the best judge of what citizens should want in order to be happy, "would be the worst conceivable *despotism*" (58; italics in original).

A public culture that defends freedom creates the ground for the flourishing of the open, reasoning intelligence that constitutes the heart of autonomy. Indeed, Kant (1980a) defends the "public use of . . . reason," by which he means a capacity that enables a person to think for oneself by being able "to use . . . [one's] own reason and to speak in . . . [one's] own person" (6). The ability "to think for oneself"—what Kant (1951, 136–137; DeLue 2002, 180) calls "*unprejudiced* thought" and what I have referred to as intellectual autonomy—only occurs when peoples' minds are freed from superstitions that void reasoned assessment as the basis for opinions. This moment is called by Kant (1951) "*enlightenment*" (137; italics in original). An enlightened person for Kant overcomes a tendency of "being guided by others," a condition that would undermine intellectual autonomy (137).

Once enlightened, however, people recognize that in order to formulate their own views in an independent fashion—as thinking for oneself requires—they need an environment that fosters intellectual pluralism. In this setting, people devise their own judgments and opinions through a process that permits them to compare and to contrast a variety of views and ideas, including opinions and judgments different from their own (Kant 1951, 136). Intellectual pluralism is highly valued because where everyone professes the same views—as is the case when people are unable to think for themselves—the basis for open, reasoned thought so central to science is impossible, and then the autonomous, rational thinking self is denied full expression.

Thus, intellectual pluralism suggests a variety of perspectives emanate from different subjectively based understandings, and Kant's point is that these understandings should be considered by people in making judgments. Despite this fact, however, Kant does not suggest that the plurality of views minimizes the place of a common point of view from which ultimately to consider matters during the course of making judgments about them. Indeed, Kant argues that independent, reasoned thinking is linked to the quest for "enlarged thought," which arises only as people overcome the limitations of "subjective private conditions of . . . [their] own judgments, by which so many . . . are confined" (Kant 1951, 137). The enlarged mind, in seeking to transcend the limitations of private, subjective thinking, acquires a *"universal standpoint,"* which, as we have seen above, is represented by the rational concepts and ideas needed to understand the natural and the human worlds (137; italics in original).

The importance of the universal standpoint for civic virtue is that it orients individuals to uphold the commitment to treat people as ends in both the public and social realms. In the public realm, this universal moral principle is manifested, as we have seen, in those political institutions and practices that secure the idea of equal freedom. In the social realm, the universal principle of respect for persons as ends is manifested in Kant's (1983, 53, 82–141) discussion of a variety of duties that people have to themselves and to others. In carrying out one's life in ways that uphold basic duties, one maintains the universal standpoint throughout one's interactions with others across the various domains of the social realm. Moreover, to act as duty requires is to act from a freely willed decision to make the moral law—and the commitment to respect persons as ends—the motivation of action as opposed to more narrow, parochial motivations arising from emotionally based feelings of self-interest. As Nieman (2002) says, for Kant, "a shopkeeper who refrains from cheating because good reputations are good for business is different from a shopkeeper who knows he can get away with cheating, and doesn't" (268; see also 76, 78). In the first case, the basis for not cheating is a motive from self-interest, but in the second, the basis for action is the moral law to which an individual conforms voluntarily and in the process manifests what is often referred to as "moral autonomy."

In achieving autonomy in the social and public realms, Kant grounds both not just on critical inquiry, freedom, and intellectual pluralism but also on the important civic virtue of toleration. And this outcome occurs for two reasons. First, the imperative to respect persons as ends would always carry a solemn obligation to uphold toleration in all the domains of the social realm, as well as in the public realm. And second, since for Kant science could not advance where imposed dogma from public or social realm agencies denied centrality of place to intellectual autonomy, a culture of toleration would be a central element of the public as well as the social realm.

Rawls, Public Reason, Toleration, and Civic Friendship

Rawls (1996, 37) advocates what he refers to as "political liberalism," a view of liberal (or what is interchangeably referred to as a constitutional) democracy that differs from the one found in Kant. Whereas Rawls (1996, xliv–xlv, 77–78) accepts the idea of Kantian autonomy, and its commitment to reasoned inquiry as it pertains to political judgments in the public realm, he does not, like Kant, think that it should be pushed deeply into all domains of the social realm. Thus, for Rawls people should make political judgments on the basis of reasoned inquiry and the central commitment to the Kantian idea of respect for persons. Rawls (1996) refers to this practice as "political autonomy," which is "the sharing with other citizens equally in the exercise of political power" (xliv). This circumstance is manifested in his view of "public reason," which, as discussed below, is the way for Rawls (1999, 133) that citizens in a liberal democracy should approach fundamental political questions—those that are central to maintaining a liberal democracy. In contrast, matters pertaining to the social realm—such as those having to do with religion—should not have to withstand the test of Kantian autonomous reason, which would require that ways of life be assessed by how well they accommodate the idea of respect for persons. Rawls (1996) refers to this practice as "moral autonomy," and points out that "many citizens of faith reject moral autonomy as part of their way of life" (xlv). Thus, for Rawls, mandating moral autonomy for all of the social realm would undermine ways of life that are justified less by open, reasoned reflection and more by a sense of comfort and belonging arising from certain habits of living and belief that embrace cherished traditions. For Rawls (1996, 14, 220), the social realm must provide a multitude of settings that permit individuals to practice their core values, including those that do and those that do not embrace moral autonomy, and those that do and those that do not embrace cherished traditions. In consequence, Rawls (1996, 37) says that it is impermissible for the state to impose onto society a particular view of the relationship between state and society that would promote through the authority of state the idea of Kantian moral autonomy throughout the social realm. Such an endeavor would be in Rawls's (1996, 37) eyes an act of "oppression," one that violates the civic virtue of toleration.

In this section, I discuss Rawls's political liberalism in some detail. I do so with the intention of demonstrating that his view of liberal democracy carries forward into the public realm, as opposed to the social realm, the Kantian values of freedom, intellectual pluralism, and the civic virtue of toleration. Moreover, Rawls's approach to these matters is the basis for fashioning the nature of contemporary public deliberation on matters of great importance to a liberal democracy, including those having to do with science. I discuss some of the ramifications of his view of public deliberation in the conclusion of this section.

Rawls's (1996, xviii–xix) political liberalism is based on the understanding that in the contemporary world the social realm consists of people who hold many diverse and often contradictory core values. The latter are referred to as "comprehensive doctrines," and each describes for its holder what is of great value in a person's life, including the moral, religious, or philosophical ideas "as well as ideals of personal virtue and character" that inform a person's way of life in the various domains of the social realm (Rawls 1996, 174–175). An example of contradictory comprehensive doctrines can be seen in matters having to do with religion, with some people advocating religious values in the social realm and others advocating secular ones. Despite the fact that the reality of life in modern society is that people hold incompatible comprehensive doctrines such as the two just cited, Rawls (1996) says that such doctrines can be "reasonable" when they do not "reject the essentials of a democratic regime" (xviii).

Rawls's (1996) chief concern is to address the question as to how people who possess "reasonable though incompatible religious, philosophical, and moral doctrines" can "live together" and make possible "over time a stable and just society" (xx, 133–134). His answer to this question rests upon the view that citizens, despite their different comprehensive doctrines, share a firm commitment to a political and thus public conception of a just society that is understood to be "a fair system of social cooperation" (9, 13–15), one in which people, in Rawls's words, are able to protect their status as "free and equal" individuals (50). The fair system of social cooperation that Rawls (1996, 11) has in mind is the "basic structure" of a constitutional democracy, including most prominently the "basic moral and political values" that are reflected in this form of government's political, economic, and social institutions (1999, 132). Moreover, the basic structure of a constitutional democracy is considered by Rawls (1996) as "one unified system of social cooperation from one generation to the next" (11), and insofar as this is true, the basic structure reproduces over time a commitment to the basic moral and political values so essential to a constitutional democracy. These values—which I refer to below as summed up in the idea of "civic equality"—are the foundation for continuing citizen support, regardless of their differing comprehensive doctrines. Citizens who give priority to and thus enable the basic values to "outweigh" other values, including their personal comprehensive doctrines, are referred to by Rawls (1996, 50; 156–157; 1999, 177) as "reasonable persons." These individuals hold what Rawls (1996, 134) calls "reasonable" comprehensive doctrines. The latter idea enables people to "endorse" the basic political values of a constitutional democracy from the point of view of a particular comprehensive doctrine (134).

People in a constitutional democracy engage in public deliberation that is designed to resolve differences, while at the same time maintaining the basic moral and political values of a constitutional democracy (Rawls 1999, 133). These objectives are approached through "public reason." The idea of public reason for Rawls (1996, l–lvii, 217, 226; 1999, 168, 133; Larmore 2003, 380) characterizes the nature of civic-oriented, public deliberation in a liberal democracy by which citizens conduct discussions of and vote on "fundamental political questions." The latter pertain to key public issues that have to do with sustaining a constitutional democracy. In this regard, then, not all issues before society fall into this category, but those that do involve matters that touch on the basic concerns of a constitutional democracy, such as the form of such a government, as well as the nature and extent of fundamental rights for citizens and the best way to make sure that the basic needs of citizens are respected and provided for (Rawls 1996, 227–230, 235; Larmore 2003, 380). In accordance with the norms of public reason, these matters are to be approached in a manner that protects and furthers the basic moral and political values of a constitutional democracy, as opposed to a particular comprehensive doctrine held by any of the citizens in the social realm (Rawls 1996, 226; 1999, 132–133). In consequence, as Charles Larmore (2003) points out, for Rawls the basic moral and political values represent the "common perspective" in terms of which citizens "justify" their decisions about fundamental political issues and questions (381).

The chief way to characterize this common point of view, as indicated above, is that it is committed to maintain throughout society the idea of civic equality. For Rawls (1996) the notion of civic equality is in tune with the basic desire reasonable individuals have for "a social world in which they, as free and equal, can cooperate with others on terms all accept" (50). To make this Kantian objective of respect for persons possible, the public culture, insofar as it supports civic equality, is designed to specify and thus secure basic core rights, liberties, and opportunities for all individuals (Rawls 1996, xlviii–l). For instance, each person should be accorded basic rights, liberties, and opportunities such as thought, religion, conscience, association, political participation, and the rule of law (Rawls 1996, 227; 1999, 141). Indeed, the basic rights, liberties, and opportunities are assigned a "special priority" and thus supersede in importance any notion of the general good that might be advocated for society as a whole (Rawls 1999, 141). These rights, liberties, and opportunities are properly embodied into the laws of a constitutional democracy only when people are accorded the "adequate all-purpose means" needed to enable them to make "effective use of their freedoms" (141). Moreover, civic equality must be protected by governmental institutions. In particular, the legislative, executive, and the judicial branches each have assigned powers and functions to preclude the abuse of authority by any one of them, as well as to ensure that the majority rule principle does not violate any person's basic rights, liberties, or opportunities (Rawls 1996, 227). Finally, a "social minimum providing for the basic needs of all citizens" must also be secured (228).

The comprehensive doctrines of specific communities can for Rawls (1996, li–lii; Larmore 2003, 385–386) become part of the public discourse guided by the standards of public reason, but only in conjunction with an effort to demonstrate how a particular approach, which manifests support for a comprehensive doctrine, works to secure the basic moral and political values of a constitutional democracy. Indeed, Rawls (1996) says that reasonable comprehensive doctrines can be introduced into the public deliberation "at any time, provided that in due course public reasons, given by a reasonable political conception [of a constitutional democracy], are presented sufficient to support whatever the comprehensive doctrines are introduced to support" (li–lii).

To provide an example of Rawls's (1999, 164–166) position, I refer to the issue of prayer in public schools. This is a fundamental political issue because it has to do with the ensuring of a form of government that protects religious choice as part of what it means to secure the status of persons as free and equal and as part of what is involved with maintaining civic equality. During the course of the discussion on this issue, various comprehensive doctrines might be entertained, including a desire for a religious culture or for a secular one. But in the final analysis, the basis for school prayer or for its absence cannot be a particular comprehensive doctrine but must be those public values that are pivotal to maintaining a constitutional democracy. The key public value in this regard is the principle of the separation of church and state. Unless this principle is protected in the discussion of such matters as school prayer, then comprehensive doctrines might be put into place that end up undermining freedom of religious choice and conscience, and in the process thwarting the commitment to civic equality. Rawls (1999) says "it [the principle of the separation of church and state] protects religion from the state and the state from religion; it protects citizens from their churches and citizens from one another" (166).

Another element of the perspective of public reason for Rawls (1996) is the commitment to make use "of the methods and conclusions of science" (224). This would require people to clarify carefully the concepts used in arguments, connect them logically, and support conclusions with a good factual case. But sometimes, after prolonged public discussion, the only results are disagreements or "standoffs," and Rawls (1999, 168) makes clear that it would be wrong for citizens, especially owing to the "duty of civility," to resolve these circumstances by invoking as the basis for their decisions particular comprehensive doctrines. Citizens should resolve their differences with a vote in a legally constituted setting, and the vote should be based on a judgment that represents each person's understanding of the best way to realize the key *public* values at stake in the discussion. Thus, Rawls (1999) claims that the outcome of the vote is "seen as legitimate provided all government officials, supported by other reasonable citizens of a reasonably just constitutional regime sincerely vote in accordance with the idea of public reason [the commitment to uphold the political values of a constitutional democracy]" (169).

But why is agreement frequently difficult to achieve in a discourse based on the common point of view of public reason? The first problem in achieving reconciliation through public reason is the existence for Rawls (1996) of contrasting comprehensive doctrines, whose very existence point "politically speaking," to competing views that cannot be reconciled and that thereby "remain inconsistent with one another" (lx). Another source of disagreements, which often cannot be reconciled, is what Rawls (1996) refers to as the "burdens of judgment" (54–58)—those complications associated with making sound, reasonable, and consensus-based judgments on many issues. What are some of the most prominent of the impediments referred to as burdens of judgment? For Rawls (1996) the concepts employed in deliberations based on public reason are often "vague and subject to hard cases" (56), which means that there is likely to be a range of interpretations among reasonable people who differ on a given issue. Also, the information used in making judgments is frequently "conflicting and complex, and thus hard to assess and evaluate," making it difficult for people to reconcile contesting claims (56). Moreover, on either side of an issue, there are different "normative considerations," and this reality—which clearly arises from the different comprehensive doctrines that may be involved—often makes "an overall assessment" of a question hard to achieve (57). As a result of these factors, by and large for Rawls, "conflicts arising from the burdens of judgment always . . . remain and limit the extent of possible agreement" (lx). I now provide an example of how this occurs in science policy.

The embryonic stem cell controversy, which involves whether public funds can be used to support research on stem cells derived from human embryos, is a matter for public reason because it touches on a fundamental issue of the basic structure of a liberal democracy. For the fact is that in any matter involved with public funding for a specific type of medical research, money spent for this endeavor is money that will not be available for other areas of need—say, public education. The consequences of such decisions may be viewed by a number of people as failing to provide critical opportunities to certain groups that are afforded to others, thus denying, on impermissible grounds, full access to fundamental rights, liberties, and opportunities to some members of society. (In 2001, President Bush authorized limited federal funds for research on sixty existing embryo stem cell lines, which were derived from embryos that had been destroyed. He prohibited further destruction of embryos in stem cell research.)

Now, differences of this sort are difficult to reconcile in discussing embryonic stem cell research. And the reason for this situation is that the question of "if or how" to spend federal funds on embryonic stem cell research, without impairing civic equality, can get bogged down in a dispute over the nature of persons. Those who object to this type of research point out that the fertilized embryo is extinguished after the stem cell is extracted. Often for reasons of particular sectarian religious belief, these people then claim that since the embryo has the moral status of a person, destroying it, even for the sake of humanitarian goals, violates the principle of treating all people as free and equal. The proponents of this research argue that these embryos do not have the moral status of persons, and thus the question of not treating people as free and equal is moot. Moreover, for proponents, not permitting this research harms the chances for a decent life for many human beings, thereby taking from these people their civic equality.

The conflicts emerging from competing comprehensive doctrines and Rawls's burdens of judgment demonstrate how agreement on embryonic stem cell research is often difficult to achieve among the contesting parties. In this regard, the first burden of judgment pertinent to this matter emerges from the different normative perspectives embedded in the argument. Thus, because there are wide differences of view over the meaning of a key concept—the moral status of persons—it is likely that the deliberation on embryonic stem cell research will be characterized by irreconcilable interpretations of what it means to treat people as free and equal. Second, as a clear burden of judgment there is the problem of the factual record that each side could use on behalf of making the case for its position. Each side could argue that the best defense of the idea of persons as free and equal is to make good use of available, but always scarce, public funds for medical research. Opponents and proponents of embryonic stem cell research might differ on the best use of these funds, with opponents claiming other areas of research are more promising and proponents arguing to the contrary. But in matters such as this, the factual record is often complex and thus does not yield a clear basis for the correctness of a particular position, and this is in part because, as in the case of embryonic stem cell research, the research record is in its incipient stage of development and thus not as complete as the record in other areas of research.

In addition to the difficulty of reaching agreement in a society with conflicting comprehensive doctrines and the reality of the burdens of judgment, another major challenge to a discourse based on public reason is the latter's potential threat to toleration, at least as claimed by some of Rawls's critics. Indeed, William Galston (2002, 116–117, 121) is concerned that being forced to frame public issues solely in terms of the public reason may deny people a chance to articulate fully their respective comprehensive doctrines in public argument. Galston (2002) says that whereas it "may well make sense to urge all citizens" to discuss issues in terms of the common standards of public reason, it is necessary not to do so in ways that "screen out the kinds of core beliefs that give meaning and purpose to many lives" (116). In this view, public reason should not frame the public discourse in a way that allows the reliance on the basic values of a constitutional democracy to deny full expression in public deliberations to people's comprehensive doctrines. Galston's (2002) position is designed to defend what he refers to as "expressive liberty," the freedom people should have "to live their lives in ways that express their deepest beliefs about what gives meaning or value to life" (28). And since liberal democratic states promote the civic virtue of toleration, it is always necessary for them to defend expressive liberty.

Rawls would more than likely respond to this critique by claiming that political liberalism never threatens expressive liberty but in fact defends it. Indeed, as we have seen above, individuals would be able to express in the public realm their comprehensive doctrines on fundamental political issues, as long as their doing so does not override a commitment to the basic moral and political values of a constitutional democracy. As Larmore (2003) says of Rawls's view, "we can argue with one another about political issues in the name of our different visions of the human good while also recognizing that, when the moment comes for a legally binding decision, we must take our bearing from the common point of view [of public reason]" (383). All that public reason expects—as a matter of general civic virtue—is that people maintain the priority of the values of a constitutional democracy, even and especially when people do not agree with decisions arising from the political process.

Still, Rawls's political liberalism leaves us with a difficult problem to resolve concerning how to maintain stability when peoples' comprehensive doctrines are not fully realized as a result of the public deliberation. For the fact is that given the strongly felt and opposing views on matters involving competing comprehensive doctrines—such as in embryonic stem cell research debate—it is not likely that a decision satisfactory to all sides can be achieved. And this circumstance may create a great degree of social instability. Rawls's (1999) response to such circumstances is to suggest that stability can be retained when reasonable persons "stand ready to offer fair terms of social cooperation between equals," and in consequence of this fact would accept these terms of cooperation even when doing so causes them to experience some degree of disadvantage (177). Furthermore, stability is aided by the fact that reasonable persons abide by a notion of "reasonable toleration in a democratic society" because they "accept the consequences of the burdens of judgment" (177). In effect, reasonable persons grasp that as a result of the burdens of judgment, public deliberations may not lead to consensus on many issues, including those of high importance to some people. Still, for the sake of maintaining a constitutional democracy, reasonable persons tolerate the lack of consensus. This position is bolstered for Rawls by the fact that the practice of guiding public discussions of contentious issues by the norms of public reason enables citizens to "learn and profit from debate and argument" and "to deepen their understanding of one another even when agreement cannot be reached" (170–171).

In my view, the civic virtue of reasonable toleration might not be strong enough to sustain stability in the face of failure to resolve differences among people who hold competing comprehensive doctrines. And the reason for this view is that the values of a liberal democracy, upon which Rawls grounds that stability, could be placed in jeopardy by public reason itself. The explanation for why this happens lies not just in the fact that people with different comprehensive doctrines win or lose on the issue at hand, but that the victory or defeat is magnified in intensity because what is also involved is acceptance or rejection of a particular interpretation—arising from a specific comprehensive doctrine—of how best to achieve the basic political values of a constitutional democracy. Thus, if the supporters of embryonic stem cell research lose, they not only lose the chance to do this research with public funds, which is bad enough. But worse still, they might come to believe that a public value so central to a constitutional democracy—the possibility of treating people as free and equal citizens—has been denied a secure place in society. In this circumstance, as a result of the discourse of public reason, those who lose a chance to engage in this research might see their opponents as threatening civic equality. Proponents of embryonic stem cell research might be moved in this context—particularly when other constraints are placed on science in areas such as denying therapeutic cloning or refusing to allow the teaching of evolution—to claim that their opponents are committed to do away with liberal democracy and its commitment to open inquiry as the basis for knowledge creation and use. The instability arising from this experience might escalate further because the opponents of embryonic stem cell research, therapeutic cloning, and the teaching of evolution might see themselves as the "true" defenders of liberal democracy against its science-oriented enemies.

As the last paragraph suggests, it is not yet settled that people, merely because they support the shared values of a constitutional democracy, would, as Rawls's doctrine of reasonable toleration suggests, put to the side their differences for the sake of securing a liberal democracy. In my view, for people to accept outcomes of public deliberation that violate their own comprehensive doctrines—especially in matters having to do with scientific research—people would have to share a commitment to the primacy of the Kantian idea of respect for persons, throughout the public and the social realms. This understanding would be the basis for a form of civic friendship that enables people to accept their differences, and maintain their commitment to a constitutional democracy, on the basis of the assumption that, explicit in the practice of intellectual autonomy, there is an outcome of highest importance to achieving a decent society. In particular, what results from a widespread social commitment to intellectual autonomy is the likelihood of the creation and provision of all those goods, mentioned in the first paragraph of this chapter, that make possible prospering lives.

Is it likely that people could value intellectual autonomy to such an extent that it would provide a basis for social stability? My contention is that this possibility is feasible in the context of the modern, enlightened world that Kant first described and that we now inhabit. After all, since the Enlightenment, our modern world has been characterized by a public culture, which holds as primary beliefs the Kantian views that rational intelligence must be used both to make it possible for science to produce knowledge and to ensure that this knowledge serves only humane purposes. Moreover, it is understood that society can achieve these goals, and attain the flourishing that results, only when it allows intellectual autonomy to manifest itself fully across the social and the public realms. Thus, attaining the degree of civic friendship needed to maintain the stability of a liberal democracy in the face of Rawls's view of public reason depends on the extent to which science is understood as necessary for progress in all dimensions of life. When this understanding is strong, then there would be an overwhelming respect for the public culture of civic friendship that sustains autonomy and its associated values—freedom, critical thinking, intellectual pluralism, and the civic virtue of toleration.

References

Beck, Lewis White. "Introduction." *Kant: On History*, edited by Lewis White Beck. Indianapolis, IN: Bobbs-Merrill, 1980.

DeLue, Steven M. *Political Thinking, Political Theory and Civil Society*. New York: Longman, 2002.

Galston, William A. *Liberal Purposes: Goods, Virtues, and Diversity in the Liberal State*. Cambridge: Cambridge University Press, 1991.

———. *Liberal Pluralism: The Implications of Value Pluralism for Political Theory and Practice*. Cambridge: Cambridge University Press, 2002.

Kant, Immanuel. *Critique of Judgement*, translated by J. H. Bernard. New York: Hafner Press, 1951.

———. *Groundwork of the Metaphysic of Morals*, translated by H. J. Paton. New York: Harper and Row, 1964.

———. *Critique of Pure Reason*, translated by F. Max Muller. New York: Anchor, 1966.

———. "What Is Enlightenment?" *Kant: On History*, edited by Lewis White Beck. Indianapolis, IN: Bobbs-Merrill, 1980a.

———. "Idea for a Universal History." *Kant: On History*, edited by Lewis White Beck. Indianapolis, IN: Bobbs-Merrill, 1980b.

———. "The Metaphysical Principles of Virtue." *Ethical Philosophy*, translated by James W. Ellington. Indianapolis, IN: Hackett Publishing, 1983.

———. "On the Old Saw: That May Be Right in Theory but It Won't Work in Practice." *Classics in Modern Political Theory*, edited by Steven M. Cahn. New York: Oxford University Press, 1997.

———. *Metaphysical Elements of Justice*, translated by John Ladd. Indianapolis, IN: Hackett Publishing Company, 1999.

Larmore, Charles. "Public Reason." *The Cambridge Companion to Rawls*, edited by Samuel Freeman. Cambridge: Cambridge University Press, 2003.

Masters, Roger D. "Introduction." *Jean-Jacques Rousseau, the First and Second Discourses*, edited by Roger D. Masters and translated by Roger D. and Judith R. Masters. New York: St. Martin's Press, 1964.

Nieman, Susan. *Evil in Modern Thought: An Alternative History of Philosophy*. Princeton, NJ: Princeton University Press, 2002.

Rawls, John. *Political Liberalism*. New York: Columbia University Press, 1996.

———. *The Law of Peoples*. Cambridge, MA: Harvard University Press, 1999.

Tinder, Glenn. *Political Thinking: The Perennial Questions*. New York: Longman, 2004.

3

Reason and Authority in the Middle Ages
The Latin West and Islam

Edward Grant

To my knowledge, no one has ever attempted to describe a relationship between scientific values and civic virtues for the Middle Ages. This is perhaps because many are unclear as to what, if anything, qualifies as "science" in the late Middle Ages, so it is unclear if there were any scientists to uphold scientific values. Moreover, what would those values have been? Indeed, a relationship between the scientists or, better, natural philosophers and civic government officials might at first glance seem nonexistent. In truth, however, there is a story to tell about these relationships.

At first glance, one naturally thinks of medicine as a discipline that unavoidably links civic virtues and scientific values, as in plagues and quarantines. But on further reflection one realizes that there were indeed numerous connections between scientific values and civic virtues throughout the Middle Ages. Like so much else in medieval intellectual life, that connection derives from the writings of Aristotle. Not only did Aristotle supply the late Middle Ages with a series of works in natural philosophy that provided a thoroughgoing description and analysis of the structure and operations of the physical world, but he also provided comprehensive writings on civil government, politics, ethics, and the economy. Aristotle had classified natural philosophy as a theoretical discipline ranked after metaphysics and mathematics. He categorized his treatises on government, politics, and ethics as practical philosophy, largely because "their purpose or aim is not merely to purvey truth but also to affect action."[1] Despite the difference between theoretical and practical subject areas, Aristotle applied the same overall methodology to both kinds of treatises. His methodology is multifaceted, but holding it all together is human reason. For Aristotle, reason held the loftiest role for the human race, as he makes clear in his *Nicomachean Ethics*, when he says "for man . . . life according to intellect [i.e., reason] is best and pleasantest, since intellect more than anything else *is* man."[2] It was not only because Aristotle elevated reason to the highest level of human activity that he was so important for the subsequent emphasis on rationality in the Western world, but also the way he actually used reason to solve problems.

When all of Aristotle's treatises were finally translated and readily available as textbooks in the medieval universities of the late thirteenth and fourteenth centuries, medieval students and teachers learned how to use reason and critical arguments in both the theoretical and practical domains over which Aristotle's works extended.

In attacking a problem, or problems, Aristotle often thought it advisable to describe the opinions of others, who were usually his predecessors. He thought it important to present a reasonable history of the problems he sought to resolve. In the first book of the *Metaphysics*, Aristotle summarizes the opinions of numerous early pre-Socratic philosophers, as well as of Plato, on the principles that constitute all things. After his lengthy summary, Aristotle says that, all told, the early philosophers named all the causes of things but did so "vaguely; and though in a sense they have all been described before, in a sense they have not been described at all. For the earliest philosophy is, on all subjects, like one who lisps, since in its beginnings, it is but a child."[3]

Aristotle's contributions derived from his ability to begin many chapters with telling questions and problems, the answers to which provided a clear understanding of his positions. Thus, in *On the Heavens* (bk. 1, ch. 8), Aristotle wrote, "We must now proceed to explain why there cannot be more than one heaven—the further question mentioned above."[4] At the beginning of chapter 9, Aristotle declares, "We must show not only that the heaven is one, but also that more than one heaven is impossible, and further, that, as exempt from decay and generation, the heaven is eternal."[5] At the beginning of chapter 10, Aristotle announces, "Having established these distinctions, we may now proceed to the question whether the heaven is ungenerated or generated, indestructible or destructible," and then in a characteristic move, declares:

> Let us start with a review of the theories of other thinkers; for the proofs of a theory are difficulties for the contrary theory. Besides, those who have first heard the pleas of our adversaries will be more likely to credit the assertions we are going to make. We shall be less open to the charge of procuring judgment by default. To give a satisfactory decision as to the truth it is necessary to be rather an arbitrator than a party to the dispute.[6]

Not only did Aristotle often proceed by considering the history of a problem, but he often enough treated philosophical problems as puzzles to be solved, where it is essential to identify difficulties and present possible solutions. In treating any problem, Aristotle advocated stating the difficulties at the outset, so as to be fully cognizant of the kinds of dilemmas that might lie ahead. In *Metaphysics*, Aristotle asserts:

> One should have surveyed all the difficulties beforehand, both for reasons we have stated and because people who inquire without first stating the difficulties are like those who do not know where they have to go; besides, a man does not otherwise know even whether he has found what he is looking for or not; for the end is not clear to such a man, while to him who has first discussed the difficulties it is clear. Further, he who has heard all the contending arguments, as if they were parties to a case, must be in a better position for judging.[7]

Aristotle then proceeds to lay out question after question that he will consider in subsequent chapters following the plan of approach he has just described.

Aristotle's approach in the practical sciences of politics and ethics was much the same as his approach to the theoretical sciences of metaphysics and natural philosophy. In the opening chapter of his *Politics*, Aristotle emphasizes the utility of resolving compound entities into their constituent elements. "As in other departments of science," he declares,

> so in politics, the compound should always be resolved into the simple elements or least parts of the whole. We must therefore look at the elements of which the state is composed, in order that we may see in what the different kinds of rule differ from one another, and whether any scientific result can be attained about each one of them.[8]

It appears that Aristotle approached the constituent elements of politics in much the same manner as he treated the physical elements in natural philosophy. In *Politics*, Aristotle used the same probing analytic, rationalistic approach he used in all his treatises, as is evident when he declares:

> Having determined these questions, we have next to consider whether there is only one form of government or many, and if many, what they are, and how many, and what are the differences between them.
>
> A constitution is the arrangement of magistracies in a state, especially of the highest of all. The government is everywhere sovereign in the state, and the constitution is in fact the government. For example, in democracies the people are supreme, but in oligarchies, the few; and, therefore, we say that these two constitutions also are different: and so in other cases.
>
> First, let us consider what is the purpose of a state, and how many forms of rule there are by which human society is regulated.[9]

Above all else, Aristotle had the scientific temperament. He valued objectivity and detachment and sought to bring all relevant evidence to bear in the resolution of any given problem. Although Aristotle did not hesitate to invoke God and gods at various points in his treatises, his citations were not for reasons of piety, but rather reflected the "sense of wonderment which nature and its works produced in him."[10]

Aristotle's Medieval Legacy

Aristotle's scientific virtues as embodied in his great range of writings began to reach the Middle Ages in the mid-twelfth century, continuing until the end of the thirteenth century. Even before Aristotle's works reached the West, significant changes were already under way. Theologians such as Berengar of Tours (ca. 1000–1088), Anselm of Canterbury (1033–1109), and Peter Abelard (1079–1142) were challenging theological authorities by the application of reason to theological problems. In natural philosophy, Adelard of Bath (ca. 1080–1142) and William of Conches (d. after 1154) also self-consciously followed the path of reason. Indeed, William thought it improper to invoke God's omnipotence as an explanation for natural phenomena. Like Adelard of Bath, William believed that God was the ultimate cause of everything, but also like Adelard, William was convinced that God had empowered nature to produce its own effects and that a natural philosopher should therefore seek the causes of those effects in nature. The world of the early Middle Ages was rapidly maturing in the twelfth century. By the end of that century, the great universities of Paris, Oxford, and Bologna were in existence. It was into this changing world that Aristotle's works were eagerly received, despite some tensions in the thirteenth century between arts masters and theologians that led at different times to various modes of censorship of Aristotle's natural philosophy.

The Study of Aristotle

For more than three centuries—from the thirteenth to the sixteenth—teachers and students studied the whole of Aristotle's works, which included his logic, natural philosophy, metaphysics, and his works on practical philosophy, namely, his ethics, politics, and economics. Thus, they were quite aware that Aristotle used much the same methodology in all his works. This similarity of approach in seemingly widely disparate subjects linked natural philosophy with ideas about government and politics. Aristotle's medieval followers were keenly aware of his elaborate division of all the sciences. Aristotle thought it important to classify different kinds of knowledge and actions into appropriate categories. He distinguished three broad categories of knowledge that he regarded as scientific: the productive sciences, the practical sciences, and the theoretical sciences. The productive sciences embraced all knowledge concerned with the making of useful objects, while the practical sciences were directed toward human conduct. Everything else fell under the jurisdiction of the theoretical sciences, which Aristotle divided into three parts. If we take them in the order of priority, they are (1) metaphysics, or theology, which considers things that are unchangeable and therefore distinct and separable from matter or body, such as God and spiritual substances; (2) mathematics also considers things that are unchangeable, but, unlike metaphysics, the objects of mathematics have no separate existence because they are abstractions from physical bodies; and finally, (3) physics or, as it was often called, natural science or, as it came to be popularly designated, natural philosophy, which is concerned only with things that are changeable, exist separately, and also have within themselves an innate source of movement and rest.[11]

With this in mind, Thomas Aquinas wrote a commentary on Aristotle's *Politics* in which he derives four things from Aristotle's remarks in the first book. The first is "the necessity of this science," that is, politics:

> For in order to arrive at the perfection of human wisdom, which is called philosophy, it is necessary to teach something about all that can be known by reason. Since then that whole which is the city is subject to a certain judgment of reason, it is necessary, so that philosophy may be complete, to institute a discipline that deals with the city; and this discipline is called politics or civil science.[12]

But where does this science of the city, or politics, belong in the overall scheme of knowledge and sciences? As his second major point, Thomas is, in effect, asking to what genus the science of politics belongs. He explains that "since the practical sciences are distinguished from the speculative sciences in that the speculative sciences are ordered exclusively to the knowledge of the truth, whereas the practical sciences are ordered to some work," it follows that the science of politics "must be comprised under practical philosophy, inasmuch as the city is a certain whole that human reason not only knows but also produces."[13] Of the practical sciences, politics belongs to the moral sciences, not the mechanical arts. As the third point, Thomas emphasizes that, with respect to all other practical sciences, "The city is indeed the most important of the things that can be constituted by human reason, for all the other human societies are ordered to it."[14]

The fourth point is extremely important, because it reveals how interrelated the methods of the speculative and practical sciences were regarded. "Fourthly," Thomas declares,

> from what has already been said we can deduce the mode and the order of this science. For just as the speculative sciences, which treat of some whole, arrive at a knowledge of the whole by manifesting its properties and its principles from an examination of its parts and its principles, so too this science examines the parts and the principles of the city and gives us a knowledge of it by manifesting its parts and its properties and its operations. And because it is a practical science, it manifests in addition how each thing may be realized, as is necessary in every practical science.[15]

It is obvious that medieval scholastic natural philosophers approached the mechanics of human government, as manifested in the cities of Europe, in much the same manner as they approached the workings of nature in the physical cosmos.

But did the scientific theories of scholastic natural philosophers about the nature and function of municipal governments in medieval Europe have any actual impact on the way cities were governed or, for that matter, in the way entire countries or regions were ruled? Many university graduates sought, and acquired, positions at the courts of various rulers, from ducal to royal, or as employees of municipal governments. Did they apply their knowledge of Aristotle's ideas about science in general, and the practical science of politics in particular, to shape and influence the behavior of the governing entities that employed them? It is likely that they did, but we shall probably never really know. The universities in medieval and Renaissance Europe had great prestige, as is evidenced by the fact that in the late fifteenth and sixteenth centuries, princes and cities established numerous universities within their domains. In these new universities, and in many of the older ones, "*Utilitarian* aims . . . increasingly took precedence over disinterested motives; universities were primarily intended to produce officials, administrators, magistrates, diplomats, and other public servants."[16] As Jacques Le Goff has declared,

> The highly theoretical and bookish character of professional training in the academy did not prevent it from responding to the needs of the public authorities. The degree of specialization required by public offices was in fact quite limited: the ability to read and write, knowledge of Latin, and familiarity with legal principles or the capacity to argue from certain texts were essential, along with some elementary accounting principles, and some still more rudimentary economics (see *De moneta* by Nicole Oresme). Furthermore, a taste for political theory on the part of princes or sovereigns, and even

a taste for "scientific" government, i.e. government inspired by scholastic principles (cf. the role of Aristotelianism at the court of Charles V of France, and at the Polish court, and the role of Aristotelianism and Platonism or an amalgam of the two in the government of the Italian oligarchies and seignieuries), coincided with the intellectual tendencies of the academics.[17]

Under these circumstances, it is highly likely that scientific values and civic virtues met and intermingled on numerous occasions, though largely with unknown results. The career of Nicole Oresme (ca. 1320–1382), mentioned by Le Goff, is a striking example of a scholastic natural philosopher who made major contributions to both science and government. Oresme belongs to that class of natural philosophers who acquired doctorates in theology and is also a member of a small class of theologians whose contributions to natural philosophy exceeded their accomplishments in theology.

Indeed, it is no exaggeration to regard Nicole Oresme as the most innovative and significant natural philosopher and mathematician in the Middle Ages.[18] He used the typical medieval questions format to comment upon all of Aristotle's works on natural philosophy. He disagreed with Aristotle on many points and presented cogent arguments for his positions. He believed that God could indeed create more than one world and that each created world would be a closed system independent of every other world. Approximately two centuries before Copernicus, Oresme argued that the earth's possible daily axial rotation was perhaps even more plausible and logical than the alternative, namely, that the earth lies immobile at the center of the world, while the celestial bodies make a daily revolution around it. He even interpreted biblical passages seemingly in favor of an immobile earth—for example, Joshua 10:12–14, where God aids the army of Joshua by making the sun stand still over Gibeon—as being just as compatible with a rotating earth. He opted for the traditional opinion, because in the absence of compelling evidence for either side, he accepted the literal meaning of the biblical texts.

In his specialized tractates, Oresme made numerous contributions. Using Euclid's theory of proportionality in the fifth book of the *Elements*, Oresme arrived at the concept of an irrational exponent. In the relationship between two ratios, $A/B = (C/D)^{p/q}$, Oresme calls the exponent, p/q, a "ratio of ratios." He treated both rational and irrational exponents, arguing that, the greater the number of rational ratios related two at a time, the greater will be the ratio of irrational ratios of ratios to rational relationships. Oresme took 100 rational ratios from $2/1$ to $101/1$ and showed that these 100 ratios taken two at a time would form 9,900 possible ratios of ratios. Since Oresme was only interested in ratios of greater inequality, that is, where the numerator of the ratio is greater than its denominator, that is, $A > B$, only half of the 9,900 ratios are relevant, namely, 4,950, which are ratios of ratios of greater inequality. Of these 4,950, Oresme shows that only twenty-five are rational, with the other 4,925 being irrational. Thus, the odds that p/q, the exponent, or "ratio of ratios," will be irrational are 197 to 1. The more rational ratios one takes, the greater the odds become that any random choice of a ratio of ratios will be irrational.

Oresme applied his fascination with ratios of ratios to traditional problems of motion. He, like so many medieval scholastics, rejected Aristotle's mathematical explanation for velocities produced by the application of a motive force to a resistance. He applied the formulations in the preceding paragraph to the velocities produced by applications of forces to resistances. Although his descriptions were verbal, they can legitimately be represented as $F_2/R_2 = (F_1/R_1)^{v2/v1}$, where F is a force applied to a resistance, R, and v_2/v_1 is the ratio of velocities generated by the two force-resistance ratios. In his French commentary on his own French translation of Aristotle's *On the Heavens*, Oresme suggests that perhaps the celestial motions are also moved by ratios of force to resistance. Perhaps

> when God created the heavens, He put into them motive qualities and powers just as He put weight and resistance against these motive powers in earthly things. These powers and resistances are different in nature and in substance from any sensible thing or quality here below. The powers against the resistances are moderated in such a way, so tempered, and so harmonized that the movements are made without violence; thus, violence excepted, the situation is much like that of a man making a clock and letting it run and continue its own motion by itself. In this manner did God allow the heaven to be moved continually according to the proportions of the motive powers to the resistances and according to the established order [or regularity].[19]

Few medieval natural philosophers would have followed Oresme. For them, the heavens were moved by angels or intelligences and offered no resistance to their motion.

In his *Treatise on the Commensurability or Incommensurability of the Celestial Motions*, Oresme first presents twenty-five propositions in which bodies are assumed to move with commensurable speeds on concentric circles, and then presents twelve propositions, in each of which at least two of the motions are incommensurable. The third part is a debate presided over by Apollo. The antagonists in this debate are the personifications of Arithmetic and Geometry, who argue whether the celestial motions are commensurable (Arithmetic) or incommensurable (Geometry).[20] There is no doubt that Oresme believed it more probable that the celestial motions were incommensurable than commensurable. For this reason, he argued that astrology was inherently implausible and in vain.

Oresme's detailed contributions to problems of celestial incommensurability have attracted the attention of modern mathematicians and philosophers. Robin Small observes that "the doctrine of eternal recurrence, which asserts that every state of affairs must come into being again on infinitely many other occasions, has attracted few supporters and many opponents."[21] Small explains that many arguments have been mustered against the doctrine of eternal recurrence. He notes that one particular counterargument was first formulated in the fourteenth century by Nicole Oresme. "Oresme constructs an example which consists of three objects moving in circular courses with incommensurable speeds, and he draws a conclusion which is the same as Simmel's: the initial position of the three objects can never recur, no matter how long they continue to move in the way described."[22] Jon Von Plato also found striking contributions in Oresme's *Treatise on the Commensurability or Incommensurability of the Celestial Motions*:

> A few of Oresme's theorems on the consequences of the possible incommensurability of the revolution times of bodies in uniform circular motion have their counterpart in the

modern theory of ergodic dynamical systems. The concept of probability plays a vital role in the latter theory. By understanding Oresme's results as anticipations of some of the simplest properties of ergodic systems, his use of the notion of probability becomes of systematic interest. But it is of interest also purely historically, since it represents a frequentist view on probabilities prior to the invention of the calculus of probability in the seventeenth century. To give at once an example of what will be studied in some detail below, let us describe one of Oresme's propositions that is relevant here. He proves that if *any portion* of the ecliptic is considered, it is *probable* that a conjunction of two planets will sooner or later visit that portion. Despite the shortcomings of Maître Nicole's conceptual apparatuses, it is obvious that a sound principle is contained in the proposition—a theorem expressing that the kinematic rotational scheme of two planets forms an *ergodic system*.[23]

Sometime around 1350, Oresme wrote his highly mathematical *Treatise on the Configuration of Qualities and Motions,* in which he represented variations in qualities by geometric figures. Among the major achievements of this treatise is the first geometric proof of the mean speed theorem, namely, that $s = 1/2at^2$, where s is distance traversed, t is time, and a is uniform acceleration. Oresme's proof was printed in numerous editions of the sixteenth century and probably influenced Galileo, who presented a similar proof in his *Two New Sciences* (1638). Finally, I mention the latest of Oresme's achievements that have come to light. In *On Seeing the Stars* (*De visione stellarum*), a treatise on atmospheric refraction, Oresme discovered that refraction of light does not require a single refracting interface between two media of differing densities and that light will be refracted along a curved path when it is in a single medium of uniformly varying density. Thus, Oresme broke with the traditional optics of Ptolemy, Alhazen, Roger Bacon, and Witelo. Oresme deduced the curved path for light by using his knowledge of convergent infinite series, showing that as line segments increased to infinity they form a curved line. Danny Burton, who first discovered Oresme's contribution to our understanding of atmospheric refraction, observes that Robert Hooke and Isaac Newton were previously thought to have been the first to argue that light is continuously refracted as it moves along a curved path through a uniformly decreasing medium. However, "while the definitive demonstration of the curvature of light in the atmosphere was Hooke's and Newton's, the original argument for such curvature was Oresme's."[24]

These were Oresme's major contributions to science and natural philosophy. Numerous other significant thoughts and ideas could be drawn from his many works, but what has been mentioned is more than enough to reveal the high quality of his scientific intellect. What scientific values can we find in his acknowledged scientific works? Certain modern scientific values cannot be applied to Oresme and his colleagues in the Middle Ages. For example, although most in the Middle Ages followed Aristotle and emphasized sensation and observation as the foundations of knowledge and science, they rarely appealed to direct observations to support an argument or a claim, perhaps, because, as Aristotle argued, our senses do not "tell us the 'why' of anything—for example, why fire is hot; they only say that it is hot."[25] To know the why of things requires theoretical explanations based on the way things had to be in order for the world to function as it did. Nor did medieval natural philosophers perform experiments in support of a theory or claim. It was never regarded as essential to do so. These habits had to await the seventeenth century.

But there were scientific values that were recognized in the Middle Ages. Indeed, some of them were first consciously emphasized on a wide scale in that period. Oresme and others, especially John Buridan, who may have been one of Oresme's teachers, believed in what Buridan called "the common course of nature." This signified that only natural causes were proper for the explanation of natural effects in the physical world. It effectively eliminated the intrusion of unpredictable, supernatural intervention. This approach was often characterized by the phrase "speaking naturally" (*loquendo naturaliter*), which meant speaking in terms of natural science, not in terms of faith or theology. Almost all who did natural philosophy in the late Middle Ages adhered to this approach: only natural explanations were legitimate for the discipline of natural philosophy.

We can better understand why medieval natural philosophers routinely invoked natural causes to explain natural phenomena if we recognize that they placed enormous emphasis on reason and reasoned argument.[26] Not only did medieval scholastics apply reason to natural philosophy, but just as significantly, they also applied it to theology to such an extent that they completely rationalized that discipline. The emphasis on reason, which is perhaps the most vital scientific value—science is impossible without it—is closely linked to another prominent value without which science cannot progress: the challenge to authority, a challenge that began in the early Middle Ages and gathered adherents in the course of the late Middle Ages.[27] I could cite numerous passages that reveal the many ways in which appeals to authority were criticized. Biblical authorities and articles of faith were all regarded as absolutely true and unchallengeable, but they were regarded as supernatural arguments that played no role in natural phenomena. Although all had to accept the creation of the world from nothing, they all acknowledged that such a creation was a supernatural act, because it made no sense in terms of Aristotelian natural philosophy, where everything that comes into being comes into being from some previously existent material entity. John Buridan, for example, posed a question in which he inquired whether every generable thing will be generated. In his response, Buridan acknowledges that one can treat this problem naturally—"as if the opinion of Aristotle were true concerning the eternity of the world, and that something cannot be made from nothing"—or supernaturally, wherein God could prevent a generable thing from generating naturally by simply annihilating it. "But now," Buridan declares, "with Aristotle we speak in a natural mode, with miracles excluded." Thus did Buridan follow the "common course of nature" and follow Aristotle rather than the faith.[28]

The real challenge to authority in the Middle Ages, however, was aimed at Aristotle himself. This may come as a surprise to moderns who are very likely to be influenced by Galileo's depiction of medieval scholastics as slavish followers of Aristotle. Although Galileo's criticisms were directed against contemporary Aristotelians, not against fourteenth- and fifteenth-century scholastic natural philosophers, his views came to be applied indifferently to the whole of medieval scholasticism.[29] Nevertheless, disagreements with Aristotle were commonplace in the Middle Ages, and there were numerous departures from his physics and cosmology. Nicole Oresme provides us with the most striking example. Oresme's assault on Aristotle, which will be described below, serves as an appropriate link between his scientific values and his involvement with the government of his day and, in effect, with civic virtues.

Nicole Oresme's intimate involvement with civic government came about largely through his rather significant relationship with King Charles V of France (1338–1380). Indeed, King John II, the father of Charles V, had already requested Oresme's help with problems of national finance that confronted his monarchy. As a consequence of John's request, Oresme wrote a famous Latin treatise on money (*De moneta;* there was a later French version) in which he shows keen understanding of the workings of government and the role of money in society.[30] It is likely that at this time Oresme came to know Charles, who was then dauphin and became king in 1364, reigning until his death in 1380. Over the years, Oresme served Charles faithfully on various royal missions. But their close relationship may well have been intellectual, since Charles had a genuine love of learning, as illustrated by the magnificent library he collected in the tower of the Louvre.[31]

Sometime around 1370, Charles commissioned Oresme to translate four Aristotelian treatises from Latin into French: the *Nicomachean Ethics, Politics, Economics* (not actually by Aristotle, but regularly attributed to him in the Middle Ages), and *On the Heavens.* By ordering the translation of the first three treatises, Charles hoped to make his councilors and courtiers better at the art of government. In the preface to his French translation of the *Ethics,* Oresme explains that

> because the books on moral subjects written by Aristotle were originally in Greek and have come down to us in Latin quite difficult to understand, the King desired, for the common good, to have them translated into French so that he and his counselors and others may understand them better, particularly the *Ethics* and the *Politics;* the first teaches how to be a good man, and the other how to be a good ruler of men.[32]

King Charles was apparently eager to use Aristotle's *Politics* as a guide to improving his own government. At the apparent urging of Oresme, Menut explains, Charles "wished to try out the idea of sharing a small part of his responsibilities as a monarch with his Council, a body of some 200 citizens of some distinction drawn from the nobility and upper ranks of the bourgeoisie to assist the king in his undertaking to represent the public sentiment and reaction to royal measures of government."[33] Indeed, Charles even urged Oresme to quicken the pace of his translations so that relevant passages might be available for his councilors to consider at a meeting scheduled for February 21, 1372. With his treatise on money, and his French translations of Aristotle's ethical and political works, Oresme was clearly heavily involved in matters relevant to the state and the economy. It seems apparent that Charles chose Oresme for the translations, and for other tasks pertaining to state government, because Oresme was a recognized Aristotelian scholar: a master of Aristotle's natural philosophy and the theoretical scientific disciplines, as well as of Aristotle's practical sciences of politics, ethics, and economics.

Although it is obvious that Charles wanted Oresme to translate the *Ethics, Politics,* and *Economics* for reasons of state, Oresme offers no reason to explain why

Charles also wanted a French translation of Aristotle's *On the Heavens*, on which Oresme conferred the title *Le Livre du Ciel et du Monde*. It is quite possible that Oresme himself suggested the translation. Why? Because he may have regarded it as important for the courtiers and councilors to view the details of earthly government against the backdrop, and within the context, of the big picture of the physical cosmos itself. Oresme was convinced that Aristotle's *On the Heavens* was the greatest book in natural philosophy ever written, as we learn at the end of his French translation, where he declares that "no mortal man has ever seen a finer or better book of natural philosophy in Hebrew, in Greek or Arabic, in Latin or French than this one."[34] If this left anyone unconvinced, Oresme concludes the entire treatise with these glorious words (in Latin) about Aristotle's *On the Heavens:* "Never in this world was there a book on natural philosophy more beautiful or more powerful."[35]

As an indication of how meaningful Oresme's translations were to King Charles, Oresme informs his readers at the conclusion of *Le Livre du Ciel et du Monde*, the final French translation, that "the very excellent Prince Charles, the fifth of this name, by the grace of God, King of France, who, while, I was doing this, has made me bishop of Lisieux." In this same final paragraph of his translation, Oresme emphasizes the great importance he placed on challenging authority, even his own, explaining that he did the translation "for the purpose of animating, exciting, and moving the hearts of those young people who have subtle and noble talents and the desire for knowledge to prepare themselves to argue against and to correct me because of their love and affection for the truth."[36]

This was not empty rhetoric placed for dramatic effect at the end of a lengthy treatise. If the courtiers and councilors, for whom the translation was made, read it with a modicum of care, they would immediately recognize that Oresme was himself the role model for challenging authority. Indeed, they could hardly avoid it. Although, as we saw, Oresme lavishly praised Aristotle's *Le Livre du Ciel et du Monde* as the greatest work on natural philosophy ever written, he challenges, and frequently opposes, Aristotle's ideas and arguments. To appreciate the full impact of Oresme's challenge to Aristotle, we need only peruse Oresme's unalphabetized list of 133 noteworthy topics that are covered in *Le Livre du Ciel* and organized in the order of their occurrence. In thirty-five of these, Oresme cites Aristotle by name and explicitly disagrees with his arguments. Most of the entries have the form "Opposing Aristotle" (*contre Aristote*). The following examples show some of the ways Oresme opposed Aristotle:

> A strong argument against Aristotle's opinion that, if another world existed, the earth of our world would move to the center of the other one, with the reply to this argument.
>
> Replies to the arguments Aristotle offers to prove that there can be but one world.
>
> How it is possible for a movement to begin and last forever, contrary to Aristotle's opinion.
>
> Opposing Aristotle, who argues that for natural reasons the heavens are living bodies.
>
> Opposing Aristotle, who says that, if the heavens move, the earth must necessarily be at rest in the middle of the heavens; the contrary is demonstrated by several arguments.

Opposing Aristotle, it is shown how it is possible in imagination and in reality that the speed of heavenly motion has been continuously increasing through infinite past time and will be continuously diminishing through infinite future time.

That air and water are not heavy in their natural places, contrary to what Aristotle says.[37]

Oresme's extensive critique of Aristotle and his exhortations to King Charles's courtiers and councilors to challenge his own opinions and interpretations should be viewed against the backdrop of the history and evolution of the medieval university, which was the home of medieval science and natural philosophy, the place where theoretical problems were discussed and analyzed by means of questions that presented the pros and cons of an argument. This analytical approach extended to problems of political science and ultimately to the fundamental problem of the relations between church and state. Some scholars trained in Aristotelian natural philosophy at the universities, or perhaps even in schools of religious orders, wrote important treatises on the relations between church and state, a problem that was prominent in the thirteenth and early fourteenth centuries. Francisco Bertelloni observes that, during the course of the thirteenth century, political argumentation was transformed by at least three basic causes: "(1) the arrival of Aristotle's writings on ethics and politics in the West, (2) the institutional consolidation of the universities and, above all, (3) the introduction of systematic theory and argumentation, which is to a great extent a consequence of the two previous causes."[38] The impact of these factors produced a series of treatises on political theory by scholastic authors, beginning with Thomas Aquinas, who wrote a treatise *On the Rule of Princes* (*De regimine principum*) in the 1260s. Of the four books of this work, Thomas contributed only the first book and part of the second (it was completed between 1274 and 1282 by Thomas's student, Ptolemy Lucques).[39] The importance of the new treatises on political theory is that they

inaugurated a tradition in political literature that can be described as the "theory of the duality of powers." This approach assumed different shapes: indirect subordination of the temporal power to the spiritual (Thomas Aquinas); direct subordination and reduction of the temporal power to the spiritual (Giles of Rome); relative independence (John of Paris); and absolute independence (Dante Alighieri). In different degrees and forms, all these authors can be included in a theoretical model that stated the existence of *two coactive powers*. In current language, this means simply two sovereignties.[40]

In radical disagreement with the idea of two coactive powers, Marsilius of Padua (1280–1343), in his *The Defender of the Peace* (*Defensor Pacis*), completed in 1324 and dedicated to Ludwig of Bavaria, "tries to show that sovereignty is only one (I, xvii), that it cannot be divided, and that it does not reside in the pope but in the *legislator humanus*."[41] Marsilius clearly went beyond his predecessors by asserting the superiority of the civil authority over church authority vested in the pope. Church and state were thus not equal, nor was the church superior to the state, but Marsilius boldly proclaimed the authority of state over church. Marsilius observes that this was not a problem that Aristotle could have known or confronted, but it is the cause of much strife. "The fruits of peace or tranquility, then, are the greatest goods, . . . while those of its opposite, strife, are unbearable evils. Hence we ought to wish for peace, to seek it if we do not already have it, to conserve it once it is attained, and to repel with all our strength the strife which is opposed to it."[42]

Marsilius proposed to end the strife between church and state by reinterpreting Christian doctrine and practice. The final authority in the Church lay with the entire community of believers acting together in a general council. It did not reside in the pope and the clergy. Indeed, only the recognized secular prince—not the pope—has the authority to call a general council. Scriptures as interpreted by reasonable men—not the pope or clergy—are the ultimate authority within the church. Marsilius insisted that the clergy are not a class distinct from the laity and should have no special authority. He granted sweeping powers to the secular state and placed the church under its authority.

The Defender of the Peace was a truly innovative treatise that influenced subsequent revolutionary figures like John Hus, John Wyclif (ca. 1320–1384), and others. Although Marsilius was an innovative thinker, his methodology and sense of organization were thoroughly scholastic (he was trained in law, medicine, and arts and was rector of the University of Paris between 1312 and 1313). After describing each of the three discourses into which he divides his treatise, Marsilius shows his scholastic roots when he explains:

> Each of these discourses I shall divide into chapters, and each chapter into more or less paragraphs depending on the length of the chapter. One advantage of this division will be ease for the readers in finding what they look for when they are referred from later to earlier discourses and chapters. From this will follow a second advantage: a shortening of the volume. For when we assume in later pages some truth, either for itself or for the demonstration of other things, whose proof or certainty has been sufficiently set forth in preceding sections, instead of trifling with the proof all over again, we shall send the reader back to the discourse, chapter, and paragraph in which the proof was originally given, so that thus he may easily be able to find the certainty of the proposition in question.[43]

We see that, in the medieval university, the training in Aristotelian natural philosophy and in the practical sciences of ethics and politics was characterized by an overall methodology that emphasized organization, analysis, and reasoned argument. The idea was to demonstrate conclusively your own ideas and to argue persuasively that the alternatives were either mistaken or inadequate. One may plausibly conclude that after 400 years—from the thirteenth to sixteenth centuries—of organized discussions of civic and cosmic problems, scholars all across Western Christendom had adopted a highly rationalistic approach to the world about them. What we have here is nothing less than the establishment of the "scientific temperament" an attribute that would eventually make Western Civilization the scientific powerhouse of the world.

Islam

Although they share a number of basic beliefs, few religions and cultures seem more contrary than medieval Western Christianity and medieval Islam. Many of the differences stem from the fact that the Christianity that evolved within the Roman

Empire accepted a separation between church and state, whereas from its inception, Islam was a theocratic state in which secularism was to play no part. Also of significance was the fact that Christianity was born within the Roman Empire, where it was disseminated slowly and therefore had time to adjust to pagan philosophical and scientific beliefs that may have been perceived as hostile or dangerous to the faith. It was not until 392 c.e. that Christianity became the state religion of the Roman Empire. By contrast, Islam, following the death of Muhammad in 632, was spread over an enormous geographical area in a remarkably short time. In less than 100 years, Islam was the dominant religion from the Arabian Peninsula westward to the Straits of Gibraltar and eastward to Persia, Balkh, Samarkand, and Khwarizm. Another striking contrast is the fact that Islam was spread by conquest, whereas Christianity spread slowly and, with the exceptions of certain periods of persecution, relatively peacefully.

Whereas Christianity spread slowly, by proselytizing, Islam came from outside the Roman world as an alien intruder, and although its converts were pagans and often former Christians, the mind-set of the invaders was one that viewed Greek learning as alien, as illustrated by the fact that Muslims distinguished two kinds of sciences: the Islamic sciences, based on the Koran and Islamic law and traditions, and the foreign sciences, or "pre-Islamic" sciences, which encompassed Greek science and natural philosophy. We might say that the slow spread of Christianity provided Christians an opportunity to adjust to Greek secular learning, whereas Islam's rapid dissemination made its relations with Greek learning much more problematic.

As the Muslim armies conquered former Christian areas such as Egypt and Syria, and parts of modern Iraq and Iran, they came into contact with Greek philosophy and science. Over the course of time, most of these Greek treatises were translated into Arabic and the great treasure of ancient learning—the foreign sciences—became readily available to scholars in Islamic lands. Within this mass of learning, Aristotle's natural philosophy was perhaps the most important. The study of his works, and the commentaries on them, gave rise to a class of scholars known as "the philosophers." In the division of Islamic scholars, three categories were usually distinguished: (1) the first level was composed of legal scholars, largely because the religious law and traditions were valued above all else—even more than theology. Next in order came (2) the *mutakallimun*, scholars who used Greek philosophy to interpret and defend the Muslim religion. The *mutakallimun* emphasized rational discourse, to which they added the authority of revelation. And, finally, at the bottom, were (3) the *falasifa*, the Islamic philosophers, who followed rational Greek thought, especially the thought of Aristotle. Not surprisingly, the philosophers placed greatest reliance on reasoned argument while downplaying revelation. The philosophers sought to develop natural philosophy in an Islamic environment and, as A. I. Sabra has put it, did so "often in the face of suspicion and opposition from certain quarters in Islamic society."[44]

The legal scholars in Islam were easily the most important group. They were traditionalists focused on the religious law who did not use philosophy in their studies and analyses of religious ideas and beliefs, largely because they were convinced that rationalistic philosophy was a threat to the Islamic religion. They were usually in direct contact with the masses and therefore exerted the greatest influence on Muslim society. The *mutakallimun* were primarily concerned with the kalam, which, according to A. I. Sabra, is "an inquiry into God, and into the world as God's creation, and into man as the special creature placed by God in the world under obligation to his creator."[45] Thus, kalam is a theology that used Greek philosophical ideas to explicate and defend the Islamic faith. The *mutakallimun* were divided into two different subgroups, but they were often criticized by the traditionalists as too rationalistic.

Of the three groups distinguished, the philosophers were the least popular. Because they used natural philosophy and logic to acquire truth for its own sake, which usually signified that they were ignoring religion, the philosophers were frequently attacked by both the *mutakallimun* and traditionalist Muslims. The famous al-Ghazali (1058–1111), and the much less known Ibn as-Salah ash-Shahrazuri (d. 1245), a religious leader in the field of tradition (*hadith*), delivered devastating attacks on philosophy and philosophers. Al-Ghazali was convinced that philosophy would lead good Muslims astray and endanger their faith. He launched major attacks on al-Farabi and Avicenna, two of Islam's greatest Aristotelian natural philosophers.

In the thirteenth century, Ibn as-Salah ash-Shahrazuri declared in a *fatwa* that "he who studies or teaches philosophy will be abandoned by God's favor, and Satan will overpower him. What field of learning could be more despicable than one that blinds those who cultivate it and darkens their hearts against the prophetic teaching of Muhammad."[46] Logic was also targeted, because, as Ibn as-Salah, put it, "it is a means of access to philosophy. Now the means of access to something bad is also bad."[47] Ibn as-Salah was not content to confine his hostility to words alone. In a rather chilling passage, he urges vigorous action against students and teachers of philosophy and logic, because

> those who think they can occupy themselves with philosophy and logic merely out of personal interest or through belief in its usefulness are betrayed and duped by Satan. It is the duty of the civil authorities to protect Muslims against the evil that such people can cause. Persons of this sort must be removed from the schools and punished for their cultivation of these fields. All those who give evidence of pursuing the teachings of philosophy must be confronted with the following alternatives: either (execution) by the sword or (conversion to) Islam, so that the land may be protected and the traces of those people and their sciences may be eradicated. May God support and expedite it. However, the most important concern at the moment is to identify all of those who pursue philosophy, those who have written about it, have taught it, and to remove them from their positions insofar as they are employed as teachers in schools.[48]

Because of these fears, philosophy and natural philosophy became marginal subjects, usually taught privately or in a minor way at this or that school. The focal point at all Islamic schools was the Qur'an and the traditions of the Islamic religion. As a consequence, the institutionalization of natural philosophy never occurred. In Islam, natural philosophy was never made a regular part of the educational process. Prior to 1500, the exact sciences in Islam had reached loftier heights than in medieval Western Europe, but they did so without a vibrant natural philosophy. In Western Europe, by contrast, natural philosophy was institutionalized, as was a highly developed logic, in the numerous medieval universities and reached a high state of development, whereas the exact sciences had merely been absorbed from

Greco-Arabic scientific literature and maintained at a modest level. I believe it is plausible to conclude that the exact sciences will not long flourish in the absence of a well-developed natural philosophy. By contrast, natural philosophy can be brought to a high state of development in the absence of significant achievements in the exact sciences. One may conjecture that the subsequent decline of science in Islam is connected to the diminished role played by natural philosophy in that society and the attendant failure to institutionalize natural philosophy within the educational process.

In light of the fate of natural philosophy in Islam and the absence of separation of church and state, it is not surprising that civic virtues in Islamic urban and state governments were drawn from the Qur'an and Islamic religious traditions. Aristotle's practical sciences, as embodied in his *Ethics* and *Politics*, could therefore play no role in guiding Muslims to an understanding of civic virtues. There were no civic virtues; there were only Islamic virtues.

A significant difference between medieval Islam and medieval Western Christendom lies in the manner in which each religion approached its sacred scriptures. Muslims made the study of the Qur'an and the hadiths, or traditional writings, the central focus of an education for all Muslims who attended educational institutions. Within this framework, there was no room for natural philosophy. In Western Christianity, by contrast, the Bible was not a subject for study in an elementary or university education. Very few were expected to read holy scripture. At the university, only students in the school of theology studied the Bible and came to memorize much, if not all, of it. But theology was one of the higher, or graduate, disciplines, just as were law and medicine. Students who began their academic careers in an arts faculty—and all did—were not expected to read the Bible or to discuss theological issues and the articles of faith. This had enormous ramifications for education. Instead of focusing on the Bible for their basic education, arts students devoted themselves to the study of natural philosophy and logic. Moreover, the study of logic and natural philosophy in the arts faculties was regarded by virtually all to be a vital preparation for those who eventually did study theology and scripture in the faculty of theology. One was expected to be competent in logic and natural philosophy to study theology and the Bible.

Not until the Protestant Reformation was the personal study and reading of the Bible advocated for everyone. At that point, and in this regard, Protestant Christianity came to resemble Islam more than it did Catholic Christianity. But by this time—in the sixteenth century—natural philosophy was so entrenched in Western Europe that it was as important for Protestants as it was for Catholics. If in the early centuries, say, from the ninth to the fifteenth centuries, Christianity had focused on Bible study in the same intensive manner as Islam focused on the Qur'an, the history of Western science would have been radically altered; we would probably still be awaiting the arrival of Copernicus, Galileo, and Newton.

One other comparison is noteworthy. In the West, a class of theologian–natural philosophers developed within the university milieu. These were scholars who, beginning in the thirteenth century, had attained proficiency in natural philosophy as masters of arts and then went on to become professional theologians—that is, doctors of theology—in a faculty of theology. It was largely their attitudes toward

Aristotle's philosophy in all its aspects that made it possible for a secular discipline such as natural philosophy to flourish in the medieval university. Without the full sanction of the theologians, Greco-Arabic science and Aristotelian natural philosophy could not have become the official curriculum of the universities. Despite some anxiety about natural philosophy in the thirteenth century, theologians not only came to endorse a secular arts curriculum, but virtually all of them believed that the study of natural philosophy was essential for a proper understanding of theology. Many theologian-natural philosophers were significant contributors to natural philosophy and science, as the names of Albertus Magnus, Robert Grosseteste, John Pecham, Theodoric of Freiberg, Thomas Bradwardine, and Nicole Oresme bear witness.

I know of no analogous development within Islam. Those who qualified as theologians, and who were students of the Qur'an and the Islamic traditions, did not contribute to natural philosophy, because they would have regarded that discipline as irrelevant to the faith, and even dangerous to it. Some *mutakallimun* may have been considered theologians and found occasion to use Greek philosophy to interpret and defend the Islamic faith. But the great majority of Islamic theologians would have regarded the application of Greek philosophy to explicate the Qur'an as blasphemous. Indeed, most would have been ignorant of Greek philosophy. By contrast, Islamic philosophers—especially the likes of al-Kindi (d. ca. 870), al-Farabi (ca. 870–ca. 950), Ibn Sina (Avicenna) (980–1037), Ibn Bajja (Avempace) (d. 1139), and Ibn Rushd (Averroes) (ca. 1126–1198)—were thoroughly acquainted with the full range of Aristotle's works, especially his natural philosophy, and wrote much on science and natural philosophy but virtually nothing on theology. In the large scheme of Islamic history, however, the Islamic philosophers played only a marginal role.

The relationship between civic virtues and scientific values in the Latin West and in Islam differed radically, largely because church and state were distinct in the former but not in the latter, which was essentially a theocracy. Civic virtues in Islam were based on the Qur'an and were not in any way drawn from Aristotle's views on the state, or from the interpretations of other secular-minded philosophers. The kinds of treatises written in the West about the relations of church and state, mentioned above, have no counterparts in the Muslim world of the Middle Ages. Within a society that distinguished between church and state, Christian theologians of the Middle Ages developed a strong regard for the importance of natural philosophy, both for its own sake and for its utility in theology. As a consequence, natural philosophy flourished and was widely disseminated throughout Western Europe between the thirteenth and sixteenth centuries. Deeply embedded in the intellectual life of Western Europe, natural philosophy shaped the "scientific temperament" that made early modern and modern science possible.

Notes

1. Jonathan Barnes, *Aristotle* (Oxford: Oxford University Press, 1982), 77.

2. Aristotle, *Nicomachean Ethics* 10.7.1178a.6, trans. W. D. Ross and revised by J. O. Urmson in *The Complete Works of Aristotle*, 2 vols. (Princeton, NJ: Princeton University Press, 1984), 2:1862.

3. I have drawn on Edward Grant, *God and Reason in the Middle Ages* (Cambridge: Cambridge University Press, 2001), 91. For Aristotle's remarks, see *Metaphysics* 1.10.993a.12–16, trans. W. D. Ross in *The Complete Works of Aristotle*, 2:1569.

4. Aristotle, *On the Heavens*, bk. 1, ch. 8, 276a.18–19, trans. J. L. Stocks in *The Complete Works of Aristotle*, 1:458.

5. Ibid., bk. 1, ch. 9, 277b.27–29, 1:461.

6. Ibid., ch. 10, 279b.4–12, 1:463.

7. *Metaphysics*, bk. 3, ch. 1, 995a.32–995b.4, 2:1572–1573.

8. *Politics*, 1.1.1252a.17–21, trans. B. Jowett in *The Complete Works of Aristotle*, 2: 1986.

9. Ibid., 3.6.1278b.6–16, 2:2029.

10. Barnes, *Aristotle*, 65.

11. For Aristotle's division of the sciences, see his *Metaphysics*, bk. 6, ch. 1.

12. Thomas Aquinas, *Commentary on the Politics*, Proemium, trans. Ernest L. Fortin and Peter D. O'Neill in Ralph Lerner and Muhsin Mahdi, eds., *Medieval Political Philosophy: A Source Book* (Ithaca, NY: Cornell University Press, 1963), 299 (Proemium).

13. Ibid.

14. Ibid., 300.

15. Ibid.

16. See Jacques Le Goff, *Time, Work, and Culture in the Middle Ages*, trans. Arthur Goldhammer (Chicago: University of Chicago Press, 1980), 148.

17. Ibid., 141.

18. Much of what follows is drawn from Edward Grant, "Nicole Oresme," in Jorge J. E. Gracia and Timothy B. Noone, eds., *A Companion to Philosophy in the Middle Ages* (Oxford: Blackwell Publishing, 2003), 475–480.

19. See *Nicole Oresme: Le Livre du Ciel et du Monde*, edited by Albert D. Menut and Alexander J. Denomy; translated with an introduction by Albert D. Menut (Madison, WI: University of Wisconsin Press, 1968), bk. 2, ch. 2, 289.

20. For the Latin edition and English translation of Oresme's treatise, see *Nicole Oresme and the Kinematics of Circular Motion: "Tractatus de Commensurabilitate vel Incommensurabilitate Motuum Celi,"* edited with an introduction, English translation, and commentary by Edward Grant (Madison: University of Wisconsin Press, 1971).

21. Robin Small, "Incommensurability and Recurrence: From Oresme to Simmel," in *Journal of the History of Ideas,* vol. 52, no. 1 (January–March 1991), 121–137. For the quotation, see 121. George Simmel gave much the same proof as Oresme in a lecture series titled *Schopenhauer and Nietzsche,* first published in 1907 (ibid., 121). Small does not cite the proof in Oresme's *Treatise on the Commensurability or Incommensurability of the Celestial Motions* but probably had pt. II, prop. 9 in mind (see *Nicole Oresme and the Kinematics of Circular Motion,* 267–269; for the analysis, see 52–53).

22. Ibid., 122.

23. Jon Von Plato, "Nicole Oresme and the Ergodicity of Rotations," in *Essays in Philosophical Analysis Dedicated to Erik Stenius on the Occasion of His 70th Birthday,* edited by Ingmar Pörn , *Acta Philosophica Fennica,* vol. 32 (1981), 1909–1191. The proposition to which Von Plato refers in Oresme's *Treatise on the Commensurability or Incommensurability of the Celestial Motions* is pt. II, prop. 4, 253–259.

24. See Danny E. Burton, ed. and trans., "Nicole Oresme's 'On Seeing the Stars' (*De visione stellarum*): A Critical Edition of Oresme's Treatise on Optics and Atmospheric Refraction, with an Introduction, Commentary, and English Translation." Ph.D dissertation, Indiana University, Bloomington, 2000, 53.

25. Aristotle, *Metaphysics* 1.1.981b.10–11, 2:1553.

26. The way this occurred is described in Grant, *God and Reason in the Middle Ages*, 115–282.

27. For the challenge to authority in the early Middle Ages to 1200, see Grant, *God and Reason in the Middle Ages*, 31–82.

28. For Buridan's remarks, see ibid., 198.

29. For some of Galileo's trenchant remarks, see Grant, *God and Reason in the Middle Ages*, 308–311.

30. See *The "De Moneta" of Nicholas Oresme and English Mint Documents*, translated from the Latin with introduction and notes by Charles Johnson (London: Thomas Nelson and Sons Ltd., 1956).

31. Here, and in what follows about Oresme and Charles, I draw on Grant, "Nicole Oresme, Aristotle's *On the Heavens*, and the Court of Charles V," in Edith Sylla and Michael McVaugh, eds., *Texts and Contexts in Ancient and Medieval Science: Studies on the Occasion of John E. Murdoch's Seventieth Birthday* (Leiden: Brill, 1997), 187–207.

32. *Nicole Oresme: Highlights from His French Commentary on Aristotle's "Politics,"* trans. Albert D. Menut (Lawrence, KS: Coronado Press, 1979), 4; also see Grant, "Nicole Oresme, Aristotle's *On the Heavens*, and the Court of Charles V," 189.

33. *Nicole Oresme: Highlights from His French Commentary on Aristotle's "Politics,"* 5; Grant, "Nicole Oresme," 189–190.

34. See *Nicole Oresme: Le Livre du Ciel et du Monde*, 731; Grant, "Nicole Oresme," 190.

35. Ibid.

36. Ibid., 191.

37. The seven examples cited above are drawn, respectively, from the following pages of Menut's translation of *Nicole Oresme: Le Livre du Ciel et du Monde*, 735, 739, 741–743, 749.

38. Francisco Bertelloni, "Marsilius of Padua," in Jorge J. E. Gracia and Timothy B. Noone, eds., *A Companion to Philosophy in the Middle Ages* (Oxford: Blackwell Publishing, 2003), 413.

39. On this, see George Sarton, *Introduction to the History of Science* (Baltimore: Williams & Wilkins Co., 1927–1948), vol. 2, pt. 2, 915.

40. Bertelloni, "Marsilius of Padua," 413.

41. Ibid.

42. "Marsilius of Padua: *The Defender of the Peace*," translated by Alan Gewirth in Lerner and Mahdi, eds., *Medieval Political Philosophy: A Source Book*, I.I.4, 442.

43. Ibid., 445.

44. A. I. Sabra, "Science and Philosophy in Medieval Islamic Theology," in *Zeitschrift für Geschichte der Arabisch-Islamischen Wissenschaften*, vol. 9 (1994), 3.

45. Ibid., 5.

46. Ignaz Goldziher, "The Attitude of Orthodox Islam Toward the 'Ancient Sciences,'" in Merlin L. Swartz, ed. and trans., *Studies on Islam* (New York/Oxford: Oxford University Press, 1981), 205.

47. Ibid.

48. Ibid., 206.

4

Civic Virtue and Science in Prerevolutionary Europe

John C. Moore

The task of relating science and civic virtue is problematic, since neither term has a clear or widely accepted meaning. A traditional Western understanding of science includes all systematic bodies of knowledge using reason as the principle instrument for organizing and expanding that knowledge. In that tradition, theology is a science. Hereafter, I will refer to that understanding of science as *scientia*. Modern science, of course, is more narrowly conceived, requiring and limited to the systematic observation of physical phenomena, the discovery of universal "laws," and, whenever possible, description in quantitative terms. It is, one might say, a species of the genus *Scientia*.

As for civic virtue, the most elementary society requires its members to observe customary practices that enable the group to survive and function. The Stone Age tribes of South America survive thanks to their own form of civic virtue, although it does seem that their societies will not be able to survive much longer, faced with the modern world. In the modern West, however, civic virtue has come to mean a good deal more than whatever behavior is necessary to preserve the community. This notion of civic virtue aims at more than survival. It is based on the belief that, to be fully human, people need the freedom to participate in communal decisions that significantly affect their lives and that people should accept the responsibility for that participation. Using their highest gifts—their ability to think, to choose, to communicate, and ideally even to love—they should engage their fellow citizens in discussion and in action in order to realize the common good. The prime virtue required to make this kind of life possible is commitment to the following habitual behaviors: (1) the use of reason in addressing public issues; (2) respect for basic human rights: political, social, and legal equality, freedom of speech, press, religion, and assembly; and (3) the acceptance of the rule of law as expressed by majority rule (with the "majority" variously defined). All other civic virtues are then put to the service of this prime virtue, virtues such as good judgment, courage, altruism, compassion, empathy, honesty, industry, per-severance.

In the history of prerevolutionary Europe, the evolution of these two sets of ideas and practices, *scientia*/science on the one hand and civic virtue on the other, is exceedingly complicated, as is the relationship between them. *Scientia*/science required the recovery of the learning of antiquity, and medieval technology such as clocks, lenses, and printing presses, together with institutions, especially universities, that permitted or even encouraged the emergence of modern science. The kind of civic virtue described above required not only the intellectual evolution of the ideal but also the institutions that made possible the implementation of the ideal: the nation-state, representative institutions, and courts protecting legal rights. It needed to overcome enormous institutional barriers: aristocratic and clerical privilege, slavery and racism, male chauvinism. Moreover, universal adult suffrage became practicable only with widespread literacy and the technological means for mass communication.

As for the relationship between the two developments, it seems that *scientia* has been essential in the formulation and transmission of the ideals of civic virtue as well as in the creation of the institutional environment necessary for those virtues to flourish. Although modern science has helped to promote civic virtue in modest, indirect ways, it has been the beneficiary of civic virtue more than its source.

The Western conceptions of politics and civic virtue had their origins, as the words themselves indicate, in the cities of Greece and in Rome. For both Greeks and Romans, there was scarcely a distinction between civic or political virtue and moral virtue in general, since service to the city-state was the basic moral requirement of the individual. And in both Greece and Rome, the very names *polis* and *res publica* indicated that the city belonged to the people, albeit a people defined so as to exclude noncitizens. Even after the Roman Republic was replaced by military strongmen called emperors, the vast powers of the ruler were theoretically based on the people. The *Lex regia* states, "What has pleased the prince has the force of law . . . , because the people have conferred upon him their *imperium*" (*Corpus Iuris Civilis* [*CIC*] 1932, 7, 227: Inst. 1.2.6; Dig. 1.4.1). And under the Romans, "the people" gradually became more inclusive until the *Constitutio Antoniniana* of 212 included all free men as citizens (Berger 1953, 389, 409–410). Theoretically, civic virtue was now expected of Celts, Egyptians, Iberians, and the many other peoples who lived within the boundaries of the Roman Empire.

After the German occupation of the western empire in the fourth and fifth centuries, Roman ideas faded from the general population but were preserved mainly in monastic libraries. The decision of the "Fathers of the Church," especially Ambrose, Augustine, Jerome, Gregory, and Boethius, to adopt and adapt the classical tradition for Christianity meant that classical texts were preserved even while the ideas lay dormant. In the early Middle Ages, roughly 500 to 1000 C.E., civic virtue outside of Italy was divorced from both city and empire and was intensely local and personal. The communal responsibility of individuals was to the village, the tribe, and the tribal leader, or even to the local strongman, armed and on horseback, who protected and exploited a rural population. Even religious loyalties tended to be local, to local shrines and saints. The principle guide to human behavior within the community was not rational theory but custom.

The emergence of Christianity had, of course, added new ingredients to the mix. Christians belonged now not only to a secular society but also to a City of God, a communion of saints, in which the prime virtues were faith, hope, and love. The primary social duty was "as you wish that men would do to you, do so to them" (Luke 6:31).[1] "Civic" virtue might even mean withdrawing from society to lead a life of poverty, chastity, and obedience. The goal was salvation after death instead of a harmonious and just life on earth. There was also the Christian commandment to "go therefore and make disciples of all nations, baptizing them in the name of the Father and of the Son and of the Holy Spirit" (Matthew 28:19), a model quite different from monastic withdrawal. The New Testament further complicated things by presenting a dual loyalty: "Render therefore to Caesar the things that are Caesar's and to God the things that are God's" (Matthew 22:21).

The *Rule of St. Benedict* (ca. 530 C.E.) called for the "performance of good works," but human effort and accomplishment were minimized: the monks should know that "the good which is in them cometh not from themselves but from the Lord" (Benedict 1948, Prologue, 7–9). Benedictine monasticism presented a Christian version of another strong theme from antiquity, one antithetical to the Ciceronian ideals of citizenship described below, namely, that the philosopher should withdraw from society and secular concerns in order to pursue wisdom. The Christian version was framed in the story of Mary, who sat at the feet of Jesus, and Martha, who "was distracted by her many tasks." The monks chose to follow Mary, rather than Martha, since, according to Jesus, Mary had "chosen the better part" (Luke 10:40–42).

But even though the new Christian values represented a departure from those of classical antiquity, Benedict was still a Roman. Obedience to the leader (the abbot) and observance of a moderate and orderly law (the Rule) made Benedictine monasticism quite different from the anchorite monasticism of the East, where hermit monks lived as the spirit moved them. Moreover, Benedict, like other Christians in the Roman Empire, adopted election as the means to select rulers (Benedict 1948, ch. 64, 163), a procedure quite different from that described in the New Testament when the apostles sought a replacement for Judas. They left the selection to God by casting lots (Acts 1:26). The Latin church of the West, however, would fill most of its offices, including the papacy, through elections. Elections are always based on the presumption that the electorate should be aware of and informed about issues of common concern.

Finally, the Rule contained an egalitarianism that went beyond that of citizenship in the late Roman Empire. The abbot was to "make no distinction of persons in the monastery . . . Let not one of noble birth be put before him that was formerly a slave, unless some other reasonable cause exist for it . . . Let the Abbot, then, shew equal love to all, and let the same discipline be imposed upon all according to their deserts" (Benedict 1948, ch. 2, 19). The Rule of St. Benedict was to reach every part of Christendom, and everywhere it went, it preserved the idea of human equality, the principle of election, and the ideal of humane and orderly governance—an inheritance part Roman, part Judeo-Christian (Colish 1997, 52–55). It might also be noted that monasteries for women kept alive the idea that women had value independent of their erotic and reproductive utility. They could aspire to the same eternal life as men and could in fact surpass men in reaching human excellence.

After a brief effluence sometimes called the Carolingian Renaissance (after Charlemagne, d. 814), Europe experienced the extraordinary blooming of the High Middle Ages (ca. 1000 to ca. 1300), a time when Europeans created most of the institutions and cultural forms still recognizable in the West today. As the population grew, agriculture, manufacturing, and commerce expanded, thanks largely to new technology. European nations, with their languages and literature, began to assume their distinctive modern forms. Romanesque and Gothic architecture became permanent parts of Western culture. A host of institutions took shape that were to last into the present: papal and secular monarchies, urban governments, English common law, continental law (based on Roman Law), representative assemblies, commercial and banking institutions, universities.

An essential part of all this blossoming was the recovery of the wisdom of pagan and Christian antiquity, including Greco-Roman ideas of civic virtue. Libraries were scoured for Latin texts, two of which in particular reintroduced Western scholars to Greek and Roman ideas about civil life: Cicero's *De officiis* (*On Duties*) and the great collection of Roman law assembled under Justinian in the sixth century C.E., the *Corpus Iuris Civilis* (hereafter *CIC*). Then in the late twelfth and thirteenth centuries, a new flood of Greek and Arabic texts, translated into Latin, swept through the schools, bringing especially the political and ethical works of Aristotle.

What did Europeans find in Cicero? In *De officiis*, Cicero discussed at length the "cardinal" virtues as developed by the Greeks, the fundamental virtues for moral goodness (and for Cicero and most of his Greek antecedents, there was really no distinction between human virtue and civic virtue): wisdom, fortitude, justice, and temperance. These virtues were to be exercised in the service of the community. Cicero discussed the contrary classical tradition that said the truly wise man would withdraw from secular concerns and devote himself to the pursuit of wisdom, but he rejected that choice as second best to the life of public service: "The life of retirement is easier and safer and at the same time less burdensome or troublesome to others, while the career of those who apply themselves to statecraft and to conducting great enterprises is more profitable to mankind and contributes to their own greatness and renown" (Cicero 1975, 1.21, 73). Although he disparaged most commerce and manufacturing as being "illiberal" (1.42, 153–155), he nevertheless asserted the basic equality of all human beings. He also recognized that individuals have distinctive gifts (1.30, 109). For those who would assume public office, he offered fundamental instructions:

> Those who propose to take charge of the affairs of government should not fail to remember two of Plato's rules: first to keep the good of the people so clearly in view that regardless of their own interests, they will make their every action conform to that; second, to care for the welfare of the whole body politic and not in serving the interests of some one party to betray the rest. (1.24, 87)

The duty of every citizen was "first, in private relations, to live on fair and equal terms with his fellow-citizens . . .; and second, in matters pertaining to the state, to labour for her peace and honour; for such a man we are accustomed to esteem and call a good citizen" (1.34, 127).

For Cicero there was no higher loyalty than that to the republic:

> But when with a rational spirit you have surveyed the whole field, there is no social relation among them all more close, none more dear than that which links each one of us with our country [*re publica*]. Parents are dear; dear are children, relatives, friends; but

one native land [*patria una*] embraces all our loves; and who that is true would hesitate to give his life for her, if by his death he could render her a service? (1.17, 59–60)

De officiis was well known by twelfth-century scholars and the cardinal virtues as enumerated by Cicero were widely discussed. For example, they were featured in the sermons of Pope Innocent III (d. 1216) (Moore 1994, 101–102). Even popes kept alive the ideal of public service, since they had for centuries been calling themselves the "servant of the servants of God," giving Christian expression to a classical ideal. Monastic withdrawal from society in order to commune with God was still held in high regard, but as the thirteenth century opened, there was clearly a new emphasis on engagement with the world. Innocent III pulled Cistercian monks from their monasteries to act as agents of his policies. In a striking paraphrase of Cicero, but with a Christian twist, he told his Cistercian legate that although contemplation in the monastery (Mary's part) was meritorious and more secure, active involvement in the world (Martha's part) was more useful. To motivate the Cistercian, he said the usefulness of the active life lay in strengthening the monk's virtue, but his own motive was clearly public utility—in this case, the elimination of heresy (Moore 2003, 154). Moreover, the important new religious orders of the thirteenth century were not monastic. The new mendicant friars went into the cities to engage and serve the people. The growing reputation of the *vita activa*, as contrasted to the *vita contemplativa*, encouraged a sense of social responsibility.

The inheritance found in the *Corpus Iuris Civilis* was more complicated, since it incorporated nearly 1,000 years of legal experience. The *Lex regia*, quoted above, summarized with admirable simplicity the whole of Roman experience: the reference to people reflected the more democratic experience of the Roman Republic; the reference to the will of the prince reflected the monarchical experience of the Empire (Berger 1953, 550–551). Both principles were to be invoked repeatedly in the history of the West (Kantorowicz 1966, 94–97; Mundy 1973, 400–404).

Perhaps the most important element in the *CIC* was the jurisprudence found therein, especially in the part called the Digest. Legal scholars in Italy toward the end of the eleventh century, and then others throughout Europe, encountered in the Digest the best legal minds of ancient Rome analyzing their rich legal tradition, using reason to interpret and reconcile real or apparent conflicts among laws, precedents, and commentaries (Bellomo 1995, 52–54, 112–117, 163–166). That skill was extremely useful to twelfth-century lawyers, and virtually the same skill was being used by scholars working in every other field of knowledge. The very heart of what is commonly called scholasticism was the application of reason, sharpened through the study of Aristotelian logic, to authoritative texts: sacred scripture, the writings of the fathers, the chaotic body of canon (church) law that had grown up over the centuries, and indeed the whole body of pagan and Christian writings already in the libraries. Then there were the new Arabic and Greek texts coming from Spain, Sicily, and the Greek East via the new translations of the twelfth and thirteenth centuries. Medieval jurisprudence and scholasticism were the ideal tools for organizing and understanding this rich, heterogeneous inheritance (Southern 1995, 11–13, 125–131).

Fundamental to all this cultural activity was the application of reason. When conservatives objected to the application of reason to sacred texts, Abelard (d. 1142) responded with *Sic et non*, a series of questions followed by ancient Christian texts that seemed to give conflicting answers to the questions. He showed that authority without reason led to contradiction, and scholasticism soon swept the field. Following Abelard's lead, Peter Lombard compiled his *Books of the Sentences* (c. 1150), posing questions, quoting authorities, and then using reason to interpret and, as far as possible, to reconcile conflicting texts. This work become the basic textbook of theology, studied and commented on by scholars well into the sixteenth century.

The intellectual flurry of the twelfth century inevitably disrupted traditional ways of thinking. Authorities were challenged; custom and customary law were now made subject to reason. When Gratian composed the legal text called the *Decretum* (c. 1140), he made custom subject to reason, quoting with approval the judgment of the Emperor Constantine (d. 337) as found in the *CIC*: "The authority of longstanding custom and practice is not insignificant; but its power is certainly not of such moment as to prevail over either reason or ordinance" (Gratian 1993, 38: D. 11 c. 4), as well as that of St. Augustine (d. 430): "Let no one prefer custom to reason or truth because reason and truth always void custom" (Gratian 1993, 26: D. 11 c. 4 and D. 8 c. 4).

Princes and popes acted accordingly. Centralizing princes, especially kings, discovered the value of educated ministers who could undermine customary restraints on princely power by invoking reason as well as principles of Roman law. The Fourth Lateran Council of 1215 forbade priests to participate in trials by ordeal, thereby forcing Latin Christians to turn to more rational means of determining guilt and innocence (Baldwin 1961). In 1234, the abundant new papal legislation that had appeared since mid-twelfth century was added to Gratian's *Decretum* to form the collection that came to be known as the *Corpus Iuris Canonici*, the basic law book of all Latin Christendom. Even after Luther threw a copy into a bonfire in 1520, the *Corpus Iuris Canonici* governed Catholicism into the twentieth century, and even in Protestant countries, the habits it had formed in Christian thinkers were not forgotten (Tierney 1982). Similarly, princes felt increasingly free to issue their own edicts, and thirteenth-century scholars organized secular law into orderly collections, seeking for their princes' laws the same prestige accorded to the ancient laws of Rome. Such collections were *The Constitutions of Melfi* in the Kingdom of Sicily (1231), Bracton's *On the Laws and Customs of England* (ca. 1230), the *Siete Partidas* in Castile (ca. 1265), and Beaumanoir's *Coutumes de Beauvais* in France (ca. 1283) (Berman 1983).

Extracting a clear sense of civic virtue from this hodge-podge was no easy matter. For the ancient Greeks and Romans, the city provided the entire identity for the citizen. It was the one native land (*patria una*). The people of twelfth- and thirteenth-century Europe, however, belonged to a maze of overlapping communities—manorial, tribal, urban, regional, diocesan—along with distant authorities claiming their loyalties: kings, emperors, popes. There were also virtues and duties distinctive to class and status. The fundamental distinction between laity and clergy involved two quite different sets of social obligations. Peasants and townsmen saw themselves as distinct groups, as the latter shook off any hint of the servitude often associated with agricultural labor. The aristocracy in much of Europe acquired its own privileged legal status and developed its own special code of virtues called chivalry: personal loyalty to one's lord, military prowess, and largesse, together with a certain refinement of manners that was developed in aristocratic courts and was celebrated in vernacular lyric poetry and romances.

Only in the communal movement of the twelfth century, when townsmen sought to establish their autonomy, was there truly fertile ground for the ideas of Greek and Roman citizenship. The communes of northern Europe drew less on Roman antecedents, each seeking its own special arrangement with the local lord. In Italy, however, Roman ideas had a special resonance. In mid-twelfth century, one Arnold of Brescia, a student of Abelard, led a rebellion in Rome against the pope. According to a contemporary, "He set forth the examples of the ancient Romans, who by virtue of the ripened judgment of the senate and disciplined integrity of the valiant spirit of youth made the whole world their own. Wherefore he advocated that the Capitol should be rebuilt, the senatorial dignity restored, and the equestrian order reinstituted" (Otto of Freising 1953, 144). His efforts cost him his life, but the memories of the Roman Republic continued to complicate the lives of popes, who considered themselves the secular rulers of Rome and central Italy.

From the twelfth century on, intellectuals familiar with urban life showed growing interest in Cicero's ideas of civic virtue. Provoked by the factional divisions in Florence, Dante invoked Cicero in defense of the Roman tradition of monarchy (Dante n.d., 2.5, 39–40). A century later, a group of humanist statesmen in Florence, called by Hans Baron the "Tuscan philosophers," embraced wholeheartedly the republican civic ideals of Cicero (Baron 1968). Even so, the actual structures of city governments in Italy from the eleventh through the fifteenth centuries show only limited Roman influence. Ideas from Roman law were available, and some Roman terminology was evident. Magistrates were "consuls," councils were commonly called "senates," and offices were commonly filled by election. But the Italian cities showed great inventiveness in shaping and reshaping their communes, with no real attempt to reproduce the institutions of ancient Rome. The most important parallel between the medieval republics and their ancient antecedents is their fate. Like the *poleis* of Greece and the Roman Republic, factional divisions within the city and competition among cities gradually led to some sort of monarchy that offered peace and security in exchange for urban independence (Waley 1969, 62–109, 221–239). Dante of Florence and Marsiglio of Padua saw monarchy as the only hope for individual rights and peace.

So there was the dilemma. Aristotle had said that the polis must be small so that the citizens could know one another, specifically so that they would be able to elect magistrates sensibly. That idea was adopted by Leonardo Bruni (d. 1444), translator of Plato and Aristotle, student of Cicero, and chancellor and historian of Florence. He dismissed any political unit larger than the city: "Liberty is possible only in the safekeeping of civic autonomy, i.e., in the small state" (Garin 1969, 26–28). The small city was essential if citizens were to have a significant role in matters of the common good, if they were to have the opportunity to use the cardinal virtues for the good of the community. But experience has shown that the city-state republic was not a viable political form, always falling under some monarch, usually one ruling a much larger unit. Florence itself fell under the sway first of the Medici despots and then of the king of France. Few small political units could stand up to a great modern nation-state. How then was the individual to have the opportunity to exercise civic virtue?

The solution to the problem, insofar as it has a solution, lay first in representative assemblies. Citizens of a large and powerful political entity, such as the nation-state, could consider the issues locally and then elect a neighbor empowered to act on their behalf in a distant representative assembly. Both on the local level with the electors and on the assembly level with the representatives, individuals are called upon to consider the common good and act accordingly. This institution, unknown in the ancient world, was the product of the twelfth and thirteenth centuries. It was to make modern democracies possible.

There were, to be sure, European antecedents of representative assemblies. The early German chieftains were expected to take council from their followers. As feudal relationships developed in parts of Europe in the ninth and tenth centuries, lords were expected to take council with their vassals. Bishops had long been meeting in councils to address problems arising in the Christian community. Then in the thirteenth century, two key legal practices emerged, both drawn from Roman law, but now given entirely new applications. The first was "what touches all should be approved by all" (*quod omnes tangit*) (Berman 1983, 221, 608 n. 54). The second was the idea that individuals—or a corporation by a majority vote—could convey to a proctor or representative the authority to act on their behalf. These principles gave a foundation for assemblies of elected representatives, first called simply to approve on behalf of their constituencies whatever a prince required of them, and then later to submit petitions for the prince's approval. Ultimately, the assemblies would make new laws with or without the prince's approval. James M. Brundage (1995) wrote:

> These various devices, then, enabled thirteenth and fourteenth-century canonists to devise an orderly law of ecclesiastical corporations, grounded on theories of representation and consent that they fabricated out of elements that they found at hand in Roman law. Other lively minds soon perceived that the intellectual foundations the canonists had constructed for church corporations could readily be adapted to fit institutions of civil government as well. (108–109)

From this beginning, combined with already existing consultative tribal and feudal councils, came the Cortes in Castile, the Estates General in France, and the Parliament in England. Full-blown theories of representative government emerged in ecclesiastical circles with the conciliar movement of the fourteenth and fifteenth centuries (Tierney 1968; Morrall 1958, 119–130). (It is noteworthy that the demographic, social, and economic disasters of the period, with famine, plague, and warfare cutting the population by a third or more did not also result in cultural reversal.) The *quod omnes tangit* principle was invoked by dozens of lay and ecclesiastical writers of the fourteenth century to argue that governments were limited by the will of the people (Marongiu 1968). Clerical intellectuals argued that popes could be called to account by councils of bishops, who in turn represented the people of their dioceses (Tierney 1968). It required no great imagination to think that perhaps kings could also be called to account—by assemblies of elected representatives such as the English House of Commons.

None of the great states of the sixteenth century was a democracy by any definition. But the intellectual inheritance and the governmental institutions necessary for modern democracies had taken shape. There remained the formidable task of recognizing religious freedom as a central civil value. Only after the bitter experience of prolonged and destructive religious wars did Westerners learn that religious dissent could not be eliminated, no matter how oppressive the methods. They would have to accept religious pluralism; they would have to provide religious freedom.

There also remained the task of championing human equality against the legal privilege of the clergy and hereditary aristocracy, a process made easier by what is commonly called the Industrial Revolution. Invoking ideals from both the classical and Christian tradition—human equality, reason, and natural law—and using the technology of modern communication, Westerners created new forms of government in which civic virtue in the modern sense could be realized. Legal equality emerged, slavery was ended, and, in the twentieth century, the franchise was extended to all adults, men and women. Civic virtue does not inevitably blossom in that environment, but the friendly environment is there.

But where do *scientia* and science fit in all this? Obviously, *scientia* had everything to do with the formulation and preservation of the ideal of civic virtue and the emergence of political forms supportive of civic virtue. Commitment to human equality, the idea of popular sovereignty, the use of reason (especially as an alternative to violence or custom) in addressing public issues, the notion of basic human rights, the very idea of civic virtue—all these ideas were articulated and kept alive by an educated minority, men and women shaped by *scientia*. *Scientia* also included a deepening understanding of human nature and human behavior through studies we would today call social sciences, especially psychology and economics (Morris 1995; Langholm 1992). Moreover, the educational institutions and the representative institutions were understood to be places for discussion, requiring some degree of freedom of speech.

Freedom of religion (and freedom from religion) was the most difficult ideal to embrace and to realize, since no Western society before the Enlightenment could conceive of a body politic divorced from religion, and since eternal salvation seemed to be at stake. Cicero had written, "Our first duty is to the immortal gods; our second, to country; our third, to parents; and so on, in descending scale, to the rest" (Cicero 1975, 1.45, 165). Socrates and Christian martyrs alike were executed for religious offenses. On this subject, people were slow learners, but ultimately Westerners learned that religious freedom should be considered a fundamental right of the citizen. Religious liberty began as a necessity begrudgingly granted and progressed to a social value greatly treasured (Strauss 1992, 198). In the official teaching of the Roman Catholic Church, that journey was not completed until the Second Vatican Council in 1965.

The physical sciences may well have played a more active role in the development of religious freedom than they did in most of the other traits of modern democracies. Medieval students of natural philosophy, the study of the changeable, sublunar universe, argued for explanations that did not depend on faith or religious belief. They called it *loquendo naturaliter,* "speaking naturally." They "sought to investigate the 'common course of nature,' not its uncommon, or miraculous, path" (Grant 1996, 195). That habit of thought, commonplace in the universities by the thirteenth century, surely made it easier to think of political life without invoking religious principles. Invoking nature and nature's laws, Enlightenment thinkers were to consider themselves "scientific" in their political writings.

Otherwise, the contributions of science in the modern sense to civic virtue seem to be limited and indirect. The intellectual virtues practiced by the scientist are not enough to make for a civil society, since so much of civil society depends on moral values and virtues that are not an essential part of science.

Charles Taylor describes how William James presented the scientific method as one that allows one "to believe a hypothesis only by first treating it with maximum suspicion and hostility" and contrasted it with the reality of human relations— "James holds, on the contrary, that there are some domains in which truths will be hidden from us unless we go at least halfway toward them. Do you like me or not? If I am determined to test this by adopting a stance of maximum distance and suspicion, the chances are that I will forfeit the chance of a positive answer. An analogous phenomenon on the scale of the whole society is social trust; doubt it root and branch, and you will destroy it" (2002, 46).

Furthermore, some of the basic principles of modern civil society are not based on rational proof (Budziszewski 1992, 49–52). No one has proved scientifically that "all men are created equal" or that they are endowed with rights of "life, liberty, and the pursuit of happiness." It has not been demonstrated scientifically that "government of the people, by the people, and for the people" should not perish from the earth. There seems to be no scientific theory to support the notions that citizens must be bound by the decisions of their elected representative, even if they did not vote for that representative, or that the minority should consider themselves bound by laws approved by the majority.

Moreover, it is not at all clear that successful scientists must manifest any personal virtues besides industry. James Watson's route to the Nobel Prize did not include a conspicuous display of virtue (Watson 1968). Scientists must have natural gifts, a willingness to apply them persistently, and a certain amount of luck. They must, to be sure, play by the rules of the profession; otherwise, they will not be allowed to play the game. But personal commitment to the common good and to civic virtues is not really essential. A successful scientist can refuse to vote or take part in political debate; he or she can defame religious and racial minorities and offer his or her services to the highest bidder, including a murderous dictator. A less serious but still regrettable lack of virtue appears when scientists use their prestige as scientists to promote opinions not based on their scientific competence.

On the other hand, it does seem true that although individual scientists of this type might flourish, the profession as a whole would not unless a sizable proportion of its members were personally committed to the common good and to civic virtue. The rational and systematic pursuit of truth, the public presentation of conclusions, and the honest and responsible criticism of the conclusions of others—all these show good example to citizens carrying out their civic duties.

Scientists who falsify their research, who resort to *ad hominem* attacks in their criticism of other scholars, who expropriate the research of their students and present it as their own—all these are likely to be condemned by their peers. In this regard, the scientific community provides a model worthy of emulation for the society at large. Indirectly, modern science probably gives citizens an additional motive for embracing freedom of speech and press: they want to enjoy the benefits of modern science. This advantage is a relatively new phenomenon. Before Francis Bacon proclaimed the practical utility of science in the seventeenth century, and well after, science did not enjoy the general prestige that it does today. In prerevolutionary Europe, the study of the physical sciences had little generally recognized utility. Rather, it was men trained in the liberal arts and in law, that is, men skilled in the use of language for administrative and judicial purposes, who were in demand. Supply followed demand (Murray 1978, 218–233). From at least the thirteenth century on, lawyers have vastly outnumbered theologians and scientists. But today, it is widely accepted that freedom to pursue research, to publish the results of that research, and to subject the research of others to informed criticism are essential for science as a whole to prosper. Surely even the most anti-intellectual citizen in the West knows the importance of science, if for nothing else, for medical treatment and for the creation of weapons of war. So the universally recognized importance of scientific research probably encourages the citizenry to value the social conditions and the civic virtues that make science possible.

Modern science, then, and to a lesser degree its predecessor natural philosophy have made modest and indirect contributions to the emergence of civic virtue. *Scientia*, however, has been essential for the development of the ideal of civic virtue and for the creation of institutions that make modern civic virtue possible.

Note

Biblical translations in this paper are based on the Revised Standard Version, but some have been modified to bring them closer to the Latin Vulgate.

References

Baldwin, John W. 1961. "The Intellectual Preparation for the Canon of 1215 against Ordeals." *Speculum*, 36:613–636.

Baron, Hans. 1968. "Cicero and the Roman Civic Spirit in the Middle Ages and the Early Renaissance." A 1938 lecture, as revised in *Lordship and Community in Medieval Europe*. Ed. Fredric L. Cheyette, 291–314. New York: Holt, Rinehart, Winston.

Bellomo, Manlio. 1995. *The Common Legal Past of Europe: 1000–1800*. Trans. Lydia G. Cochrane. Washington, DC: Catholic University Press.

Benedict. 1948. *The Rule of St. Benedict*. 5th ed. with English trans. by D. Oswald Hunter Blair. Scotland: Fort Augustus Abbey Press.

Berger, Adolf. 1953. *Encyclopedic Dictionary of Roman Law*. Philadelphia: *Transactions of the American Philosophical Society*, n.s., 43:331–808: "*Civitas Romana*," 389; "*Constitutio Antoniniana de civitate*," 409–410; "*Lex de imperio*," 550–551.

Berman, Harold J. 1983. *Law and Revolution: The Formation of the Western Legal Tradition.* Cambridge, MA: Harvard University Press.

Brundage, James A. 1995. *Medieval Canon Law.* London: Longman.

Budziszewski, J. 1992. "Religion and Civic Virtue." In *Virtue.* Ed. John W. Chapman and William A. Gaston, 49–68. New York: New York University Press.

CIC (*Corpus Iuris Civilis*). An English translation can be found in Samuel P. Scott, trans., *The Civil Law.* 17 vols. Cincinnati, OH: Central Trust Co., 1932. For Institutes: 1.2.6, see 2:7; for Digest: 1.4.1, see 2:227.

Cicero. 1975. *De officiis.* Trans. Walter Miller. Cambridge, MA: Harvard University Press.

Colish, Marcia L. 1997. *Medieval Foundations of the Western Intellectual Tradition: 400–1400.* New Haven, CT: Yale University Press.

Dante. N.d. [ca. 1955]. *Monarchy and Three Political Letters.* Trans. Donald Nicholl. New York: Noonday Press.

Garin, Eugenio. 1969. *Science and Civic Life in the Italian Renaissance.* Trans. Peter Munz. Garden City, NY: Doubleday.

Grant, Edward. 1996. *The Foundations of Modern Science in the Middle Ages.* Cambridge: Cambridge University Press.

Gratian. 1993. *The Treatise on Laws.* Trans. Augustine Thompson. Washington, DC: Catholic University Press.

Kantorowicz, Ernst H. 1966. "Kingship under the Impact of Scientific Jurisprudence." In *Twelfth-Century Europe and the Foundations of Modern Society.* Ed. Marshall Clagett, Gaines Post, Robert Reynolds, 89–111. Madison: University of Wisconsin Press.

Langholm, Odd. 1992. *Economics in the Medieval Schools: Wealth, Exchange, Value, Money and Usury According to the Paris Theological Tradition: 1200–1350.* Leiden: Brill.

Marongiu, Antonio. 1968. "The Theory of Democracy and Consent in the Fourteenth Century." In *Lordship and Community in Medieval Europe.* Ed. Fredric L. Cheyette, 404–421. New York: Holt, Rinehart, Winston.

Moore, John C. 1994. "The Sermons of Pope Innocent III." *Römische Historische Mitteilungen,* 36:81–142.

———. 2003. *Pope Innocent III (1160/61–1216): To Root Up and to Plant.* Leiden: Brill.

Morrall, John B. 1958. *Political Thought in Medieval Times.* New York: Harper.

Morris, Colin. 1995. *The Discovery of the Individual: 1050–1200.* Repr. of 1972 edition. Toronto: University of Toronto Press.

Mundy, John H. 1973. *Europe in the High Middle Ages: 1150–1309.* New York: Basic Books.

Murray, Alexander. 1978. *Reason and Society in the Middle Ages.* Oxford: Clarendon.

Otto of Freising. 1953. *The Deeds of Frederick Barbarossa.* Trans. Charles Christopher Mierow. New York: Columbia University Press.

Southern, R. W. 1995. *Scholastic Humanism and the Unification of Europe.* Vol. 1: *Foundations.* Oxford: Blackwell.

Strauss, David A. 1992. "The Liberal Virtues." In *Virtue.* Ed. John W. Chapman and William A. Gaston, 197–203. New York: New York University Press.

Taylor, Charles. 2002. *Varieties of Religion Today: William James Revisited.* Cambridge, MA: Harvard University Press.

Tierney, Brian, 1968. *Foundations of the Conciliar Theory.* London: Cambridge University Press.

———. 1982. *Religion, Law, and the Growth of Constitutional Thought, 1150–1650.* Cambridge: Cambridge University Press.

Waley, Daniel. 1969. *The Italian City-Republics.* New York: McGraw-Hill.

Watson, James D. 1968. *The Double Helix: A Personal Account of the Discovery of the Structure of DNA.* New York: Atheneum.

5

Virtues and the Scientific Revolution

Rose-Mary Sargent

The scientific revolution introduced fundamental conceptual changes in the explanatory categories, methods, and goals of natural philosophy. In England a significant expression of the new philosophy was reflected in the founding of the Royal Society of London. According to its charter of 1663, the "studies" of the Royal Society were "to be applied to further promoting, by the authority of experiments, the sciences of natural things and of useful arts, to the glory of God the Creator, and the advantage of the human race" (*Record of the Royal Society* 1912, 82–83). Along with the introduction of organized experimental research, members of the early Royal Society recognized that their project would require the compilation of a large factual foundation, the development of criteria for testing inferences drawn from the foundation, and a cooperative social structure to coordinate research efforts and to ensure the safe and effective use of knowledge. As a social institution, the Royal Society also required standards of conduct to govern the behaviors and practices of its members and to ensure that knowledge in the public interest was properly disseminated. The standards they adopted were based on the traditional civic virtues of honesty, civility, toleration, and intellectual modesty that Francis Bacon (1561–1626), one time Lord Chancellor of England, had elaborated in the previous generation.

Royal Society Fellows often referred to the works of Bacon as a major source of inspiration. In his *Scepsis Scientifica*, for example, Joseph Glanvil (1665) maintained that Bacon's fictional account of a scientific society in *The New Atlantis* provided the "Prophetic Scheam of the ROYAL SOCIETY" (22). When Thomas Sprat's *History of the Royal Society* was published in 1667, most editions carried an engraving by another fellow of the Society, John Evelyn, that prominently featured a likeness of Francis Bacon. In 1912, the editors of the third edition of *The Record of the Royal Society of London* continued to trace their major inspiration to Bacon and another of his works, *The New Organon*. Bacon, they wrote, had encouraged an "insatiable curiosity ... to pry with eager enthusiasm into every department of nature" for "discovery and invention in all that concerns the material well-being of society" (33).

Accordingly, the Royal Society was "one of the earliest practical fruits of the philosophical labors of Francis Bacon" (1). Given this recurrent theme, it will be helpful to look first at those aspects of Bacon's philosophical advice that proved to be so influential.

Bacon's Philosophical Project

Bacon is perhaps best known today for his attempt to move away from what he saw as the empty speculation of previous philosophers and ground a new philosophy within the realm of practice. To convey his ideas about how the advancement of learning could contribute to improvements in human health, welfare, and society, he often wrote of the "power" or "utility" of knowledge. It would be a mistake, however, to conflate Bacon's ideas with the type of utilitarianism developed in the nineteenth century. In *The New Atlantis*, his fable about a utopian island society governed by a scientific elite, Bacon attributed the islanders' scientific, technological, economic, and political successes to the fact that they were a peace-loving people who did not seek conquest or great wealth, but merely self-sufficiency (1874, vol. 3, 141–147; see vol. 3, 151). Criticisms of Bacon as a prophet of Western capitalism, imperialism, colonialism, and other forms of political and social power struggles, therefore, are questionable at best (e.g., Achinstein 1988; Martin 1992; Merchant 1980; Weinberger 1976; Whitney 1990). In his preface to *The Great Instauration*, Bacon wrote explicitly that readers should "consider what are the true ends of knowledge" and "seek it not either for pleasure of the mind, or for contention, or for superiority to others, or for profit, or fame, or power, or any of these inferior things; but for the benefit and use of life; and that they perfect and govern it in charity" (1874, vol. 4, 20–21).

Bacon's philanthropic attitude had roots in both the Christian and humanistic traditions. As befitted a person who held high political office in England, he was a practicing Anglican, yet he was also influenced by his mother's devotion to Calvinism, especially to the doctrine of good works. Bacon consistently maintained that it was the duty of natural philosophers to "cultivate truth in charity" (1874, vol. 4, 20). To accomplish his goal, he "fervently" prayed to "God the Father, God the Son, and God the Holy Ghost" that "they will vouchsafe through my hands to endow the human family with new mercies" (20). As a statesman, Bacon also adhered to the Renaissance Humanist ideal of the improvement of the moral and social worlds, and he sought to extend the concerns of morality and the promotion of an active life into the sphere of natural philosophy. In 1592 he wrote to his uncle, Lord Burghley, that he wished to take "all knowledge for his province" (vol. 8, 108). Throughout his life he continued to develop his multiple interests, guided by ideals of a virtuous *vita activa* and the promotion of the common good. The civility, charity, and religious toleration displayed by the citizens of *The New Atlantis* further illustrated the social and political benefits that Bacon believed would accrue from a reformed natural philosophy (vol. 3, 270–273; see Peltonen 1992, 1996; Sargent 1996, 2002; Shapiro 1983).

Bacon also shared the humanists' critical attitude toward logical manipulation and dogmatic adherence to theoretical systems not founded on experience. In *The*

Great Instauration he maintained that logical syllogisms yield propositions that are "barren of works, remote from practice, and altogether unavailable for the active department of the sciences" (1874, vol. 4, 24). Bacon desired "to command nature in action," and "all those specious meditations, speculations, and glosses in which men indulge are quite from the purpose" (24). Because "it is from the ignorance of causes that operation fails," however, experiments of "light," those designed to yield true causal knowledge, were as important as experiments of "fruit" (32; see 47). Thus, his ideal of usefulness played both a social and an epistemic role (48–49). If a theory, tested by experiment, is found to be fruitful of works, then that can be taken as one sign of the theory's truth. As Bacon maintained, "fruits and works are as it were sponsors and sureties for the truths of philosophies" (73; see also 110).

Although Bacon expressed confidence that the work could be completed in a short time in parts of *The New Organon*, his extensive experience of compiling natural and experimental histories ultimately led him to formulate a fallibilistic and dynamic stance toward knowledge. For more than thirty years, he learned not only about nature but also about how to study nature. By 1620 he had come to realize that the construction of the factual foundation was "a kind of royal work" because it is "of very great size, and cannot be executed without great labour and expense" (1874, vol. 4, 251). At best he could only hope to achieve partial and tentative truths. Yet he also saw that the more truth one could find, even if it were local or tentative, the more ability one would have to aid humanity. He had "no entire or universal theory to propound." Instead, he saw his role as the modest one of "sowing . . . for future ages the seeds of a purer truth and performing my part towards the commencement of the great undertaking" (104). Indeed, even the methods that he advocated could require future alteration because "the art of discovery may advance as discoveries advance" (115).

In addition to the massive amount of information to be collected, the significance of the material in the factual foundation had to be determined. Bacon argued that the senses are not subtle enough for this task (1874, vol. 4, 58). Reason is required for the interpretation of data, yet reason as well is no clear light. The mind is a "false mirror" beset by "idols" that result from natural proclivities or are acquired through linguistic practice and theoretical speculation (53–69). These idols of the mind give rise to the prejudgment of data and thus lead to biased interpretations. Bacon did not believe that the idols could be totally eliminated, but making people aware of their influence could mitigate their ill effects. Diversifying the experiential basis by expanding the class of investigators would also help to guard against the particular biases of any one individual or group. Cooperation on a large scale had been made possible by recent technological innovations. Printing and navigation, for example, had produced an "openness of the world" and disclosed "multitudes of experiments and a mass of natural history" (vol. 3, 476; see also vol. 4, 82–84, 100–101). The time was right, therefore, for philosophers to lay aside their "prejudices" and "join in consultation for the common good" (vol. 4, 21). To enhance this consultation, effective communication would be essential.

Bacon advised that experimental results and factual observations should be recorded in clear and precise language. His reports in his *Natural and Experimental Histories* and the *Sylva Sylvarum* served as models for scientific communication.

In these works, he provided detailed descriptions of the methods he used, the observations and experiments made, suggestions about the significance of the observations for current theoretical speculations, and reminders for practice (1874, vol. 5, 133–36; vol. 2, 339–680; see Sargent 1999). It is true that Bacon made extensive use of rhetorical tropes in other works, such as *The New Organon*. The different purposes for which he composed these works can explain any apparent inconsistency between his advice and his practice. The *Histories* were designed as contributions to the factual foundation for natural philosophy, whereas *The New Organon* was meant to persuade readers to participate in his project. In his *De Augmentis*, he noted that even poetry could be an effective way to excite curiosity about questions concerning nature (vol. 4, 318–335; see Sargent 2002). As the leading propagandist for the new science, Bacon provided the methodological advice as well as the excitement needed for a revolution in learning (for an eighteenth-century assessment of Bacon's contribution, see Voltaire 1732, 46–51). His appeals to humanistic virtues were at once rhetorical and justificatory. If one's goal is to advance useful knowledge through a cooperative research effort, then virtues such as honesty, civility, toleration, and modesty will be essential. Bacon set the agenda for the next generation of philosophers who would go on to establish the "brotherhood of scientists" that he had envisioned (Bacon 1874, vol. 3, 323).

The Royal Society of London

After the turmoil of the civil wars that divided England into numerous factions for two decades, monarchy was restored in 1660. At this time, a number of men who had previously met in smaller groups to discuss natural and experimental philosophy joined together in an ambitious program for establishing a national research community. The Royal Society of London was to be the institutional embodiment of Bacon's proposed "marriage of the empirical and rational faculty" where individual members would contribute according to their differing abilities as simple observers, fact gatherers, experimenters, or interpreters (Bacon 1874, vol. 4, 19). Methodological diversity was not their only goal, however. When Sprat (1667) recounted the history of the Royal Society a few years later, he described how the contributions of all social classes were to be employed. Indeed, part of the external justification for the Society's incorporation consisted of appeals to how philosophical and social tolerance would ultimately result in the civil stability and economic advantages that had been so glowingly described in Bacon's *New Atlantis* (see Hunter 1981; Sargent 1995).

In addition to such rhetorical flourishes concerning the social justification of experimental science, however, Bacon's advice about the necessity of an extensive cooperative research effort also played a role in the internal justification of the Royal Society's methods and was practically implemented in the Society's statutes. In statute 4, for example, three-hour weekly meetings were scheduled for members

> to order, take account, consider, and discourse of philosophical experiments and observations; to read, hear, and discourse upon letters, reports, and other papers, containing

philosophical matters; as also to view, and discourse upon, rarities of nature and art; and thereupon to consider, what may be deduced from them, or any of them, and how they, or any of them, may be improved for use or discovery. (*Record of the Royal Society* 1912, 119)

Furthermore, in order to extend the exchange of information and ideas to the international community, Charles II granted that the Royal Society "shall have full power and authority ... to enjoy mutual intelligence and knowledge with all and all manner of strangers and foreigners, whether private or collegiate, corporate or politic, without any molestation, interruption, or disturbance whatsoever" (68).

Among the offices established by the Society's statutes, a secretary was assigned to keep a record of communication in registers, journals, and letters books. Henry Oldenburg, secretary from 1662 until his death in 1677, significantly expanded the position when he established the regular publication of its *Philosophical Transactions of the Royal Society of London* in 1665. Although published in English to encourage a wider audience at home, the *Transactions* were immediately translated into Latin as well for the international exchange of experimental and theoretical considerations. Such free communication was not the only means of acquiring information, however. Members could also direct particular experimental investigations according to explicitly Baconian methods and goals. Statute 5 stipulated that for "the propounding and making of Experiments for the Society, consideration shall be had of the importance of any Experiment, to the discovery of any truth or axiom in nature, or to the use and benefit of mankind." When the results of these experiments were reported to the Society, "the matter of fact [i.e., what occurred during the process of the experiment] shall be barely stated, without any prefaces, apologies, or rhetorical flourishes." Precise language concerning facts was requisite, but, if a fellow thought "fit to suggest any conjecture, concerning the causes of the *phaenomena* in such Experiments," they were encouraged to do so in a separate report (*Record of the Royal Society* 1912, 119).

The Society initially planned that a number of directed experiments would be performed by an official curator who would receive a stipend of £200 per year. According to the description of this position in Statute 11, curators had to be fellows of the Royal Society "of good fame and virtuous conversation, knowing in philosophical and mathematical learning, addicted to and well versed in observations, inquiries, and experiments concerning natural and artificial things" (*Record of the Royal Society* 1912, 125). Robert Hooke, a member of the Society who often performed the role of curator, albeit without receiving the title or stipend, combined the requisite philosophical and experimental virtues. Although remembered today primarily for his mechanical ability, experimental ingenuity, and microscopic observations, Hooke also propounded theoretical conjectures such as his pulse theory of light in opposition to Isaac Newton's particulate theory. Newton himself also merged the rational and empirical approaches that Bacon had favored. He followed a highly deductive and axiomatic style in his *Principia Mathematica*, but he also employed experiments in this work as well as in his *Opticks*. Indeed, in his first letter to the Royal Society on a "New Theory about Light," Newton used Bacon's concept of an "instance of the cross" to describe what he believed to be the "crucial experiment" that proved the truth of his theory (Newton 1672, 3078; also

Bacon 1874, vol. 4, 180–190). Shortly after this he became a member of the Society and, with the publication of the *Principia* in 1687, he became its leading figure. For the thirty years prior to Newton's ascendancy, however, Robert Boyle, a founding member of the Society, had served as the primary model of an experimental and natural philosopher.

Boyle's public advocacy of a Baconian dual approach to the study of nature was evident in his numerous natural and experimental histories as well as in his more speculative works. In his *Origin of Forms and Qualities* (1666) and *Excellency and Grounds of the Corpuscular or Mechanical Philosophy* (1674), he combined a discussion of how the corpuscular hypothesis could account for empirical evidence with a detailed theoretical justification based on rational criteria relating to its simplicity and intelligibility (Boyle 1772, vol. 3, 1–112; vol. 4, 67–78). Boyle also had a lifelong humanistic concern for practical studies and composed many methodological and programmatic works that emphasized the themes of civic virtue (Hunter 2000). In his *Usefulness of Natural and Experimental Philosophy* (1663), for example, Boyle discussed at length the charitable uses to which he hoped his work would contribute, and he often prefaced his experimental histories with suggestions for how his investigations into the properties of bodies could aid human health and welfare (Sargent 1995, 35–41). Of equal significance was his extensive attempt to foster a cooperative research effort that would ultimately contribute to the common good.

Boyle taught others how to perform and judge both simple and complex experiments in his *Certain Proëmial Essays* (1661). He also pointed out the numerous difficulties that surround attempts at experimental manipulation. Because of the contingencies of experiment, he warned his readers against speculating on single experimental results. Extreme caution in theorizing and frequent repetition and variation of experimental trials would be requisite (Boyle 1772, vol. 1, 298–353). Even with scrupulous attention to detail, however, errors could still occur. Theoretical hubris had to be reigned in by a full appreciation of the limitations of human sense and reason. Intellectual modesty would also be necessary for an adequate collection and assessment of information. Boyle ridiculed those of his contemporaries who thought that mechanical work or commerce with tradesmen was beneath them. As a member of the English aristocracy, Boyle was well positioned to argue for the inherent dignity of a hands-on experimental approach and he freely displayed his own laboratory collaborations with paid laborants as well as his personal visits to the workhouses and shops of artisans. More so than their learned counterparts, craftsmen were valuable sources of information about the ways in which materials may be manipulated because their livelihood depended on an accurate attention to detail (Sargent 1995, 149–158). Thus, such commerce was of crucial methodological importance. It not only increased the quantity of information but also improved its quality because data were gathered from a broad basis of observers whose varied perspectives could mitigate the effect of individual prejudices.

The civic virtues expounded by Bacon, Boyle, and the Royal Society contributed both to the internal logic and the external justification of the experimental method. In recent popular accounts, however, the role of these virtues has been largely misunderstood. Focusing their attention on themes of gentlemanly conduct and trust, for example, some writers have contended that experimenters' appeals to civic virtue served primarily as a rhetorical device designed to hide the political and social ambitions peculiar to individuals of Restoration England (e.g., Shapin and Schaffer 1985; Shapin 1995). Yet, when seen in broader historical context, it is clear that such issues were not unique to Restoration society. Rather, they reflected the Renaissance humanistic vision that Bacon had advocated earlier in the century. Furthermore, the use of rhetoric and metaphor was largely limited to the realm of propagandistic attempts to generate excitement for the overall project and not for scientific proof, which consisted of experimental and rational criteria. The presence of rhetoric, therefore, cannot automatically be used to impugn theoretical and factual truths generated by the program.

The studies of social historians typically betray an anachronistic imposition of twentieth-century categories onto seventeenth-century concerns. Natural philosophers were explicit about the political, moral, and social implications of their scientific proposals and did not attempt to disguise covert motives behind a disinterested language of "objectivity." In addition, the Royal Society itself was not a highly unified professional organization (see Hunter 1981). Although it represented the institutionalization of the new science and embodied the shared ideals of utility and moral progress, tensions within the Society were immediately apparent. As we have seen, Bacon's multifaceted plan for the advancement of learning explicitly eschewed philosophical systematizing and included rational and empirical methods for discovering truths of nature. Unlike Boyle, Hooke, and Newton, who shared Bacon's universal interests and abilities, most of the early members of the Royal Society had more narrow concerns that influenced divergent views of the Society's mission. Some members believed that its main goal should be the development of theoretical knowledge as Bacon had advised in *The New Organon*, whereas others felt that most effort should be given to the construction of natural histories and practical inventions on the model of Bacon's *Sylva Sylvarum* (Sargent 1999, xxiii).

Bacon's proposals for cooperative research and the free exchange of ideas also contained inherent inconsistencies. Although he had called for a rather democratic approach to inquiry in *The New Organon*, his example of Solomon's House in the *New Atlantis* displayed a hierarchical division of labor. Moreover, the secrecy practiced by the fathers of Solomon's House conflicted with the ideal of open communication. These tensions came to the fore in the Royal Society. The lower classes, to which tradesmen and some merchants belonged, were not widely represented among the Society's ranks, and some fellows believed that membership ought to be more selective and restricted. Members also disagreed about the extent to which information should be released to the public. Some argued that in order to improve human welfare they had a duty to restrict the dissemination of knowledge that would have a detrimental effect. Others argued that in order to increase the stock of practical inventions, modes of production had to be kept secret. Tradesmen and artisans, for example, would be reluctant to share the details of the processes by which they made their living unless they had the assurance that these secrets would not in turn become public knowledge (McMullin 1985; Sargent 1996, 1999).

Conclusions

As modern science and its narrative developed in the nineteenth and twentieth centuries, the above tensions became more pronounced. Scientific knowledge was no longer generally accessible but instead became the domain of highly specialized experts and professional societies. When decisions concerning the disbursement of limited research resources came to be determined on the basis of a project's fit with the interests of governmental or corporate funding agencies, it is not surprising that the original spirit of science as a cooperative and charitable enterprise would be adversely affected. Today's national security concerns have served to add yet another incentive for secrecy among and between various scientific communities. When the moral imperative to develop science for the common good is usurped by such nationalist and capitalist desires for increased security and profit, competition replaces cooperation and obvious problems arise. As a brief look at recent editorials in *Science* reveals, these developments set the stage for conditions that can hinder virtuous behavior (Beachy 2003; Kennedy 2003a, 2003b; Wallerstein 2002).

A common response to such conditions has been to call for increased objectivity. Such a response serves primarily to obscure the problems, however. The quest for objectivity reinforces a positivist-style distinction between facts and values and perpetuates the misguided idea that science is autonomous from the social and moral worlds within which it exists. The ideal of value-free inquiry actually represents a perversion of the import of Bacon's idols. Bacon urged that we should guard against the idols' influence so as to avoid the prejudgment of favored outcomes. That does not mean that we must exclude all consideration of human interests. For Bacon and the early members of the Royal Society, experimental practice required an expanded and inclusive society of investigators that strengthened the habits of discourse in a civil society and explicitly recognized and addressed the social and political purposes of scientific inquiry. As we have seen, moral progress and scientific progress were linked in the social and epistemic roles that usefulness played in the justification of early experimental practice. Value considerations, as well as the civic virtues of honesty, civility, toleration, and intellectual modesty, were and ought to be central.

A more appropriate response, suggested by the above historical considerations, would call first for the explicit recognition that tensions and conflicts of interest are inherent within the complex enterprise of science and will often reflect similar tensions within society as a whole. Second, the values that actually guide scientific practice must be identified and evaluated. While matters internal to scientific practice may not be open for general inspection and judgment, the values that guide the work can and should be a matter of public debate. Scientific knowledge has indeed brought with it great power. But, of course, having power does not give one the right to use it. As the early Baconians would argue, power must be tempered by intellectual modesty and charity. Hubris and naked self-interest are as misplaced within the scientific community as they are within a democratic society. Members of professional scientific societies have long been responsible for the standards of conduct that govern their behavior. As citizens, they continue to be responsible for making explicit the ways in which priorities in research are set and carried forward. Although inherent conflicts may not be eliminated, subsequent ill effects can be mitigated by keeping in mind considerations drawn from the civic virtues that were so influential at the inception of the modern scientific enterprise.

References

Achinstein, Sharon. 1988. "How to Be a Progressive without Looking Like One: History and Knowledge in Bacon's *New Atlantis.*" *Clio* 17: 249–264.

Bacon, Francis. 1874. *The Works of Francis Bacon.* 14 vols., edited by James Spedding, Robert L. Ellis, and Douglas D. Heath. London: Longman.

Beachy, Roger N. 2003. "IP Policies and Serving the Public." *Science* 299: 473.

Boyle, Robert. 1772. *The Works of the Honourable Robert Boyle.* 6 vols., edited by Thomas Birch. Reprint, Hildesheim, Germany: Georg Olms, 1965.

Glanvil, Joseph. 1665. *Scepsis Scientifica*, London.

Hunter, Michael. 1981. *Science and Society in Restoration England.* Cambridge: Cambridge University Press.

———. 2000. *Robert Boyle (1627–91): Scrupulosity and Science.* Woodbridge, UK: Boydell Press.

Kennedy, Donald. 2003a. "An Epidemic of Politics." *Science* 299: 625.

———. 2003b. "Two Cultures." *Science* 299: 1148.

Martin, Julian. 1992. *Francis Bacon, the State and the Reform of Natural Philosophy.* Cambridge: Cambridge University Press.

McMullin, Ernan. 1985. "Openness and Secrecy in Science: Some Notes on Early History." *Science, Technology, and Human Values* 10: 14–23.

Merchant, Carolyn. 1980. *The Death of Nature.* New York: Harper and Row.

Newton, Isaac. 1672. "New Theory about Light and Colours." *Philosophical Transactions of the Royal Society of London* 80: 3075–3087.

Peltonen, Markku. 1992. "Politics and Science: Francis Bacon and the True Greatness of States." *Historical Journal* 35: 279–305.

———. 1996. "Bacon's Political Philosophy." In *The Cambridge Companion to Bacon*, edited by Markku Peltonen. Cambridge: Cambridge University Press, 283–310.

Record of the Royal Society of London. 1912. 3rd ed. London: Oxford University Press.

Sargent, Rose-Mary. 1995. *The Diffident Naturalist: Robert Boyle and the Philosophy of Experiment.* Chicago: University of Chicago Press.

———. 1996. "Bacon as an Advocate for Cooperative Scientific Research." In *The Cambridge Companion to Bacon*, edited by Markku Peltonen. Cambridge: Cambridge University Press, 146–171.

———. 1999. "General Introduction." In Francis Bacon, *Selected Philosophical Works*, edited by Rose-Mary Sargent. Indianapolis, IN: Hackett, vi–xxxvi.

———. 2002. "Francis Bacon and the Humanistic Aspects of Modernity." *Midwest Studies in Philosophy* 26: 124–139.

Shapin, Steven. 1995. *A Social History of Truth.* Chicago: University of Chicago Press.

Shapin, Steven, and Simon Schaffer. 1985. *Leviathan and the Air-Pump: Hobbes, Boyle, and the Experimental Life.* Princeton, NJ: Princeton University Press.

Shapiro, Barbara. 1983. *Probability and Certainty in Seventeenth-Century England.* Princeton, NJ: Princeton University Press.

Sprat, Thomas. 1667. *The History of the Royal Society of London, for the Improving of Natural Knowledge*. Reprint, edited by Jackson I. Cope and Harold Whitmore Jones. St. Louis, MO: Washington University Press, 1958.

Voltaire. 1732. *Philosophical Letters*. Translated by Ernest Dilworth. Indianapolis, IN: Bobbs-Merrill, 1961.

Wallerstein, Mitchel B. 2002. "Science in an Age of Terrorism." *Science* 297: 2169.

Weinberger, Jerry. 1976. "Science and Rule in Bacon's Utopia." *American Political Science Review* 70: 865–885.

Whitney, Charles. 1990. "Merchants of Light: Science as Colonization in the *New Atlantis*." In *Francis Bacon's Legacy of Texts*, edited by William A. Sessions. New York: AMS Press, 255–268.

Part II

Values Revealed in the Work of Scientists

My intention is not to prove that I was right but to
find out *whether* I was right.

—Bertolt Brecht's *Galileo*

Part I detailed the high standards that scientists set for themselves. But how well does the allegiance to these noble ideals bear up in practice? We cannot attempt here a systematic, empirical study of the epistemological and ethical behavior of researchers. But what we will do is present four essays that analyze numerous cases of actual scientific practice. These examples richly illustrate the complexity of the decisions that scientists are forced to make and the nature of the pressures they experience from both their peers and society at large. Not all of these scientists are perfect saints (as indeed is the case with religious saints!), but one cannot help but be impressed with how laborious scientific research is and how dedicated scientists are to the quest of understanding the natural world.

In chapter 6, Gerald Holton shows the variety of ways the virtue of probity figures in the lives of two Nobel Prize–winning physicists, the American P. W. Bridgman and the Dane Niels Bohr. Their talents and taste in research problems were quite different. Bridgman was an experimenter par excellence, one who gloried in collecting huge amounts of extremely accurate data. His laboratory notebooks show that in his published articles he would sometimes understate the precision of his measurements just to make sure that he didn't mislead the reader. Those who associate Bridgman's name with the concept of "operationalism"

will not be surprised to learn that he was determined to clarify anything that puzzled him, whether it was in science or in his private life, and to express it as clearly as possible. In 1939, after much self-scrutiny, he published a manifesto in which he announced that his laboratory would be closed to any visiting scientist from a totalitarian county who was cooperating with an authoritarian government. Holton presents Bridgman as a striking exemplification of the virtue of candor.

Niels Bohr's writings are anything but models of lucidity. His scientific interests lay in theorizing, sometimes on a rather grand scale, as when he attempted to extend his controversial concept of complementarity from the domain of quantum mechanics into the study of cultural conflict. Although he is different from Bridgman, Holton argues, Bohr is also a man of great integrity. From the risks he took in defending an unpopular theory of the atom at the beginning of his career to the missionary zeal with which he attempted (unsuccessfully) to head off a nuclear arms race with the Soviet Union, Bohr shows a marked awareness of the scope and seriousness of the scientific quest and the responsibilities of a citizen-scientist.

In chapter 7, Michael Ruse analyzes the nature of the trust that cements the scientific community together—unlike intelligence agencies, which are supposed to be suspicious of what their informants tell them, scientists assume that the reports of experiments sent into journals are intended to be veridical. Ruse argues that although there are strong self-serving reasons not to fake your results, this atmosphere of trust is also maintained by a learned visceral repugnance at the very idea of cheating. Scientists find it perverse. (Once in a graduate seminar I asked my students how difficult it would be to fake their dissertation results. One social scientist who was doing survey research admitted it would be very easy, but added that it would be a ridiculous thing to do because he really wanted to know what people thought about the issues on his questionnaire.)

Ruse shows how scientists' assumption that real scientists would never deceive leads to very interesting dynamics in scientific debates. In general, scientists don't impugn the integrity of their opponents even when they think they are dead wrong. However, in certain special kinds of controversies (which Ruse delineates), scientists may accuse their opponents not just of sloppiness or error but of practicing a kind of scientific perversion that ought to exclude them from the scientific community. Ruse then tests his analysis on a wide variety of examples from the history of evolutionary biology, beginning with pre-Darwinian quarrels and ending with the vitriolic attacks on E. O. Wilson and sociobiology. Ruse's theory also predicts when potential controversies would not be expected to materialize, and he illustrates that situation nicely with his account of how the Darwin–Wallace episode never turned nasty and the reaction of the scientific community to Mendel's spruced-up results.

In chapter 8, Allan Franklin tells a remarkable story about how a physicist, Emil Konopinski, challenged Enrico Fermi's theory of beta decay and in 1935 proposed an alternative account, called the K-U theory, which appeared to fit the data better. The K-U theory became the received view, and dozens of experiments produced results that fit it better than Fermi's. After a few years, however, scientists discovered there were errors in calculation and faults with the experimental setups. When these were corrected, Fermi's theory was clearly superior and the K-U account was clearly wrong—and it was Konopinski himself who announced the demise of his own theory in 1943.

Franklin's detailed account of this episode provides many insights into how science works: how difficult it is to design an experiment that produces unambiguous results, how confusing it can be to make sense of the sheer wealth of data, and the blend of creativity and detective work required when bizarre discrepancies develop among seemingly reliable experimental and theoretical procedures. All in all, it is another case illustrating scientists' unrelenting efforts to attain a clear picture of the operations of nature.

Nowhere is the pursuit of clarity more difficult than in the scientific study of people. In chapter 9, Frederick Churchill looks at the intellectual and societal challenges faced by Alfred Kinsey in his research on human sexual behavior. Kinsey's first contributions were in biology, and he adapted the taxonomic methods he had used in studying gall wasps to the study of human sexuality. Huge numbers of specimens were required in order to capture all the variations exhibited in nature and document the frequency of their occurrence. Churchill argues that evolutionary ideas also informed Kinsey's work—human sexual behavior had to be viewed in the context of its phylogenetic past.

As recent Kinsey biographers have established, Kinsey's monumental research efforts were fueled not just by scientific curiosity but also by a conviction that a scientific understanding of the varieties of sexual behavior should have an impact on the value judgments that society made about sexuality. Churchill argues that he was less successful in this enterprise, in part because Kinsey may not have fully understood the logical and philosophical difficulties that beset any attempt at devising an evolutionary ethics. Once again, we see a scientist maintaining a high degree of integrity while confronting problems of enormous complexity and depth.

6

Candor and Integrity in Science

Gerald Holton

In the pursuit of researches and in the reporting of their results, the individual scientist as well as the community of fellow professionals relies implicitly on the researcher embracing the habit of truthfulness, a main pillar of the ethos of science. Failure to adhere to the twin imperatives of candor and integrity will be adjudged intolerable and, by virtue of science's self-policing mechanisms, rendered the exception to the rule. Yet both as philosophical concepts and in practice, candor and integrity are complex, difficult to define clearly, and difficult to convey easily to those entering on scientific careers. Therefore, it is useful to present operational examples of two major scientists who exemplified devotion to candor and integrity in scientific research.[1]

When scientists communicate with one another, they may be sometimes reticent on details, for example, about painfully acquired methods still needed in their current research or about matters that have not yet been settled finally in their own minds or laboratories. But they rarely are not candid in what they convey to colleagues or even rivals in their field. For in scientific research there is a mechanism at work that may get one found out rapidly for improbity—a mechanism and an ethos much attenuated in most other professions (as the daily news tends to make clear, be they politics, the military, industrial enterprises, the public media, lawyers, financial gurus, accountancies, even the priesthood). That mechanism is the ability of sufficiently trained, skeptical scientists to confirm or deny in principle, and sometimes quite quickly in fact, the veracity of a communication offered to them.

Thus, while scientists are generally born no better or worse with respect to the general human tendencies to exaggerate or to deny, to misremember or to avoid sharing everything they know quite freely, in the acculturation process they learn to suppress those natural instincts and try to put on what Jacob Bronowski named "the habit of truth," which is the key for the successful program of science as a whole. To be sure, when a nuclear scientist is asked about the details of a particle accelerator that is still being built, she may not always be forthcoming, but at least will reply quite appropriately—perhaps "sorry, I can't tell you yet"—a negative sort of candor.

Candor, of the positive or negative kind, is not the same as integrity, but the two notions are related, as indicated in my copy of *Roget's Thesaurus*, where both notions are listed under "probity," together with rectitude, honesty, loyalty, truth, scrupulosity, and the like. Perhaps I can here illustrate each, and the interplay between them, in terms of two historical examples of major scientists: one from the thoughts and works of P. W. Bridgman, and the other from those of Niels Bohr, respectively experimenter and theoretician. They also may serve as actual case studies in a collection that may concentrate more on the abstract notions.

Percy W. Bridgman (1882–1961) won the 1946 Nobel Prize in Physics for his investigations of the changes in materials subjected to extremely high pressures. He is also widely remembered for his contributions to the philosophy of science, which changed the intellectual landscape of many scientists. His philosophy of "operationalism," first elaborated in *The Logic of Modern Physics* (1927), attempted to brush away indefinable elements by proposing that concepts should be defined in terms of experimental procedures, or operations—an approach that influenced economics and psychology also.

I had the privilege of knowing Bridgman, first as his dissertation student in experimental high-pressure physics, and then as a colleague. It seems to me that his life and work were constructed along about half a dozen ordering ideas. Watching him at work, one might have been reminded of Michael Faraday in the simplicity of the experiment and the thoroughness of detail of the research accomplished with it. When I first entered Bridgman's laboratory at Harvard, fresh from doing wartime research with advanced pulse circuits, I was astounded to see nothing but DC electrical measurements of resistances and potentials, and Kelvin Bridges instead of electronics. Yet the experiments—on tiny samples the size of a nail paring, conducted inside small presses that were themselves inside bigger presses, and all the information on the changing physical properties coming out on one wire to an old galvanometer—were top-drawer.

The work Bridgman did was always personal, hands on, faster and with more data points per day than seemed humanly possible. He said that physics is the quantitative exploration and analysis of physical experience. Those words meant what they said: quantitative, exploration, experience. He was guided not by fashionable new theories but by thermodynamics, and the prospect of huge areas of new physical phenomena to be conquered. He gave the impression of wanting to harvest field upon field of new data while keeping his eye on yet more remarkable ones constantly appearing on the horizon as he increased the pressure range. And one could rely on his every word. It even went beyond that, as I discovered when, after his death, I was asked to archive his laboratory notebooks. There I found that in the interest of not misleading anyone, he had kept himself from publishing the last decimal in each reading, that being the region where uncertainties could enter.

Like some other scientists I have studied, Bridgman saw no fundamental difference between science and philosophy if properly conceived, or really between his life and his work, or between public and private science. He made no distinction between a novice with interesting ideas and willingness to work and take risks and an elder statesman of science on a courtesy visit. He seemed to be curious about every subject in science and outside, but by the same token, he was never satisfied that he had really exhausted any deep question. He would not have been surprised to learn that his own extensive work (seven technical books and some 200 scientific papers, plus seven more books and about sixty papers on philosophy and the study of social science) is useful today in a great variety of natural sciences—physics, chemistry, geology, engineering, even in biology, as in the study of the properties of protein under high pressure—as well as in psychology, economics, philosophy, and history of science.

Bridgman loyally stayed with his university from the day he entered as a freshman in 1900 until he retired from his professorship fifty-four years later. He persisted in the same field of research throughout and saw it grow in power as he reluctantly drove the range of attainable pressures in his laboratory from a few thousand atmospheres at the start, to ultimately more than 400,000. The same persistence came out in the short run as in the long. A famous example is a sentence from one of his scientific papers, describing how to make a thin hole as narrow as the lead in a pencil but in a big block of very hard steel: "It is easy, if all precautions are observed, to drill a hole ... 17 inches long, in from 7 to 8 hours."

Anyone who knew him can immediately see him, wearing his well-used lab coat, at the lathe or at the forepump of the press, pumping up the pressure, always by hand, undeflectable by anything while taking data. I can attest to that. On a morning in the fall of 1946, I was in the workshop constructing apparatus for my dissertation problem, which he had agreed to supervise as long as I would not bother him too often. The telephone rang, and I happened to be the one to take it. A voice from the Associated Press asked me to bring Mr. Bridgman to the phone. (Bridgman, of course, did not tolerate a telephone in his laboratory.) I explained it was impossible to get him out while he was taking data. The voice at the other end, now quite agitated, demanded an interview with him because the announcement had just come from Stockholm that Bridgman had won the Nobel Prize. Of course, I ran into Bridgman's lab to convey the great news. Not missing a single stroke, he continued at the pump and said quite simply, "Tell them—I'll believe it—when I see it." Here, indeed, was the operational approach in action, and also a test of the equanimity of his spirit.

Plato said that "clear ideas drive away fantastic ideas," but in Bridgman the need to clarify his ideas in honest self-evaluation was not merely therapeutic; it was a biological necessity. He had an ethos of lucidity and candor of the most difficult kind: with himself. In 1938, at the peak of his powers, he wrote, "As I grow older, a note of intellectual dissatisfaction becomes an increasingly insistent overtone in my life. I am becoming more and more conscious that my life will not stand intellectual scrutiny, and at the same time my desire to lead an intelligently well-ordered life grows to an almost physical intensity."

So, for Bridgman, another all-too-frequent barrier was removed—that between moral and intellectual issues. Compelled by his insistence to be clear and candid about one's stand, and acting visibly as a citizen-scientist, he published a manifesto in *Science* (Bridgman 1939) in which he announced the closing of his laboratory to visiting scientists of totalitarian countries, because he saw that they had subordinated their loyalty to science to the demands authoritarian governments might make on their work. But we also see in the preceding quotation a mainspring, a force driving several apparently disparate achievements. His attractions to high-pressure physics seem to have started with his attempt to give instrumental meaning to the concept of high hydrostatic pressures inside a sealed enclosure. He never tolerated the use of "black boxes" that required the experimenter to believe a manufacturer's calibration or circuit diagram. His work on dimensional analysis was in the nature of a self-interrogation. His book on thermodynamics starts with the question, "What are the most basic variables to choose and how do we define them?"

Bridgman may not have read Charles S. Peirce's essay of 1878, "How to Make Our Ideas Clear," but he had a deeply rooted affinity with the American empiricist philosophers. Here, too, was the source of his sympathy with the philosophy of the displaced Vienna Circle, as brought by refugee scientists and philosophers who began to come to the United States in the 1930s.[2]

The Logic of Modern Physics was his first major contribution to the critical analysis of the foundations of physics. To this day, anyone with scientific interest who reads it for the first time finds it an electrifying experience. As must be true for many, I clearly remember the exact place in the library where, as a student, I happened upon the book, and then found myself standing there, reading the first chapters right away. Key phrases burn in one's memory: "In general, we mean by any concept nothing more than a set of operations; the concept is synonymous with the corresponding set of questions." Or, "The true meaning of a term is to be found by observing what a man does with it, not by what he says about it." Or, "If a specific question has meaning, it must be possible to find operations by which answers may be given to it. It will be found in many cases that the operations cannot exist, and the question therefore has no meaning."

All the traits of Bridgman's mind were there: the lucidity of style, the lack of philosophical self-consciousness, the uncompromising drive to the foundations. It was a message of immense power for scientists, at least in the English-speaking world, and as in many such cases, the explanation of its power is not that the book brings to the reader a message never thought of before, but rather that it lays open, with clarity, what the reader has been trying to formulate on his or her own. The most fruitful way of understanding Bridgman's philosophical writings is to see them as a record of continual self-interrogation and self-discovery. That is why they have also been such an effective tool of self-recognition for other scientists.

It is not surprising that Bridgman had to clarify for himself philosophical problems before he could feel satisfied with his solution of scientific problems. For the typical task of science, to put it very simply, is to relate the world of appearances, or data, and the world of conceptions, or ideas. And the usual way scientists do this is to construct an arch that starts from the ground of direct observation, then rises up to the region of theory, or concepts and other thought constructs, and then comes again back to the level of the immediately given, to a new set of verifiable observations.

The question that always nags the honest mind is this: how can one be sure whether or not the arch connecting initial and final data is not merely fantasy? Roughly, Bridgman's answer was that there are two tests. There must be formal connections among the thought elements in the upper region; they must be able to stand the tests of logic and of "mental" or "paper-and-pencil" operations. And second, each of the physical concepts used must, in principle, be supported from the world of experience below, by having meaning in terms of physical or instrumental operations. This is how the operational attitude determines the shape and direction of a possible theory and the type of data relevant to it at each end. But this process of construction is, of course, not restricted only to science. In Bridgman's straightforward way, he wrote: "It would doubtless conduce greatly to clarity of thought if the operational mode of thinking were adopted in all fields of inquiry." Even so, the critique and elaboration of his conceptions by other scholars sometimes astonished Bridgman. Once, at the end of a long symposium with philosophers, he said, with unusual candor:

> As I listened to the papers I felt that I have only a historical connection with this thing called "operationalism" . . . I have created a Frankenstein, which has certainly got away from me. I abhor the word operationalism . . . which seems to imply a dogma, or at least a thesis of some kind. This thing I have envisaged is too simple to be dignified by so pretentious a name; rather, it is an attitude or point of view generated by continued practice of operational analysis . . .
>
> The date usually associated with this is 1927, the year of publication of my book, *The Logic of Modern Physics,* but preparation for this in my own thinking went back at least to 1914, when the task of giving two advanced courses in electrodynamics was suddenly thrust upon me . . . The underlying conceptional situation in this whole area seemed very obscure to me and caused me much intellectual distress, which I tried to alleviate as best I could . . . The dimensional situation proved comparatively simple, and I was able to think the situation through to my own satisfaction—an experience that perceptibly increased my intellectual morale.[3]

In this quotation there is, I believe, a clue to Bridgman's key motivation. It is the sentence, "I was able to think the situation through to my own satisfaction." To clear his own ever-active mind of intellectual disquietude and the possibility of self-deception—that was a basic driving force, whether designing an experiment or analyzing the foundations of thermodynamics or of society. He never bothered to answer seriously the charge of philosophical solipsism, but I think that the answer has to be this: one cannot, by any other criterion, hope to get maxims that are more generally valid than those one can get by letting questions rise up in a mind that habitually subjects itself to exceptional intellectual disquietude, and that habitually is given to uncompromising, candid self-examination.

First and last, his science was his individual struggle to discern "the way things are," which phrase is, in fact, the title of one of his last books. Indeed, he told me he had preferred to call this book "The Way It Is." "But," he said, "the publisher doesn't like it; however, I am still not sure that 'things' really exist." To him, the mark of a scientist was the willingness to devote oneself fully to finding out the way it is, regardless of the consequences.

Bridgman clearly placed the highest value on the most difficult way of achieving veracity: trying at all costs to be clear and honest in his own mind—a paradigmatic case of internal candor. His direct, plain-spoken, unambiguous writings and speeches were a result of that clearing of his own mind. Turning now to Niels Bohr (1885–1962), we find, by contrast, a rather different situation. Bohr's writings were usually the result of a painful struggle, sometimes lasting for many years of drafting and redrafting, to put into the languages of science and everyday speech his complex thoughts, and yet many of these publications and public addresses were, as he knew, difficult to unravel. I had the opportunity to discuss this problem with him. He explained it to me in a moving sentence: ''I do not choose to speak or write more clearly than I think.'' In this case, candor consisted in conveying with honesty the insufficiency of ordinary language to represent fully the internal state of a superb mind. However, as if to make up for this difficulty, Bohr became the paradigmatic example of the twin brother of candor—namely, integrity.

Again, first a brief overview of his scientific career. It is commonly agreed that it may be divided roughly into five periods. During the first decade of his professional life, his main concern was with spectra, the absorption and emission of light, the structure of the periodic table, and the chemical properties of matter. During the second period, from the early 1920s for about a decade, he was the leader of his Institute for Theoretical Physics in Copenhagen, devoting himself to the conquest of quantum mechanics, working with furious energy, and surrounded by a remarkable group of young scientists from all over the world. This was the time of concern with the wave–particle puzzle, the uncertainty relation, complementarity, the discovery of the loss of visualizable physics, and the clarification of problems ranging from the structure of crystals to the chemical bond. By the late 1920s, it seemed that, in principle, all properties of atoms and molecules were understandable by the single force of electromagnetism.

In the third period, from the early 1930s until the occupation of Denmark by the Germans in April 1940, Bohr and his collaborators worked on what came to be known as field quantization, elementary particle physics, and the structure of the atomic nucleus. After Bohr's narrow escape from Denmark to Sweden in 1943, followed by his trip to England and then to the United States, his career entered a fourth phase as he consulted with the British scientists, and later with those at Los Alamos, who had entered upon the huge effort to preempt the German attempt to make a nuclear weapon—an attempt on which the Germans, as recent documentation shows, had in fact embarked first. But at the same time Bohr also became more and more concerned with planning for the postwar world, including his tragically unsuccessful efforts to open the eyes of Roosevelt, Churchill, and later of the United Nations leadership to opportunities that might well have averted the nuclear arms race.

In his last twenty years, Bohr was chiefly occupied with applying the lessons of his science not only to further research in physics but also to all spheres of life, ranging from philosophy to international politics. He also devoted himself to the internationalization of scientific cooperation, as in the founding of CERN, the European center for research in high-energy physics, and to encouraging scientists in third-world countries.

Studying Bohr's work and life, I see four principles of integrity in science that possessed him to the end, four principles that can be emulated in our time. The first of these is simply this: try to get it right at all costs, sparing no effort. You may have to seek help and advice where possible, but do all you can to prove to yourself and others that your scientific idea is correct. This norm or principle of integrity of science in the narrowest interpretation of the phrase can nevertheless be very hard and may even drive one to the edge of despair if one has selected a really worthy problem. I have been surprised how often the word "despair" comes up in the autobiographies and letters of some of our best scientists. Heisenberg once recalled his collaboration with Bohr in 1926 and 1927, saying, "We couldn't doubt that this [quantum mechanics] was the correct scheme, but even then we didn't know how to talk about it. [These discussions] threw us into a state of almost complete despair" (Heisenberg 1975, 569).[4]

Obedience to this norm can force one to take risks on behalf of a hard-won scientific idea before it is fashionable or safe. Again, Bohr's life and work contain many powerful illustrations. On arriving in Manchester, he soon saw that Ernest Rutherford's idea of a nuclear atom was right and, moreover, that the atom "seemed to be regulated from inner part to the outer by the quantum."[5] This recognition immediately became the basis of Bohr's first great work. But think what it entailed at the time. Although Rutherford himself was at the first Solvay Congress in 1911, nobody mentioned his discovery of the nucleus during that summit meeting of the major physicists of the day. It took a few more years, including Bohr's and Henry Moseley's work, for scientists to catch on generally. But Bohr had staked everything on it at once, and on the quantum ideas of Planck and Einstein that also were only beginning to be accepted by physicists. The result was the "Bohr atom" in Bohr's paper of 1913. It has long ago made its way into all the schoolbooks, but the reception at the time was quite different. Otto Stern is reported to have remarked, "If this nonsense is correct, I will give up being a physicist." Bohr said later, "There was even a general consent that it was a very sad thing that the literature about spectra should be contaminated by a paper of that kind."[6] The risk young Bohr took in his 1913 paper could well have endangered his career. It was a physics so very different from that of Newton, Maxwell, Planck, Thomson, and even Rutherford.

It is a part of the first principle of integrity that one must submit oneself to the dialogue with others to find out whether one is right. New science starts in the head of an individual, but it does not survive unless it becomes part of the consensus of the community. Bohr knew this well. When his mentor Rutherford received Bohr's paper in manuscript, he agreed to send it on to be published despite his objections, but he wrote to Bohr, "I suppose you have no objection to my using my judgment to cut out any matter I may consider unnecessary in your paper?" (Moore 1985, 50).

Poor Rutherford! A considerably extended version of the earlier manuscript was already on its way to him, and soon thereafter Bohr himself appeared at his door, having come from Denmark where he had gone to establish himself. For many long evenings they discussed every point. Bohr reported that at the end, Rutherford declared he had not realized Bohr would prove so obstinate, but "he consented to leave all the old and new points in the final paper" (French and Kennedy 1985, 79). Then Bohr went to Göttingen and Munich and succeeded in bringing some of the older, skeptical physicists around.

That Einstein never gave in to the Copenhagen view on quantum mechanics was to Bohr a source of real unhappiness. Indeed, very few others escaped Bohr's almost missionary zeal. His collaborators such as Leon Rosenfeld were overawed by Bohr's unrelenting effort to attain clarity of fundamentals. Bohr's favorite quotation was from Schiller: "Only fullness leads to clarity / And truth lies in the abyss." To gain the real treasures one must be ready to descend into the abyss, that dangerous place at the bottom where two huge slopes (representing contrary theories) push against each other.

I have already begun to move into the second of the principles of integrity in science. It concerns the difference between choosing the narrowly specialized problems—relatively safe but at the cost of a fragmenting and disintegrating tendency for the subject—versus choosing the more difficult problem that has some promise to bring coherence to the field, and with it integrity in the second sense of that word. To put it succinctly, the second principle might run as follows: try to be a scientist first, a specialist second. If you have it in you to make more than individual bricks that others might use, throw your life's energies into work on what Einstein called the great temple of science.

Again, Niels Bohr can give us all the examples we need, even in his 1913 paper, where he introduced the correspondence principle in its early form precisely in order to connect quantum physics with classical physics in the limit of large orbits. It is a powerful bridge that Bohr used to great advantage for years, for example, for the theory of stopping fast-moving particles in matter, in his 1948 survey. Similarly, he dealt with the puzzle of light and matter for more than two decades, trying ways to reconcile the discontinuity shown by quantum effects with the continuity shown in classical physics.

Dealing with science in a coherent way also led him to think about scientific fields far beyond physics, in a manner that few had dared to do since the days of Helmholtz and Ernst Mach. He struggled constantly with what he called "the epistemological lesson which the modern development of atomic physics has given us, and its relevance for [the other] fields of human knowledge" (Bohr 1961, v). One chief lesson of quantum mechanics was that atomic processes did not have to be described in fragmentary ways, with different theories for different effects, but that through quantum mechanics we could see the wholeness of the processes in and among atoms.

Could this lesson not be applied to wider fields? Bohr thought it could. Therefore, his essays dealt often with "biological and anthropological problems," stressing the features of wholeness distinguishing living organisms and human cultures—at least insofar as such "problems present themselves against the background of the general lesson of atomic physics" (Bohr 1961, 2).

To some extent, Bohr's pursuit of the second principle was part of the old hope of the "unity of all sciences," a phrase he often used. But it is not merely a phrase, an empty dream. That the various branches of science form one organic, interlocking picture of the world shows up in almost any substantial scientific research today. A modern paper on cosmology is really a jigsaw puzzle of which the pieces might well carry individually such labels as "elementary particle physics," "general relativity," "applied mathematics," and "observational astronomy." An experiment in neurophysiology brings together physics, chemistry, biology, computer technology, mathematics, and engineering, all at once. Such examples are becoming the rule. As Bronowski (1956) wrote, "Science is not a set of facts, but a way of giving order and therefore giving unity and intelligibility to the facts of nature" (710).

If Bohr himself did not work directly in fields outside the physical sciences, he did persuade some of his younger collaborators. A major example is Max Delbrück, who gladly confessed that the prime motivation of his own early work in biology was "Niels Bohr's suggestion of the complementarity principle in biology as a counterpart to the complementarity principle in physics" (Kay 1985).

As we come to the third principle of integrity in science, as exemplified in Bohr's life and work, the area of action, opportunity, and obligation for the responsible scientist widens still further, and so does the challenge to follow Bohr's example. Both the findings of modern science and its "habit of truth to experience" have penetrated deeply into the world of culture as a whole. The third principle of integrity in science might go like this: "Science is, and should be, part of the total world view of our time. This is a vision you should imaginatively explore, defend, and contribute to."

There are various ways of implementing such a vision, and Niels Bohr was active in each of them. There is of course the task of pedagogy, the need to bring scientific understanding to all parts of society, not least because persons in this modern world who do not know the basic facts that determine their very existence, functioning, and surroundings are in fact living in a dream world. Such persons are, in a sense, not sane.

Then there is the link between science and policy. If that link is not understood, if the technical implications for good and ill are not made clear, democracy is at risk because the leadership can be caught up in fantasies—whether technocratic or Luddite—and the citizenry cannot participate in the basic decisions that have technical components.

But for Bohr, the third principle asserted itself also in an almost compulsive pursuit, during the last twenty years of his life, to find bridges between scientific knowledge and such nonscientific fields as ethics, the arts, and philosophy. Bohr was interested in philosophy from early youth on, looking for "great interrelationships" among all areas of knowledge.[7] This ambition eventually took a different and grander form, based chiefly on the complementarity principle he announced in 1927. There are various statements of it. Bohr's own briefest formulation goes like this: "Any given application of classical concepts precludes the simultaneous use of other classical concepts which, in a different connection, are equally necessary for the elucidation of the phenomena" (quoted in Wheeler 1963, 30). The issue behind all this, as Robert Oppenheimer and many others have stressed, concerns the three great overlapping questions: What is objectivity? What is reality? Is the world deterministic or not? For classical physics, it was possible to say that the world was deterministic in the sense that if the positions and momenta of all objects were precisely measured, the future course of all history would be known. But, Bohr asked, would this be true on the atomic scale? Could that world be known more and more certainly, independent of our own predilections, or decisions, or our laboratory arrangements?

As we know, Bohr, Heisenberg, and others of that circle gave a resounding "No" to that question in the 1920s. Objective knowledge of a phenomenon, in Bohr's terms, is what you learn from the full reports of all experimental arrangements that probe into the phenomenon—arrangements, be it noted, of apparatus on the scale of everyday life and describable in ordinary human language (with mathematics merely a compact and refined extension of it). There is no firm boundary between that which is observed and the observing machinery; the boundary is movable, and the different descriptions that result from different placements of the boundary are complementary. Together, they give an exhaustive account of whatever one means by reality. Objectivity, according to the Copenhagen school, is therefore, in Oppenheimer's phrase, not an "ontological attribute"—that is, not a description of the property of being—but becomes a problem of communication.

Bohr saw in his complementarity principle the hope of extending the concept of complementarity beyond physics, in dealing with such opposing concepts or mutually exclusive experiences as thought and introspection, justice and charity, the processes in the living cell and the biophysical, biochemical analysis of organisms. By describing his ambitious attempt for examination, I am, of course, not proposing that Niels Bohr's own solution to meet the obligation of the third principle of integrity be universally adopted. Rather, I am illustrating the challenge that genius sets for itself. We scientists, in our more humble ways, should also do what we can to explore the links between the sciences and with other areas of scholarship, or we shall be pushed out of the common culture. The laboratory remains our workplace, but it must not become our hiding place.

The full grandeur of Bohr's ambition was to apply the complementarity point of view also to the understanding and toleration of differences between traditional cultural systems. What gave it all such urgency for him was his perception that the most time-honored method of conflict between societies was chiefly the attempt by one to annihilate the other, and that in the atomic age this method had become a guarantee for universal catastrophe, for mutual suicide. As Bohr put it, the main obstacle to a peaceful relation between various human societies is "the deep-rooted differences of the traditional backgrounds . . . which exclude any simple comparison [or accommodation] between such cultures. It is above all in this connection that the viewpoint of complementarity offers itself as a means of coping with the situation" (Bohr 1961, 30).

He never gave up the hope that this could be achieved, although he knew it would not be done soon. In his last interview, on the day before his death, he said, "There is no philosopher who really understands what one means by the complementarity description. It has to go [into] the schools." The Copernican system was, for a long time, also not accepted by the philosophers. But eventually, "the school children didn't think it was so bad. [This is how it got into] common knowledge. I think it will be exactly the same with the complementarity description."[8]

With this I have come to the fourth, the last, and most demanding of the principles of integrity: the special obligation scientists have to exercise sound citizenship. There are many reasons why that obligation is special, and the very opposite of elitist arrogance. The most obvious one is simply this: having been helped to become scientists and to live as scientists in this suffering world, we are the beneficiaries of unusual privilege, of scarce resources, and of the painful labors of our scientific parents. The mechanics we learned in school came to birth in the anguish of Galileo, dictating his book in his old age, disgraced, blind, and under house arrest. Kepler died on a highway like a dog, on one of his futile journeys to find money to pay for printing the books from which we have learned about his laws. Indeed, many of the formulas we rely on every day were distilled from the blood and sweat of our distant forebears, most of them now forgotten. We stand not only on the shoulders of a few, but also at the graves of thousands.

Science by its nature is cumulative and consensual, a social activity across space and time. In addition, any new scientific finding has the potential of changing, sooner or later, some part of the life of mankind, and not in every case for the better. Under these circumstances, one must conclude that science has a just claim to moral authority when it is widely seen as an activity that honors both truth and the public interest. By this I do not mean that each individual scientist must be active beyond science on behalf of the welfare of society, as were Bohr and Bridgman in their different ways. But I do mean that when we look over the profession as a whole, we must be able to say that this group, through the activities of enough of its members, is responding to its special responsibilities—special for all the reasons I have given, but also because on certain issues our scientific knowledge does give us an opportunity to make essential policy suggestions.[9] And special too, some may wish to add, simply because the flow of so much good brain power into science and technology today may have caused a corresponding deficit or opportunity cost in the rest of the polity.

Here again, Niels Bohr is an exemplar of the good citizen within the republic of science. This came through in so many ways, earliest perhaps by his openness to and encouragement of new talent, no matter from where it came. But from the many illustrations we must finally select the example he gave us through his dedication to oppose the arms race.

More than most others, Bohr thought of the atomic bomb not only as decisive in countering any such German effort; as his memoranda to President Roosevelt and later his letter to the United Nations show, Bohr also thought of such weapons as ending at last the tolerability of war itself. Thus, he wrote, "The expectations for a future harmonious international cooperation...remarkably correspond to the unique opportunities which...have been created by the advancement of science" (Bohr 1985). For this to happen, as he saw very clearly, one had to preempt a nuclear arms race after World War II. To achieve that, in turn, meant capturing the energies of the world's scientists, as well as of the atom itself, for peaceful purposes. And that inevitably meant we would need an "open world," for the verification of arms control agreements, for sharing technical information for peaceful uses, and also for sharing more in one another's cultures.

The main stumbling block, he knew well, would be dealing properly with the Soviet Union. Often invaded, and again deeply ravaged by war, its citizens viewed themselves as a great nation, beleaguered but not to be coerced. To avoid a fatal increase in hostility and suspicion on their part, Bohr argued again and again in 1944 and early 1945 that one would have to bring them in before the end of the war, while they were still allies, to reach an understanding of the world's common interests, including the industrial uses of atomic energy, based on concessions on each side.

Bohr saw a unique opportunity before the full development and deployment of a new weapons system, an opportunity in which historically based rivalries and contrary traditions could be submerged and their negative potential defused. He urged also that scientists of different countries, used to international collaboration and having bonds across national frontiers, could prove especially helpful with the deliberations of their respective governments. Finally, he hoped that the world's political leadership would contain sufficiently many statesmen to whom scientists could speak on such matters and who would understand them.

We know, of course, how very differently it all came out. In early 1944 Churchill and, at his urging, Roosevelt agreed that the Soviet leadership be faced with a fait accompli of the atomic bomb's development. Thereby they were betting that secrecy was really working, and that any Soviet buildup of a similar system later on would be slow. Neither turned out to be true. Incidentally, they also agreed that Bohr should be carefully watched because of his eager interest in international collaboration on arms control. If it had been up to Churchill alone, Bohr would probably have been interned after Bohr visited Churchill in an attempt to convert him to Bohr's view.

Scholars will debate for years whether a break through the fears on both sides, and particularly through the alienation of Stalin and his circle (about whom Bohr had no illusions), could have resulted from the vision of a harmonious and progressive world that Bohr urged. With his usual eloquence, Robert Oppenheimer summed up the hopeful view in these words: "I think that if we had acted wisely and clearly and discreetly, in accordance with Bohr's views, we might have been freed of our rather sleazy sense of omnipotence, and our delusions about the effectiveness of secrecy, and turned our society toward a healthier vision of a future worth living for" (Oppenheimer 1963). Even as yet other potentially destabilizing weapon systems are being designed, these words should remind us how fatefully the world today is facing a moment of history that has close analogies to the situation then. And once more, as Niels Bohr and others have shown at similar points, the moral authority of scientists as citizens will be tested by the seriousness, courage, and eloquence with which they inform the current debate.

With candor and integrity in mind, when our students and colleagues inquire about probity in science, let us tell them of Bridgman and Bohr. Let us tell them that such probity is not achieved merely through fear of sanctions against dishonor, but must be earned through positive acts—acts motivated by thorough intellectual self-examination and the adoption of the merciless habit of truth; motivated by some understanding of the grand history of our science, and of our privileged place in it; motivated by the scope and seriousness of the quest as scientists; motivated by the hope that science will help build a coherent world picture; and not least motivated by our responsibilities, as citizen-scientists, to the larger society that has nourished us, the society which we must help to flourish, or with which we shall perish.

Notes

1. Portions of this chapter have been adapted from my essay, "A Personal View of Percy W. Bridgman, Physicist and Philosopher," *Methodology and Science*, 26:01 (1993), and from chapter 12 of my *Thematic Origins of Scientific Thought: Kepler to Einstein*, rev. ed. (Harvard University Press, Cambridge, MA, 1988).

2. For the transplantation of elements in the Vienna Circle to the United States, and Bridgman's role in it, see Holton (1993, ch. 1) and Holton (1995).

3. Bridgman (1961), 75–76, a work first published in Boston by Beacon Press in 1954. Bridgman also published an article titled "The Struggle for Intellectual Integrity" in *Harper's Magazine* (December 1933), which was reprinted in Bridgman 1955.

4. On Einstein's case of "despair," see Einstein (1949, 51–53).

5. Interview 1 with Bohr, October 31, 1962, p. 10, in American Institute of Physics (1962).

6. Interview 2 with Bohr, November 7, 1962, p. 1, in American Institute of Physics (1962).

7. See Moore (1985), 406–407. For another example, see the discussion of Einstein's search for a coherent world picture in Holton (1998, ch. 4).

8. Session 5 with Bohr, November 17, 1962, in American Institute of Physics (1962).

9. Remarkably, many of the best scientists have collaborated, without relying on a call from the government, to form organizations through which citizen-scientists can promote the welfare of society. Profiles of several dozen of these can be found in Sonnert and Holton (2002). Bohr and Bridgman each helped to found one of these organizations.

References

American Institute of Physics. 1962, Interviews with Niels Bohr, in Sources for the History of Quantum Physics (on deposit, unpublished).

Bohr, N. 1961, *Atomic Physics and Human Knowledge,* Science Editions, New York.

———. 1985, "The Ideal of an Open World," *Impact of Science on Society* 35, 30 (reprint of letter of June 9, 1950).

Bridgman, P. W. 1927, *The Logic of Modern Physics,* Macmillan, New York.

———. 1933, "The Struggle for Intellectual Integrity," in Bridgman, P. W. (1955): *Reflections of a Physicist,* 2nd ed., Philosophical Library, New York, 361–379.

———. 1939, "Manifesto by a Physicist," *Science* 89, 179.

———. 1961, "The Present State of Operationalism," in Frank, P. G. (ed.): *The Validation of Scientific Theories,* Collier Books, New York.

Bronowski, J. 1956, "The Educated Man in 1984," *Science* 123, 710.

Einstein, A. 1949, "Autobiographical Notes," in Schilpp, P. A. (ed.): *Albert Einstein: Philosopher-Scientist,* Library of Living Philosophers, Evanston, IL.

French, A. P., and Kennedy, P. J. (eds.). 1985, *Niels Bohr: A Centenary Volume,* Harvard University Press, Cambridge, MA.

Heisenberg, W. 1975, "Discussion with Heisenberg," in Gingerich, O. (ed.): *The Nature of Scientific Discovery,* Smithsonian Institution Press, Washington, DC.

Holton, G. 1993, *Science and Anti-science,* Harvard University Press, Cambridge, MA.

———. 1995, "On the Vienna Circle in Exile: An Eyewitness Report," in Köhler, E., et al. (eds.): *The Foundation Debate,* Kluwer, Dordrecht, 269–292.

———. 1998, *The Advancement of Science, and Its Burdens,* Harvard University Press, Cambridge, MA.

Kay, L. E. 1985, "Conceptual Models and Analytical Tools: The Biology of Physicist Max Delbrück," *Journal of the History of Biology* 18, 207.

Moore, R. 1985, *Niels Bohr: The Man, His Science, and the World They Changed,* MIT Press, Cambridge, MA.

Oppenheimer, R. 1963, "Niels Bohr and His Times," The George B. Pegram Lectureship, Brookhaven, NY, Oppenheimer Collection, Box 267, Library of Congress, Washington, DC.

Sonnert, G., and Holton, G. 2002, *Ivory Bridges: Connecting Science and Society,* MIT Press, Cambridge, MA.

Wheeler, J. 1963, "Fugitive and Cloistered Virtue," *Physics Today* 16, 30.

7

Evolutionary Biology and the Question of Trust

Michael Ruse

M y dictionary offers many meanings for the word "trust," but the first and
presumably primary seems the most pertinent for a discussion about the nature and practice of science and scientists. *Trust* is "firm belief or confidence in
the honesty, integrity, reliability, justice, etc. of another person or thing; faith;
reliance." There seems to be a two-part reason why trust, as thus defined, is an
absolutely crucial component to the practice of science.

The Nature and Significance of Trust

First, trust is important in science because science is essentially a *social* activity
(Hull 1988). To do science, you are trained by others, you often work with others,
you use and make judgments on the results of others, and if you are any good as a
scientist, you have others pick up your results and use them for their own ends. As
a scientist, a far worse fate than disagreement is indifference. It is undoubtedly true
that the science of the twentieth century has been much more social than previously, but one suspects that the stories of lonely geniuses working away in garrets
have always been 90 percent mythological. Charles Darwin, that sick man buried
away for forty years in the Kent countryside, carried on an absolutely massive
correspondence with his fellow scientists, and anybody who doubts that Darwin
was keen to pass on his ideas has simply not read his *Autobiography*. (Actually, the
publication of Darwin's complete correspondence shows that, as student and as
adult, Darwin mixed with his fellow scientists much more than we had ever
dreamed.)

The second factor is that, given the peculiar nature of science's sociality, you
simply could not do science without trust. I presume that you could have a social
situation without a great deal of trust. A poker game is social in a sense—I have
friends who really look forward to gathering with their buddies once a week—but
you would be a damn fool to trust anyone in the game. Less extremely, I can

imagine a mart and exchange situation—a flea market, for instance—where trust would not be the first quality I would find useful. (I am not saying that everyone is immoral. Rather, *caveat emptor*.)

But in science, you have got to have trust. You simply cannot spend your time checking everybody's experiments and calculations. When you submit a paper to a journal, you have no choice but to accept that the editor and the referees will not use your work to their own ends, and that to the best of their ability they will judge your work fairly. The editor in turn must assume as a norm that a paper submitted is by the person or persons on the title page—that there has been no plagiarism, for example—and also that the results are not simply a function of creative imagination. Students must trust their supervisors not to use the students' labors for the greater glory of the supervisors' well-being. And much, much more (especially today) is the trust that your co-workers are not dragging you down into the mud (Broad and Wade 1982).

What I want to suggest, and in a way this is the central unifying hypothesis of this chapter, is that scientists regard violations of trust as more than simply moral lapses, if indeed the central reaction is a moral one at all. There is more of an aesthetic reaction, which is akin to the reaction that we all have when we are faced not so much with a moral violation but with something that we would label "perverse." (I shall not discuss here whether violations of trust are in fact perversions, although this is something to consider.)

In another context, I characterized a perversion as something that we, as responsible human beings, could not imagine wanting to do even if we had full freedom of action—if we owned Gyges' ring, for instance (Ruse 1988). We can imagine ourselves or someone else stealing, for example, even though we will presumably think such an action immoral and it may not be something we have ever done. But we cannot imagine ourselves sexually violating a small child, nor can we imagine a responsible person wanting to do such a thing. It is for this reason that perversion has an aesthetic dimension, in particular, what I have called the "ugh" factor (i.e., a sense of revulsion), because it violates our humanity. (My paradigm case is drinking out of a urinal, because it stresses that perversion is more than just a matter of morality, if indeed such a practice—surely labeled by one and all as "disgusting"— is immoral at all.)

Note how crucial is the notion of "humanity." A tiger that killed and ate a small child would be "dangerous" but no pervert, whereas a human who did the same would undoubtedly be labeled "perverted." Note also that, because perversion has such an emotive and value-laden sense, we are most reluctant simply to slap such a label on people. Much of the recent trouble in dealing with stories of Catholic priests and altar boys has not been because the evidence was not there—it usually is there, abundantly—but because it is simply unthinkable that men of such integrity and trust would do such vile things. We would be a lot less reluctant, on the same evidence, to draw conclusions about heterosexual adultery or about pinching the church funds to support a fondness for the horses.

My hypothesis is that violations of trust in the scientific context are very much akin to acts of perversion in the general sense. They are things that the scientist cannot imagine wanting to do, even if he or she could do them. Gyges ring would not make one into a plagiarist or set one to the stealing of others' ideas from a paper that one was sent to referee. It is not so much that it would be immoral, but rather that one would no longer be playing the game that one had freely chosen to enter into—a game that would be spoiled for everybody if one cheated.

(In the case of plagiarism, the spoiling is not quite the same as if someone uses false findings. David Hull suggests that it is for this reason that scientists do not judge plagiarism with quite the same severity as faking. As a matter of empirical fact, I am not sure that this is so, but as in games, if someone steals your achievements, it does rather spoil things. In science, the monetary rewards do count for less than the brownie points of prestige for a successful move. Does anybody really think that it is the cash that makes the Nobel Prizes so important? For this reason, plagiarism, no less than fraud, is a violation of what the scientist stands for.)

I am not sure whether the disgust felt at trust violation is innate or learned. Probably a bit of both. Certainly, the young scientist is warned of the inequities of breaking the rules, and much is made of the sorry examples of those who have sinned. But one suspects that there must be an innate human factor here, too, probably centering on basic feelings of fairness and justice. In this respect, the parallel with perversion is strong. There is an innate human factor often associated with what is thought to be unnatural—like child molestation. But learning goes on, too. My parents' generation recoiled in disgust from oral sex, but it is wonderful what a couple of sex manuals and a little soap and water will do to change one's mind.

In the discussion here, I shall assume without detailed argument that there is a commonsense plausibility in what I am saying about trust violation being like a perversion. On the one hand, scientists do not regard trust violation as being simply immoral. If, say, a scientist steals from his grant to take his mistress off on foreign holidays, you may condemn—you may be very mad, especially if you lost out in the granting competition—but at some level you can understand. To fake your results is just not understandable. "Why would you do it? You only hurt yourself. Even if you don't get found out, you know that your work is worthless."

On the other hand, because it is so unbelievable, scientists are very unwilling to condemn. This is not just a matter of cowardliness or laziness or closed shop. It is a matter of reluctance to deny that another is a real human being in a scientific sense. It is a matter of speaking the unspeakable, and, of course, since no man is an island, it is to admit the possibility of flaws in one's own human design. "Ask not for whom the bell tolls, it tolls for thee." There may be elements of racism or sexism or some such things, but I do not find it at all surprising that (until recently at least) many scientists would make comments such as, "Well, of course, fraud isn't really a problem in North America. Just a few cases among Iranians [or plug in your own least favored group or nation] and the like." The point is that one could readily deny that Iranians were full scientific beings. One could not as readily do the same for Americans.

Perhaps one place where you do have a difference between perversion and trust violation is over the question of morality. Usually, morality enters into both sides. I would say that a child rapist is both perverse and immoral, and the same of a plagiarist. But I have allowed that perhaps perversion and morality can be separated—drinking from a urinal, perverse but not immoral, being a case in point. Note, however, that this separation occurs because I, unlike the Kantian, do not think that we necessarily have duties to ourselves. I say that if it is only you, then it is your (nonmoral) business. It may be that in science, being always social, the duties-to-oneself issue does not arise. However, perhaps a case of trust violation that is not immoral is that of the scientist who spends all of his or her life coming up with the most wonderful (and good) theories and then burns them unread on his or her deathbed. Would we want to say that Gogol was immoral because he burnt the second part of *Dead Souls*? But I do note that a major reason why (in this particular case) we think he was mad was because we cannot imagine a responsible being freely doing such a thing.

I am almost finished with setting the framework for discussion in this chapter, but I must introduce one more corollary, as it were, from my hypothesis—in a way, perhaps the most important of all. I have said that scientists will be loath to bring charges of trust violation. But truly this is only the case of those who are disinterested, having no stake in the issue. One place where we might expect to find such accusations made more readily is where we have really violent disagreements about the facts or the theories of science. If these occur, might there not be a temptation to claim untrustworthiness simply because if the charge can be made to stick, then one can exclude one's opponents and their ideas from the realm of science? Conversely, there may be desperate urges to deny trust violation, precisely because this would cast aspersions, as a scientist, on oneself or on someone one admired.

If this last point is true, then perhaps (at a general level) the matter of trust violation is very much more than that of a few postdocs caught faking their findings. Over time, we do get lots of violent disagreements. Hence, perhaps in a deep sense the question of trust pervades, possibly haunts, the culture of science. If this be so, then it might be a reason why in recent years we have had such a gulf between the critics of science—congressmen and journalists, for instance, for whom questioning a source's integrity is such a straightforward matter—and scientists who so often seem casual, even indifferent, about trustworthiness.

Spelling things out, and returning again to the disinterested, my point is that the use of trust as a weapon may make for another reason why people would be disinclined to rush in with (or to accept) charges of trust violation. Experience of science and of its history may make for a certain cynicism about all such charges, since so often they have been used as political tools of attack. Especially, there will be (at the very least) caution, since so often in such cases (where the factor of trust is raised in the course of a dispute) there is an ambiguity about whether there has actually been a violation of trust. It is not that the scientists not directly involved are indifferent to violations of trust—this is the last thing that is true. It is just that they are experienced in the ways of science.

Enough now of simply laying out my hypothesis. I am a philosophical naturalist (Ruse 1986). I want my claims to be understood as empirical realities and not just as theoretical constructs. Hence, it is always important for me to test my ideas against real science, past or present. In this particular case, I choose evolutionary theory taken as a whole, down through its history. I should say that I do not know whether evolutionists have been particularly extreme about trust violation, one way or the other. But it is a theory whose history I know rather well, and there are some interesting episodes against which I can play my philosophical claims.

Let us therefore turn to evolutionism, and in order to do so, let me tell you that, roughly speaking, you can divide the history of evolutionary theory into three parts (Ruse 1979, 1996). The first 100 years, from the birth of the idea in the middle of the eighteenth century until the mid-nineteenth century and the publication of Charles Darwin's *On the Origin of Species* in 1859, saw evolutionary ideas regarded in serious scientific circles as being pseudoscience or less. They were on a par with phrenology or *Naturphilosophie*. Then, thanks to Darwin, evolutionism became respectable, although one cannot truly say that it became at that time a fully professional or mature science, with journals, students, and so forth. In some respects, it became more of a popular science, a metaphysics, a secular religion to put matters at the most extreme. Finally, around the 1930s and 1940s, thanks to the efforts of such scientists as Theodosius Dobzhansky, author of *Genetics and the Origin of Species* (1937), evolution became a fully professional functioning science, even if one that had to fight (not always entirely successfully) for its place in the sun against such competitors as molecular biology. This is much the position we find today.

To start our survey, I turn to an episode in the pre-Darwinian era, even though as a matter of strict historical fact it occurred after Darwin had discovered his mechanism of evolution through natural selection.

Vestiges of the Natural History of Creation

In 1844, the Scottish businessman Robert Chambers published (anonymously) the evolutionary tract *Vestiges of the Natural History of Creation*. In many circles it was wildly popular. Tennyson, for instance, used its message of upward progression to and beyond our species to infuse with hope the closing passages of his great poem *In Memoriam*. There is little surprise that the book sold really well—much better than Darwin was to do fifteen years later. Yet, the respectable scientific community hated *Vestiges*. I think that its reception in this quarter was a major reason why Darwin hesitated for so long to publish his evolutionary ideas. As a very professional scientist himself (in the early years, as a geologist), Darwin had no desire to be associated, even remotely, with such a nonscientific work. We were, as I have said just above, in the era of pseudoscience.

What, then, would one expect, if my hypothesis about scientific trust be well taken? There was no question of flagrant fraud or plagiarism (or the like) as such. Nevertheless, the hypothesis may well apply, especially since Chambers was anonymous and so unlikely to fight back and accusations would not involve one being offensive to a named individual (in particular, to an individual of proven scientific worth). In particular, one might expect that the scientific community would want to label the author of *Vestiges* not just as a bad scientist but also as an untrustworthy one or, at least, as untrustworthy judged as a scientist. In other words, it would want to exclude him from the domain of science on the grounds that he was not a true entity or being. *Vestiges*, therefore, would be not just bad science but nonscience—not something, that is, which lifts evolution out of the slough of pseudoscience.

This is precisely what we do find. I will refer simply to the 1845 review of *Vestiges* written by the Cambridge professor of geology Adam Sedgwick. Right through his review, we find Sedgwick harping on the theme that, if the author of *Vestiges* be a scientist, he must be dishonest—he must have broken trust with the values of science. However, given the opprobrium that such an accusation would bring, one cannot accuse even the *Vestiginarian* of this. Hence, the only conclusion is that he is no genuine scientist—he has no human standing within the community—and so *Vestiges* cannot be genuine science.

The review is 85 pages long, and then, five years later, Sedgwick returned to the theme for another 700 pages! There is much from which one can choose, so let me quote only the following passage, where the notion of trust is actually invoked:

> One of the most intrepid men [Newman!] of the Oxford half-Popish School has told us plainly, that candour is not the leading virtue of a Saint. But there are fanatics of other schools, and many a man has been a fanatical idolater of his own material hypothesis. In such a state of mind, he is like one afflicted with monomania. We cannot trust him for a single moment. But he is an object of pity far more than blame. It is not that he hates the form of truth; but either his vision is so false that he sees her out of bearing; or he has, unfortunately, such a film before his senses, that he cannot behold her figure though she stand upright before his face. He has not read to us the book of nature, as we have seen it written; but he has given us, instead, a strange set of readings, and made her tell a story most foreign to her simple meaning. In common cases, we should call this a very grave offence against truth and reason. Had he told us that our geological documents were mutilated and obscure—that, like the worm-eaten parchments of an old record-office, they were so far gone that no mortal could make a connected history out of them—and that he would work up a historical tale from his imagination—using the old documents now and then to eke out a hypothesis, or to give a savour of reality to a fictitious narrative:—Had he done this, we could have understood him, and we might have admired his lucid style, and the air of sober systematic reality which seems to refresh us while we read his pages. But this he has not done. He professes to write a history in conformity with our old documents. He has interpolated them, again and again; he has falsified their dates; and he has not condescended to tell his readers what part of his narrative is based on written records of old date, and what part is pure invention. If the works of nature are thus to be turned upside down, and every principle of sound Inductive Reasoning is now to be held in abeyance, it is high time for our men of science to strike work; and we must henceforth cull our philosophy from John Dee, and our history from George Psalmanazar. (Sedgwick 1850, 44)

As a matter of historical fact, I am not sure that Sedgwick succeeded in his aim of expelling or keeping *Vestiges* from the halls of pure science. Indeed, there is reason to think that he protested too much, drawing people's attention to *Vestiges* and to conclusions very different from his own (Secord 2000). But the strategy is clear for all to see. Science does not demand freedom from error. It does demand trust. Anyone who behaves as does Chambers cannot, *qua* scientist, be considered trustworthy. Hence, Chambers is no true scientist, and *Vestiges* is no true science. Just the reasoning and conclusion that I predicted.

Charles Darwin and the Wallace Factor

I turn next to Charles Darwin. It is difficult to write briefly on Darwin and his work. For every person who would judge Darwin one of the all-time geniuses of creation, there is a critic who finds all sorts of demeaning features in the man's life and work. For everyone who stands in amazement at Darwin's creative powers, there is another who cringes before Darwin's plodding and pedestrian nature. For each who thinks the *Origin* a masterpiece of style, there is another who finds it long and tedious and badly written.

But, positive or negative, genius or plodder, there is near-universal agreement that Charles Darwin was a man of the utmost integrity, as a person and as a scientist. Whether agreeing with him or not, whether admiring him or not, all must allow that Darwin was a gentleman. And never more so than when he was writing such works as *On the Origin of Species*. Either the brilliance shines through or the stupidity is there without attempt at concealment. But what you find is there truly and honestly—hooray or alas!

None of this seems very promising grist for our mill. Fortunately (for us!) there is one discordant note in this symphony of praise. It is made by the supporters—fanatics is not too strong a term—of the co-discoverer of natural selection, Alfred Russel Wallace. What motivates the charge is not easy to see, although it surely has something to do with the contrast between the two men, Darwin and Wallace. This could not have been more extreme. Darwin was rich, well educated, and firmly entrenched in the scientific network. Wallace was always searching for ways to make ends meet, was indifferently taught, and was ever a man on the edge of scientific respectability— enthusiasms for such things as spiritualism and socialism did not help.

Most important and most resented is the fact that Darwin was the author of *On the Origin of Species* and Wallace was pipped at the post. And therein lies the rub, at least in explicit charge if not in implicit motive. Given the fact that, for all of his oddities, perhaps because of his oddities, there was something strongly appealing about Wallace—he combined the innocence of a child with an absolutely rocklike determination over what he believed to be morally right; there has long been a tradition of those who would argue that Darwin deprived Wallace of his true inheritance—plagiarism of the most vile kind.

The charge centers always on the fact that, in 1858 after he had had his brainstorm of discovery, Wallace sent his ideas on evolution and selection to—of all people—Charles Darwin! Nor was this done in some public manner, to an office, for example, where secretaries could take note. Rather, it was to Darwin's home in the village of Downe, where there were only family and servants. The Wallace groupies, therefore, offer us involved scenarios of Darwin having stolen the central causal themes of evolution—something that they claim was possible, since Darwin was powerful and Wallace was not, Darwin was in England and Wallace was not, and (most important) Darwin had Wallace's communication and others did not. In short, Darwin was tempted by the most gross violation of scientific trust that one can imagine—a temptation before which he duly fell. (Brackman [1980] is representative of this position. Kohn [1981] scotches it.)

I shall not pause here to defend Darwin's integrity. Let me simply say categorically that there is no truth to the charge. We have simply masses of documentary counterevidence, taking us back to private notebooks of the late 1830s when Darwin first became an evolutionist and hit upon natural selection, and bringing us forward to detailed study of the postal practices of the late 1850s when Wallace sent his package to Darwin. What does interest me here, rather, is the actual behavior of Darwin and his chums, particularly Charles Lyell and Joseph Hooker, who counseled Darwin when Wallace's paper arrived and who arranged for the joint publication of Wallace's paper and some pieces by Darwin at the beginning of July 1858 (two weeks after Wallace's paper arrived) in the *Journal of the Linnaean Society*.

My questions are the very opposite of the critics. Why did Darwin not destroy Wallace's paper, or at least sit on it for a good long while? Why did Lyell and Hooker arrange for quick publication of *both* the Wallace and the Darwin pieces, given that everyone knew that Darwin had had his ideas for a long time? Why did Darwin always speak openly of Wallace and of his contribution, even after publication of the *Origin*, when it was clear to all that it was the *Darwinian* revolution, and not the Darwin/Wallace revolution? Why, in fact, was everyone so keen not merely to be trustworthy, but to make a very point of it?

The answer, I think, is that—apart from the fact that Darwin and friends were professional scientists and had deeply internalized the rules of proper conduct—they realized that they simply had to be purer than pure. They were pushing a radical revolutionary theory, one that had already drawn down scorn and vitriol from professional scientists and many others in Victorian Britain. It was part of the Darwinians' strategy to present themselves as the very epitome of solid, respectable, ultramoral, middle-class Englishmen, as scientists of the highest order. However upsetting evolutionary theory had been in the past—often made deliberately upsetting by its proponents—it was not to be seen as such in the future. You may not want your daughter to be a biologist, but Darwinism had to be something that even she could discuss and endorse in polite society.

Hence, the treatment of Wallace: there must not be the slightest scandal here. Justice must be done and must be seen to be done. Darwin even panicked and thought that he must give all major credit to Wallace, being content just to pick up the crumbs. Wiser heads prevailed—after all, the point of the enterprise was to give Darwin full credit—but the wisdom was to inflate Wallace to even greater status than he really deserved, content in the realization that such generosity would rebound to the Darwinians, who would be judged as altogether too modest. There was to be no further silliness about Darwin's failing to sit down to write the *Origin*—which he at once did, in the space of fifteen months, after twenty years of prevarication. But, equally, there was to be no way that scandal would stain the sacred enterprise. (Browne [1995, 2002] is excellent on these matters.)

As a strategy, given that the criticisms I am considering were very much late comers to the tale, the Darwinians succeeded brilliantly. Darwin did end up getting the major (and in my opinion, deserved) credit. Wallace got his dues, which I am sure everyone wanted him to have. The Darwinians came out of the exercise with a reputation for the highest moral and scientific probity. Wallace himself, for instance, always thought that the treatment he received at the hands of Darwin's clique was exemplary in the extreme. And evolution started its climb up to something endorsed and extended by real scientists and not just charlatans on the fringe. As trust pushed *Vestiges* away from genuine science, so trust pushed the *Origin* toward genuine science.

(I have not checked this prediction, but I would be prepared to gamble that today's enthusiasts for Wallace have their own axes to grind. I would be not at all surprised to learn that they think that Wallace's more "holistic" attitude to evolution is preferable to that of the somewhat "reductionistic" Darwin. If this be so, then the matter of trust is cutting two ways, with its being used to promote Wallace and belittle Darwin.)

Huxley and Owen on the Brain

I move next to the great hippopotamus controversy (as it was described by the Reverend Charles Kingsley in his *Water Babies*). This was the vicious clash on the nature of the human brain, just around and after the time of the publication of the *Origin*, between Darwin's supporter Thomas Henry Huxley and the great anatomist and Darwin opponent Richard Owen (Desmond 1982, 1994, 1997; Rupke 1994).

The big debate over evolution was over its implications for the status of our own species, *Homo sapiens*. No one really cared very much about where frogs had come from. But they did care about us. Coincidentally, this was the time when explorers were just sending back specimens of that unsettling creature the gorilla, and so expectedly there was much interest in the anatomical and other differences between the great apes and humankind. For the Darwinians, any differences had to be minimized. For the opponents, the differences had to be maximized, and so Owen entered the fray, publishing a lecture in 1859 titled "On the Gorilla," staking the claim that there are indeed fundamental differences of type between apes and humans. It is a question not just of quantity but also of quality. In particular, argued Owen, the ape brain (unlike that of humans) lacks the lobe known as the "hippocampus minor," and the cerebral hemispheres never completely cover the cerebellum.

It seems now, as indeed it seemed then, that in his most extreme pronouncements, Owen had made a serious mistake, probably a combination of in part seeing what he wanted to see and in part working with poorly preserved specimens. There are fundamental differences of proportion between ape brains and human brains, but not the postulated differences of type. We humans are not unique, at least not in this way. But instead of admitting to his mistake, Owen stuck to it—at least, he fudged the issue with definitions—and left the way open for the Darwinians to criticize, as they did at length and, Huxley (1863) in particular, with great vigor.

It was almost as if Darwin's critics had set out to give away the game, for Owen's opponents were able to attack him right at the most basic level of his competence and authority. If Owen could be discredited as an anatomist, then this would pass on to anything that he might say about evolution. But, Huxley in particular wanted a more decisive and savage victory. He wanted to push Owen right out of science, showing not just that Darwin's opponents were mistaken scientists, not just that they were inadequate scientists, but that in some fundamental way they did not deserve the name of "scientist" at all.

To do all of this, Huxley moved to make the dispute between himself and Owen not just a matter of scientific disagreement, but also of trustworthiness as a scientist and hence as a man. I should say that Huxley was somewhat given to making this link, having (in private correspondence) at the time of the *Origin* denied that any of the French could be good scientists on account of their general immorality! Less sweepingly and more publicly, he too had cut his teeth on *Vestiges*. In the early 1850s, when Huxley was asked to review one of the late revisions of the *Vestiges*, he criticized not just the science but also (after the fashion of Sedgwick) the integrity of the man:

> It would be no less wearisome than unprofitable to go into a detailed examination of all of the blunders and mis-statements of the "Vestiges"—to drag to light all of the suggestions of the false and suppressions of the true, which abound in almost every page, and which, in a work of such pretension, of such long elaboration, and so filled with whining assertions of sincerity, are almost as culpable if they proceed from ignorance, as if they were the result of intention. (Huxley 1854, 2)

Thus, when the hippocampus dispute blew up, Huxley was ready to try the same gambit, refusing to take the dispute as simply one of honest difference between two dissenting scientists. The stakes were raised to that of a matter of integrity and trustworthiness as a practitioner. For instance, when there was a question of putting Owen up for the Council of the Royal Society, Huxley stated bluntly that he thought this a mistake. Given that

> one of us two is guilty of wilful and deliberate falsehood, I did not expect to find the Council of the Royal Society throwing even a feather's weight into the scales against me. But of the fact that Owen's selection onto the Council at this particular time will be received and used in that light there cannot be doubt.

To the secretary of the Royal Society (William Sharpey), Huxley spelled out that what is at issue here is no mere scientific dispute but something going to the very core of what it is to be a scientist and a human being. We must ask "whether any body of gentlemen should admit within itself a person who can be shown to have reiterated statements which are false and which he must know to be false" (This comment is from the correspondence of the Royal Society, in London, and quoted in Rupke 1994).

I do not want to claim an exclusive lien on explanation. There are clearly various ways in which one can interpret Huxley's attack, and the most obvious—that Huxley hated Owen and he really thought him to be a cheat—is probably that with the most truth. But there is surely another dimension that my approach to scientific trust clarifies and highlights (and that in turn supports my approach). I have noted how, at the least, Darwin moved evolution from the status of pseudoscience to the higher level of respectable popular science, the kind of background metaphysics or secular religion of the working biologist. For people like Huxley, although I doubt that he (unlike Charles Darwin himself) ever really wanted to make a fully functioning mature science of evolution, this new status of evolution was very important. Hence, whatever evolution itself may have been, it was crucial to destroy the critics of Darwin.

Evolution had to be defended for its own sake. But there was surely more than this. We are just at the time when, regardless of the precise status and fate of evolution, Huxley and his friends were making major efforts to professionalize science in general, to make it a working enterprise for the full-time and science-employed practitioner. In Huxley's case, professional biology meant professional anatomy and physiology (and embryology a little later). Hence, although evolution may have been background, it was essential background. It therefore had to be defended for the sake of the whole, as well as for itself.

In addition, however—and this is the really key factor, which is almost aside from evolution as such—as Huxley and friends were professionalizing biology (and indeed the rest of science), it was crucially important for them to define the precise mode of being a professional scientist. Here, the trust factor was absolutely vital, both in its own right—a professional scientist must be a person who realizes that to hold onto a false hypothesis moves from the foolish to the wrong—and, coincidentally in this case, because Huxley could use it to try to lever out of professional science a powerful figure whose very philosophy (German Idealism) went against the kind of science (British Empiricism) that Huxley and his second-half-of-the-nineteenth-century pals were trying to promote. If the integrity factor could be used to get rid of Owen and his updated *Naturphilosophie*, then all to the good.

Of course, if what I am saying is correct, then if my earlier suppositions are well taken, we should expect to find that the reactions to Huxley would be far from clear-cut. People knew of the row between Huxley and Owen, and (unless they were right in Huxley's corner) would want to discount the personal factor somewhat. Also—especially given that (at the time) the facts of the dispute were at least somewhat murky—even those keen on professionalizing biology and defining out the nonmembers would recognize both Owen's past achievements and his earned right to be considered part of the professional community, however defined. In addition, they would hardly be oblivious to the obvious support that one such as he would give to a professionalized biological community.

History certainly seems to bear out my predictions. Although in later years the Huxleyites were to conquer the Royal Society, on this occasion, Huxley's protestations notwithstanding, Owen was elected to the council. Moreover, some felt that Huxley had gone altogether too far in his charges against Owen. The president of the Royal Society, Edward Sabine, thought Huxley's charge "a *very painful* one" and hoped that "we have no occasion to believe that one or other of those in controversy have been 'guilty of wilful and deliberate falsehood'. It would indeed be a painful position for the Society to be obliged to take either side in a *moral* dilemma of so serious a character" (quoted in Rupke 1994, 77).

My interpretation is that this represents, not so much prevarication or weak-mindedness on the part of Sabine—although there may well have been this—but rather a very standard reaction to charges of trust breaking. On the one hand, the charges are so very serious: if proven, then people are declared unfit for the kingdom of science. On the other hand, the issues are far from clear-cut and are very much bound up with other motives, such as one's ideal of a science and who should be incorporated within it. It was a painful position and not wanting to take sides was understandable. This is especially so when, as in a case like this, the ulterior motives are not really that far from the surface:

> Is it not high time that the annual passage of barbed words between Professor Owen and Professor Huxley, on the cerebral distinctions between men and monkeys, should cease? Surely the British and every other Association have heard enough of the *personality* side of this discussion. Continued on its present footing, it becomes a hindrance and injury to science, a joke for the populace, and a scandal to the scientific world. Both parties have said all they can say; and the more they say, the more firmly do they retain the correctness of their original propositions and opinions. (quoted in Rupke 1994, 298)

My three cases from the nineteenth century suggest, as does this passage quoted from the *British Medical Journal*, that the trust factor functions very much as I had hypothesized. Hence, although the century had almost four decades to run after the Huxley/Owen hippocampus debate, I shall now move forward rapidly. I am sure there were other episodes where trust breaking and integrity were involved. But I am trying to test a hypothesis, not rewrite the history of evolutionary theory. Therefore, I shall now turn toward our century, to see what light it throws on my claims.

The Biometrician/Mendelian Controversy

As we draw nigh to the twentieth century, the most important conceptual events in the history of evolutionary theory center on genetics: the rediscovery of Mendel's rules, the development of the theory of genetics based on these rules, the initial feeling that genetics and evolution through natural selection are in conflict, followed by the realization that the two are complementary and necessary components the whole picture. This all prepares the way for the key social event in the 1930s and 1940s, the professionalization of evolutionary studies around a "paradigm" Darwin–Mendel synthesis.

Staying, as before, in the Anglo-Saxon world, the twentieth century's opening is spanned by a major conflict about the nature of the raw stuff of evolution, the building blocks of change. I refer to the controversy between the biometricians, especially Raphael Weldon and Karl Pearson, who thought that the nature of evolution is always gradual and based on microchanges, and the Mendelians, especially William Bateson, who thought that lasting moves in evolution are necessarily fairly large and significant—evolution proceeds through one-step macrochanges (Provine 1971; MacKenzie 1981; Ruse 1996, from which the correspondence that follows is quoted).

The dispute was bitter in the extreme. It had a patricidal element in that Bateson had been Weldon's student and in that Weldon died, a relatively young man, in 1906, undoubtedly in major part from the strain of the controversy. By now I am sure it will come as no surprise that, as in the Huxley/Owen dispute, it rapidly moved from the purely scientific, where one debated mere matters of fact, to one where the key issues were integrity and trust. Weldon accused Bateson of omitting "from his account of these records [of a certain kind of plant] some passages which materially weaken his case." Bateson took this personally (which he was obviously supposed to do, even though Weldon was careful not to make an explicit charge of fraud): "Weldon's position in writing is therefore that of the accomplice who creates a diversion to help a charlatan. I cannot at all understand his motives, or how he can bring himself to play this part." And Weldon responded in kind:

> Dear Bateson,
> I can do no more.
>   First, you accuse me of attacking your personal character; and when I disclaim this, you charge me with a dishonest defense of some one else.
>   I have throughout discussed only what appeared to me to be facts, relating to a question of scientific importance.
>   If you insist on regarding any opposition to your opinions concerning such matters as a personal attack upon yourself, I may regret your attitude, but I can do nothing to change it.
>
>   Yours very truly,
>   W.F.R. Weldon

And so the battle lines were set, with the biometricians insisting that one work with small variations and selection and (as a consequence) use fairly sophisticated mathematics, and the Mendelians insisting that discrete variations are the key to change and that the mathematics can confuse as much as enlighten. There is no need for details. The Huxley/Owen dispute can serve as our norm, including the fact that those on the edge had a somewhat cynical view about all of the charges being launched and counterlaunched. Hence, having noted that (in the quotation above) Bateson confirms my reading of trust breaking as something inhuman ("I cannot at all understand his motives"), I will conclude with more from Bateson confirming that this is something akin to what (in the broader domain) we think of as perverse, rather than simply wrong:

> We have been told of late, more than once, that Biology must become an *exact* science. The same is my own fervent hope. But exactness is not always attainable by numerical precision: there have been students of Nature, untrained in statistical nicety, whose instinct for truth yet saved them from perverse inference, from slovenly argument, and from misuse of authorities, reiterated and grotesque. (Bateson 1902, 71)

The Piltdown Hoax

Chronologically, the next item we ought to consider is the Piltdown hoax, the supposedly genuine but in fact fabricated prehuman skull, found in England in 1911. However, although there are many items of interest in this hoax, including reactions by various parties to its discovery (not the least being that it was an *English* discovery), from our perspective (trying to see how trust operates in a broader context in science) it is perhaps too obviously a hoax to be that interesting and informative—especially given that it was not unveiled until after the principal characters were long dead.

The one point that I will make about Piltdown, with an eye to the next episode that I shall discuss, is the fact that even today emotions are raised over who precisely was responsible for the hoax. Moreover, in the broader context, the hoax is still used to support arguments about what should and should not be included in proper (and by implication, good) science. In this respect, particularly interesting is Stephen Jay Gould's claim (Gould 1980) that the perpetrator was the Jesuit priest and paleontologist Teilhard de Chardin. I do not know if Chardin was involved—others think not—but what is interesting is the way that Gould was clearly using this claim of gross trust violation to make his own case for science.

In particular, although once a biological progressionist, since the sociobiological controversy (on which, more below) Gould has been convinced that such progressionism is both false and a social barrier to the improvement of lower and deprived classes in our society. In attacking Teilhard, explicitly Gould was attacking one of the most powerful and eloquent of recent spokesmen for biological progress. If Teilhard's status as a reliable authority could be diminished, so much the better for Gould's vision of science. (It is worth adding that, having accused Teilhard, Gould was happy to conclude that the priest was able to do the dark deed because, back in those days, judged as a scientist, he was no true professional—he was a mere amateur. This explains how a man of undoubted general integrity could have done such a thing and at the same time saves Gould from making a grave personal attack on a fellow scientist, considered as a scientist.)

We have always known how history can be used for our own ends. No one is a greater master at this than Gould, and nowhere more so than in this case.

Mendel's Fishy Figures

More central to evolutionary thought, although likewise involving attitudes toward a figure of the past, is the case of Gregor Mendel and the suspicious statistics. By the 1930s, thanks to the efforts of the theoretical population geneticists, Mendel had been brought firmly within the evolutionary fold. Indeed, it is not too much to say that, after Darwin, he was seen as the most important figure in its history. Not that this was a matter of pure history, any more than was Gould's attack on Teilhard. It is undeniable that scientists (and evolutionists are no exception) make great use of the important figures from their past—they help to give a sense of identity, inspiring young and old along the rough path of discovery. Mendel particularly had (and still has) a special place among scientists, since in his lifetime he was ignored and unknown, his genius being discovered only after his death. Even the most discouraged and unappreciated among us could (and still can) take heart from his story.

Yet, no sooner had Mendel been welcomed into the fold than it was discovered—and announced to the world in 1936 by the leading geneticist/statistician Ronald Fisher—that, beyond any shadow of doubt, Mendel's results are fraudulent. It is not that his laws are wrong—they are probably right—but that his results are far too good. In real life you simply do not get the kind of perfect readings that Mendel reported. We have gone beyond a little rounding off to outright fakery.

The obvious response is that Mendel was a fraud. But the implications of such a conclusion were (and probably still are) too frightening to contemplate. The whole science of genetics, and evolution, too, is besmirched. Something must be done and something is done: the gardener is blamed!

> A serious and almost inexplicable discrepancy has appeared . . . in that in one series of results the numbers observed agree excellently with the two to one ratio, which Mendel himself expected, but differ significantly from what should have been expected had his theory been corrected to allow for the small size of his test progenies. To suppose that Mendel recognized this theoretical complication, and adjusted the frequencies supposedly observed to allow for it, would be to contravene the weight of the evidence supplied in detail by his paper as a whole. Although no explanation can be expected to be satisfactory, it remains a possibility among others that Mendel was deceived by some assistant who knew too well what was expected. This possibility is supported by independent evidence that the data of most, if not all, of the experiments have been falsified so as to agree closely with Mendel's expectations. (Fisher 1936, 164)

One gathers from the last sentence that the more the forgery, the less the likelihood that Mendel committed it. One gathers also, from responses to Fisher's article, that all agreed that Fisher's reaction was essentially the correct one. No one in the scientific community wanted (or yet wants) to charge Mendel, although the more charitable tend to find the mistake simply in the methodology and less in the assistant (see Stern and Sherwood 1966).

Again, I find confirmation for my position on trust and integrity in science. It is a mistake to think that this attitude by Fisher and other evolutionists (and geneticists generally) is simply a cover-up by the scientific community. Or rather, if it is a cover-up (and I have expressed elsewhere my feelings that probably Mendel is guilty), I want to know why it was so readily and generally committed. Fisher was a difficult man, but he was not a dishonest one. As you may expect by now, my feeling is that the answers lie in the broader picture. Mendel plays an important part in the definition of genetics (and hence evolution) as a science. To depose him as a cheat is to devalue one's science. If it has to be done, then it has to be done. Certainly, one cannot conceal unpleasant facts (the revelation of which was precisely what Fisher was at). But no one is going to thank you for rushing in and doing an integrity-bashing hatchet job if it is not strictly necessary.

Dobzhansky's Russian Temperament

I come now to the man who was probably the most important figure in evolutionary biology in this century, the already-mentioned Russian-born, American-residing Theodosius Dobzhansky. I cannot overemphasize the influence that this man, especially through his ground-breaking book *Genetics and the Origin of Species*, has had on the field. It was he and his work that truly laid the foundation of a working professional discipline of evolutionary studies (aided, let me rush to add, by a number of others, including Ernst Mayr, George Simpson, and Ledyard Stebbins). For a host of reasons, then and now, it was and is important that this man be seen clearly as a reputable scientist.

Yet, judged by standards that many would feel appropriate today, in at least two areas Dobzhansky skated perilously close to behavior that verges on the dishonest—the sorts of things that a trustworthy scientist simply would not do. The first occurred in his authorship of articles, or rather, his joint authorship of articles, especially those with the theoretical population geneticist Sewall Wright. Today, in the opinion of many who think about these things, if your name is on the paper, then unless there is a specific disclaimer or qualification, you get credit and you take responsibility for the lot. However, Dobzhansky was famously—notoriously—unable to handle more than the simplest mathematics. How was it, then, that he could happily put his name on work that was (at least for that time in biology) quite ferociously mathematical? He had not the first idea of what was going on in his papers, except for the empirical bits at the beginning and end. Not much disclaiming going on here to the person who came across his work cold, as it were.

Second, there was the question of the quality of Dobzhansky's empirical findings, that area in which he did work and excel, if anywhere. By any standards, he churned out incredible amounts of material, simply clogging the agendas of the theoreticians (primarily Sewall Wright) to whom he turned. He and his students, both in the field and in the laboratory, produced data batch after data batch, as they poked into the life and times of that geneticists' favorite organism, the fruit fly. But, right from the beginning, there were complaints about the sloppiness of Dobzhansky's methodology and recording methods, and these were complaints that persisted. It is true that poor-quality work is in itself perhaps not an immediate matter of integrity, but as we have seen in the case of the Huxley/Owen dispute, ongoing poor-quality work (especially in the face of criticism) does tend to be judged that way. And in the case of Dobzhansky, there were those prepared to make precisely such a complaint.

You will have realized that, in this chapter, it is not my aim to make judgments about integrity as such. Rather, I want to test my own hypotheses about trust and integrity in the light of history. Recognizing, then, that it is not my (self-imposed) mandate to say what *I* think that Dobzhansky should have done, turning to the first issue—that of joint authorship—one must point out that, at that time (or since, for that matter), no one did come across the Dobzhansky/Wright work cold, as it were. Everybody knew that Dobzhansky was incapable of handling the mathematics and that it was all done by Wright. No one concealed the fact, least of all Dobzhansky, who (on every possible occasion) happily told people that, with respect to mathematics, "Papa [i.e., Sewall Wright] knows best" (see Mayr and Provine 1980).

In other words, the point is that, although by today's standards some might critique Dobzhansky, no one then felt the need to do so. Nor, given Dobzhansky's general importance in his field, was this a case of covering up. It was just not an issue. As others have pointed out in the context of physics, it was only just at this time (the 1930s) that we start (in any major sense) to get the collaboration of theoreticians and experimentalists. Hence, people were feeling their way forward on all of these matters, not the least of which was the writing of jointly authored articles and the assignment of credit. Clearly, things have changed since those days, and probably today people do feel the need to be more formal in their behavior. But then, it was a non-issue and was treated as such.

The sloppy work was certainly no non-issue, although it does seem fair to say that (as in the credit case) when Dobzhansky was working (especially in the late 1930s and 1940s), people were not quite as sensitive on these matters as they have become since. It is surely in part for this reason that people were able and prepared to put the inaccuracies down to simple "sloppiness," explaining it away as a function of Dobzhansky's almost childlike (well, certainly Russian) "enthusiasm" and the like (as they were to do for other things judged embarrassing in a professional scientist, such as his eagerness to embrace the ideas of Teilhard de Chardin).

However, just as the critics were looking rather sourly on Dobzhansky's aim to move from a strict genetics to a genetics-based evolutionism, feeling that he was moving out to something on the fringe of real science, one suspects that the defenders were bound and determined not to let integrity charges stick to so important a figure. It is certainly the case that something analogous was happening in the case of the religion. Putting Dobzhansky's faith down to his peculiar Russian temperament was not simple racism on the part of his American colleagues. Rather, they were trying to defend the idea that he could be a good and proper scientist, despite these lapses—lapses that would be cause for concern in an American-born scientist. I think, indeed, that Dobzhansky himself played this card to an extent.

One final, rather interesting point: as I have already noted, scientific standards have tightened up today. Perhaps, it is therefore not insignificant or coincidental that the question of Dobzhansky's accuracy has again become a matter of discussion and that at least one alternative excusing explanation—an explanation as much in the spirit of the present day as is the criticism—has been offered. This is that Dobzhansky was moving into a new field, a field that required a different kind of data gathering, and that consequently should not be judged by the standards of the old field. In particular, Dobzhansky's *evolutionary* genetics required massive amounts of material, gathered (primarily) from the wild, as opposed to a few detailed readings from laboratory experiment (as one gets and desires in traditional genetics). At the level he was working, the precision is simply not possible, nor is it needed.

I do not want to read too much into all of this. Perhaps even the politically correct can continue to speak of "Russian enthusiasm," and it is just coincidental that matters to do with the relationship between theory and evidence have become a hot philosophico/historical topic. But I do find it interesting that history can be, if not rewritten, then reinterpreted, in order to preserve certain ideals or facts (in this case the integrity of Theodosius Dobzhansky) even as present-day customs and mores change. And with respect to my overall thesis about integrity and trust being bound up with our ideal of a scientist, given the continuing importance of Dobzhansky as the founder of modern evolutionary studies, I take as confirmation the ongoing effort to defend him as a proper thinking and behaving scientist (see also Adams 1994).

Human Sociobiology as Pseudoscience

Bringing my trip through the history of evolutionism down to the present, I come to the final episode that I want to discuss. The biggest controversy in evolutionary theory in recent years has been over human sociobiology, the attempt to explain human social behavior in terms of our genetic heritage as shaped and preserved by natural selection. And at the heart of this controversy was *Sociobiology: The New Synthesis* (Harvard University Press, 1975), by the Harvard entomologist Edward O. Wilson. For a good ten years from the date of its publication, Wilson and his supporters were attacked and belittled by the widest range of critics—feminists, Marxists, social scientists, philosophers, and more (Segerstrale 2000).

Among these critics were some very eminent scientists, evolutionists even, including some of Wilson's fellow Harvard biology department members, notably Richard C. Lewontin and Stephen Jay Gould. For these men, the sociobiology debate could never be a simple matter of science, for it struck deeply at views that went to the very core of their being, both as people of the left and, being Jewish, as members of a group that felt (with some justification) that, throughout this century, it had been oppressed by biological theories of humankind. (This last point comes through very clearly in Gould [1981]. See also Ruse [1999].)

Expectedly, it did not take long for the debate to move (degenerate?) into one of personal integrity, with Lewontin, for example, being quite open in his belief that Wilson had betrayed the trust of a scientist. In the following interview, Lewontin is speaking of a review that he penned of a book coauthored by Wilson and a young physicist, Charles Lumsden:

> I don't really think we are engaged primarily in an intellectual issue. I do not think that what he [Wilson] has doing for the last ten years has been primarily motivated by a genuine desire to find out something true about the world, and therefore I don't think it is serious. One of the reasons my book review of Lumsden and Wilson had a kind of sneering tone is that it is the way I genuinely feel about the project, namely that it is not a serious, intellectual project. Because I have only two possibilities open to me. Either it is a serious intellectual project, and Ed Wilson can't think, or he can think, but it is not a serious project and therefore he is making all the mistakes he can—he does. If it is a really deep serious project, then he simply lowers himself in my opinion as an intellectual . . . It is a question of what kind of intellectual work you have to do to meet a certain intellectual pretension to explanation about the world. If I am going to sit down and write a theory about how all of human culture is explained by biology, I have a lot of epistemological groundwork to learn, I mean, a fantastic amount . . . I mean, those guys have just jumped feet first into a kind of naive and vulgar kind of biological explanation of the world, and the consequence is a failure. It is a failure as a system of explanation because they haven't done their homework . . . I have to say that my chief feeling—I'll be honest about my chief feeling when I consider all this stuff—it's one of disdain. I don't know what to say, I mean, it's cheap! (Segerstrale 1986, 75)

No one could accuse Wilson of outright fraud or plagiarism. He is the model of southern courtesy and generosity. He bends over backward to give credit, and his own empirical work is a paradigm for young researchers. But the stakes are too high. Wilson's personal probity may not stop the critics. Hence, if they cannot get him directly, then they will do so indirectly. Most informative in this respect is a book coauthored by Lewontin, *Not in Our Genes* (Lewontin et al. 1984). Prominent in the early chapters is the story of one of the most discussed and unambiguous cases of fraud in recent science, that of Sir Cyril Burt and of his faking the data on IQ scores. Then, having set the scene, we move on to a nice juicy discussion of Edward O. Wilson and of human sociobiology. Thus, the reader not only is offered all sorts of criticisms specifically against human sociobiology itself but also is presented with these in the context of (straight after having read about) a blatant unapologetic violation of the most basic standards of science. If this is not a textbook case of imputing guilt by association, then I do not know what is.

My intent here is not to raise moral indignation, in you or in me. I am not concerned about the outrageous act of linking Wilson with Burt—although how else one would judge the connection I do not know. I simply want to use this linking as my final episode in the history of evolutionary theory, showing how readily scientists move to matters of trustworthiness in their aims to delimit and define science as they would have it, and how trust and integrity are used in the attempt to include or (more often) to exclude certain people from the domain of science, as it is properly to be understood and practiced.

Conclusion

Let me simply restate my main hypothesis and its corollaries. Science being social depends essentially on trust. I see violation of trust being more than simply a moral failing, but akin rather to perversion, where one does something that takes one from the area of natural human (in this case scientific human) action and status. This being so, we should expect to find scientists under normal circumstances (especially if they are themselves disinterested) very loath to launch or accept charges of trust violation, simply because the very charges are themselves so grave.

However, given the way I have characterized trust, we should expect to find that it pervades the whole culture of science. The integrity factor impinges on more than a few notorious cases such as Piltdown man, or a handful of foreign students publishing in obscure medical journals. In particular, we should expect to find that when scientists disagree very strongly about matters of science, there will be a temptation to move to charges of trust violation, precisely because, if accepted, one will thereby be removing one's opponents (and their ideas) from the domain of science.

One expects that those under attack (real or potential) will defend themselves against violations of trust, especially since the charges will probably be based on matters that are less than sharply black or white. Hence, my hypothesis implies that charges and countercharges will be batted back and forth. And it suggests, as a final consequence, that people on the sidelines will probably have their natural inclination to reject charges of trust violation reinforced by a certain cynicism based on experience about the way in which trust violation is used as a weapon against scientific enemies. It is not moral insensitivity that makes people loath to charge untrustworthiness but a knowledge of the history of science.

Simply put, I argue that this hypothesis and its implications make sense of my rapid trip through the history of evolutionary theorizing and, conversely, is supported by that trip. What better conclusion could be desired by a philosophical naturalist such as myself?

References

Adams, M., ed. 1994. *The Evolution of Theodosius Dobzhansky*. Princeton, NJ: Princeton University Press.

Bateson, W. 1902. *Mendel's Principles of Heredity*. Cambridge, UK: Cambridge University Press.

Brackman, A. C. 1980. *A Delicate Arrangement: The Strange Case of Charles Darwin and Alfred Russel Wallace*. New York: Times Books.

Broad, W. J., and N. Wade. 1982. *Betrayers of the Truth: Fraud and Deceit in the Halls of Science*. New York: Simon and Schuster.

Browne, J. 1995. *Charles Darwin: Voyaging. Volume 1 of a Biography*. New York: Knopf.

———. 2002. *Charles Darwin: The Power of Place. Volume II of a Biography*. New York: Knopf.

Desmond, A. 1982. *Archetypes and Ancestors: Paleontology in Victorian Britain, 1850–1875*. London: Blond and Briggs.

———. 1994. *Huxley, the Devil's Disciple*. London: Michael Joseph.

———. 1997. *Huxley, Evolution's High Priest*. London: Michael Joseph.

Fisher, R. A. 1936. Has Mendel's work been rediscovered? *Annals of Science* 1: 115–137.

Gould, S. J. 1980. The Piltdown conspiracy. *Natural History* 89 (August): 8–28.

———. 1981. *The Mismeasure of Man*. New York: Norton.

Hull, D. 1988. *Science as a Process*. Chicago: University of Chicago Press.

Huxley, T. H. 1854. [Review of] Vestiges of the Natural History of Creation, Tenth Edition, British and Foreign Medico-Chirurgical Review, 13, 425–439. In *The Scientific Memoirs of Thomas Henry Huxley, Supplementary Volume*. Edited by M. Foster and E. R. Lankester, 1–19. London: Macmillan, 1903.

———. 1863. *Evidence as to Man's Place in Nature*. London: Williams and Norgate.

Kohn, D. 1981. Review of Brackman, *A Delicate Arrangement*. *Science* 213: 1105–1108.

Lewontin, R. C., Steven Rose, and Leon J. Kamin. 1984. *Not in Our Genes: Biology, Ideology and Human Nature*. New York: Pantheon.

MacKenzie, Donald A. 1981. *Statistics in Britain 1865–1930. The Social Construction of Scientific Knowledge*. Edinburgh: Edinburgh University Press.

Mayr, Ernst, and William Provine, eds. 1980. *The Evolutionary Synthesis: Perspectives on the Unification of Biology*. Cambridge, MA: Harvard University Press.

Owen, R. 1859. On the gorilla. *Proceedings of the Royal Institution* 3: 10–30.

Provine, W. B. 1971. *The Origins of Theoretical Population Genetics*. Chicago: University of Chicago Press.

Rupke, N. A. 1994. *Richard Owen: Victorian Naturalist*. New Haven, CT: Yale University Press.

Ruse, M. 1979. *The Darwinian Revolution: Science Red in Tooth and Claw*. Chicago: University of Chicago Press.

———. 1986. *Taking Darwin Seriously: A Naturalistic Approach to Philosophy*. Oxford: Blackwell.

———. 1988. *Homosexuality: A Philosophical Inquiry*. Oxford: Blackwell.

———. 1996. *Monad to Man: The Concept of Progress in Evolutionary Biology*. Cambridge, MA: Harvard University Press.

————. 1999. *Mystery of Mysteries: Is Evolution a Social Construction?* Cambridge, MA: Harvard University Press.

Secord, J. A. 2000. *Victorian Sensation: The Extraordinary Publication, Reception, and Secret Authorship of Vestiges of the Natural History of Creation.* Chicago: University of Chicago Press.

Sedgwick, A. 1845. Vestiges. *Edinburgh Review* 82: 1–85.

————. 1850. *Discourse on the Studies at the University of Cambridge.* 5th ed. Cambridge: Cambridge University Press.

Segerstrale, U. 1986. Colleagues in conflict: An in vitro analysis of the sociobiology debate. *Biology and Philosophy* 1: 53–88.

————. 2000. *Defenders of the Truth: The Battle for Science in the Sociobiology Debate and Beyond.* New York: Oxford University Press.

Stern, C., and E. R. Sherwood, eds. 1966. *The Origin of Genetics: A Mendel Source Book.* San Francisco: W. H. Freeman.

8

The Rise and Fall of Emil Konopinski's Theory of β Decay

Allan Franklin

George Levine, a sympathetic and critical commentator on science, once asked, "What if important scientific discoveries were often made because the scientist *wanted* something to be true rather than because he or she had evidence to prove it true?" (Levine 1987, 13). In this chapter I tell the story of Emil Konopinski, who in the 1930s was a coauthor of an alternative to Fermi's theory of β decay. Although his theory initially seemed to be supported by the existing experimental evidence, further work provided considerable evidence against the theory. If anyone would have wanted the theory to be correct and to make a judgment against the evidence, it would have been Konopinski. As I will show, he didn't.

The history illustrates both the fallibility of science and the ability of science to overcome errors. The early experimental results on β decay, which suggested the need for an alternative to Fermi's theory, were, in fact, incorrect. The electrons emitted by the radioactive element lost energy in escaping from the thick sources used, giving rise to an excess of low-energy electrons. There was, in addition, an incorrect theory–experiment comparison. A correct, but inappropriate, theory was being compared to the experimental results. It was only when both of these errors were corrected that a valid experiment–theory comparison could be made. When it was, Fermi's theory was supported.

I begin the story with β decay, the process in which an atomic nucleus emits an electron, simultaneously transforming itself into a different kind of nucleus. In the early twentieth century, it was thought that the final state of β decay involved only two bodies (the daughter nucleus and the electron). The laws of conservation of energy and conservation of momentum require that the electron emitted in such a two-body decay be monoenergetic. For each radioactive element, all of the electrons emitted would have the same energy. Considerable experimental work on β decay in this period culminated in the demonstration by Ellis and Wooster (1927) that the energy spectrum of the emitted electrons was in fact continuous. The electrons were emitted with all energies from zero up to a maximum, which depended on the particular element. Such a continuous spectrum was incompatible with a two-body decay process. The conservation laws were threatened. In 1931, Wolfgang Pauli proposed that a third particle, one that was electrically neutral, had a very small mass, and had spin of one-half, was also emitted in β decay. This solved the problem and saved the conservation laws because in a three-body process the electron is not required to be monoenergetic, but can have a continuous energy spectrum.[1]

Fermi's Theory of β Decay

Enrico Fermi named the proposed new particle the neutrino, little neutral one, and immediately incorporated it into a quantitative theory of β decay (Fermi 1934a, 1934b). Fermi assumed the existence of the neutrino, that the atomic nucleus contained only protons and neutrons, and that the electron and the neutrino were created at the moment of decay. Fermi's theory gave a reasonable, although not exact, fit to the energy spectrum of electrons emitted in β decay. He also explained other features of that decay. In particular, his theory predicted that the product of the integral of the energy spectrum, $F(Z, E_o)$, and the lifetime of the transition, τ_o, would be a constant for each type of transition ($F\tau_o$ is a constant). Fermi cited already-published experimental results in support of his theory, in particular, the work of Sargent (1933). Sargent had found that if he plotted the logarithm of the disintegration constants (inversely proportional to the lifetime) against the logarithm of the maximum electron energy, the results for all measured decays fell into two distinct groups, known in the later literature as Sargent curves (figure 8.1). Although Sargent had originally

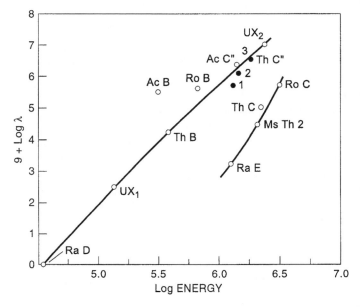

Figure 8.1 Logarithm of the decay constant (inversely proportional to the lifetime) plotted against the logarithm of the maximum decay energy (the Sargent curves). From Sargent (1933).

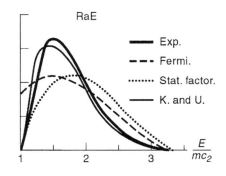

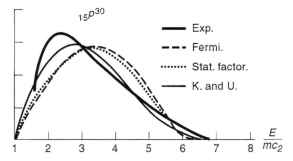

Figure 8.2 The energy spectra for the β decay of RaE and ^{30}P, respectively. The curve labeled Exp. is the experimental result, Fermi. is the Fermi theory, and K. and U. is the Konopinski-Uhlenbeck theory. From Konopinski and Uhlenbeck (1935).

remarked, "At present the significance of this general relation is not apparent" (Sargent 1933, 671), this was what Fermi's theory required, namely, that $F\tau_o$ be approximately constant for each type of decay. "Fermi connects the two curves of Sargent's well-known graph relating the lifetime and maximum energy with 'allowed' and 'forbidden' transitions" (Konopinski and Uhlenbeck 1935, 7).[2]

Although, as Konopinski and Uhlenbeck pointed out, Fermi's theory was "in general agreement with the experimental facts," more detailed examination of the decay energy spectra showed that there were discrepancies. Fermi's theory predicted too few low-energy electrons and an average decay energy that was too high. Konopinski and Uhlenbeck cited as evidence the energy spectrum of ^{30}P obtained by Ellis and Henderson (1934) and that of radium E (RaE; bismuth, ^{210}Bi) measured by Sargent (1933) (figure 8.2). It is clear that the Fermi theory curves are not a good fit to the observed spectra.

The Konopinski-Uhlenbeck Theory and Its Experimental Support

Konopinski and Uhlenbeck proposed a modification of Fermi's theory that would eliminate the discrepancy and predict more low-energy electrons. "This requirement could be fulfilled in a simple, empirical way by multiplying [the energy spectrum] by a power of the neutrino energy $E_o - E$'' (E_o is the maximum decay energy and E is the electron kinetic energy; Konopinski and Uhlenbeck 1935, 11).[3] As shown in figure 8.2, the curves labeled "K and U" (Konopinski-Uhlenbeck theory) fit the observed spectra far better than do the Fermi curves. Konopinski and Uhlenbeck also noted, "Our modification of the form of the interaction does not of course affect Fermi's explanation of Sargent's law" (12).

The Konopinski-Uhlenbeck theory was almost immediately accepted by the physics community as superior to Fermi's theory, and as the preferred theory of β decay. In a 1936 review article on nuclear physics, which remained a standard reference and was used as a student text into the 1950s, Bethe and Bacher (1936), after surveying the experimental evidence, remarked, "We shall therefore accept the K-U theory as the basis for future discussions" (192).[4]

The K-U theory received substantial additional support from the results of the cloud-chamber experiments of Kurie, Richardson, and Paxton (1936). They found that the observed β-decay spectra of several elements (^{13}N, ^{17}F, ^{24}Na, ^{31}Si, and ^{32}P) all fit the K-U theory better than did the original Fermi theory. It was in this paper that the Kurie plot, which made comparison between the two theories far easier, made its first appearance. The Kurie plot was a graph of a particular mathematical function involving the electron energy spectrum that gave different results for the Konopinski-Uhlenbeck theory and for the Fermi theory. It had the nice visual property that the Kurie plot for whichever theory was correct would be a straight line. If the theory did not fit the observed spectrum, then the Kurie plot for that theory would be a curve. The Kurie plot obtained by Kurie and his collaborators for ^{32}P is shown in figure 8.3. They described the results as follows: "The (black) points marked 'K-U' modification should fall as they do on a straight line. If the Fermi theory is being followed the (white) points should follow a straight line as they clearly do not" (1936, 377).

Kurie and his colleagues concluded:

> The data given above indicate that the Konopinski-Uhlenbeck theory gives a very good account of the distribution curves of the β-rays from the light radioactive elements. We have cited cases of three electron emitters (^{24}Na, ^{31}Si, ^{32}P) and two positron emitters (^{13}N, ^{17}F) where deviations from the theoretical shape of the curve of the observed points are surprisingly small. The spectra of the three elements Cl, ^{41}A, ^{42}K can be resolved into two components each of which is very closely a K-U curve. (380)[5]

Interestingly, Kurie and his collaborators had initially obtained results that were in agreement with the Fermi theory. Their experimental apparatus used a cloud chamber placed in a magnetic field. The electron tracks produced in the cloud chamber have a radius of curvature proportional to the momentum of the electrons. This also determined the energy of the electrons. Kurie and his collaborators attributed their incorrect result to the preferential elimination of low-energy decay electrons by one of their selection criteria; one that eliminated events in which the electron tracks in the cloud chamber showed a visible deflection.[6] Low-energy electrons are scattered more frequently than are high-energy electrons and will therefore have more tracks with visible deflections. The scattering was greatly reduced by filling the cloud chamber with hydrogen rather than the original oxygen.

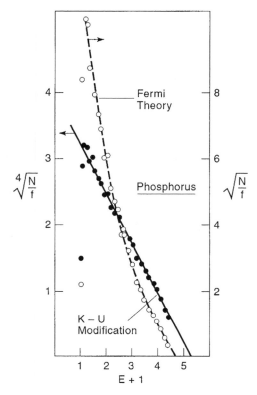

Figure 8.3 The Kurie plot for the decay of ^{32}P, based on Kurie et al. (1936). "The (black) points marked 'K-U modification' should fall as they do on a straight line. If the Fermi theory is being followed the (white) points should follow a straight line as they clearly do not" (377).

Last spring we examined the Fermi theory to see if it predicted the shape of the distributions we were getting and reported favorably on the agreement between the two...with the reservation that we did not feel that our experiments were good enough satisfactorily to test a theory. At that time we were using oxygen as the gas in the chamber as is usual in β-ray work. In measuring the curves we had adopted the rule that all tracks with visible deflections in them were to be rejected. That this was distorting the shape of the distribution we knew because we were being forced to discard many more of the low energy tracks than the high energy ones. This distortion can be reduced to a very great extent by photographing the β-tracks in hydrogen instead of oxygen. The scattering is thus reduced by a factor of 64...[7]

We found with the hydrogen filled chamber that the distribution curves were more skew than they had appeared with the oxygen filled chamber. This is not surprising: our criterion of selection had been forcing us to discard as unmeasurable a large number of low energy tracks. The number discarded increased as the energy of the track decreased. The apparent concordance between our early data and the Fermi theory was entirely traceable to this because the Fermi distribution is very nearly symmetrical so that when the number of low energy tracks was measured this apparent asymmetry in the experimental distributions was lost. (Kurie et al. 1936, 369)

Similar problems affected other cloud-chamber experiments. Paxton found a different solution: he measured all tracks of sufficient length. "Because β-ray scattering becomes increasingly serious as the energy decreases, all tracks of sufficient length were measured as well as possible in spite of bad curvature changes, in order to prevent distribution distortion from selection criteria" (Paxton 1937, 177).[8]

Despite its general support of the K-U theory, the Kurie et al. paper also discussed a problem with the K-U account. The maximum decay energy extrapolated from the straight-line graph of the Kurie plot seemed to be higher than the value obtained visually from the energy spectrum (figure 8.4). Konopinski and Uhlenbeck had, in fact, pointed this out in their original paper. Kurie et al. found such differences for ^{30}P and for ^{26}Al, but found good agreement for RaE and ^{13}N. With reference to the latter, they stated, "The excellent agreement of these two values of the upper limits [obtained from the K-U extrapolation and from nuclear reactions] is regarded as suggesting that the high K-U limits represent the true energy changes in a β disintegration" (370). The evidence of the endpoints was, however, uncertain and did not unambiguously support the K-U theory.

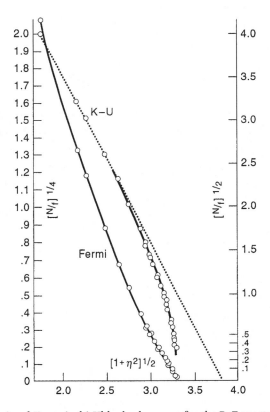

Figure 8.4 The Fermi and Konopinski-Uhlenbeck curves for the RaE spectrum. Redrawn from Langer and Whittaker (1937).

Additional support for the K-U theory came from several further measurements on the RaE spectrum, but the support provided for the K-U theory by all of the available evidence was not unequivocal. Richardson (1934) pointed out that scattering and energy loss by electrons leaving the radioactive source could distort the energy spectrum, particularly at the low-energy end:

> The failure of theory to explain the continuous spectrum makes it of interest to obtain all possible experimental information, and although much is now known about the high energy part of the curve, the low energy region has remained obscure owing to certain experimental difficulties. The chief of these has been the contamination of the low energy end of the curve by rays reflected with unknown energy from the material on which the radioactive body was deposited. (442)

There were other uncertainties in the measurement of the RaE decay spectrum. O'Conor (1937) remarked, "Since the original work of Schmidt in 1907 more than a score of workers have made measurements on the beta-ray spectrum of radium E with none too concordant results" (305). He cited twenty-seven different measurements of the high-energy endpoint energy, for which the largest and smallest values differed by more than a factor of two. By 1940, however, a consensus seems to have been reached and, as Townsend (1941) stated, "the features of the β-ray spectrum of RaE are now known with reasonable precision" (365). The future would be different. The spectrum of RaE would be a constant problem.[9]

The Support Erodes

The discrepancy between the measured maximum electron energy and that extrapolated from the K-U theory persisted and became more severe as experiments became more precise. In 1937, Livingston and Bethe remarked,

> Kurie, Richardson, and Paxton, have indicated how the K-U theory can be used to obtain a value for the theoretical energy maximum from experimental data, and such a value has been obtained from many of the observed distributions. On the other hand, *in those few cases in which it is possible to predict the energy of the beta decay from data on heavy particle reactions, the visually extrapolated limit has been found to fit the data better than the K-U value.* (emphasis added)

They noted, however, the other experimental support for the K-U theory and recorded both the visually extrapolated values and those obtained from the K-U theory.

The difficulty of obtaining unambiguous results for the maximum β-decay energy was illustrated by Lawson (1939) in his discussion of the history of measurements of the ^{32}P spectrum in which different experimenters obtained quite different experimental results:

> The energy spectrum of these electrons was first obtained by J. Ambrosen (1934). Using a Wilson cloud chamber, he obtained a distribution of electrons with an observed upper limit of about 2 MeV. Alichanow et al. (1936), using tablets of activated ammonium phosphomolybate in a magnetic spectrometer of low resolving power, find the upper limit to be 1.95 MeV. Kurie, Richardson, and Paxton (1936) have observed this upper

limit to be approximately 1.8 MeV. This work was done in a six-inch cloud chamber, and the results were obtained from a distribution involving about 1500 tracks. Paxton (1937) has investigated only the upper regions of the spectrum with the same cloud chamber, and reports that all observed tracks above 1.64 MeV can be accounted for by errors in the method. E. M. Lyman (1937) was the first investigator to determine accurately the spectrum of phosphorus by means of a magnetic spectrometer. The upper limit of the spectrum which he has obtained is 1.7 Å 0.04 MeV. (131)

Lawson's own value was 1.72 MeV, in good agreement with that of Lyman. The difficulties and uncertainties of the measurements are clear. Measurements using different techniques disagreed with one another and physicists may have suspected that the discrepancy might be due to the different techniques used. Even measurements using the same technique differed.

Another developing problem for the K-U theory was that its better fit to the RaE spectrum required a finite mass for the neutrino. This was closely related to the problem of the energy endpoint because the mass of the neutrino was estimated from the difference between the extrapolated and observed endpoints. Measurement of the RaE spectrum in the late 1930s had given neutrino masses in the range from 0.3 to 0.52 m_e, where m_e is the mass of the electron. On the other hand, the upper limit for the neutrino mass from nuclear reactions at that time was less than 0.1 m_e.[10]

Toward the end of the decade, the tide turned and experimental evidence began to favor Fermi's theory over that of Konopinski and Uhlenbeck. Tyler (1939) found that the ^{64}Cu positron spectrum observed using a thin radioactive source fit the original Fermi theory better than it did the K-U theory. "The thin source results are in much better agreement with the original Fermi theory of beta decay than with the later modification introduced by Konopinski and Uhlenbeck. As the source is made thicker there is a gradual change in the shape of the spectra which gradually brings about better agreement with the K-U theory than with the Fermi theory" (125). Similar results were obtained for phosphorus, sodium, and cobalt by Lawson (1939; figure 8.5):

> In the cases of phosphorus and sodium, where the most accurate work was possible, the shapes of the spectra differ from the results previously reported by other investigators in that there are fewer low energy particles. The reduction in the number of particles has been traced to the relative absence of scattering in the radioactive source and its mounting. The general shape of the spectra is found to agree more satisfactorily with that predicted from the original theory of Fermi than that given by the modification of this theory proposed by Konopinski and Uhlenbeck. (131)

The superiority of the Fermi theory in accounting for these results is evident.[11] Richardson's earlier warning concerning the dangers of scattering and energy loss in spectrum measurements had been correct. These effects were causing the excess of low-energy electrons. Compare the later, thin-source results for ^{32}P shown in figure 8.6 with the earlier, thick-source results, also on ^{32}P, shown in figure 8.3.

There was yet another problem with the evidential support for the K-U theory. This was pointed out by Lawson and Cork (1940) in their study of the spectrum of indium (^{114}In). Their Kurie plot for the Fermi theory is shown in figure 8.7. It is clearly a straight line, again indicating that the Fermi theory is the correct one. They pointed

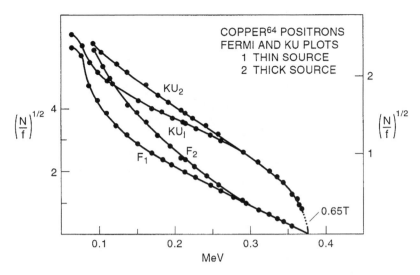

Figure 8.5 Fermi and K-U plots of positrons from thick and thin ^{64}Cu sources. Redrawn from Tyler (1939).

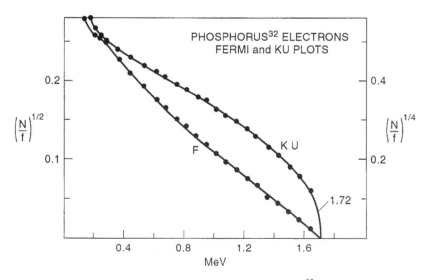

Figure 8.6 Fermi and K-U plots for electrons from phosphorus ^{32}P. Redrawn from Lawson (1939).

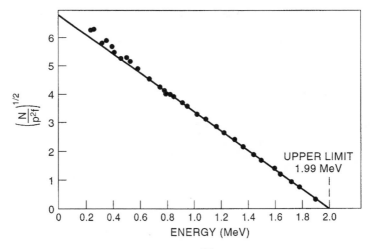

Figure 8.7 Kurie plot for electrons from the decay of ^{114}In. Redrawn from Lawson and Cork (1940).

out, "*However, in all of the cases so far accurately presented, experimental results for 'forbidden' spectra have been compared to theories for 'allowed' transitions*. The theory for forbidden transitions [for Fermi's theory] has not been published" (Lawson and Cork 1940, 994; emphasis added). An incorrect experiment–theory comparison had been made. The wrong theory had been compared to the experimental results. Similar cautions concerning this type of comparison had been made earlier by Langer and Whittaker (1937) and by Paxton (1937). Langer and Whittaker (1937) noted that "the K-U plot was made *without considering the fact that radium E is a forbidden transition*. A correction to the theory has been worked out by Lamb and [by] Pollard from which it appears that the extrapolated endpoint is brought into somewhat better although not complete accord with the experimental value" (717; emphasis added). Paxton (1937), remarking on the discrepancy between the K-U theory and the experimental measurements at the high-energy end of the ^{32}P spectrum, stated, "Accordingly this work is best interpreted as indicating a sharp deviation from the K-U relation near the high energy limit ... This discrepancy might be eliminated by modifying the K-U formula to apply to a *doubly forbidden type of disintegration*" (170; emphasis added). Little attention seems to have been paid to these comments. The β decay of ^{114}In was an allowed transition, which allowed a valid comparison between theory and experiment. That valid comparison favored the Fermi theory.

Konopinski and Uhlenbeck Assist Fermi

The spectrum of so-called forbidden transitions for the original Fermi theory was finally calculated by Konopinski and Uhlenbeck (1941). They noted that some of the evidence from the β-decay spectra that had originally supported their theory now tended to support the Fermi theory. "The authors made a criticism of Fermi's formula on the basis

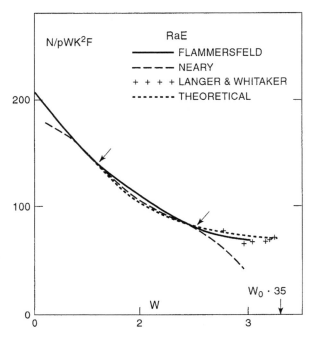

Figure 8.8 The ratio of the number of electrons emitted by RaE per unit energy range to the relative number expected according to Fermi's allowed formula, for different experiments. The theoretical prediction is the dotted curve. Redrawn from Konopinski and Uhlenbeck (1941).

of a comparison with older experimental data and advanced a modification of the Fermi theory which seemed to represent the data better. The technical improvements in the most recent measurements [including those of Tyler (1939) and of Lawson and Cork (1940), discussed above], particularly in eliminating scattering, have withdrawn the basis for the criticism" (309). They remarked that these new measurements had also confirmed the maximum spectrum energy as derived from nuclear masses. "The so-called K-U modification had led to values that were distinctly too large" (309).

They noted, however, that there were still discrepancies between Fermi's theory and other experimental results so that the choice between the two theories was still unresolved:

> Fermi's formula however still does not represent a great number of observed β-spectra. Many of these disagreements are undoubtedly due to the superposition of spectra, as has lately again been emphasized by Bethe, Hoyle, and Peierls. Nevertheless all the disagreements cannot be explained in this way. The well investigated spectra of RaE and ^{32}P show definite deviations form Fermi's formula. (309; figures 8.8, 8.9)

Konopinski and Uhlenbeck attributed the discrepancies to the fact the RaE and ^{32}P were forbidden decays. Unlike the case of allowed transitions, for which the shape of the energy spectrum was independent of the mathematical form of the decay

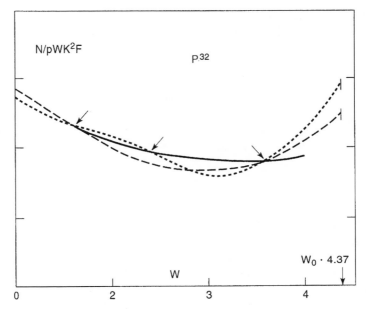

Figure 8.9 The ratio of the number of electrons emitted by ^{32}P per unit energy range to the relative number expected according to Fermi's allowed formula, for different experiments. The theoretical prediction is the dotted curve. Redrawn from Konopinski and Uhlenbeck (1941).

interaction, the shape of the forbidden spectra did depend on the mathematical form. They calculated the spectrum shapes for the various possible forms of the interaction and noted that "there is, therefore, no a priori reason to expect them to obey the allowed formula" (309).

Konopinski and Uhlenbeck compared their calculated spectra to the available experimental results. They reported that they could obtain good fits to the observed spectra of ^{32}P and RaE. The agreement of the RaE spectrum with the K-U theory was also explained when Konopinski and Uhlenbeck calculated the spectra expected for forbidden transitions.

> The one encouraging feature of the application of the theory [for forbidden transitions] to the experiments is that the decided deviation of the RaE from the allowed form can be all explained by the theory . . . *The theory gives a correction factor approximately proportional to* $(E_o - E)^2$ for an element like RaE. This accounts for the surprising agreements found by the experimenters between their data and the so-called K-U distribution. (320; emphasis added)

In 1943 Konopinski published a review article on β decay. He noted, "For β-decay theory, next in importance to the confirmation of the general structure of the theory itself, has been the making of a choice between the Fermi and K-U ansätze . . . *The K-U criticism and modification of Fermi's theory seems now to be definitely disproved by the following developments*" (Konopinski 1943, 243; emphasis added). The evidence cited by Konopinski included the evidence of the β-decay energy spectra discussed earlier: *"Thus, the evidence of the spectra, which has previously comprised the sole support for the K-U theory, now definitely fails to support it"* (218; emphasis added).

Discussion

It was only eight years between the original publication of the Konopinski-Uhlenbeck theory and the public, and published, declaration by one of its authors that it was incorrect. Konopinski, and the rest of the physics community, agreed that it did not accurately describe β decay. Based on the best experimental evidence available at the time, the observed energy spectra from ^{32}P and RaE decay, Konopinski and Uhlenbeck had proposed a modification of Fermi's theory that better fit that evidence. Experiment had, albeit incorrectly, called for a new theory.

Experimental work continued and physicists found that these early experimental results were incorrect. It was quickly realized that scattering and energy loss in the radioactive sources used in such experiments had distorted the spectra. Thinner sources were then used, and the new results favored Fermi's theory. At the time, these were technically very difficult experiments. In the early stages of an experimental investigation, it is often difficult to identify sources of background that might mask or mimic the effect one wishes to observe. When physicists realized that scattering and energy loss were a problem, and they did so rather quickly, they took corrective action. The sources were made thinner.

Similarly, the incorrect experiment–theory comparison was eliminated. Konopinski and Uhlenbeck calculated the theoretical spectra needed to solve the allowed–forbidden transition problem. Ironically, after the calculation was done, a correct experiment–theory comparison argued that Fermi's theory, rather than their own, was correct. In addition, Lawson and Cork performed an experiment on an allowed transition for which a valid experiment–theory comparison could be made. That, too, favored Fermi's theory. Konopinski was convinced by the experimental evidence.

This is not, I believe, an unusual episode in the practice of science. Despite claims by postmodern and constructivist critics, no cases have been presented in which scientific decisions have gone against the weight of evidence.[12] What makes this case noteworthy is that we have a public record in which the author of a theory argued that the evidence showed that his own theory was wrong. In this episode, and, I believe, in the general practice of science, George Levine's worry, cited at the start of this chapter, is unfounded. Konopinski became the chief critic of his own theory: *"Thus, the evidence of the spectra, which has previously comprised the sole support for the K-U theory, now definitely fails to support it."*

Notes

1. Bohr and others proposed an alternative explanation, that energy was not conserved in β decay. That was rejected on experimental grounds. The history of this episode is more complex. For details, see Franklin (2000, chs. 1, 2).

2. β-Decay transitions come in several types depending on the mathematics that describes the state of the particles involved. "Allowed" transitions occur more quickly than do "forbidden" transitions.

3. In terms of the formalism of the Fermi theory, this was accomplished by introducing derivatives of the neutrino wave function into the mathematical expression for the interaction energy.

4. This article was often referred to as the "Bethe Bible."

5. For radioactive isotopes of chlorine, argon, and potassium, the observed spectra fit two straight lines for the K-U theory. These were due to complex decays, in which the original nucleus decayed into one or the other of two final states of the daughter nucleus.

6. One cannot get an accurate measurement of the electron momentum (energy) using an entire track that contains a large deflection. Not only does the momentum change, but the deflection makes fitting the observed track to a single track with constant momentum inaccurate. For a more detailed discussion of selectivity in the production of experimental results, see Franklin (1998).

7. The Coulomb scattering of an electron by a nucleus is proportional to Z^2, where Z is the charge on the nucleus. Thus electron scattering from oxygen, $Z = 8$, is sixty-four times larger than that from hydrogen, $Z = 1$.

8. Measuring a track with such a curvature change will usually result in an incorrect value of the momentum or energy of the particle. In addition, it will increase the uncertainty of that determination.

9. For example, Petschek and Marshak (1952) analyzed the spectrum of RaE and concluded that the interaction describing β decay must include a pseudoscalar term, one of the possible mathematical forms of the decay interaction. That led physicists to conclude that the decay interaction was a combination of the scalar, tensor, and pseudoscalar forms of the interaction. That analysis was later shown to be incorrect.

10. Contemporary experiments show that the neutrino actually has a mass. The current upper limit is approximately one ten millionth of the mass of the electron.

11. Recall that the correct theory is the one that gives the best fit to a straight line in the Kurie plot.

12. Nick Rasmussen (private communication) has suggested that I am holding constructivists to an impossibly high standard. He says that examination of the published record will never show scientists making a decision that goes against experimental evidence. This is because scientists always give reasons for their decision that will appeal to and persuade the scientific community. Why such reasons are persuasive to members of the scientific community is not discussed by constructivists. Rasmussen states that constructivists will never be able to show that the situation was different or that it should have been different, using such evidence.

References

Alichanow, A. I., A. I. Alichanian, and B. S. Dzelepow. 1936. "The Continuous Spectra of RaE and P^{30}." *Nature* 137: 314–315.

Ambrosen, J. 1934. "Uber den aktiven Phosphor und des Energiesspektrum seiner β-Strahlen." *Zeitschrift fur Physik* 91: 43–48.

Bethe, H. A., and R. F. Bacher. 1936. "Nuclear Physics." *Reviews of Modern Physics* 8: 82–229.

Ellis, C. D., and W. J. Henderson. 1934. "Artificial Radioactivity." *Proceedings of the Royal Society (London)* A146: 206–216.

Ellis, C. D., and W. A. Wooster. 1927. "The Average Energy of Disintegration of Radium E." *Proceedings of the Royal Society (London)* A117: 109–123.

Fermi, E. 1934a. "Attempt at a Theory of β-Rays." *Il Nuovo Cimento* 11: 1–21.

———. 1934b. "Versuch einer Theorie der β-Strahlen." *Zeitschrift fur Physik* 88: 161–177.

Franklin, A. 1998. "Selectivity and the Production of Experimental Results." *Archive for the History of Exact Sciences* 53: 399–485.

———. 2000. *Are There Really Neutrinos? An Evidential History.* Cambridge, MA: Perseus Books.

Konopinski, E. 1943. "Beta-Decay." *Reviews of Modern Physics* 15: 209–245.

Konopinski, E., and G. Uhlenbeck. 1935. "On the Fermi Theory of Radioactivity." *Physical Review* 48: 7–12.

———. 1941. "On the Theory of β-Radioactivity." *Physical Review* 60: 308–320.

Kurie, F. N. D., J. R. Richardson, and H. C. Paxton. 1936. "The Radiations from Artificially Produced Radioactive Substances." *Physical Review* 49: 368–381.

Langer, L. M., and M. D. Whittaker. 1937. "Shape of the Beta-Ray Distribution Curve of Radium at High Energies." *Physical Review* 51: 713–717.

Lawson, J. L. 1939. "The Beta-Ray Spectra of Phosphorus, Sodium, and Cobalt." *Physical Review* 56: 131–136.

Lawson, J. L., and J. M. Cork. 1940. "The Radioactive Isotopes of Indium." *Physical Review* 57: 982–994.

Levine, G., Ed. 1987. *One Culture: Essays in Science and Literature.* Madison: University of Wisconsin Press.

Livingston, M. S., and H. A. Bethe. 1937. "Nuclear Physics." *Reviews of Modern Physics* 9: 245–390.

Lyman, E. M. 1937. "The Beta-Ray Spectrum of Radium E and Radioactive Phosphorus." *Physical Review* 51: 1–7.

O'Conor, J. S. 1937. "The Beta-Ray Spectrum of Radium E." *Physical Review* 52: 303–314.

Paxton, H. C. 1937. "The Radiations from Artificially Produced Radioactive Substances. III. Details of the Beta-Ray Spectrum of P^{32}." *Physical Review* 51: 170–177.

Petschek, A. G., and R. E. Marshak. 1952. "The β-Decay of Radium E and the Pseudoscalar Interaction." *Physical Review* 85: 698–699.

Richardson, O. W. 1934. "The Low Energy β-Rays of Radium E." *Proceedings of the Royal Society (London)* A147: 442–454.

Sargent, B. W. 1933. "The Maximum Energy of the β-Rays from Uranium X and other Bodies." *Proceedings of the Royal Society (London)* A139: 659–673.

Townsend, A. A. 1941. "β-Ray Spectra of Light Elements." *Proceedings of the Royal Society (London)* A177: 357–366.

Tyler, A. W. 1939. "The Beta- and Gamma-Radiations from Copper[64] and Europium[152]." *Physical Review* 56: 125–130.

9

The Evolutionary Ethics of Alfred C. Kinsey

Frederick B. Churchill

R ecent works in the history and philosophy of science have explored anew the
possible connection between science and ethics.[1] They follow a well-established
tradition that has dogged modern science since David Hume questioned whether a
moral claim (i.e., an "ought") might be derived from a factual claim (i.e., an "is"). In
the post-Darwin period, as biologists wrestled with explanations for evolution, evolutionary ethics became a major issue for promoters of species descent. T. H. Huxley
and Herbert Spencer locked horns in a well-known exchange over how the new
materialistic evolution theory might have changed the moral/factual relationship.[2]
The eminent Victorian zoologist tended to sympathize with Hume, while the self-
trained natural philosopher maintained that morality, just like every other human
attribute, was a natural part of the cosmic evolutionary process and thus derived
from it. Shortly after the turn of the century, the professionally trained English
philosopher G. E. Moore rejected Spencer's ontology, along with the utilitarian
ethics of John Stuart Mill and the idealistic ethics of Kant, in an elaborate presentation published as *Principia Ethica*. All such science-based or rationalized ethical
systems, according to Moore, committed "a naturalistic fallacy"; that is, they represented efforts to derive the foundations of ethics and personal feelings of obligation from ethically neutral claims. The gulf between the two, for Moore, could not
be bridged.[3]

It is doubtful that many practicing evolutionists followed the ensuing philosophical arguments, pro and con, that responded to Moore's elaborate and in places
confusing presentation, but the naturalistic fallacy, with respect to evolutionary
ethics, remains a formidable hurdle.[4] In 1987, historian of science Robert J. Richards
presented an extensive survey of the reactions of selected nineteenth- and twentieth-
century biologists and philosophers to construct or deny an evolutionary ethics. He
concluded his volume with a challenging appendix in which he provided an elaborate effort of his own to establish a "revised version" of evolutionary ethics
based on modern biological arguments for kin and group selection.[5] More recently,
Paul Farber has also detailed the efforts of biologists of the twentieth century to

reintroduce an evolutionary ethics. Julian Huxley, C. D. Waddington, Warder Clyde Allee, Alfred Edwards Emerson, and after 1975 E. O. Wilson, in Farber's critical account, relied to differing degrees on the validity of specific scientific notions, such as progress, physiological development, ethology and psychology, social cooperation, and population genetics, to anchor a global standard for ethics to their evolutionary commitments. Likewise, Farber considered Richards's "revised version" "highly problematic."[6] Marga Vicedo has demonstrated that the American pragmatists William James and John Dewey, in less formalized deliberations on evolution and ethics, did have an impact on eugenicist Charles Davenport, plant geneticist Edward East, embryologist E. G. Conklin, and geneticist and experimental protozoologist Herbert Spencer Jennings—all of whom wrote popular treatises endorsing an evolutionary ethics. There were a few prominent biologists, such as George Gaylord Simpson, who revealed an uneasy sense, which independently and informally echoed Moore's critique that the task could not be done.[7]

What follows is not an attempt to examine the success or failure on the part of particular philosophers, historians, or biologists to resolve the complex issues associated with evolutionary ethics. Instead, I present a somewhat different case study, in which a twentieth-century American evolutionary biologist of the first rank was forced to confront moral issues on several levels, whether he wanted to or not. Far more than the research of any of the biologists mentioned above (with the possible exception of Davenport), he had to deal directly with a range of ethically controversial human behaviors and place them within his own beliefs about what was right and wrong and his personal commitment to social progress.

I focus on the career of Alfred Kinsey, on his research on sexual behavior in humans, and on the first of two specialized volumes he published of his research.[8] This volume, published in 1948, quickly made Kinsey famous around the world, and by the time of the arrival of the second volume five years later, he had gained such acclaim that his portrait appeared on the cover of *Time Magazine*.[9] Kinsey was not only toasted for having broached with scientific objectivity the secret sexual lives of 12,000 Americans and having unveiled in the process a complex world of tensions and hypocrisy but he was also castigated for having turned a deeply personal, even sacrosanct, subject into the object of a statistical and materialistic science. Much has been made of the shortcomings of Kinsey's statistics. Two recent biographers who have looked at this issue conclude that Kinsey generally did the best he could given the circumstances, which compelled him to fashion new techniques for interviews and in sampling procedures.[10]

My concern, however, is to explore the ethical implications of Kinsey's work—particularly with respect to the naturalistic fallacy. It is an issue that has received less scrutiny despite the fact that early critics railed on the matter as soon as *Sexual Behavior in the Human Male* (1948) appeared. Witness Henry P. Van Dusen, the scholarly Presbyterian minister and president of Union Theological Seminary in New York City, who responded in a short review that "the most disturbing thing is the absence of a spontaneous ethical revulsion from the premises of the study, and inability on the part of its readers to put their fingers on the falsity of those premises."[11] Lionel Trilling, professor of literature at Columbia University and one of the celebrated authors and critics of his generation, echoed a similar concern: "Nothing in the [Kinsey] Report is more suggestive in a large cultural way than the insistent claims it makes for its strictly scientific nature, its pledge of indifference to all questions of morality at the same time that it patently intends a moral effect."[12] Neither of these critics referred directly to the naturalistic fallacy; they were, however, only two of the many reviewers to complain about the mix of science and ethics in Kinsey's work. Additional complaints from both ministers of the church and lay observers were written after *Sexual Behavior in the Human Female* appeared five years later.[13] Here is a final example, written by the liberal and eccentric Episcopalian minister W. Norman Pittenger:[14]

> Dr. Kinsey is not a philosopher nor a moralist; he claims to be an "objective" scientist, whatever that means. But this very quality produces its accompanying defect. He cannot see that sexuality in man is not the same as sexuality in animals, nor can he grasp what for him must be a very subtle distinction between the idea of norm as a simple report of what people do and the idea of norm as what people *ought* to do.[15]

Pittenger, in fact, was delivering a spiritual lesson on the "the theology of sex," by which he meant that when sex was viewed in a Christian context, "it cannot be regarded as an isolated biological phenomenon which has no relation to our social situation; neither can it be seen as a simple urge which we share with the other animals."[16] Instead, the sexologist must be concerned with the "inner" love that brings a married couple to understand themselves and God, through *Agape* or a theocentric "brotherly concern" and adoration rather than through *Eros* or an egocentric passion and desire for others—including God.[17] No wonder Kinsey's sexology collided with even the progressive wing of western theological and intellectual traditions; no wonder Kinsey ran the danger of committing the naturalist fallacy in their eyes.

Before plunging into Kinsey's studies on sexual behavior, it is important to examine briefly his career as an evolutionary zoologist, for that is where those premises Van Dusen identified lie and that is the subject in which Kinsey established his scientific methods and made his name before turning to the study of sexual behavior.

Gall Wasp Studies

Kinsey had completed his dissertation in 1919 at Harvard's Bussey Institute, where he worked under the famous scholar of ant societies William Morton Wheeler. For his dissertation, he chose to study the taxonomy of gall wasps of the genus *Cynips*—which comprises species of small wasps that lay their eggs on the leaves and twigs of oaks and a few other woody-stemmed plants. The hatched larvae stimulate the host to form a protective tissue around them (i.e., a gall), which also serves as a food supply for the larvae. As mentioned above, Kinsey's approach was taxonomic, but of a modern sort. For his dissertation and then for the next twenty years as professor of zoology at Indiana University, he collected wasps and their galls throughout the continent. In the process, he traveled thousands of miles by auto and many hundreds by foot in order to understand the ranges and changes of as many species as possible.

(After his death, Kinsey bequeathed more than a million specimens to the American Museum of Natural History in New York.)[18]

Kinsey understood modern taxonomic techniques to include the following strategies. (1) Only by collecting enormous numbers of individuals and systematically recording the precise location, the species of oak involved, the minute details of the insects' morphology and behavior, and even the different structures of the galls, could he even begin his task. (2) Only by the plotting and comparing of variables in statistical format could he appreciate the range of a single variation and make rightful claims about varieties, species, higher taxa, their distribution, and their life cycles. (3) Only after recognizing the aggregate structure of a natural population could he understand its phylogeny and draw conclusions about the evolutionary path and geographic progression of close varieties and related species as the genus evolved. Eventually, Kinsey insisted, "if the taxonomic arrangement brings together species of common ancestry and accurately portrays the varying degrees of relationship between those species, a classification becomes one of the most powerful tools available for the evolutionary interpretation of biologic phenomena."[19]

Given Kinsey's broad experience with the technical details of taxonomy, given his conviction that taxonomy must be based on evolution theory and explore phylogenesis, given, too, his obsession with the massive collection of specimens from natural populations of gall wasps and their galls, and finally, given his penchant of establishing the range of variations of numerous traits of these natural populations, it is understandable why Kinsey was considered in the 1930s to be in the first tier of American zoologists.[20] As we turn to Kinsey's research in sexual behavior, we need to bear in mind two questions: What elements of his taxonomic methods and beliefs get transferred to his research on human sexuality? How does the taxonomic approach help us interpret his moral judgments about sexual behavior?

Sexual Behavior in the Human Male: The Data

The canonical account of Kinsey's conversion from a gall wasp specialist to a human sexologist may be found in the opening pages of *Sexual Behavior in the Human Male*. The story begins in 1938, when Kinsey was asked by undergraduates at Indiana University to resurrect what was called the "marriage course."[21] With the approval of the new president of the university, Herman B Wells, a committee of eight faculty members chaired by Kinsey taught the revised course for the first time in the summer of 1938. Kinsey and a young zoology colleague delivered six lectures on the biological aspects of sex. The other faculty members gave lectures that addressed the social, medical, economic, legal, and religious dimensions of the subject. The course, open only to married or engaged students, was enormously successful, and Kinsey's own lectures were particularly so. Again, according to the traditional story, it was during this summer that Kinsey was consulted by students about their own sexual concerns, and from these encounters a questionnaire, which initially was developed to help other students in the class, quickly emerged as an important instrument for sexual research. The course continued on a semester basis through the spring of 1940, when medical, sociological, and religious leaders in Indiana

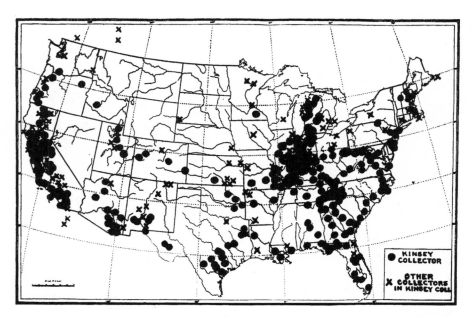

Figure 9.1 American collections of Cynips. From page 12 of Kinsey (1930). Reproduced by permission of The Kinsey Institute for Research in Sex, Gender, and Reproduction, Inc.

complained about the direction in which Kinsey was taking it. Wells, who was very supportive of him in general, presented Kinsey with an ultimatum that in the future he would be authorized either to teach the course or focus on his sexual research. He would not be allowed to pursue both tracks in tandem. After some hesitation, Kinsey chose research.

What is not generally told in this traditional story is that Kinsey had from the early 1930s, if not earlier, acquired a scholarly familiarity with classical and contemporary literature on sexuality; he had for a long time discussed sexual matters with his graduate students and had been appalled at student and colleague ignorance of the basics of human sexual drives and techniques. Furthermore, from the first presentation of the marriage course, Kinsey had gone to Chicago and elsewhere on exploratory research trips. The marriage course may have provided the immediate opportunity for Kinsey to reorient his professional career, but it certainly was not the introduction to his scholarly interest in the subject.[22]

Kinsey pointed out that his concentration on the range of variations in natural populations of gall wasps led to his focus on variations in human sexual behavior.[23] (It is interesting to compare the formatting of the diagrams and distribution of sites where he collected specimens of gall wasps [figure 9.1] and data on sexual behavior [figure 9.2].) The development of a questionnaire and a successful technique for carrying out interviews transferred the spirit of his taxonomy to sexology.[24] The questionnaire was expanded over a few years, so that by 1948 it contained more than 500 items about the details of a subject's life and sexual behavior. The format consisted of a single-paged matrix through which Kinsey and his highly trained fellow interviewers might maneuver with ease in response to the subject's free-flowing

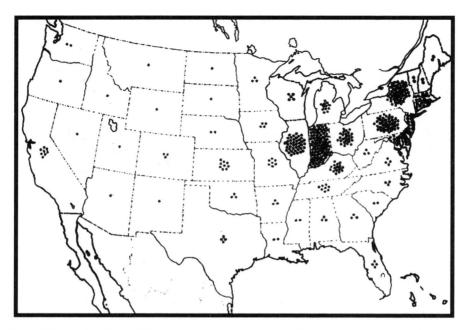

Figure 9.2 Sources of sexual histories. One dot represents fifty cases. From page 5 of Kinsey, Pomeroy, and Martin (1948). Reproduced by permission of The Kinsey Institute for Research in Sex, Gender, and Reproduction, Inc.

account of his or her own sexual experiences. The questionnaire was filled out in code and remained—and still largely remains—secret and completely confidential. The questionnaire probed into the broad range of human sexual experiences, the frequency of such experiences over the subject's lifetime, and the age when the subject became aware of such biological events as pregnancy, coitus, fertilization, menstruation, and venereal diseases. It elicited responses about the vital statistics of an individual's religious commitments, family and marital status, level of education, rural and urban background, and recreational habits.

As mentioned above, a lot has been made about the statistical shortcomings, the sampling problems, and general interpretation of the data Kinsey collected.[25] Recently, much has also been made of Kinsey's personal sexual orientation, particularly his developing homosexual preference in later life. Both of these issues are important in evaluating the results of Kinsey's research, but these aspects of his life and work strike me as largely irrelevant to the posed question about his naturalistic ethics.

Now, Kinsey repeatedly made the point that he and other interviewers, and for that matter the entire project, meticulously avoided passing moral judgment on any of the histories provided by the volunteer subjects and that his summary conclusions were a matter of statistical fact, not ethics. It was this neutral stance that won him the confidence of his first student subjects and in part allowed his research to be financially supported and to succeed. Nevertheless, there is hardly a human preoccupation in the Judeo-Christian tradition, let alone all of human history, that has lent itself more to moral judgments than sexual behavior. Is it conceivable that Kinsey really avoided such judgments? Does the outrage of critics, such as Van Dusen, Trilling, and Pittenger, fairly testify otherwise? Our problem is to examine whether or not there is an unstated ethics embedded in Kinsey's sexual studies.

One must recognize *Sexual Behavior in the Human Male* as a sober, scientific book at the outset. When it appeared in 1948, it was stolidly clinical in appearance.[26] It possessed a dull, dark maroon cover with the title and authors' names prominently displayed on the spine in gilt lettering on a black background. Its eight hundred pages were studded with tables and bar and line graphs, and its twenty-three chapters were frankly yet solemnly entitled. It had the requisite aspects of the serious scholarly work that it indeed was. The preface, written by Dr. Alan Gregg of the Medical Sciences Division of the Rockefeller Foundation, which had indirectly supported Kinsey's research, captured the sober and yet compelling message of the entire volume. "Certainly," Gregg wrote,

> no aspect of human biology in our current civilization stands in more need of scientific knowledge and courageous humility than that of sex. The history of medicine proves that in so far as man seeks to know himself and face his whole nature, he has become free from bewildered fear, despondent shame, or arrant hypocrisy. As long as sex is dealt with in the current confusion of ignorance and sophistication, denial and indulgence, suppression and stimulation, punishment and exploitation, secrecy and display, it will be associated with the duplicity and indecency that lead neither to intellectual honesty nor human dignity.[27]

With these words, Gregg captured Kinsey's personal motivation and beliefs and, indeed, the tone of the work he was introducing. There can be little doubt that Kinsey was on a crusade—with "courageous" determination, if not always "humility," to present scientifically established data to change the current state of "ignorance," "denial," "punishment," "secrecy," and so forth. What Gregg's words do not capture is the second dimension of Kinsey's revolution, his attack on the foundations of moral judgments about sexual behavior. In order to understand this claim, I first provide a sketch of Kinsey's book.

The project was not just data, and Kinsey's conclusions were not simply generalized descriptions. The male volume is structured in three parts. The first part shows considerable erudition and methodological reflection as Kinsey and his co-workers presented chapters on the historical background to their project, on their interviewing technique and its associated problems, and on the enormous statistical obstacles inherent in gathering such sensitive material from thousands of volunteer contributors and the validity of the data they were able to collect.[28] As controversial as Kinsey's statistical analysis turned out to be, he had certainly labored to address many of the dilemmas in collecting such material, and he improved his statistical analysis in the second volume on the human female.

The second part of the male volume, consisting of nine chapters, introduced Kinsey's conception of sexual outlets (behavior) and discussed the various biological and social factors that were to be compared with them. Six in all, the sexual outlets designated general types of male sexual experiences; they included masturbation, nocturnal emissions, heterosexual petting, heterosexual intercourse, homosexual relations, and animal intercourse. For the purposes of the study, a sexual incident signified any time a subject experienced a sexual orgasm. Thus, the outlets were unambiguous; the incidents were countable, and correlations of the incidents over the subject's life history with the different outlets and with other social attributes, such as religion, education level, and recreational interests, could be measured in terms of frequency and compared in both table and graphic forms. Kinsey sprinkled his discussions with anecdotal material drawn from the case histories, but as a taxonomist he knew all too well that any worthwhile study had to be based on counting and measurement.

The third part discussed each of the outlets individually and focused on the incidents and their frequencies over the aggregate lifetimes of the males involved. At the end of each chapter, Kinsey provided a qualitative assessment of techniques and consequences. As he explained,

> These chapters will be especially concerned with interpretations of the data, and will summarize the nature of each type of behavior, emphasize the individual variation that occurs, discuss the correlations of each type of activity with each other source of outlet, and show something of the significance of these factors to the individual and to society of which he is a part.[29]

Notice particularly the last clause of this passage, for Kinsey's interest in "the significance of these factors to the individual and to society of which he is a part" opened a space for moral judgments to enter.

The Biological Nature of *Sexual Behavior in the Human Male* and Some Normative Statements

As he frequently mentioned, Kinsey considered his research into sex to be "biologic" in nature. It is important to pin down what "biologic" in this context actually implied, in terms of methods, anti-essentialism, de animalibus, the normal–abnormal distinction, and temporal and regional differences.

Methods

Both Jones and Gathorne-Hardy (see n. 10) have argued that Kinsey transported his taxonomical method into his study of human sexual behavior. This meant collecting, comparing, counting, and measuring frequencies. These mechanical procedures led to mapping and establishing populations with given attributes. In both fields of study, Kinsey was interested, above all, in the range of variations within given populations. For his gall wasps, such an understanding led to the lumping or splitting of populations into species and to the delineations of phylogenetic lineages. With his sex studies, it meant identifying accessible groups for study and bringing into the open the full variety of their social and physiological distributions—all for the purpose of achieving a better understanding of the diversity of sexual behavior within the human species as a whole.

Anti-essentialism

This aspect of both taxonomic domains makes it clear that Kinsey rejected typological characterizations of populations based on privileged attributes. In his endeavor, he showed himself to be abreast of contemporary biology as it moved through the 1920s and 1930s into the 1940s toward an outspoken advocacy of a population concept of species. I believe Kinsey's study of gall wasps might have become a classic in the so-called evolutionary synthesis that followed if he had integrated his population studies with chromosomal genetics and had disentangled better the action of the environment and natural selection, as his fellow graduate student at Harvard and life-long friend Edgar Anderson had done with plants. Nevertheless, Kinsey's statistical studies of sexual behavior were an extension of his anti-essentialistic convictions, that is, his belief that there were no particular sexual attributes that defined his human male subjects.[30]

His anti-essentialism invited him to be critical of pre-established definitions of acceptable behavior. For example, he described with reference to a frequency distribution of "total sexual outlets" that, at the one extreme, his histories had uncovered "one male who, although apparently sound physically, had ejaculated only once in thirty years," while at the other extreme, they revealed that another "male (a scholarly and skilled lawyer) has averaged over 30 [incidents] per week for thirty years. This is a difference of several thousand times."[31] The vast majority of interviewed males fitted somewhere in between.

Note especially Kinsey's positive descriptors for the two extremes: "apparently sound physically" and "a scholarly and skilled lawyer." Kinsey's words appear to defuse any shocked conclusions about assumed stereotypes that held that the extremes should be classified differently from the main body of the population. Instead of judging the extremes, Kinsey was embracing them, along with everyone in between, as part of the given diversity in nature. It might be asked to what extent this factual presentation and anti-essentialist view of human behavior provided a screen for moral judgments, and whether there were demarcations between glory and infamy. I return to these questions in a moment.[32]

De Animalibus

Kinsey was without question a confirmed evolutionist. Both his gall wasp and human sexual behavior assumed a continuum in the phylogenetic process, but in slightly different ways. In his gall wasp studies, Kinsey used his data to speculate upon the evolutionary lineages of his collected species and upon the meaning of higher taxonomic categories. In his study of human sexual behavior, Kinsey drew parallels between the sexual behavior of humans, primates, and other mammals. His commitment to the phylogenetic continuum warranted this attention, and references to animal behavior, particularly to the anthropoid apes, appeared here and there in the male volume. For example, he compared preadolescent sex play and adolescent or premarital sex in both groups.[33] In one exemplary passage, he commented upon particular human sexual behaviors that traditionally were considered psychotic or neurotic and asserted that "in actuality, they [i.e., the "psychotic" and "neurotic"] are more often expressions of what is biologically basic in mammalian and anthropoid behavior, and of a deliberate disregard for social conventions."[34] Such a statement raised the specter of sexually active humans behaving like apes and so left the message, for those who wanted to find it, that Kinsey was affirming that human sexual behavior was being sanctioned by the phylogenetic past. Once man was brought into the picture, the Darwinian continuum favored an argument *de animalibus*. What animals were physically and how they acted presaged what *Homo sapiens* was and should be. The social and moral implications shocked Kinsey's public just as Darwin and Huxley had shocked their Victorian contemporaries.[35]

Normal–Abnormal Distinction

Kinsey was very much a modern evolutionary biologist when he rejected the traditional use of the adjectives "normal" and "abnormal" with respect to sexual behavior. In their place, he substituted the terms "common" and "rare," and his terminology was in keeping with the developments of contemporary population and classical genetics, which were concerned with common and rare genes and with chromosomal and point mutations. For example, when considering the range in individual variations in the frequency of the total sexual outlet in different age groups, Kinsey focused on the continuity in the curves of frequency of his aggregate data. "No individual," he explained, "has a sexual frequency which differs in anything but a slight degree from the frequencies of those placed next on the curve." He immediately added, "Such a continuous and widely spread series raises a question as to whether the terms 'normal' and 'abnormal' belong in a scientific vocabulary."[36]

His insistence that the normal–abnormal dichotomy be replaced did not mean, however, that Kinsey believed anything and everything goes. As a zoologist, he would have been aware that the majority of mutations and developmental aberrations were deleterious to the individual and neutral or harmful to the population.[37] The same argument might hold with respect to sexual coercion or violence. While discussing Kinsey's study of pedophilia, Gathorne-Hardy asserted "that Kinsey was fiercely against any use of force or compulsion in sex."[38] Nevertheless, Gathorne-Hardy also points out, I believe rightly, that Kinsey seemed more concerned about the impact of laws on sex offenders than on the harm such offenders might cause to their objects of desire. Kinsey promised to discuss the problem in a special volume on sexual offenses, which he never lived to write.[39]

Temporal and Regional Differences

Finally, a biological relativism played out in Kinsey's identification of temporally and regionally different attitudes toward sexual behavior. For the most part, he was concerned with the religious, social, and legal guardians of society, whose beliefs stretched back in time and place to antiquity and who were still shaping social opinions about sexual behavior in different contemporary settings. Kinsey felt that a synergistic relationship existed between society and its guardians, which established the moral codes. "In the broadest sense," he argued, "the mores may become systems of morals and systems of morals are formalizations of the mores . . . Sexual mores and systems of sexual morality are no exceptions to this general rule."[40] These codes and the moral standards, interacting and congealing with one another, became inflexible products of history and its contingencies. Time and again, Kinsey rebuked our concreted moral heritage because it had caused tensions and even neuroses and psychoses among individuals whose sexual drives lay outside of the narrowly prescribed band of tradition.[41]

Levels of Prescriptive Statements and
the Naturalistic Fallacy

Did Kinsey construct an evolutionary ethics with his studies of human sexual behavior? This is the question I began with. I find it instructive to pursue this question on three levels: (1) prescriptive statements or lessons aimed at the individual, that is, the identification of individual obligations; (2) prescriptive statements or lessons relevant to society as a whole; and (3) prescriptive statements or lessons targeting orthodox sexual standards. All three levels are reflected in a long exemplary passage in which Kinsey discussed human sexual interaction with animals:

> Anglo-American legal codes rate sexual relations between the human and animals of other species as sodomy, punishable under the same laws which penalize homosexual and mouth-genital contacts. The city-bred judge who hears such a case is likely to be unusually severe in his condemnation, and is likely to give the maximum sentence that is possible. Males who are sent to penal institutions on such charges are likely to receive unusually severe treatment both from the administrations and from the inmates of the institutions. All in all, there is probably no type of human sexual behavior which has been more severely condemned by that segment of the population which happens not to have had such experience, and which accepts the age-old judgment that animal intercourse must evidence a mental abnormality, as well as an immorality.

To this heartfelt statement, Kinsey adds another perspective drawn from his interviews:

> On the other hand, in rural communities where animal contacts are not infrequent, and where there is some general knowledge that they do commonly occur, there seem to be few personal conflicts growing out of such activity, and very few social difficulties. It is only when the farm-bred male migrates to a city community and comes in contact with city-bred reactions to these activities that he becomes upset over the contemplation of what he has done. This is particularly true if he learns through some psychology course or through books that such behavior is considered abnormal. There are histories of farm-bred males who have risen to positions of importance in the business, academic, or political world in some large urban center, and who have lived for years in constant fear that their early histories will be discovered. The clinician who can reassure these individuals that such activities are biologically and psychologically part of the normal mammalian picture, and that such contacts occur in as high a percentage of the farm

population as we have already indicated, may contribute materially toward the resolution of these conflicts.[42]

Evident in these extended passages is Kinsey's deep concern for the plight of the "farm-
bred" male who moves from a rural community with a particular set of behavioral
standards to the city with another. Kinsey neither condemns nor promotes but claims
that the sexual experience is a variation that falls within a distribution curve established by his data. Here, too, we find Kinsey's prescription of how society, as a whole,
should deal with the moral dissonance experienced by such an individual. Included is a
plea for better understanding and an argument *de animalibus*. Kinsey, in short, is
urging a social agenda, which envisions a new world order with respect to sexual
behavior. It is a world order that, given his research, is based on reality and ought to be
reflected in our moral response. Finally, Kinsey's wrath is unleashed upon the legal and
orthodox guardians of morality who, through an antiquated, biologically uninformed
tradition, may emotionally and physically destroy an unwitting individual. Evolution,
phylogeny, a range of variations, anti-essentialism, and a caveat about "abnormality"
are mixed into the argument and influence all three levels of moral persuasion.

I find no question about the normative nature of Kinsey's remarks with respect to
the second and third levels of his discussion. Kinsey's appeal for appropriately
trained "clinicians" in the above passages denotes an ethical imperative for the
second level, that of society. Gathorne-Hardy affirms this in a general caveat: "It is,
I [i.e., Gathorne-Hardy] think, now generally accepted by all commentators, and has
been seen for some time, that Kinsey had a range of social and legal reforms—his
'social agenda' in today's jargon."[43] With regard to the third level, that of orthodox
standards, Kinsey's dismissal of the "city-bred judge," penal institutions, and an
"age-old judgment" provides just one example of his condemnations of traditional
morality that pervade the entire volume.[44]

With respect to the first level, that of the individual, the question of moral
judgments becomes more complicated. Was Kinsey simply providing a description
when he presents the dilemma of the farm boy? Was he neutral and simply accepted
the behavior as a fact of nature? Or did he condone the intercourse between human
and animal in a normative manner? Did he encourage the reader, who may have
been concerned about his own experiences, to accept his sexual appetites as variations in the range of natural and hence permissible behaviors? Did the facts of
nature condone certain individual behavior?

On the side supporting the exclusive descriptive nature of Kinsey's collection
and presentation of data, it is worth considering that the hundreds of interviews,
the nature of his questionnaire, and the accounts of his persuasive manner all
indicate that Kinsey was true to his claim of being nonjudgmental when confronting
the realities of the diverse world. He is explicit about this in his chapter on interviewing.[45] In the body of the volume, he also recognized that scientists should
avoid moral judgments. Thus, while examining different frequencies of masturbation, he insisted that "the moral desirability of eliminating masturbation is, of course,
an issue whose merits *scientists are not qualified to judge*,"[46] and using similar language with respect to the medical treatment of homosexual tendencies, he reflected
that "whether such a program is morally desirable is a matter on which a scientist is

not qualified to pass judgment."[47] Such statements lead one to believe that Kinsey is fully conscious of the difference between descriptive and normative claims, between scientific and moral judgments.

On the other side of the question, the very nature of his statistical study allowed Kinsey to present a large range of sexual behavior as acceptable because it was natural, a product of evolution, and a consequence of the unique physiological sexual drives of each individual. Because he dealt so directly with a controversial human behavior, his factual statements could not remain neutral. They prescribed a tolerance that had not previously been permitted when the facts did not exist. This circumstance led inevitably to the commission of the naturalistic fallacy that drew the fire of his morally outraged critics.

When we put his beliefs into a loose syllogistic form, the linkage between Kinsey's descriptive and normative claims may be schematized in the following fashion. His biological and sexual researches together boil down to four propositions:

1. Variations of all traits within species are natural.
2. Such variations, collectively, are important for a species' survival and are a universal feature of its evolution.
3. Mankind, as a naturally evolved species, exhibits variations in its sexual behavior.
4. Therefore, these variations are important for mankind, should not concern sexually active individuals, and ought to be tolerated by human society.

In this logical, pedagogical format, we can see claims 1–3 are descriptive whereas claim 4 has a descriptive and two normative clauses. Kinsey, in the eyes of his critics, therefore committed the naturalistic fallacy. We may also see that there is a play on words in the syllogism. The "important" in proposition 2, besides having no normative implication, has a proximate teleological connotation that is perfectly acceptable as a descriptive claim in twentieth-century biology. If we changed "important" to "good," the teleological connotation becomes stronger. The "important" in proposition 4 is more ambiguous because of its ascription to "mankind;" while the "should" and "ought" in the same proposition are outwardly normative. There is, in other words, a two-step move from description to prescription, from living nature to a moral human individual and society.

For comparison, we might characterize the beliefs of Kinsey's moral critics, whom he considered representative of the orthodox Judeo-Christian tradition, with a contrasting syllogism:

1. A combination of scriptures, law, and tradition describes what constitutes acceptable human sexual behavior in human societies.
2. Any other human sexual behavior constitutes unacceptable behavior.
3. All unacceptable human sexual behavior is proscribed by scriptures, law, and/or tradition.
4. Therefore, all unacceptable human sexual behavior ought to be proscribed in human societies.

Here we can see that 1–3 are ostensibly descriptive claims; claim 4 is a normative one about current unacceptable sexual behavior. There is, however, ambiguity in this syllogism, too. In claims 1–3 "acceptable" and "unacceptable" are presented as descriptive predicates, but they unavoidably possesses a normative connotation. Claim 4 only follows from the previous claims if one agrees to the normative implications of the term "unacceptable." Substituting the term "abnormal" for "unacceptable" makes the hidden normative implications somewhat more obscure but does not make them disappear. As described above, Kinsey objected to the use of the abnormal–normal distinction because of its moral implications.

I conclude this section with the claim that Kinsey committed the naturalistic fallacy on two levels: with regard to individual obligations and with regard to social standards. Moreover, on the third level, he identified his critics as introducing metaphysical norms into the scientific domain where they did not belong. What may we infer from these conclusions?

Shifting the Moral Boundaries

As one who admires Kinsey's taxonomy, who appreciates his evolutionary biology, and who believes that a more liberalized world with respect to sexual diversity is a fairer and less hypocritical world, must I nevertheless dismiss Kinsey's moral transgressions because they appear to violate the naturalistic fallacy? I believe not. Kinsey may have sympathized with his subjects and desired a new social order with respect to their sexual behavior, but he had also shifted the bedrock beneath the traditional reasoning.

When Kinsey described the social contexts of sexual acts, he did so primarily in terms of the opportunities and prohibitions they encountered, and he drew explicit moral conclusions about incidents on the second and third levels described above. When it came to the first, the personal level, he claimed to have divorced sex, as a biological function, from the realm of moral consideration altogether. So he assumed *Sexual Behavior in the Human Male* to be an aseptic study of sexual incidents, defined by the biological function of an orgasm and reduced to unspecified physiological functions of sexual "drives," "energies," and "capacities."[48] It is also true that Kinsey did not describe this behavior in terms of the traditional human values associated with sexual acts, such as love, personal commitments, reproduction, and family loyalties, all of which have moral implications. The only condemnation of particular sexual acts and values was, as described above, Kinsey's condemnation of "pathological behavior," by which he meant sexual acts that were not consensual, may harm another person, or were consequences of unequal power.

I have argued that Kinsey was not fully successful with this separation of the evolutionary/physiological and moral sides of individual sex behavior, and I suspect that if he succeeded completely, he would have had to deny, unless he followed William James or John Dewey, the human agent of free will at the point physiological sexual drives took over.[49] After all, where there is no volition, there can be no moral choice. From the point of view of the Judaic-Christian tradition and our legal codes, this separation of the biological and physiological from the social and spiritual violated centuries of moral ideals. As unrealistic (Kinsey would say, "hypocritical") as these ideals may have been and continue to be, this separation seemed to have been both an intended goal and an illusion in Kinsey's revolution.

Nevertheless, Kinsey's attempted demarcation between the moral, on the one hand, and the evolutionary and physiological, on the other, suggests that we must also re-examine the premise of the naturalistic fallacy. It was framed by G. E. Moore at a time when biology—although evolutionary—was still gripped by essentialistic understandings, which could not accommodate to the actual range of biological and social variations. So can the very concept of a naturalistic fallacy allow for the shifting boundary between the domains of ethics and science over time? If the moral bedrock beneath Kinsey's work—Ruse calls it the "metaethical level" (1999, 216–221)—has shifted, do discussions about the naturalistic fallacy not require a recognition that what is normative for some may become descriptive for others? Finally, when the scientist attempts to deal with behavior that both is rooted in evolved passions and is idealized by our metaphysics, can the descriptive and normative ever be completely disentangled? That is, can the "Eros" and "Agape" in Pittenger's essay be truly disassociated from one another in this world? At least, both Kinsey and most of his moral critics found it difficult to disentangle the sexual behavior of his analytic studies from his genuine concern for his subjects and the social world embracing them all.

Notes

1. This chapter first appeared under the same title *in History and Philosophy of the Life Sciences*, 24 (2002), 391–411. The version in this book has been edited further for the sake of clarity and two diagrams and associated comments have been added. Permission to republish is courtesy of *HPLS*.

2. See Spencer (1879, 1893) and Huxley (1893, 1894). Both of Huxley's essays have been republished in *Evolution and Ethics* (J. Pardis and G. C. Williams, eds.; Princeton University Press, 1989), with a long historical introduction by Pardis.

3. Moore (1903); Baldwin (1990) points out the confusion and inadequacies in Moore's presentation, which were immediately identified by Bertrand Russell and other contemporary philosophers.

4. See the collection of papers in Paul Thompson (1995) and Jane Maienschein and Michael Ruse (1999). Thompson, in his introduction, presents a thumbnail sketch of the history of the naturalistic fallacy. See also Michael Bradie (1994).

5. Robert J. Richards (1987), especially appendix 2, "A Defense of Evolutionary Ethics" (595–627).

6. Paul Farber (1994, 163).

7. Michael Ruse (1999) has detailed the contrast between J. S. Huxley and Simpson. For a comparison of Simpson with Theodosius Dobzhansky, see Farber (1994).

8. Kinsey et al. (1948, 1953).

9. *Time*, August 24, 1953. The cover bore the enticing subtitle "Alfred Kinsey. Reflections in the mirror of Venus."

10. James H. Jones (1997) and Jonathan Gathorne-Hardy (2000). The latter biography is the American edition of the same work published by Chatto and Windus Ltd. in Great Britain in 1998. Gathorne-Hardy comments on Trilling and other fierce moral critics of Kinsey, including Margaret Mead and Lawrence Kubie (271–276). He does not, however, pursue the philosophical question about Kinsey or his critics committing the naturalistic fallacy.

11. Van Dusen (1948, 81–82).

12. Trilling (1950, 224).

13. The Kinsey Institute Library in Bloomington contains many scrapbooks of domestic and foreign reviews of both of Kinsey's volumes, which date back to the period when Kinsey was director of the institute.

14. W. Norman Pittenger (1905–1997), professor of Christian apologetics at the General Theological Seminary in New York City, was a recognized scholar of ethics in both American and English theological circles. After his retirement in 1966, he lived in Cambridge, England, where he became senior member at King's College. He wrote more than ninety books in his long career and was associated with process theology and with an advocacy for the rights of homosexuals, among whom he included himself. This background makes his criticism of Kinsey all the more interesting.

15. W. Norman Pittenger (1954, 16; italics in original).

16. Ibid., 18.

17. The Greek word *Eros,* meaning "sexual love," was taken from the Greek God of the same name. It implies a desire or yearning for another human or for God. *Agape* is the Greek word for God's love for humanity and man's surrender to it and hence to God's grace. See Anders Nygren (1953) for a full discussion of the Agape and Eros motifs in antiquity and the Middle Ages. I thank John C. Moore for this reference and for the use of his personal copy of his own book on the subject. Here he points out that in the twelfth century, "the Christian legacy on sexual love was ambiguous"—at times considered evil; at times accepted as a normal and sanctioned activity of men and women (Moore 1972, 31–38).

18. Gathorne-Hardy (2000, 442).

19. Kinsey (1930, 61). *Cynips* provided the principal illustration of variations in Kinsey's basic biology textbook; at the same time, Kinsey indirectly associated the genus with the study of Mendelian heredity and Darwinian evolution. See Kinsey (1938, pt. V).

20. Gathorne-Hardy (2000, 116–118) points out that Kinsey received four stars in *American Men of Science* and argues that he was seriously considered for induction into the National Academy of Science.

21. Kinsey, Pomeroy, and Martin (1948, 3–4). The "marriage course" was framed to be an introduction to all aspects of married life and was restricted to advanced undergraduate students who had gotten, or were about to be, married. The story is amplified by Cornelia V. Christenson (1971, 96–115).

22. Some of this has been hinted at in Christenson (1971), but it has been Jones (1997) and Gathorne-Hardy (2000) who have fully detailed Kinsey's long-standing interest in human sexuality.

23. See particularly Kinsey (1939).

24. Kinsey, Pomeroy, and Martin (1948, chs. 2, 3); see Jones (1997, 351–368) for the most detailed historical account of the questionnaires and interviews. Also Gathorne-Hardy (2000, 178–184).

25. There is a long list of this literature evaluating Kinsey's methodology. Cochran et al. (1954) was the most exhaustive examination of Kinsey's first volume done in Kinsey's lifetime (Gathorne-Hardy 2000, 279–286). For an excellent recent professional reevaluation of Kinsey's, see Bancroft (1998).

26. The publisher, W. B. Saunders, was an established firm specializing in medical books. The recent reprint by Indiana University Press (1998), by way of contrast, sports a popular beige cover with reflective red lettering on the spine.

27. Kinsey, Pomeroy, and Martin (1948, v).

28. Kinsey dedicated the volume to the 12,000 persons who had already contributed data to their research and to 88,000 more who, "someday, will help complete this study."

29. Kinsey, Pomeroy, and Martin (1948, 497).

30. Jones also describes Kinsey's taxonomy as "anti-essentialist," but he then goes on to associate this philosophical position with Kinsey's methodological tendency to be a "splitter" rather than a "lumper" in his designation of species (Jones 1997, 146–147). As I understand the terms essentialism and anti-essentialism, they have no logical connection with the practice of splitting or lumping but have to do with species as natural kinds and with their permanency or flux.

31. Kinsey, Pomeroy, and Martin (1948, 195)

32. See Gould (1985, 155–166), a delightful essay discussing Kinsey's anti-essentialism and its implications for moral judgments.

33. Kinsey, Pomeroy, and Martin (1948, 222, 549). See also the passage on self-fellation on 510.

34. Kinsey, Pomeroy, and Martin (1948, 201).

35. For Kinsey's interest in the sexual behavior of many species of mammals, see Jones (1997, 302–309) and Gathorne-Hardy (2000, 375–376, *passim*). Important for this subject and for evaluating Kinsey's early efforts to associate biological and sexual behavior, and for his support of eugenics, see Kinsey (1935). A handwritten note explaining that this draft was written prior to the "marriage course" in the fall of 1938 and "given as paper, April 1, 1935, to Discussion Group he belonged to CVC [Cornelia V. Christianson]" helps identify the date and circumstance of this lecture. Jones (1997, 153–154, 194–195, 305–309, 809 fnn. 78–82) also discusses this manuscript.

36. Kinsey, Pomeroy, and Martin (1948, 199). It was characteristic of Kinsey's work that he considered the normal–abnormal distinction only in the context of frequencies of traits in a population rather than in a context of embryonic development, where it would have made perfect sense—this despite his repeated reference to individual clinical cases.

37. It is doubtful that Kinsey would have fully appreciated the debate going on among evolutionists at the time about the importance of hidden variations (often identified as cryptic mutations) in increasing the plasticity and adaptability of a population.

38. Gathorne-Hardy (2000, 220–225, 376–377; quotation on 223). His sources, listed in fn. 26 (488) are from Kinsey et al. (1953, 17–18) and from Kinsey's associate, Paul Gebhard, "int. A" and "lectures." In a recent telephone conversation and two letters, Gebhard affirmed that Kinsey drew the line of morally permissible sexual behavior at the point when harm was done or when there existed an undue disparity in "power" as in the case of adult–child relationships. "In summary," Gebhard explained, "Kinsey's personal attitude was that what consenting adults did sexually in private was no one else's business. He was opposed to violence or duress" (personal communication and letters, December 21 and 30, 2002).

39. Paul Gebhard, Kinsey's successor at the Institute for Sexual Studies, published *Sex Offenders* in 1965. According to Gathorne-Hardy (2000, 440–441), Gebhard used Kinsey's data.

40. Kinsey, Pomeroy, and Martin (1948, 465).

41. Kinsey, Pomeroy, and Martin (1948, 468, 483–487, 663–666).

42. Kinsey, Pomeroy, and Martin (1948, 677). No one can read this passage without becoming aware of what Kinsey felt was morally right. Note Kinsey's use of the term "normal" in the last sentence.

43. Gathorne-Hardy (2000, 259, 480 fn.)

44. For lengthier remarks against traditional social mores, see Kinsey, Pomeroy, and Martin (1948, 263–268, 483–487).

45. See, e.g., Kinsey, Pomeroy, and Martin (1948, 35).

46. Kinsey, Pomeroy, and Martin (1948, 513; emphasis added). The next sentence hints at a possible prescriptive role for scientists: "Whether such a program is psychologically or

socially desirable or physically possible for any large number of males is a question that can be submitted to scientific examination."

47. Kinsey, Pomeroy, and Martin (1948, 665). Kinsey completed his sentence with, "but whether such a program is physically feasible is a matter for scientific determination."

48. Kinsey does not detail systematically the physiological, including hormonal, factors that influence the frequency of sexual outlets, but he does refer to sexual "drives," "capacities," and "energies" in his general discussion of "factors effecting variations" and his critique of the psychological notion of sublimation. Kinsey, Pomeroy, and Martin (1948, 203–213).

49. Marga Vicedo (1999) draws a connection between the American pragmatists and the four biologists she discusses. Jones (1997, 30–31) mentions that Kinsey attended a high school that was supervised by Henry W. Foster, a graduate of the University of Chicago and admirer of Dewey, but he does this in the context of Kinsey's later pronounced empiricism rather than with respect to Dewey's discussion of materialism and free will.

References

Baldwin, T. 1990. *G. E. Moore*. London: Routledge.

Bancroft, J. 1998. "Alfred Kinsey's Work 50 Years Later" (introduction to facsimile reprint of Kinsey et al. [1953]). Bloomington: Indiana University Press.

Bradie, M. 1994. *The Secret Chain. Evolution and Ethics*. Albany, NY: State University of New York.

Christenson, C. V. 1971. *Kinsey a Biography*. Bloomington: Indiana University Press.

Cochran, W. G., F. Mosteller, and J. W. Tukey (Eds.). 1954. *Statistical Problems of the Kinsey Report on Sexual Behavior in the Human Male*. Washington, DC: American Statistical Association.

Farber, P. 1994. *The Temptations of Evolutionary Ethics*. Berkeley: University of California Press.

Gathorne-Hardy, J. 2000. *Sex the Measure of All Things. A Life of Alfred C. Kinsey*. Bloomington: Indiana University Press.

Gould, S. J. 1985. "Of Wasps and WASPs," in *The Flamingo's Smile. Reflections in Natural History*. New York: W. W. Norton, 155–166.

Huxley, T. H. 1893. *Evolution and Ethics* [Romanes lecture]. In Pardis, J., and G. C. Williams, *Evolution and Ethics*. Princeton, NJ: Princeton University Press, 1989, 57–103.

———. 1894. *Prolegomena*. In Pardis, J., and G. C. Williams, *Evolution and Ethics*. Princeton, NJ: Princeton University Press, 1989, 104–116.

Jones, J. 1997. *Alfred C. Kinsey. A Public/Private Life*. New York: W. W. Norton.

Kinsey, Alfred C. 1930. *The Gall Wasp Genus Cynips. A Study in the Origin of Species*. Waterman Institute for Scientific Research Publication no. 42 [Indiana University Studies, vol. 16]. Bloomington: Indiana University Press.

———. 1935. "Biologic Aspects of Some Social Problems," ms. in the Kinsey Institute Library, series I.E.I, folder 2.

———. 1938. *A New Introduction to Biology*. Philadelphia: J. B. Lippincott.

———. 1939. "Individuals," Phi Beta Kappa address, delivered June 5, 1939, reprinted in Christenson (1971), 3–9.

Kinsey, Alfred C., Wardell B. Pomeroy, and Clyde E. Martin. 1948. *Sexual Behavior in the Human Male*. Philadelphia: W. B. Saunders.

Kinsey, Alfred C., Wardell B. Pomeroy, Clyde E. Martin, and Paul Gebhard. 1953. *Sexual Behavior in the Human Female*. Philadelphia: W. B. Saunders.

Maienschein, J., and Ruse, M. (Eds.). 1999. *Biology and the Foundation of Ethics*. Cambridge: Cambridge University Press.

Moore, G. E. 1903. *Principia Ethica*, 2nd ed., edited with introduction by Thomas Baldwin. Cambridge: Cambridge University Press, 1993.

Moore, J. C. 1972. *Love in Twelfth-Century France*. Philadelphia: University of Pennsylvania Press.

Nygren, A. 1953. *Agape and Eros*, trans. Philip S. Watson. Philadelphia: Westminster Press.

Pittenger, W. N. 1954. *The Christian View of Sexual Behavior. A Reaction to the Kinsey Report*. Greenwich, CT: Seabury Press.

Richards, R. J. 1987. *Darwin and the Emergence of Evolutionary Theories of Mind and Behavior*. Chicago: University of Chicago Press.

Ruse, M. 1999. "Evolutionary Ethics in the Twentieth Century: Julian Sorell Huxley and George Gaylord Simpson," in Maienschein and Ruse (1999, 198–224).

Spencer, H. 1879. *Data of Ethics*, 2nd ed. London: Williams and Norgate.

————. 1893. *Principles of Ethics*. London: Williams and Norgate.

Thompson, P. 1995. *Issues in Evolutionary Ethics*. Albany, NY: State University of New York.

Trilling, L. 1950. "The Kinsey Report," reprinted in L. Trilling, *The Liberal Imagination. Essays on Literature and Society*. New York: Viking Press, 223–242.

Van Dusen, H. P. 1948. "The Moratorium on Moral Revulsion." *Christianity and Crisis*, 8: 81–82.

Vicedo, M. 1999. "The Laws of Inheritance and the Rules of Morality. Early Geneticists on Evolution and Ethics," in Maienschein and Ruse (1999, 225–256).

Part III

Sites of Struggle

Downgrading Science While Weakening Democracy

The preceding chapters have presented a positive appraisal of the values that animate scientific research and an optimistic picture of how they reinforce the civic virtues necessary for a liberal democratic society. We now turn to the views of those who find the traditional values of both science and civil society to be dangerous or inadequate.

In chapter 10, Keith Parsons reviews, and then rebuts, criticisms from both the postmodernist left and the religious right. Sandra Harding faults the traditional concept of objectivity from a feminist perspective. She argues that the scientific ideal of disinterested, impartial inquiry is a delusion that produces biased results. She recommends that scientists stop trying to produce value-free science and adopt instead a "standpoint epistemology" that is centered on the experiences and political needs of the oppressed. In his reply in chapter 10, Parsons points out that oppression is unlikely to confer cognitive benefits and that in a pluralistic society there is unlikely to be agreement on which standpoint should be privileged.

As a case in point, Parsons looks at two different arguments that science should become more "religion-friendly." Phillip Johnson holds that science is committed to a form of philosophical naturalism that biases it against "creation science" and the newer intelligent design theories. Alvin Plantinga believes the Christian community should

pursue science by starting from and taking for granted "what we know as Christians." Plantinga may think that only slight emendations would be required to Christianize science, but Parsons provides a long list of traditional Christian beliefs that would wreak havoc if current science had to accommodate them; for example, how could historical linguistics be reconciled with the tower of Babel account of the origin of different languages?

Chapters 11 and 12 show the detrimental effects that such proposals to "improve" science are having on North American society. In chapter 11, Philip Sullivan provides an interesting Canadian perspective on the operation of postmodernism in universities and other social institutions. Some of his examples are at first so silly as to be amusing, such as the attempt to produce politically correct versions of Aesop's fables or proposals to let children discover scientific claims by listening to corn popping. But the accumulative effect of the episodes recounted in his essay is sobering. He describes the chilling effect on free speech when universities cater to the comfort level of hypersensitive students. Is it really beyond the pale to expect law students to debate both sides of cases about pornography or lesbian custody in mock court classes? A similar philosophy informs Canadian laws against "hate speech," which have turned out to have most unfortunate consequences.

In chapter 12, Barbara Forrest and Paul Gross trace in detail the political agenda of an influential group of intelligent design creationists called the Wedge. The scientific foundations of intelligent design theory have been summarily criticized by scientists and philosophers. But it will be less easy to counter the Wedge's strategy for incorporating not only Christian values but also specific tenets of Christian faith into all aspects of American society. We are all familiar with attempts to mute the teaching of evolutionary theory in schools, but I was astounded at the comprehensiveness of the Wedge's strategy. They are working out a "premodernist" philosophical system that will simultaneously replace the allegedly faulty, naturalistic approach of enlightenment science and restore theocratic elements into our political system. The "secular academy" must obviously be challenged, but so must "mainline" theological seminaries. The Wedge theorists are intelligent adversaries and deeply committed to instantiating a faith-based society of their own design. The last two chapters give us a preview of what would ensue if they were to succeed.

In chapter 13, Pervez Hoodbhoy describes the unfortunate effects of attempts in Pakistan to produce Islamic science. In part because the Qur'an is held to be the *literal* word of God (for traditional Christians the Bible is only inspired by God), Islamic fundamentalism is extremely intransigent. Sutras that speak of natural phenomena must take precedence over science textbooks. Sometimes the claim is that modern scientific discoveries were prefigured in the Qur'an; other times the Qur'an is used to prove science wrong. (The American website http://Islamicbooks.com offers monographs using scripture to prove that Darwinian evolution cannot be correct, in part because of the role of chance mutations. There are also picture books correcting what children are taught in secular schools; for example, it is by Allah's will that lake water turns into vapor and rises into the atmosphere—it is wrong to say that the sun *causes* the evaporation.)

The detrimental effects on social policy of constraining science by religion can be serious—how can modern banks operate if charging interest is banned? How can building codes be enacted if the damage caused by earthquakes is viewed as divine retribution? Hoodbhoy's examples sound eerily familiar to the American ear, and they remind us of what the outcome could be if the Wedge group described by Forrest and Gross were to win majority support.

In chapter 14, Meera Nanda describes strange crossties between a variety of movements in India that would distort or constrain science. India has welcomed and contributed to modern technology. Yet it has for the most part resisted the values of modern science. The result is what Nanda calls "reactionary modernism." Hindu nationalists have developed what they call "Vedic science." Like their Islamic counterparts, religious scholars claim that the important truths of science are all to be found in ancient Hindu writings. In the case of "Vedic mathematics," there are in fact some simple mathematical facts to be discovered. (These are computational tricks encoded in Sanskrit slogans; however, the texts are actually quite recent.) But most of the parallels between the Vedas and modern science are forced indeed. For example, the three qualities, or *gunas*, of matter–spirit (purity, impurity, and activity) are said to correspond to the positive, negative, and neutral charges of fundamental particles. Having thereby established the scientific credentials of the Hindu scriptures, one then affirms a scientific basis for astrology, menstruation taboos, and goddess worship as a cure for smallpox.

The picture gets more complex because leftist Indian intellectuals who have bought into postmodernism argue that all ways of seeing nature are on a par and have come out in defense of such "local knowledges." Some members of the religious right have picked up these philosophical ideas and now use them to defend the appropriateness of Hindu science for Hindus. "Creation scientists" in America despise postmodernism because they believe their theory is the uniquely correct one. Partisans of "Vedic science," on the other hand, are comfortable with relativism because of their doctrine that "truth has many names." But the effect of adopting either kind of ersatz science is the same: the scientific values of candor and integrity are put under attack and the possibilities for rational debate on public policy are put in jeopardy.

10

Defending the Radical Center

Keith Parsons

In Harper Lee's *To Kill a Mockingbird*, the narrator, Scout, defined "democracy" as "equal rights for all, special privileges for none." Scout was right; it is contrary to democratic principles for a privileged caste to enjoy unearned benefits at the expense of others. It is equally repugnant when some groups are arbitrarily excluded or marginalized. The central issue of this volume is whether the principles and practice of science promote, or at least are consonant with, the practice of democracy. But what if the scientific community were systematically and pervasively guilty of giving undeserved advantages to some groups while unfairly excluding others?

Critics from both the left and the right charge that science is indeed guilty of such affronts to democracy. From the left, Sandra Harding charges that scientific reasoning, in the name of a specious notion of objectivity, systematically excludes women's perspectives, and consequently that science privileges males and favors male interests. From the right, proponents of intelligent design theory (IDT) such as Phillip Johnson and Alvin Plantinga argue that the scientific establishment, in the name of a dogmatic metaphysical and methodological naturalism, unfairly dismisses intelligent-design hypotheses and their defenders. Both kinds of critics therefore recommend the radical overhaul of scientific practice to redress these alleged inequities. In this chapter I examine and rebut both sets of charges. I argue that both the left-wing and the right-wing critics present a distorted picture of science and that the adoption of their recommendations would result in a less rational and, in fact, less democratic science.

The title of this chapter reflects the current standing of science in our society. Science still occupies a central place in our intellectual culture, but in recent years it has had to weather increasingly strident ideological attacks. The ongoing "science wars" pit critics from the "academic left"—philosophical relativists, social constructivists, radical feminists, postmodernists, and others—against scientists and many philosophers of science. At issue is the claimed objectivity of scientific knowledge and science's image as the pre-eminently rational human enterprise. From the other end of the political spectrum, many conservative Christians have repudiated young-earth fundamentalism in favor of IDT, which they think can make a serious bid for academic respectability. As Philip Kitcher likes to say, theories of intelligent design are no longer hick, but chic. Some recent proponents of IDT boast impressive scientific credentials and count among their supporters several noted philosophers.

Daniel Dennett (1995) has characterized Darwinism as the "universal acid." He means that Darwinian explanations potentially subvert doctrines all across the ideological spectrum, from feminism to fundamentalism. Actually, what he says about Darwinism applies to science in general. Science has always made a radical claim, namely, that humans are capable, at least on occasion, of transcending sectarian bias and of acquiring objective knowledge. Science stands for intellectual sobriety in a world besotted with dangerous doctrinal intoxicants. Small wonder it is the perennial target of zealots and ideologues.

Sandra Harding argues that the idealization of science as a disinterested, impartial, value-neutral inquiry—which she identifies as the stated ideal of male-dominated science—is a delusion that prevents science from achieving true objectivity. The traditional standard of science is what she calls "weak objectivity"—the rule that science must remain strictly neutral respecting all political, religious, and ideological agendas. Harding alleges that such "weak" objectivity never has been and never will be practiced in science since it is impossible to achieve. She offers references to the work of Thomas Kuhn and the social study of the natural sciences to back this claim (Harding 1991, 115).[1] She concludes:

> Modern science has again and again been reconstructed by a set of interests and values—distinctively Western, bourgeois, and patriarchal . . . Political and social interests are not "add-ons" to an otherwise transcendental science that is inherently indifferent to human society; scientific beliefs, practices, institutions, histories, and problematics are constituted in and through contemporary political and social projects and always have been. (119)

Thus, political and social interests are not pollutants that can be filtered out by adopting stricter epistemological standards or more rigorous scientific methods and experimental protocols. According to Harding, such interests and their concomitant values are essentially *constitutive* of science, so the idea that things could be otherwise is a dangerous delusion.

Harding claims that it is "weak objectivity" that is dangerous because it employs the rhetoric of impartiality to mask its own hidden agendas. Harding charges that the pursuit of "value-free" research has only served to protect the interests of the privileged (118). Harding recommends that "weak" objectivity be replaced by "strong" objectivity, which will be achieved only when science adopts the feminist standpoint. Feminist standpoint epistemology (FSE) holds that women's experience, articulated and analyzed from a specifically feminist perspective, has profound cognitive significance. FSE contends that feminist analysis, by raising women's experience of oppression to a level of critical self-consciousness, turns that experience into a source of insight. Men, as the beneficiaries of such oppression, will not share women's experiences and so will not gain such insights. For Harding, therefore, since the practice of science inevitably serves political interests and social values, it should be explicitly done from the standpoint of feminism, since serving feminist interests and values will produce a less "partial and distorted" science than does traditional research (104).

There is something very odd about a position that claims to represent a feminist standpoint while viewing women's experience of oppression as conferring a cognitive benefit. I cannot see that the experience of oppression—except perhaps for the particular types of oppression routinely imposed on graduate students—is likely to enhance one's scientific acumen. Perhaps living under oppression will force victims to develop "street smarts," the sorts of practical cognitive skills necessary to survive in a hostile environment. However, it is likely that one deleterious effect of oppression is to deprive its victims of the full opportunity to develop the kinds of disciplined, critical, abstract thinking necessary for scientific reasoning. It is hard to see that any amount of feminist consciousness raising could compensate for these disadvantages. Consequently, I would expect that, on the whole, women would be more likely to make good scientists *after* they are freed from oppression and marginalization.

Various critics have addressed other elements of Harding's arguments. Cassandra L. Pinnick (1994) has taken issue with Harding's attack on traditional "weak" objectivity. She notes that Harding, typical of those who make such critiques, simply assumes that Kuhn and the Strong Program sociologists have succeeded in showing that science is ineluctably driven by politics, social agendas, ideology, and so forth. Pinnick points out that a number of distinguished philosophers of science have disputed such claims and have argued that the traditionally rational, epistemic factors still prevail in science (see, e.g., Lakatos 1970; Laudan 1977; Newton-Smith 1981; Brown 1989). She further notes that the assertion that feminists will do better science is an empirical claim that could be substantiated by various types of evidence, yet Harding has so far offered no such evidence. Ellen R. Klein (1996) likewise disputes Harding's characterization of objectivity, arguing that it is a caricature. She quotes a remark of Stephen Toulmin's that being *dis*interested does not imply being *un*interested. Objectivity does not require that scientists display a detached and value-neutral attitude toward their work or that they not have strong hopes and expectations about projected results. Objectivity requires us to admit that we *are* biased by our values and interests and to seek those scientific methods and standards that will, insofar as possible, limit the effects of such bias and permit the intersubjective ratification of scientific claims.

Harding could concede some of the points and distinctions made by Pinnick and Klein yet still insist that they have missed her main claim. Pinnick and Klein still assume that bias is something that can be filtered out of science by sufficiently rigorous methods and standards. Yet Harding insists that political and social interests are not "add-ons" that can be subtracted out, but are fundamentally constitutive of science. She endorses various sociologists of science who claim to show that the content of science is a social construct *through and through*. In other words, the very methods and standards of science are merely "rules of the game" adopted to serve local social and political interests (see, e.g., Shapin and Schaffer 1985). Harding could therefore insist that feminist values should explicitly determine the methods and standards of science—since, again, these must be determined by *some* set of social values.

Yet Harding (1991) cannot consistently argue this way. The central claim of FSE as applied to science is that the feminist standpoint will ground a science that is less "partial and distorting" than are "Western, bourgeois, and patriarchal" values and interests (104). Harding says that all science is "socially situated" and that we must determine which of these social/ideological loci generate the most objective knowledge (117). However, to conduct such an evaluation, we must have criteria for identifying instances of objective empirical knowledge and for determining which social "situations" are most conducive to such knowledge. Obviously, upon pain of vicious circularity, these criteria must be grounded *independently* of those "situations." Yet the existence of such independently grounded criteria would belie the claim that social values and interests determine *all* such epistemic criteria.

Thus, Harding apparently must claim two incompatible things: (a) that science, down to its root methods and standards, is thoroughly constituted by social interests and values; and (b) that, nevertheless, there exist *non-socially determined* methods and standards that permit us to identify instances of objective knowledge and to ascertain which social "situations" are most conducive to acquiring such knowledge. If Harding rejects (a), she must admit that there exist trustworthy methods and standards that are not products of social interests and values. If she rejects (b), she has no non-question-begging way of saying that the feminist standpoint will ground a less partial and distorting science than do competing values and interests.

I think that the above considerations show that Harding's project is fundamentally incoherent, but could she still argue that science would be more democratic in spirit if it adopted the feminist standpoint? It all depends on what precisely would be involved with adopting the feminist standpoint. It is plausible that, in some branches of science, sexist bias has skewed research in ways that harm women, and that a strong dose of feminism might be a corrective. Similarly, perhaps the Marxist convictions of scientists such as Stephen Jay Gould and Richard Lewontin made them more vigilant in exposing the fallacies of IQ testing. In cases such as these, ordinary people's interests are served by scientists who, motivated by their left/liberal convictions, are energized to expose the scientific errors supporting harmful racial and gender stereotypes (see Brown 2001, 191–193).

On the other hand, perhaps many critics have badly overstated the distorting effects of racism and sexism in science (as argued by Gross and Levitt 1994). Moreover, where such distortion has occurred, as in the disturbing history of craniometry recounted by Stephen J. Gould in *The Mismeasure of Man* (1981), it is questionable whether Harding has identified the best corrective. As Pinnick's criticism implies, Harding must show that in the historical instances when such distortion occurred, they were set right in the way she recommends—by the infusion of a new set of values and interests—and not due to the development of *more* neutral, *less* interested, and *less* value-laden methods. Finally, as we shall see below, conservatives can argue just as plausibly that basing science on the values of evangelical Christians would also serve to correct bias.

When Harding recommends that science adopt the feminist standpoint, she seems to mean something much deeper—and darker—than that feminism should serve to correct occasional lapses from scientific objectivity. FSE insists that women's experience, *explicitly as interpreted by feminist analysis*, should become central to the epistemology of science. The danger here is that scientific results could become hostage to whatever doctrines are then prevalent in feminist theory. For instance, in his book *The Blank Slate* (2002), Steven Pinker argues that "gender feminism," which he identifies as the presently predominant feminist creed, vehemently endorses a *tabula rasa* view of the human mind and bitterly contests the quite strong empirical evidence to the contrary (337–371). If Pinker is right, and he makes a very good case, gender feminists would seem to cast themselves in the role Urban VIII played to Galileo—that of proscribing findings contrary to sacrosanct tenets. In this case, it is hard to avoid the harsh conclusion of Gross and Levitt (1994) about the real motivation behind radical feminists' efforts to "reform" science:

> Science-as-it-is becomes, for such critics, an intolerable constraint, a terrible danger. To radical feminists as to dreamers of teleportation and transluminal space-travel, it represents abhorrent limits . . . It is liable at any moment to produce results that de-molish one or another cherished preconception of ideology. (147)

To obviate the danger, science-as-it-is must be transformed so that it can no longer threaten sacred doctrine. However, putting science to the service of ideology invites unflattering comparisons with Lysenkoist genetics and "Aryan science" in Nazi Ger-many. Of course, Harding would reply that feminism is a liberating ideology, unlike Nazism or Soviet-style Communism. However, making *any* ideology sacrosanct by in-sulating it from empirical criticism is contrary to the spirit of democracy. Granting unearned privileges to ideas seems equally, or more, repugnant than, for example, special tax breaks for the obscenely wealthy. Besides, privileging ideas means that you inevi-tably privilege people. Could Harding claim that gender feminism has earned a privileged status among ideologies, so that we should now simply presume it true and act on that assumption? But ideas earn the privilege of being presumed true only by having faced, *and by continuing to face*, all of the challenges that have or will arise against them. John Stuart Mill (1952) spoke what should have been the final words on this matter:

> There is the greatest difference between presuming an opinion to be true, because with every opportunity for contesting it, it has not been refuted, and assuming its truth for the purpose of not permitting its refutation. Complete liberty of contradicting and disproving our opinion is the very condition which justifies us in assuming its truth for purposes of action; and on no other terms can a being with human faculties have any rational assurance of being right. (276)

Though they come from the opposite end of the political spectrum, the complaints against science voiced by Phillip Johnson and Alvin Plantinga sound remarkably like Harding's. Like Harding, they think that the standards of science have been skewed to serve certain interests and exclude others. According to Johnson (1991), a dogmatic commitment to metaphysical naturalism (MN) has corrupted the practice of science. MN may be taken either as the strong claim that only physical reality exists, or as a weaker claim that does not rule out the existence of the supernatural but insists on the causal closure of the natural, that is, that the physical world is impervious to super-natural influence. In either form, MN excludes from science any hypothesis that offers supernatural explanations of natural phenomena. Thus, Johnson (2001) claims, non-naturalistic theories, such as creationism, are dismissed *tout court*:

> Creationists are disqualified from making a positive case, because science by definition is based upon naturalism. The rules of science also disqualify any purely negative

argumentation designed to dilute the persuasiveness of evolution. Creationism is thus ruled out of court—and out of classrooms—before any consideration of evidence. (67)

With creationism ruled out by fiat, evolution must triumph, despite the shoddy evidence supporting it (Johnson 1991). But Johnson argues that this ban on supernatural hypotheses rests upon philosophical biases, assumptions that are neither implied by nor required for good scientific practice (Johnson 2001, 73).

The upshot, as Johnson sees it, is that a scientific elite gets to enjoy the privilege of having its philosophical biases enshrined as scientific truth. A degree of populism has always characterized democracy. Creationists point to the fact that in numerous polls the American people favor creationism and hold that school textbooks should present it on an equal basis with evolution. One could, of course, reply with a Menckenesque aphorism about the scientific perspicacity of the American people, but if Johnson is right that evolution mostly rests on philosophical bias, the creationists would have a point.

But many scientists, at least since T. H. Huxley, have denied that science is based upon MN. In his 1868 essay "On the Physical Basis of Life," Huxley (1868) explains that the materialism he advocates is methodological, not metaphysical. He argues that science must employ a materialist vocabulary and accept only materialist explanations. However, he regards this as a methodological requirement, not a statement about the nature of ultimate reality. In fact, he holds the strong version of MN—the claim that all that exists is matter and physical force—to be a groundless metaphysical conjecture, just as bad as the worst theological dogmas (161–162). In his view, *all* metaphysical doctrines about ultimate reality are equally groundless. Science should favor the use of materialist terminology for both practical and epistemological reasons:

> With a view to the progress of science, the materialistic terminology is in every way to be preferred. For it connects thought with the other phaenomena of the universe, and suggests inquiry into the nature of those physical conditions, or concomitants of thought, which are more or less accessible to us, and a knowledge of which may, in future, help us to exercise the same kind of control over the world of thought as we already possess in respect of the material world; whereas, the alternative, or spiritualistic terminology, is utterly barren, and leads to nothing but obscurity and confusion of ideas. (164)

In other words, science seeks to *understand*, and materialist hypotheses are comprehensible in ways that supernatural hypotheses—with their postulation of vague, inscrutable beings and occult forces—are not. Also, materialist hypotheses can be empirically evaluated while supernatural hypotheses are notoriously intractable when it comes to testing. Further, materialist hypotheses connect with other such hypotheses, and with diverse sorts of observable phenomena, in ways that suggest new and promising lines of inquiry. On the other hand, spiritualistic "explanations"—God, souls, vital forces, etc.—tend to be explanatory dead ends that obstruct and obscure by placing their explananda permanently beyond the reach of further inquiry.

If the naturalism of science is methodological and not metaphysical, and if it is justified by legitimate philosophical and pragmatic reasons, as Huxley argues, then Johnson's charge of elitism is baseless. More recent philosophers, such as Robert T. Pennock (1999), have also vigorously defended the claim that scientific naturalism is methodological, not metaphysical. As Pennock cleverly puts it, "Science is godless in the same way that plumbing is godless" (282). Unless we can expect things to happen in predictable ways, we cannot test hypotheses in either plumbing or physics. Prediction requires that theoretical posits be postulated to connect with phenomena in regular and lawlike ways. By contrast, God proverbially works in mysterious ways, and scripture even explicitly warns us not to put the Lord to the test (Deuteronomy 6:16). So, *pace* Johnson, methodological naturalism does not rest upon the blithe assumption that only material beings are real. Scientists and philosophers have argued at length that methodological naturalism is justifiable independently of metaphysical assumptions.

Alvin Plantinga, however, is not buying it. He argues that naturalism as a methodological prescription is groundless, and certainly not binding on Christians. The Christian community should "pursue science in its own way, *starting from* and taking for granted what we know as Christians" (Plantinga 2001a, 340; italics in original). Thus, for instance, since Christians *know*, prior to any scientific inquiry, that God created the universe and that human nature is fallen and sinful, they should employ this information as background knowledge in the evaluation of scientific claims (347). And since Christians *know*, by revelation, that God is the Creator, they are justified in a skeptical attitude toward evolutionary theories that would undermine God's creative role (347). Unlike Johnson, Plantinga is not demanding that mainstream science be changed so that supernatural theories get equal consideration with naturalistic theories. Plantinga is saying that Christians who are scientists should feel free to break from the mainstream and form communities where science is pursued on the basis of Christians' *own* epistemological and methodological principles. Johnson is an integrationist; Plantinga is a separatist.

Plantinga offers a number of arguments against methodological naturalism. Though these arguments have many holes (as Michael Ruse [2001] points out), I think we should concede that, *in principle*, supernatural hypotheses could be evaluated scientifically. I agree with Theodore Schick, Jr. (2000), on this point:

> The supernatural is, by definition, outside of the natural world, But that doesn't mean that it is unknowable or beyond the reach of science. The supernatural can be known by its effects just as sub-atomic particles can. What's more, if the supernatural exists, it's real, and if it's real, I believe it can be investigated scientifically. There are no a priori barriers to scientific inquiry. (37)

For instance, if, contrary to fact, we found that the geological evidence indicated that the earth is only six to ten thousand years old, and if we found dinosaur, human, and trilobite fossils together in the same strata, and if archaeologists found the remains of a giant wooden ship on Mount Ararat, we should start to take the claims of young-earth creationists seriously (Schick 2000, 36). The upshot is that science does not presuppose naturalism as a methodological requirement (and certainly not as a metaphysical dogma).[2]

In fact, creationist hypotheses do make many empirical claims, and these have been subjected to extended, meticulous, point-by-point refutations (see, e.g., Futuyma 1982; Kitcher 1982; Newell 1982; Ruse 1982; Godfrey 1983; McGowan 1983; Wilson 1983; Montagu 1984; Strahler 1987; Berra 1990; Pennock 1999, 2001; Miller 1999; Eldredge

2000; the National Center for Science Education website; and, of course, the magnificent archives at www.talkorigins.org). Darwin himself, in the final, glorious chapter of *Origin*, demonstrates again and again that natural selection explains organic phenomena far better than special creation does. Darwin did not appeal to metaphysical or methodological naturalism in rejecting special creation; he beat it in a fair fight vis-à-vis the empirical facts.

So Johnson's claim that creationism is dismissed by a priori fiat is simply false. There is nothing biased, undemocratic, or elitist in mainstream scientists' hostility toward creationist hypotheses. These hypotheses were not arbitrarily dismissed. On the contrary, they have received extensive, careful, detailed empirical scrutiny—far more attention than they deserved, in fact.

But what about Plantinga's recommendation that Christian separatists should form their own scientific communities? Actually, his advice is somewhat belated since a number of Christian groups have been doing just that for some years now. They have formed their own well-funded "research" institutions and think tanks, such as the Institute for Creation Research in San Diego and the Discovery Institute of Seattle. They have their own journals and organize their own learned conferences. They keep trying to break into the scientific mainstream, but so far with negligible success.[3]

Plantinga does not seem particularly perturbed by the fact that creationism has made little headway in mainstream science and has no reasonable prospect for doing so in the foreseeable future. He has often exhorted Christians to abide by their *own* epistemological criteria and not to care a fig if others, like pesky atheists, reject those criteria. Consider his defense of Reformed Epistemology, which claims that Christians have the epistemic right to regard belief in God as properly basic:

> There is no reason to assume in advance that everyone will agree on the examples [of properly basic beliefs]. The Christian will of course suppose that belief in God is entirely proper and rational; if he does not accept this belief on the basis of other propositions he will conclude that it is basic for him and quite properly so. Followers of Bertrand Russell or Madelyn Murray O'Hare [sic] may disagree; but how is that relevant? Must my criteria, or those of the Christian community, conform to their examples? Surely not. The Christian community is responsible to *its* set of examples, not to theirs. (Plantinga 1983, 77, italics in original)

Surely, though, if Christians can do science based on what they "know" as Christians, then they must concede the same epistemic rights to everybody else. For instance, surely Sandra Harding could just as reasonably appeal to some special extrascientific "women's way of knowing" to ground the truth of gender feminism and thereby establish a basis for feminist science. Suppose, then, that *everybody* takes Plantinga's advice—Christians, Marxists, feminists, Muslims, Orthodox Jews, Wiccans, and indefinitely many cultists and kooks—and each community does its own kind of "science" based on what it "knows," *qua* Marxist, Christian, Wiccan, Raelian, and so on. The anarchic, ultrabalkanized mess that would result would bear little resemblance to the scientific enterprise as we now know it. Such epistemological anarchism might have pleased Paul Feyerabend, but would it please Plantinga?

Actually, Plantinga recognizes that a balkanized science would be a bad thing and denies that his position leads to that condition. Plantinga notes that Pierre

Duhem argued that if we base our assessments of physical theory on our metaphysical (or religious, political, or ideological, I might add) commitments, then science becomes partisan and loses its status as pre-eminently *public* knowledge that strives for universal assent. Plantinga (2001a) concedes that this is a strong argument and comments approvingly:

> It is important that we all, Christian, naturalist, creative antirealist, whatever—be to work at physics and the other sciences together and cooperatively. Therefore, we should not employ in science views, commitments, and assumptions only some of us accept, that is, we should not employ them in a way that would make the bit of science in question unacceptable or less acceptable to someone who did not share the commitment or assumption in question. (354)

So, Plantinga agrees with the Duhemian ideal—up to a point. He thinks that Christians could certainly do physics, chemistry, and most of biology in the Duhemian spirit, but he draws the line with evolutionary biology and much of the human sciences. For instance, Christians must object to "declarations of certainty and the claims that evolutionary biology shows that human and other forms of life must be seen as a result of chance (and hence cannot be thought of as designed)" (Plantinga 2001a, 355). In this one brief passage Plantinga commits two straw man fallacies. First, there is no evidence (despite certain notorious *obiter dicta* uttered in polemical passion by some evolutionists) that evolutionary science claims any greater certainty for its findings than any other scientific field. Second, a standard canard against evolution is that it claims that everything is due to chance ("the law of higgledy-piggledy," said John Herschel), when the essence of natural selection is that survival is *not* random.

Plantinga here also begs the question by assuming that if organisms came about by evolution, they cannot be designed. He needs to explain why Christians must disagree with the position that evolutionary biologist, and devout Christian, Kenneth Miller (1999) takes. Further, it is odd that Plantinga would think that Christians would reject evolution but have no problem with physics. Physics seems to be a far bigger threat than evolutionary science. After all, it was Stephen Hawking's bestseller *A Brief History of Time* (1988) that proposed the "no-boundary" cosmology that makes a Creator otiose. As for chemistry, is Plantinga justifiably confident that no promising naturalistic theory of the origin of life will be proposed? Plantinga has dismissed origin of life research as "arrogant bluster" (Plantinga 2001b, 128), but Ruse (2001) shows that the bluster is Plantinga's own.

In fact, there are innumerable points in many areas of science that some Christians will see as doctrinally inadmissible. For instance, Douglas J. Futuyma (1982) lists some of the sciences that fundamentalist young-earth creationism (appropriately abbreviated YEC) would find objectionable:

> Physicists, too, will find themselves under fire: they may be able to discover the structure of the atom, but according to the fundamentalists, physicists are wrong in claiming that radioactive atoms break down at a constant rate. All of geology is under siege: the entire petroleum industry may be built on geological knowledge, but geologists' evidence on the earth's age and the forces that have shaped it is, according to the fundamentalists, all worthless. Astronomers may be able to measure the speed of stars billions of light years

away, but when it comes to their evidence of the age and origin of the universe, they are all wrong . . . Linguistics is also anathema: the notion that human languages have developed from one another is an evolutionary doctrine that contradicts the Biblical story of the tower of Babel. In short, all the sciences are under attack. (5)

Now Plantinga might side with nonfundamentalist old-earth creationism against YEC, but on whose authority would Plantinga get to decide just what it is that Christians "know?" Mormon archaeologists would appeal to the Book of Mormon to evaluate hypotheses about Mesoamerican civilizations. Physicians who are Jehovah's Witnesses will reject medical theories that do not imply the unacceptability of blood transfusions. Southern Baptist psychologists will reject psychological theories that exonerate homosexuals from responsibility for their sexual proclivities, since they already "know" that homosexuality is a sin. Liberal Episcopalian psychologists, on the other hand, would incline to accept such theories. In short, though he genuflects in Duhem's direction, it is hard to see how Plantinga's arguments do not lead directly to the extreme balkanization of science, and the epistemological anarchism that goes with it. Given Plantinga's (1993) explicit epistemological commitments, it is hard to view him as a closet Feyerabendian, but that is where his argument seems to go.

Suppose, then, that Plantinga bites the bullet and concedes that his epistemological separatism, if adopted by all interested parties, would mean the end of science as we know it. Would a balkanized, epistemologically anarchic science be more democratic than science as it is currently practiced? Feyerabend claimed with great vehemence that it would (Feyerabend 1975, 1980). He argued that a genuinely democratic society would respect a complete epistemological libertarianism. That is, members of different traditions should be free to follow only the epistemological standards of their own traditions and to act accordingly (Feyerabend 1980). To insist that they act on scientists' standards when those conflict with their own epistemological traditions would be sheer elitism (Feyerabend 1980).

But Feyerabend's vision is completely unrealistic. Society *cannot* be merely a farrago of sects, each hermetically sealed within its own exclusive set of standards, and each pursuing only its own good in its own way. In every society, however pluralistic or individualistic, there have to be cooperative, collective actions that are done for the sake of the *common* good—wars fought, taxes collected, criminals apprehended and punished, lawsuits litigated, health, education, and welfare programs enacted. Therefore, there must be some basis for cooperative, collective action. These cooperative actions require collective decisions that have to be based on some particular set of standards. In performing collective actions, therefore, societies have *no choice* but to act on some particular standards rather than others.

Perhaps the greatest internal danger to a democratic society is factionalism—the usurpation, by those serving a narrow sectarian agenda, of laws and institutions that are supposed to serve the common interest. For a democracy to work, its citizens have to be willing to transcend factionalism by curbing sectarian demands when the common good is at stake. For instance, the religious devotee, however deeply committed, must be willing to forgo employing the power, prestige, or authority of the state to impose his or her creed. Judges cannot be allowed, not even in Alabama, to turn courthouses into theaters for evangelization. The reason is simply that the courts, and all such public places, belong to everybody, not just to fundamentalist jurists. It follows that the Duhemian virtues are essential for citizens of a democracy. They must be willing to eschew excessive partisanship and participate in collective actions based upon a broad consensus of standards and values.

The true service of science to democracy is that it provides the best example of how sectarian bias can be overcome, and how a highly heterogeneous group of people can agree to be led by a set of common standards. Science is the supreme example of how people of all sorts—Hindus, Muslims, Christians, Jews, atheists, pagans, liberals, conservatives, men, women, and persons of every nationality—can set aside ideological differences and pursue a cooperative enterprise of inestimable value.

Notes

1. The page numbers in this chapter refer to Harding (1991) as reprinted in the anthology *The Science Wars: Debating Scientific Knowledge and Technology* (Cornell University Press, 2003), edited by Keith M. Parsons.

2. This does not mean that I reject the arguments of Huxley and Pennock, only that I regard their premises as supporting a weaker conclusion. I do not think that naturalism is a methodological *requirement* of science. It is conceivable that a supernatural hypothesis could be scientifically evaluated vis-à-vis a naturalistic one—as Darwin showed. I see naturalism as a *heuristic* principle that has proven a fruitful and reliable rule guiding science. That is, I see heuristic naturalism as much like heuristic reductionism. Much of the most successful scientific inquiry has proceeded upon the heuristic assumption that complex wholes are best understood in terms of the properties and behaviors of their constituents. Thus, the macroscale properties of materials are explained in terms of the microscale properties of their molecular or atomic constituents. Similarly, the inheritance of biological traits has been explicated in terms of DNA. However, the success of reductionism as a heuristic does not mean that good science is inevitably reductionistic. Aristotle and other premodern scientists certainly did not think so. Surely, though, in those fields where a reductionist heuristic has been most fruitful, an especially heavy burden of proof must fall on anyone proposing a more holistic approach. Similarly, I think that Huxley and Pennock's arguments establish that scientists are copiously justified in disregarding supernatural hypotheses. As the critical essays in Pennock (2001) show, the latest attempts to revive supernaturalism in science are dismal failures.

3. For many years now antievolutionists have been charging that evolution is a "theory in crisis" (Denton 1985), that Darwin is once again "on trial" (Macbeth 1971; Johnson 1991), and that creationist theories such as "intelligent design" are viable scientific alternatives (Dembski 1998). If these claims were true, there should be some evidence in the professional scientific literature by now. However, as John R. Staver (2003) reports in a recent issue of *The Science Teacher*:

> Leslie Lane, a biologist at the University of Nebraska–Lincoln recently conducted an electronic search of the Science Citation Index over the past 12 years. Approximately 10,600,000 published articles were searched in 5300 journals. "Intelligent design" was only a keyword in 88 articles; 77 of these were in various fields of engineering, exactly where one should expect design to be a prominent concept. The remaining 11 articles included 8 that criticized the scientific foundations for ID [Intelligent Design]; 3 of those articles appeared in nonresearach journals. "Specified complexity" and "irreducible complexity," two important concepts of ID theory, appeared in 0 and 6 articles

respectively . . . On the contrary, approximately 115,000 articles used "evolution" as a keyword, primarily referring to biological evolution, and natural selection was a keyword phrase in 4100 articles. (34)

Clearly, there is nothing in the refereed scientific literature indicating that evolution is in a state of crisis, that Darwin is "on trial," or that mainstream scientists are considering creationist hypotheses as viable alternatives.

References

Berra, T. M. 1990. *Evolution and the Myth of Creationism: A Basic Guide to the Facts in the Evolution Debate*. Stanford, CA: Stanford University Press.
Brown, J. R. 1989. *The Rational and the Social*. London: Routledge and Kegan Paul.
———. 2001. *Who Rules in Science? An Opinionated Guide to the Science Wars*. Cambridge, MA: Harvard University Press.
Dembski, W. 1998. *The Design Inference*. Cambridge: Cambridge University Press.
Dennett, D. C. 1995. *Darwin's Dangerous Idea: Evolution and the Meanings of Life*. New York: Simon and Schuster.
Denton, M. 1985. *Evolution: A Theory in Crisis*. Bethesda, MD: Adler and Adler.
Eldredge, N. 2000. *The Triumph of Evolution and the Failure of Creationism*. New York: W. H. Freeman.
Feyerabend, P. 1975. *Against Method*. London: Verso.
———. 1980. "Democracy, Elitism, and the Scientific Method." *Inquiry*, vol. 63.
Futuyma, D. J. 1982. *Science on Trial: The Case for Evolution*. New York: Pantheon Books.
Godfrey, L. R., ed., 1983. *Scientists Confront Creationism*. New York: W. W. Norton.
Gould, S. J. 1981. *The Mismeasure of Man*. New York: W. W. Norton.
Gross, P. R., and Levitt, N. 1994. *Higher Superstition: The Academic Left and Its Quarrels with Science*. Baltimore: The Johns Hopkins University Press.
Harding, S. 1991. *Whose Science? Whose Knowledge? Thinking from Women's Lives*. Ithaca, NY: Cornell University Press.
Hawking, Stephen. 1988. *A Brief History of Time*. New York: Bantam.
Huxley, T. H. 1868. "On the Physical Basis of Life." In *Selected Works of Thomas H. Huxley*, New York: D. Appleton (n.d.), 130–165.
Johnson, P. E. 1991. *Darwin on Trial*. Washington, DC: Regnery Gateway.
———. 2001. "Evolution as Dogma: The Establishment of Naturalism." In Pennock (2001), 59–76.
Kitcher, P. 1982. *Abusing Science: The Case against Creationism*. Cambridge, MA: MIT Press.
Klein, E. R. 1996. *Feminism under Fire*. Amherst, NY: Prometheus Books.
Lakatos, I., 1970. "Falsification and the Methodology of Scientific Research Programs." In *Criticism and the Growth of Knowledge*, I. Lakatos and A. Musgrave, eds., Cambridge: Cambridge University Press, 91–196.
Laudan, L. 1977. *Progress and Its Problems: Towards a Theory of Scientific Growth*. Berkeley: University of California Press.
Macbeth, N. 1971. *Darwin Retried: An Appeal to Reason*. Boston: Gambit.
McGowan, C. 1983. *In the Beginning: A Scientist Shows Why the Creationists Are Wrong*. Toronto: Macmillan of Canada.
Mill, J. S. 1952. *On Liberty*. In *The Great Books of the Western World,* vol. 43, Robert Maynard Hutchins, editor-in-chief, Chicago: Encyclopedia Britannica, Inc.
Miller, K. R. 1999. *Finding Darwin's God: A Scientist's Search for Common Ground between God and Evolution*. New York: HarperCollins.
Montagu, A. 1984. *Science and Creationism*. Oxford: Oxford University Press.

Newell, N. D. 1982. *Creation and Evolution: Myth or Reality?* New York: Columbia University Press.

Newton-Smith, W. H. 1981. *The Rationality of Science*. Boston: Routledge and Kegan Paul.

Pennock, R. T. 1999. *Tower of Babel: The Evidence against the New Creationism*. Cambridge, MA: MIT Press.

————, ed., 2001. *Intelligent Design Creationism and Its Critics: Philosophical, Theological, and Scientific Perspectives*. Cambridge MA: MIT Press.

Pinker, S. 2002. *The Blank Slate: The Modern Denial of Human Nature*. New York: Viking.

Pinnick, C. L., 1994. "Feminist Epistemology: Implications for Philosophy of Science." *Philosophy of Science*, 61, 647–657.

Plantinga, A., 1983. "Reason and Belief in God." In *Faith and Rationality: Reason and Belief in God*, A Plantinga and N. Wolterstorff, eds., Notre Dame, IN: University of Notre Dame Press, 16–93.

————. 1993. *Warrant and Proper Function*. New York: Oxford University Press.

————. 2001a. "Methodological Naturalism?" In Pennock (2001), 339–361.

————. 2001b. "When Faith and Reason Clash: Evolution and the Bible." In Pennock (2001), 113–145.

Ruse, M. 1982. *Darwinism Defended: A Guide to the Evolution Controversies*. Reading, MA: Addison-Wesley.

————. 2001. "Methodological Naturalism under Attack." In Pennock (2001), 363–385.

Schick, T., Jr. 2000. "Methodological Naturalism vs. Methodological Realism." *Philosophy*, 3(2), 30–37.

Shapin, S., and Schaffer, S. 1985. *Leviathan and the Air-Pump*. Princeton, NJ: Princeton University Press.

Staver, J. R. 2003. "Evolution and Intelligent Design." *The Science Teacher*, 70(8), 32–35.

Strahler, A. N. 1987. *Science and Earth History: The Evolution/Creation Controversy*. Buffalo, NY: Prometheus Books.

Wilson, D. B., ed., 1983. *Did the Devil Make Darwin Do It? Modern Perspectives on the Creation-Evolution Controversy*. Ames: Iowa State University Press.

11

Are Postmodernist Universities and Scholarship Undermining Modern Democracy?

Philip A. Sullivan

No opinion should be held with fervour... Fervour is only necessary in commending an opinion which is doubtful or demonstrably false.
— Bertrand Russell, quoted in Johnson, *Intellectuals*, 209

It may one day seem strange that, in our own time of extraordinary and revolutionary innovation in the physical sciences, from the human genome to the Hubble telescope, so many "radicals" spent so much time casting casuistic doubt on the concept of verifiable truth.
— Christopher Hitchens, *Why Orwell Matters*, 199

On December 6, 1989, Marc Lepine, who failed to gain admission to the University of Montreal's École Polytechnique, took revenge by shooting twenty-seven of the school's women students before turning his gun on himself. Fourteen died of their wounds, including one he dispatched with a knife. The Montreal Massacre, as this rampage came to be termed, is commemorated annually in Canada with a solemnity approaching that reserved for World War One Armistice Day. In the immediate aftermath, the public media reported widespread soul searching about the male propensity for violence. Engineering schools and the profession were subject to extensive criticism because, in contrast with the advances that women had made in other professions, their participation in engineering seemed stuck at traditionally negligible levels. The putative sexist attitudes of male engineering faculty and the antics of male engineering students were subject to harsh criticism by feminist advocates. Many of Canada's engineering schools found themselves engaged in protracted bouts of introspection. The University of Toronto's Faculty of Applied Science and Engineering struck a committee to find ways of making the student experience more hospitable for women. As a committee member attempting to understand the issue, I read feminist critiques, but this led me down a totally unexpected path. I came to doubt their quality: much of feminist scholarship seems corrupted by advocacy. This led to a broader concern: the uncritical acceptance of relativist epistemologies, or theories of knowledge, has fostered irrationalism in certain disciplines, thus undermining the vital role of universities as sources of knowledge essential to the functioning of modern democracies.[1]

In this respect, it has been said that a representative or parliamentary democracy is actually a dictatorship that is constrained by time and by the knowledge that, if laws and policies introduced by the government of the day do not adequately reflect the concerns of the governed, the rulers will be turned out of office. As historian Barbara Tuchman's (1985) account of the U.S. government's decision-making process for the Vietnam War poignantly demonstrates, even in an era of widespread education and professionalism, the functioning of modern democracies cannot rely upon political elites to formulate government laws and policies. It must instead involve widespread participation of all citizens in the decision-making process. As philosopher Paul Kurtz (1996) observes, democracy is thus "rooted in a method of inquiry," and, to be most effective, "this means that we need to cultivate in the ordinary person the arts of intelligence, an appreciation of critical thinking, and some rationality" (493). With many others, I interpret this as requiring that public debate should resemble as much as possible the methods of the natural and historical sciences in that it should rely on rational argument applied to the evaluation of evidence.

But the historical record clearly shows that such a mode of debate is difficult to achieve. The reasons seem to be rooted in universal human propensities for irrationalism and for taking offense on religious, political, or other grounds. Humanity's capacity for irrationalism is well known; astronomer Carl Sagan (1995) gives an informative account of its many current manifestations in the United States. Examples include transcendental meditation (TM), astrology, channeling and other forms of necromancy, and faith healing. The TM movement promises adherents that they can learn to levitate or reduce crime rates through meditation, with the worldwide TM organization having an estimated value of $3 billion. A quarter of all Americans apparently believe the predictions of astrologers, and there is evidence that this credulity is spreading. Belief in astrology even reaches to high office; the late President Ronald Reagan and his wife Nancy are said to have consulted a personal astrologer in public and private matters (Sagan 1995, 16, 19, 303). The Canadian-born magician James Randi (1989) has used his professional knowledge to expose in spectacular and often hilarious ways the charlatanism and outright fraud involved in the lucrative business of faith healing.

Some irrational beliefs may be dismissed as anodynes, possibly helping us cope with the capriciousness of life, but others exact huge economic and social costs. Perhaps the worst of the latter is the so-called recovered memory (RM) movement. Denying the large body of scientific evidence that our recollections of events in the distant past are partial, imaginative, and often erroneous reconstructions, RM therapists claim that they can elicit from their patients accurate repressed memories of alien abductions, parental sexual abuse, or forced participation in satanic rituals involving child murder and cannibalism. Psychologists Elizabeth Loftus and Richard Ofshe give detailed accounts of the rise of this phenomenon since the early 1980s, including discussions of scientific evidence that memories can be falsified, descriptions of therapists' use of techniques tantamount to brainwashing, and harrowing accounts of the effects on patients and their families (Loftus and Ketcham 1994; Ofshe and Watters 1994). Since 1979, there has been a veritable explosion in the diagnosis by RM therapists of multiple personality disorder (MPD), the proponents of which allege that "childhood trauma cause children and young adults to 'split' into new personalities" (Ofshe and Watters 1994, 205). These false memories have provided the rationale for civil damage awards and criminal convictions. This is despite the fact that the allegations are usually improbable or even bizarre, that they are almost always unsupported by credible corroborative evidence, and that the patients' symptoms invariably deteriorate under the therapists' ministrations. It has become a latter-day witch-hunt, differing from those of centuries past only in that the accused are not physically executed.

The RM phenomenon is relevant to the present discussion because a contributing factor appears to have been exaggeration by feminist advocacy researchers of the extent of family violence together with misrepresentation of its causes. Many of these advocates are academics (Van Til 1997). Combined with public recognition that genuine cases of incest and other forms of assault have, in the past, not been taken seriously, this has created what professor of English John Fekete calls a "moral panic." Philosopher Christina Hoff Sommers (1994, 188–226) and Fekete (1994, 25–169) give detailed accounts of the exaggerations and misrepresentations in U.S. and Canadian feminist analyses, thus providing textbook examples of the corrupting effects of advocacy on scholarship.

The idea that informed rational debate by an educated public is essential to the health of our democracies is hardly new; in introducing his education bill, U.S. President Thomas Jefferson wrote that "every government degenerates when trusted to the rulers of the people alone" (in Hirsch 1996, 18). In this context, journalist Jonathan Rauch (1993) has provided a useful classification of various modes of thought now operating in Western societies, most of which are not conducive to a democracy:

The Fundamentalist Principle: Those who know the truth should decide who is right.

The Simple Egalitarian Principle: All sincere persons' beliefs have equal claims to respect.

The Radical Egalitarian Principle: The beliefs of persons in historically oppressed classes or groups are to receive special respect. ·

The Humanitarian Principle: When evaluating claims, the first priority is to cause no hurt.

The Liberal Principle: When there are competing claims, the only legitimate way is to decide which is right is to have everyone check the arguments of everyone else.

Rauch (1993) suggests that "the last principle is the only one which is acceptable [in a modern democracy], but ... it is now losing ground to the others, ... [that] this development is extremely dangerous ... [and that] impelled by the notions that science is oppression and criticism is violence, the central regulation of debate and inquiry is returning to respectability—this time in a humanitarian disguise" (6). Motivated by the obvious successes of the natural sciences, and seeing certain parallels with the intellectual methods of these disciplines, he uses the term "liberal science" for such a mode of inquiry. More recently, in a speech criticizing Canada's restrictive hate speech law, criminal lawyer Edward Greenspan echoed Rauch's classifications and expressed identical concerns (Giroday and Seligman 2004).

As Rauch suggests, the first four modes of thought are threats to rational, informed debate, and thus to university scholarship. Traditionally, such threats have come from sources external to the university, and the first is well understood. Typical recent Canadian examples are attacks made on Sikh studies programs, first at the University of Toronto and then at the University of British Columbia. In both cases, on the basis of historical scholarship, academics had drawn conclusions about the origins of Sikhism that were contrary to the accepted dogma. The protests and actions taken by the respective Sikh communities, which partly funded these programs, effectively destroyed them (Sodhi 1993; Gill et al. 1999).

But a relatively new phenomenon is increasing the emphasis on the second, third, and fourth principles, combined with the active participation of universities in their advancement. In order to make North American academia more inclusive of women and ethnic minorities, we have seen the institution of speech codes, anti-harassment policies focusing on sex and race, employment equity policies, and student admission policies based on nonacademic considerations. Often introduced by white male administrators, these have usually been generously motivated by a desire to avoid offense to colleagues and students, and to reinforce values of co-operation and collegiality. A more sinister aspect, however, is the politicization of the concept of offense in a way that demonstrably inhibits scholarship and disrupts university life.

Two spectacular Canadian examples of this politicization are the "chilly climate" investigations of the political science departments at the Universities of Victoria and British Columbia. In these debacles scholarly objections to feminist ideas and practices were portrayed as a form of harassment (Fekete 1994, 286–318; Borovoy 1999, 93–96). This conflation may be directly traced to the adoption of relativist epistemologies as an "integral [part] of the official corpus of feminist theory" (Patai and Koertge 2003, 142).

In this chapter, I explore the sources of such phenomena. I argue that the uncritical acceptance of relativist epistemologies in certain disciplines has led to various forms of shoddy scholarship, including destruction of the distinction between impartial investigation and advocacy, pseudoscience, and even outright charlatanism. Following a brief discussion of the epistemology of science, I review the attributes of pseudoscience, and use the latter perspective to comment on developments in certain disciplines.

Ancient and Modern Censorship

History is replete with examples of the destructive effect of censorship on scholarship in the name of religion or other ideology. Perhaps the most notorious example of censorship in the Western world is the Roman Catholic Church's Index of Forbidden Books, which was instituted by Pope Paul IV in 1559 and abolished only in 1966. Its sole purpose was to stifle freedom of thought. For example, included in the first list was Giovanni Boccaccio's 1353 masterpiece, the *Decameron*, which depicted fourteenth-century life in all its licentiousness. An expurgated version bearing the Vatican's *Imprimatur* appeared in 1573; the censor "cleaned up the entire book by a very simple device: any cleric compromised in Boccaccio's text was replaced by a layman" (De Rosa 1988, 172). In 1869 the German Church historian J. H. Ignaz von Dollinger published under a pseudonym *The Pope and the Council*, which "tried to show how false and exaggerated were papal claims to infallibility. [It] was put on the Index less than two weeks before [the first session of Vatican I, the Council at which the doctrine of infallibility was proclaimed]" (175).

That equally destructive censorship can occur in the modern democratic states is demonstrated by historian Diane Ravitch's (2003) account of the treatment that U.S. publishers routinely give K–12 school texts in reading, English literature, and history. To increase the likelihood that their books will be adopted by educational authorities, many of the major publishers have quietly developed elaborate codes containing extensive lists of forbidden words, topics, activities, and portrayals that might offend one advocacy group or another. Battles over the content of school texts is nothing new but, in recent decades the publishers' lot has been complicated by pressures from both the religious right, which takes offense at discussion of such topics as evolution and abortion, and groups on the political left, including militant feminists and ethnic groups seeking to eliminate anything that they deem uncomfortable.

Ravitch's litany of examples range from the petty to outright falsification. One publisher's bias panel rejected Aesop's fable of the fox and the crow as unsuitable for a reader anthology because it "represented the stereotypical depiction of women as overly concerned about their appearance and easily deceived by flattering men." In a move uncannily reminiscent of the "cleansing" of Boccaccio's *Decameron*, the panel would only accept the fable if the "genders" of the animals were changed. Another publisher requires art in history texts to portray women as taking leading roles, thus requiring, in some instances, "artists to tell lies" (Ravitch 2003, 11, 44).

This intellectual vandalism is not confined to text publishers. In 2002 the New York state education officials "expurgated literary passages on the Regents English examinations for high school students." Typically, in a passage from Isaac Bashevis Singer's memoir of his life in Poland, "the state excised references to Jews and Gentiles ... [thus] completely obliterating the cultural context of Singer's story." Standardized test companies have also been vigilant. One gives an example of an unacceptable item: a multiple-choice question asking students to identify which of four ethnic groups has the highest birth rate. The company "guidelines note that the item is 'cognitively accurate' but ... may be 'offensive to various minority groups'" (Ravitch 2003, 59, 115–116). This pervasive censorship is an Orwellian exercise in dumbing down, forgetting, and falsification!

This is bad enough, but it is especially disturbing when censorship to satisfy the ideological concerns of special-interest groups occurs in universities; yet U.S. civil liberties advocate and author Nat Hentoff (1992) is just one of many writers to document many examples. One concerns the classroom discussion of a Hawaii divorce proceeding in which a family court judge awarded custody of a child to the mother who was then living in a lesbian relationship. A Supreme Court judge in that state subsequently gave the father leave to appeal. The New York University Law School chose the case for a prestigious student moot court competition that is adjudicated by practicing judges, sometimes from the U.S. Supreme Court. Women law students assigned to argue the father's case objected that it was offensive to their views. After a campus brouhaha, the law school withdrew the case because, for some faculty members, the issue "was not an open question in a law-school community that has a policy of condemning anti-gay biases" (Hentoff 1992, 201–204).

A similar Canadian example occurred at York University's Osgoode Hall law school in the mid 1980s. Instructor Richard Devlin—a self-described male feminist—asked students taking his course to prepare legal briefs on the constitutionality of a hypothetical antipornography law. He randomly divided the class into two groups, asking one to argue for the law and the other against. He was investigated by the university's sexual harassment center, which asserted that some women were offended by the notion that they should argue against their personal beliefs. Some were even said to be undergoing "identity crises" as a result of the assignment. In commenting on both the undue breadth of York University's sexual harassment definition and the willingness of authorities to use it, Canadian Civil Liberties Association lawyer Alan Borovoy (1999) observed that "the official policy of a university [was] threatening a law teacher for employing laudable pedagogy" (85–86). Commenting on such incidents, Hentoff (1992) recalled the words of a journalist colleague: "Censorship is the strongest drive in human nature; sex is a weak second" (1).

On Science and Pseudoscience

As a prelude to discussing the issue of shoddy scholarship, I briefly explore the nature of scientific knowledge and contrast it with pseudoscientific reasoning. As Rauch (1993) observes, the obvious success of the natural sciences provides a basis for thinking critically about other disciplines, some of which border on the pseudoscientific.

Scientists in physics and cognate disciplines practice the doctrine of *scientific realism*. It is generally agreed that there are two core attributes to this doctrine: an independence thesis, and a knowledge thesis (Papineau 1996). Specifically, there is an external world existing independently of humans, and this world can be described with a certain degree of accuracy as it is, and not just as it appears to our senses. Philosophers have made many attempts to characterize scientific knowledge; of these, I suggest that the most fruitful, promoted by Ronald Giere (1988) and others, is to view such knowledge as a type of cognitive map. Through a complex process involving the observation of nature, theoretical speculation, experiment, and social negotiation, scientists construct their theories. Being human artifacts, the form that scientific theories assume may well be culture specific; also, like maps, they are always approximate and subject to revision. But, again like maps, successful theories—those which have become stable and have a track record of verified predictions—contain objective information in three senses: first, once the coding used to specify the theory is established, there is universal agreement on what that coding means; second, theories can be used to successfully negotiate their referent; and third, they often contain information missed by their creators, but subsequently noticed by others.

Some scientific ideas are purely instrumentalist; an example is the discipline of fluid mechanics, which ignores the molecular nature of matter completely, assuming that all matter is a continuum, with the properties of the smallest part no different in essence from those of matter in bulk. But many scientific ideas prove to have ontological significance; a modern illustration is the accumulation of evidence for the existence of the stellar objects known as black holes. Einstein's equations of general relativity are complex and difficult to solve, and it was the German astrophysicist Karl Schwarzchild who, between 1915 and 1916, was the first to explore their properties by obtaining solutions for an idealized case: a nonrotating spherically symmetric mass. This solution was initially considered to be a mathematical curiosity; Einstein and many of his colleagues denied that they might actually represent a real astronomical object (Thorne 1994). Evidence, the most recent of which has been obtained from the Hubble orbiting telescope, has since convinced the most skeptical of astrophysicists that they exist (Sullivan 2004).

One of the characteristic features of physics and related disciplines is a reliance on the interpretation of events that can be repeated. It is this repeatability that enables scientists to achieve a consensus of interpretation, which transcends culture and which is one of the striking features of a science-based discipline. A second feature of those disciplines making extensive use of mathematics to express basic principles is an ability to predict events never before observed. An example is the accurate specification of trajectories and timing of space missions.

In the historical sciences, including astrophysics, archaeology, paleontology, and history itself, repeatability and prediction are not possible. The main feature of these sciences is the search for a critically informed consensus on the interpretation of evidence. As physicist Alan Cromer (1997) puts it, "As long as investigators can search for their own bones and pots, or can examine those found by others, the critical re-examining process of science remains intact" (58). It is in this sense that Rauch (1992) uses the term liberal science: "The whole liberal intellectual system, from the hard sciences to history and even to journalism is really little more than an endless self-organizing hunt for error." And, in a discussion of the scientific status of the discipline of history, historian Keith Windschuttle (1997) observes that "Western science has trumped all other cognitive styles . . . [It] works, and none of the others do with remotely the same effectiveness" (281).

While there are no precise rules for distinguishing pseudoscience from science, examination of belief systems such as astrology and parapsychology suggests certain clear signs of pseudoscience. Following the discussion of political scientist Jack Grove (1989), we may say that a pseudoscience

- Lacks an independently testable framework of theory that is capable of supporting, connecting, and hence explaining the claims
- Lacks progress
- Tends to evaluate the quality of evidence, not on its intrinsic merits, but on its consistency with a preordained conclusion
- Usually constructs its ideas in such a way as to resist any possible counterevidence

As noted by Grove and others, including Sagan (1995, 21), the last characteristic is often the most noticeable. Good examples are Marxism and Freudianism; in his detailed critique of the scientific status of Sigmund Freud's ideas, psychologist Hans Eysenck (1986) demonstrates Freud's "overwhelming desire to avoid refutation" (93) and notes Marx's extensive reliance on "interpretation, rather than on direct verification through observable facts" (94). RM therapists' tactics provide classic illustrations of this gambit. In discussing parental sexual abuse allegations, Loftus and Ketcham (1994, 16) note therapists' use of the phrase "in denial" to counter doubts by patients or demands by accused parents for corroboration; indeed, therapists have been known to portray parents' denials as evidence of their own repressed memories. When one former multiple-personality-disorder patient asked her therapist, "Don't you think it is odd that no one is getting better and that everyone wants to cut and kill themselves after they get into therapy with you?," her therapist's response was, "Which personality am I talking to now?" (Ofshe and Watters 1994, 223).

The third characteristic in Grove's list is often an easily discernible feature of pseudosciences such as creationism and has invaded university disciplines such as anthropology. Anthropologist Derek Freeman's (1983) critique of Margaret Mead's flawed investigation of Samoan culture notes that, by the time she left for Samoa in 1925, cultural anthropology had become "an ideology that, in an actively unscientific way, sought to exclude biology from the explanation of human behavior." Known as *cultural determinism*, this ideology continues to be influential in certain social science disciplines, with its adherents dismissing or denigrating research showing evidence of a biological influence. An example is the work of psychologist Doreen Kimura (1999), which provides persuasive evidence of subtle but distinct sexual differences between female and male cognitive abilities that are associated with biological factors such as fetal hormonal balances. Yet feminist scholars generally continue to "refuse to grant any explanatory power to biology" (Patai and Koertge 2003, 135).

Windschuttle gives many examples of an uncritical reliance on reference to Marxism and psychoanalysis in such trendy areas as literary theory and cultural studies; I take this to be a tell-tale sign of pseudoscience, and suggest that—on close examination— they will be shown to possess the characteristics I list above. In this respect, Windschuttle's (1997) description of the current crop of literary and social theories is instructive:

> Large-scale generalizations about human society or human conduct are taken as given before either research or writing starts . . . Any evidence that might be brought into play is used to confirm the theory that is already chosen . . . The [currently fashionable theories are] quite hostile to most of the traditional [i.e., narrative and inductive] assumptions of historians. (19–20)

From Relativism to Irrationalism

A characteristic feature of twentieth-century Western thought is the growing influence of the doctrine of *relativism*, which denies "that there are certain kinds of universal truths" (Audi 1999, 790). Historical journalist Paul Johnson (1984) suggests that experimental confirmation just after World War I of Einstein's theory of relativity in physics played a major role in spreading acceptance of the doctrine among intellectuals, but, as others have noted, it actually has no philosophical relationship to Einstein's theory. The most prominent scholarly manifestation of relativism is the doctrine of *postmodernism*, which, for this discussion, may be taken as maintaining that "there are no facts, only interpretations, and no objective truths, only the perspectives of individuals and groups" (Windschuttle 1996, 25).

An extension of this idea is the concept of *social* or *cultural constructivism*, which has been described as

> any of a variety of views which claim that knowledge . . . is the product of our social practices and institutions, or of the interactions and negotiations between relevant social groups. Mild versions hold that social factors shape interpretations of the world . . . [Stronger versions insist] that the world is accessible to us only through our interpretations, and that the idea of an independent reality is at best an irrelevant abstraction and at worst incoherent. (Audi 1999, 855)

In describing scientific knowledge, I use the term "construct" because, as noted in the discussion of RM therapy, it is now widely accepted that the human mind is not a passive receptacle into which knowledge is transferred, as in loading a dictionary onto a computer. It is instead active in the interpretation of perceptions in the light of many factors, and memory involves an active reconstruction based on partial information and the use of such criteria as plausibility, personal beliefs, and past expectations (Matthews 1993; Hirsch 1996, 133–134). However, when the term "constructivism" is used in current debates, it is almost always strong constructivism that is implied; in the following, I use constructivism in this sense.

Constructivists make some very specific claims about science as practice and as knowledge; following a commentary by philosopher Susan Haack, they may be succinctly summarized as follows (as reported in Zurcher 1996):

- Social values are inseparable from scientific inquiry.
- The purpose of science is the achievement of social goals.
- Knowledge is nothing but the product of negotiation among members of the scientific community.
- Knowledge, facts, and reality are nothing more than [cultural] constructions.
- Science should be more democratic.
- The physical sciences are subordinate to (i.e., a subdiscipline of) the social sciences.

Haack emphatically denies every one of these claims.

Windschuttle's (1997, 12) description of the major tenets of the currently fashionable theories in what have been called the "new humanities" bears many similarities; the major elements are as follows:

- Inductive reasoning and empirical research cannot provide a basis for knowledge.
- Truth is relative rather than absolute, so different intellectual and political movements create their own form of knowledge.
- Scientific theories are inventions and not discoveries, so they can never be value-free or objective.
- The traditional divisions of academic disciplines are inappropriate.

The widespread acceptance of these ideas in the humanities and social sciences has led to predictable consequences. For example, many constructivists claim that one cannot legitimately distinguish between science and pseudoscience, and that allegedly alternative sciences such as creationism, afrocentrism, and even astrology must be treated with respect, especially by our educational system. As noted above, constructivism in one form or another is a basic tenet of women's studies programs.

A bizarre example is the debate over the origins of Native American populations. Archaeological evidence suggests that humans first entered North America from Japan, Polynesia, or Asia. But this conflicts with Native American beliefs, which teach that their ancestors emerged spontaneously from a subterranean world of spirits. According to at least one archaeologist, these contrary explanations should be viewed as equally valid relative to their respective cultures (described in Sokal 2000). In a 1994 Status of Women Supplement to the Canadian Association of University Teachers' *CAUT Bulletin*, Jill Vickers argues that anthropology texts should present the two explanations as "parallel belief systems," because she worries that the accepted archaeological explanation is offensive to aboriginal peoples (Bercuson et al. 1997). This is a classic illustration of an academic's use of Rauch's humanitarian principle.

A second consequence, described in detail by biologist Paul Gross and mathematician Norman Levitt (1994), is the presumption by humanist critics of science that they do not need to understand the content of a scientific subject in order to pronounce upon it. A third, documented by Windschuttle (1997), is that crucial classifications such as the distinction between history and fiction are erased. A fourth, following the precepts of postmodernist historian and philosopher Michel Foucault, is to treat all knowledge as contaminated by power relationships (Audi 1999, 321).

The fourth idea in Haack's list of indictments is especially pernicious: it politicizes scholarship, leading to two predictably disastrous consequences. First, it leads to the replacement of evaluation of the intrinsic merits of evidence by ad hominem argument. Hence, following traditional Marxist tactics, in order to dismiss an argument as being unworthy of consideration, it is only necessary to identify the political or social group to which the argument's proponent belongs; as Windschuttle (1997, 132) puts it, talk about issues is replaced by "talk about talk." The second consequence is a tendency to take seriously only the work of like-minded individuals, a phenomenon I call "intellectual tribalism." The insiders' account of women's studies programs provided by Daphne Patai and Noretta Koertge (2003) graphically illustrates the extent to which feminist scholarship is contaminated by these practices.

As might be expected, these ideas have also led to the abandonment of any pretense at standards—anything goes. In particular, all of these developments open the door for a descent into irrationalism. This development is attracting attention from outside of academe; for example, in an essay entitled *Culture and the Broken Polity*, art critic Robert Hughes quotes a fifty-year-old prediction by poet W. H. Auden: "Reason will be replaced by Revelation . . . Knowledge will degenerate into a riot of subjective visions" (Hughes 1993, 3). Hughes argues that Auden's prediction has come true; he describes absurdities produced by academics in the name of cultural criticism, together with an enthusiastic approval of this sorry development. In a commentary that seems impossible to parody, Chicago professor of English and education Gerald Graff states: "Narrow canons of proof, evidence, logical consistency and clarity of expression have to go. To insist upon them imposes a drag on progress. Indeed, to apply strict canons of objectivity and evidence in academic publishing today would be . . . [to cause] the immediate collapse of the system" (quoted in Hughes 1993, 77).

Wake-up calls have been made in the humanities; Windschuttle's analysis of the effects on history is devastating. An amusing example of the shoddy scholarship inspired by postmodernist methodology, he describes Foucault's description of an animal taxonomy supposedly taken from an ancient, but unnamed, Chinese encyclopedia. This evidence is, apparently, widely cited by constructivists to bolster their position that there are equally valid alternatives to taxonomies based on evolutionary principles. But it turns out that there is no such classification; as Foucault himself apparently acknowledges, the taxonomy is merely a hypothetical possibility taken from a work of fiction (Windschuttle 1997, 253–255).

A second example illustrates the determination of social scientists, and particularly the feminist variants, to impose the doctrine of cultural determinism on anthropology by finding evidence of matriarchal cultures. In a 1935 text anthropologist Margaret Mead described the men of the (head hunting) Tchambuli tribe as "effete," and the women as "comradely," hinting that this society had matriarchal elements. After much criticism, however, she retracted this view, and repeatedly denied that her findings could be interpreted in this way. Yet, more than fifty years later, sociologist Steven Goldberg surveyed thirty-eight introductory sociology texts and found that thirty-six quoted Mead's 1935 remarks as evidence of matriarchal influence. As Goldberg (1991) puts it, "[It is the social sciences] that first, most completely and most nakedly exhibited the contemporary tendency for ideological wish to replace scientific curiosity" (172).

Constructivist critics have also attempted to portray the content of successful physical and mathematical science as containing cultural artifacts. Many are fatally flawed by their ignorance of the science they discuss (Gross and Levitt 1994). But numerous historical case studies, prepared by sociologists of knowledge, are not easily dismissed. Nevertheless, philosopher James Brown's (2001) recent critique of the better known of these studies leaves little doubt that the conclusions the sociologists draw from these studies are, at best, controversial. I cite an example with which I am familiar: an analysis by sociologist Donald MacKenzie (1978, 1999) of an acrimonious early-twentieth-century dispute between two statisticians over the interpretation of data on the effect of vaccination on the mortality rate arising from diseases such as smallpox.

MacKenzie's protagonists, Karl Pearson and George Yule, developed different estimators that could lead to opposite interpretations of the effectiveness of vaccines. Wanting to show that social factors enter the content of statistical knowledge, and to relate the preferences of the protagonists to their opposing attitude to the then fashionable eugenics, MacKenzie (1978) claimed that "logic and mathematical demonstration alone were insufficient to decide between the two positions" (52). I examined this study, raising a number of objections regarding both the completeness of the historical record and MacKenzie's interpretations (Sullivan 1998). Regarding the latter, MacKenzie (1999) evades a fundamental issue relating to epistemic norms of mathematical reasoning, making his attempts to link the protagonists' attitudes to eugenics implausible. Pearson and a colleague argued that, because Yule had not derived his estimator from the fundamental principles of statistics, it was arbitrary; in other words, Yule had not solved the problem he had posed. Pearson was a strong advocate of eugenics, but any mathematician, including those totally opposed to eugenics, would have accepted that Pearson's objections had to be addressed. I suggest that many such studies are pseudoscientific in character, because a social explanation seems to be taken as a foregone conclusion. As Haack (1996) puts it, by "ignoring or denigrating the relevance of evidential considerations [they are] invariably *debunking* in nature" (259, italics in original).

Constructivism in Mathematics and Science Education

These problems of scholarship would be bad enough if they were merely confined to universities, but they are now having a broader impact. For example, in Australia, architectural schools have been influenced to such an extent that many of their graduates are described by potential employers as "very well versed in postmodernist theory but poorly educated in structure, construction and budgeting and, as a result, barely fit for practice" (Windschuttle 1997, 13). Worse still is the widespread influence of constructivism on science and mathematics education in schools; because of its importance, I discuss it here.

For decades U.S. and Canadian education faculty have been viewed by their academic colleagues with suspicion or even outright contempt. This perception is exacerbated by undeniable evidence of a steady decline in elementary and secondary school standards, both relative to other countries and absolutely, as indicated by such data as the decline of SAT scores and the introduction of university remedial courses. According to University of Virginia's Eric Hirsch, this is a direct result of the propagation in teachers' colleges of an "orthodoxy masquerading as reform." Hirsch's critique implies that the ideology has all the hallmarks of pseudoscience. This includes caricaturing of conventional teaching practices, an absence of rigorous criticism within the field of education combined with ad hominem response to external critics, and denigration of evidence of failure by such devices as "mounting furious attacks on standardized tests" (Hirsch 1996, 48, 63–66, 177, 117).

Given this prevailing ideology, it is no surprise that education faculty have seized upon constructivism as a means to advance their agenda in the teaching of mathematics and science. In an excellent critique of the philosophical underpinnings of constructivist teaching methods, professor of education Michael Matthews (1993) recognizes that mild constructivism "is far superior to the behaviorist theory of mind and learning . . . [and] its stress on understanding as the goal of science instruction is a major advance over the rote learning . . . that characterizes so many science class rooms." But Matthews also emphasizes that the epistemology is "individual centered, experience-based and relativist," with the leap from the useful observation that the "'mind is active in knowledge acquisition' to the epistemological conclusion 'we cannot know reality' [being] endemic in constructivist writing" (359, 360, 362, 365).

This philosophy means that the instruction concept of teaching is abandoned in favor of a system in which, through their own activities, students construct their own individual version of their perceptions of reality. Each student is encouraged to develop concepts that are said to "make sense" or are "viable" in the light of that individual's past experience. Consequently, as education professor Jere Confrey puts it, it is the student who "must decide on the adequacy of his/her construction" (quoted in Davis et al. 1990, 112). As Matthews (1993) notes, "This talk of making sense . . . is fraught with grave educational and cultural implications . . . It is a very unstable plank with which to prop up curriculum proposals" (368).

A collection of essays by constructivist mathematics educators edited by Davis et al. (1990) makes for disturbing reading: it suggests ignorance of both the history and the philosophy of the subject and, by implication, depicts the typical secondary school mathematics teacher as not very competent. For example, in arithmetic, students are encouraged to develop their own methods for basic manipulations; thus, two essays discuss the difficulties students might have with the standard column-borrowing technique for subtractions such as $200 - 87$ (Davis et al. 1990, 58, 100). One hints at using a trial-and-error approach by adding up from the smaller number. To anyone having a sense of the history of mathematics, this is tantamount to reversion to the clumsy methods that were forced on the ancient Egyptians and other cultures because of the limitations of their numeral systems. Given the long history of developments leading to the universal adoption of the decimal-positional system, which is unmatched in terms of flexibility and power, it is preposterous to think that, on their own initiative, students would develop methods for such operations as efficient as those now routinely used. The Hindu development of the decimal-positional system, completed by the sixth century C.E., was not fully understood in the West until after the fifteenth century; "as late as 1299 the city of Florence issued an edict prohibiting the commercial use of Hindu-Arabic numerals; they were thought to be too easy to falsify on accounts" (Hollingdale 1989, 101). Should we really expect students to recapitulate this development on their own?

Similar problems arise in science teaching. Apparently as a motivational device, social constructivist educators encourage students to work from the complex to the simple. Thus, when introducing the concept of pressure in the physics of fluids, instead of working with configurations that are amenable to interpretation with simple mathematics applied to well-controlled configurations, and leading to convincing demonstrations of such precise and proven ideas as Pascal's principle, pressure is to be introduced when talking about weather phenomena such as hurricanes. The role of the teacher as a source of expert knowledge is deliberately suppressed; they become, as the jargon would have it, "facilitators."

Cromer (1997, 176) describes an example from a recent U.S. introductory textbook that graphically illustrates the problems that constructionism creates. The book instructs students to listen to the sound of popcorn popping. They are told to crouch beside their desks and to move up and down according to their perception of the intensity or rate of popping. They are then expected to draw a graph—with their eyes closed! What is the point of this exercise? It can hardly be to demonstrate concepts of experimental design, measurement, and repeatability. Apparently, it is meant to demonstrate the variability of naive personal perceptions of a complex event such as corn popping. This could conceivably be a worthwhile activity if it was used to make the point that scientific observations have to transcend subjective impressionistic reports. But the textbook draws the opposite conclusion—that diversity of reports is the essence of science.

Needless to say, when working scientists are apprised of this philosophy, they are invariably aghast. Science has not progressed by attempting to "make sense" of the confusing phenomena of direct personal experience; it has progressed by developing concepts and principles that are almost always antithetical to everyday commonsense but that ultimately prove successful in organizing our knowledge of the physical world. This understanding usually involves initiation into a specialized technical language and abstractions teased out of the results of many experiments.

In spite of these obvious difficulties, constructivist educators have taken control of elementary science education in many Western countries. In the United States, individuals having, at best, a rudimentary education in the sciences are now developing policies, curricula, and textbooks, with predictably disastrous consequences. The current crop of U.S. elementary school science texts are riddled with elementary errors, undefined terms, misconceptions, and assertions having absurd consequences. New Zealand is so committed to nonobjectivity that it has removed laboratory demonstration tables for specially designed experiments from all classrooms. Apparently, "this is to prevent teachers from claiming to know more than their students, thus unduly influencing how the students construct their own knowledge" (Cromer 1997, 11–12). According to Matthews (1995), the country is being led "into an educational and scientific abyss" (12).

In the United States, this method of teaching is being actively promoted by the Education Directorate of the National Science Foundation (NSF) through grants to various state boards of education. Comments by NSF grant recipients reveal clearly that constructivist teaching methods are based on a well-defined ideological agenda: to "transform science from 'a white male domain' to an undertaking more in tune with 'the sensibilities and values orientations of the under-represented' [and to] 'expand the caricatured image of science' from 'logical' to 'creative' and from 'competitive' to 'cooperative' " (Cheney 1988).

It is important to note that there is a groundswell of revolt against constructivist teaching methods. Cromer (1997) notes that, when science teachers were sequentially exposed to experimental demonstration workshops run by a constructivist and by an academic scientist, they immediately rejected constructivism; as one put it, the "difference between the [constructivist's] demonstration on buoyancy and [the scientist's] was like night and day" (14). In 1993, following legislation enacted as a direct result of pressure from the Massachusetts business community, faculties of education lost most of their roles in training teachers (181). Also, accumulating evidence shows that, instead of benefiting women and minorities, constructivist teaching methods lower basic skills in all groups. In late 1997 the California State Board of Education voted unanimously to revert to traditional approaches of teaching math (Cheney 1988).

Effects of Postmodernism on Civil Society

The strange complex of epistemological and political doctrines we have been discussing is spreading from the university into the larger society. Two Canadian developments illustrate these influences. The first is a provision in Canadian law making it a criminal offense to "engage in the willful promotion of 'hatred' against people distinguished by race, religion, or ethnicity" (Borovoy 1999, 40). U.S.

constitutional protection of free speech would likely disallow equivalent laws, so that the Canadian experience is a textbook illustration of the problems they create. The second is the influence of relativist legal doctrines on Canada's appeal courts, leading them to make controversial, even antidemocratic, judgments.

Canada's hate-speech law has its origins in the emergence in the 1960s of a tiny and ineffectual but vocal group of Holocaust deniers, the most prominent being the German immigrant Ernst Zundel, who publicized his claims in various ways such as recorded telephone messages. As was only to be expected, there was widespread dismay in the Jewish community; Nazi death camp survivors demanded action (Borovoy 1999, 39). The Canadian Criminal Code, which already had a provision against spreading "false news," was, as a result, modified to include hate speech. In the three decades that have since elapsed, there have been just two convictions of Holocaust deniers, but there have also been a large number of cases showing how the so-called humanitarian principle described by Rauch undercuts liberal democracy. One, particularly egregious, was the charging of young protesters at a Shriners parade in Toronto because they distributed literature containing the phrase "Yankees go home." The crown attorney had the good sense to withdraw the charge but, as Borovoy (1999) notes, "In the meantime, those young people suffered the suppression of their perfectly legitimate political protest and they spent a couple of days in jail" (41).

Borovoy describes other cases that, in hindsight, seem ridiculous, but perhaps the most grotesque was an attempt to convict Zundel under the false news provision. At the trial, defense counsel put death camp survivors through searing cross-examinations, deniers claimed that Auschwitz was a Jewish holiday camp (sic!), and the *prosecution* found it necessary to summon a Gentile banker to ask him if he was paid by a Zionist conspiracy (Borovoy 1999, 44). Apart from the obscenity of this spectacle, it graphically illustrates the inappropriateness of using courts to investigate history.

Canada's Supreme Court eventually disallowed the "false news" provision, but the "hate speech" provision remains on the books. Its dismal record notwithstanding, advocacy groups such as the Canadian Jewish Congress continue to campaign for broadening of the conditions under which charges can be laid. Such advocates acknowledge the vagueness inherent in the concept of hate speech but like to point out that unreasonable prosecutions usually fail, or at least are overturned on appeal. But, as Borovoy (1999)—himself a Jew—observed, one should not be unnecessarily put through the harrowing process of a criminal trial; furthermore, "[If] we cannot speak our minds publicly without the fear of facing a criminal charge, we are not enjoying a meaningful freedom of speech" (41). The U.S. courts have been more vigilant in recognizing the "chilling effect" of such laws.

The second example grew out of recent changes in Canada's Constitution, which, until transferred to Canada 1982, was an 1867 Act of Britain's Parliament. The 1982 transfer included, for the first time, a formal Charter of Rights and Freedoms equivalent to the Bill of Rights embedded by 1789 in the U.S. Constitution. But the 1982 charter is not universally accepted as advancing democratic ideals; according to political scientists F. Morton and Rainer Knopff (2000), it promotes judicial activism and replaces "a long tradition of parliamentary supremacy . . . [with] a regime of constitutional supremacy verging on judicial supremacy." As an example, the contentious issue of sexual orientation was deliberately excluded from the 1982 charter's list of prohibited grounds of discrimination, but Canada's Supreme Court read it in. As a result, when in 1994 Ontario's Attorney General could not get legislative assent for a bill allowing, *inter alia*, homosexual adoption, she successfully resorted to the courts. Whatever one may think of the intrinsic merits of this particular issue, the rise of what Morton and Knopff call "jurocracy," implicit in these developments, poses troubling questions about the functioning of democracy (Morton and Knopff 2000, 13, 119, 142). Two aspects are pertinent to the present discussion.

The first is the replacement of the give and take of parliamentary debate on contentious issues with rights claiming in courts. As the Zundel hate speech trial illustrates, courts are almost always unsatisfactory forums for resolution of questions of history and other matters of great social importance. They are intrinsically unsuited to disinterested debate, tending to polarize and oversimplify issues and encouraging replacement of evidence by casuistic argument. The second aspect is closely related: it is the growing influence of postmodernism on our appeal courts. As Morton and Knopff (2000) put it, postmodernist advocates are "convinced of their own unique virtue and the corruption of all who disagree or question." This influence enters in two ways: through court clerks, who assist judges in researching and writing opinions and who often base their drafts on dubious advocacy research, and through special interest groups who, on acquiring intervener status, also use the results of advocacy research (131, 145–146). Following developments in U.S. law schools, postmodernism in the form of *critical legal studies* has been particularly influential in Canada. One Canadian law professor describes this legal philosophy as follows:

> The untenability of legal formalism resides in its never-to-be-realized quest for some rational and objective grounding for the decisions . . . and choices that courts make . . . [It] is blind to the fact that it can do no more than give effect to and to legitimate the established distribution of power relations . . . It will remain so because the Enlightenment quest for some epistemological grounding of Truth and Knowledge [sic!] is unrealizable. (Hunt 1988, 896)

Court clerks are invariably recent graduates of law schools heavily influenced by this philosophy.

In the United States, postmodernism has promoted such trends as encouraging juries to ignore evidence and acquit black defendants as a way of protesting racism in the justice system. In Canada, the National Bar Association released a report alleging widespread racism in the legal system; a subsequent investigation revealed that this allegation was based not on any evidence but on the unfounded assertions of a postmodernist philosophy known as "critical race theory" (Morton and Knopff 2000, 133).

The impact of the combination of postmodernism and advocacy research on the rule of law in Canada is graphically illustrated by a case that reached Canada's Supreme Court. Angelique Lavalee fatally shot her violent husband in the back of the head as he left the room in which they just had an argument. He had just threatened to kill her. In the ensuing trial she claimed self-defense, but "for obvious reasons [this defense is normally] strictly limited by the requirement that grievous bodily harm to the accused be imminent, and that there is no alternative to the use of deadly force" (Morton and

Knopff 2000, 143–144). Consequently, her lawyers introduced a theory known as the "battered wife syndrome" (BWS), which holds that women subject to physical abuse and fearing that violence is imminent are nevertheless psychologically incapable of leaving their abusers. On the strength of this theory she was acquitted, and the Supreme Court subsequently confirmed this acquittal. Who was the authority for BWS? The justice writing the majority opinion for the Court cited none other than the U.S. psychologist Lenore Walker, the source of the notorious 1993 Super Bowl wife-beating hoax (Martin 2003; Sommers 1994, 189–192).

Conclusion

To succinctly state the issues, I can do no better than use the words of two philosophers quoted by Matthews in the conclusion of his critique of science education in New Zealand. The first is Michael Devitt: "I have a candidate for *the* most dangerous contemporary intellectual tendency, it is . . . constructivism. Constructivism attacks the immune system that saves us from silliness" (quoted in Matthews 1995, 210). The second is Karl Popper:

> The belief in the possibility of a rule of law, of equal justice, of fundamental rights and a free society can easily survive the recognition that judges are not omniscient and may make mistakes about facts . . . But the belief in the possibility of a rule of law, of justice, and of freedom, can hardly survive the acceptance of an epistemology which teaches that there are no objective facts. (quoted in Matthews 1995, 211)

Next, I quote one of the most influential political leaders of the modern age:

> We are now at the end of the Age of Reason . . . There is no truth either in the moral or the scientific sense . . . Science is a social phenomenon . . . The slogan of objective science has been coined by the professorate to escape from the very necessary supervision of the power of the State. (quoted in Cromer 1997, 22)

These are the words of Adolf Hitler.

The message is clear: universities and colleges must renew their roles as standard-bearers for society in rational debate and the evaluation of evidence; decline in this function is no less than a serious threat to western civilization.

Note

1. A preliminary version of this chapter was presented at the Society for Academic Freedom and Scholarship Conference titled "Academic Issues in Higher Education: Focus on Fundamentals," held at the University of Toronto June 20–21, 1998. I am grateful to Christine Furedy of York University and to Noretta Koertge of Indiana University, for comments and suggestions for improvements.

References

Audi, Robert, editor. *The Cambridge Dictionary of Philosophy* (2nd ed.). Cambridge: Cambridge University Press, 1999.

Bercuson, David, Robert Bothwell, and J. L. Granatstein. *Petrified Campus: The Crisis in Canadian Universities*. Toronto: Random House of Canada, 1997: 105–107.

Borovoy, A. Alan. *The New Anti-Liberals*. Toronto: Canadian Scholars' Press Inc., 1999.

Brown, James R. *Who Rules in Science? An Opinionated Guide to the Science Wars*. Cambridge, MA: Harvard University Press, 2001: 118.

Cheney, Lynne. "Whole Hog for Whole Math" [press release]. Washington, DC: American Enterprise Institute, 4 February 1988.

Cromer, Alan. *Connected Knowledge: Science, Philosophy and Education*. New York: Oxford University Press, 1997.

Davis, Robert, Carolyn Maher, and Nel Noddings, editors. *Constructivist Views on the Teaching and Learning of Mathematics*. Reston, VA: National Council of Teachers of Mathematics Inc., 1990.

De Rosa, Peter. *Vicars of Christ: The Dark Side of the Papacy*. London: Bantam Press, 1988.

Eysenck, Hans. *Decline and Fall of the Freudian Empire*. London: Penguin Books, 1986.

Fekete, John. *Moral Panic: Biopolitics Rising*. Outremont, Quebec: Robert Davies Publishing, 1994.

Freeman, Derek. *Margaret Mead and Samoa: The Making and Unmaking of an Anthropological Myth*. Cambridge, MA: Harvard University Press, 1983: 282.

Giere, Ronald. *Explaining Science: A Cognitive Approach*. Chicago: University of Chicago Press, 1988.

Gill, Gurbaksh Singh. "Are Sikh Chairs Serving Sikh Interests?" www.sikhnet.com, 1999.

Giroday, Gabrielle, and Steven Seligman. "Should Hate Speech be a Crime?" *Society for Academic Freedom and Scholarship Newsletter* (2004), 37: 13–14.

Goldberg, Steven. *When Wish Replaces Thought*. Buffalo, NY: Prometheus Books, 1991.

Gross, Paul R., and Norman Levitt. *Higher Superstition: The Academic Left and Its Quarrels with Science*. Baltimore: The Johns Hopkins University Press, 1994.

Grove, Jack W. *In Defence of Science: Science, Technology and Politics in Modern Society*. Toronto: University of Toronto Press, 1989: 147–148.

Haack, Susan. "Towards a Sober Sociology of Science." *The Flight From Science and Reason*. Paul R. Gross, N. Levitt and M. Lewis, editors. Baltimore: The Johns Hopkins University Press, 1996: 259–264.

Hentoff, Nat. *Free Speech for Me but Not for Thee*. New York: Harper Perennial, 1992.

Hirsch, Eric D., Jr. *The Schools We Need and Why We Don't Have Them*. New York: Doubleday, 1996.

Hitchens, Christopher. *Why Orwell Matters*. New York: Basic Books, 2002.

Hollingdale, Stuart. *Makers of Mathematics*. London: Penguin Books, 1989: 2–8, 96, 101.

Hughes, Robert. *Culture of Complaint: The Fraying of America*. New York: Oxford University Press, 1993.

Hunt, Alan. "Living Dangerously on the Deconstructive Edge." *Osgoode Hall Law Journal* (1988) 26: 867–896.

Johnson, Paul. *A History of the Modern World*. London: Weidenfeld and Nicolson, 1984: 1–11.

———. *Intellectuals*. London: Weidenfeld and Nicolson, 1988.

Kimura, Doreen. *Sex and Cognition*. Cambridge, MA: MIT Press, 1999.

Kurtz, Paul. "Two Sources of Unreason in Democratic Society: The Paranormal and Religion." *The Flight from Science and Reason*, Paul R. Gross, Norman Levitt, and Martin W. Lewis, editors. Baltimore: The Johns Hopkins University Press, 1996: 493.

Loftus, Elizabeth F., and Katharine Ketcham. *The Myth of Repressed Memory*. New York: St. Martin's Press, 1994.

MacKenzie, Donald. "Statistical Theory and Social Interests: A Case Study." *Social Studies of Science* (1978) 8: 35–83.

————. "The Zero-Sum Assumption: Reply to Sullivan." *Social Studies of Science* (1999), 29(2): 223–234.

Martin, Robert I. *The Most Dangerous Branch: How the Supreme Court of Canada Has Undermined Our Law and Our Democracy.* Montreal: McGill-Queens University Press, 2003: 151–152.

Matthews, Michael. "Constructivism and Science Education: Some Epistemological Problems." *Journal of Science Education and Technology* (1993) 2(1): 359–370.

————. *Challenging New Zealand Science Education.* Palmerston North, New Zealand: Dunsmore Press, 1995.

Morton, Frederick L., and Rainer Knopff. *The Charter Revolution and the Court Party.* Peterborough, Ontario: Broadview Press, 2000.

Ofshe, Richard, and Ethan Watters. *Making Monsters: False Memories, Psychotherapy, and Sexual Hysteria.* New York: Charles Scribner's Sons, 1994.

Papineau, David. "Introduction." *Philosophy of Science.* D. Papineau, editor. Oxford: Oxford University Press, 1996: 2.

Patai, Daphne, and Noretta Koertge. *Professing Feminism: Education and Indoctrination in Women's Studies.* Lanham, MD: Lexington Books, 2003.

Randi, James. *The Faith Healers.* Buffalo, NY: Prometheus Books, 1989.

Rauch, Jonathan. *The Outnation: A Search for the Soul of Japan.* Boston, MA: Harvard Business School Press, 1992: 134.

————. *The Kindly Inquisitors: New Attacks on Free Thought.* Chicago: University of Chicago Press, 1993.

Ravitch, Diane. *The Language Police: How Pressure Groups Restrict What Students Learn.* New York: Alfred A. Knopf, 2003.

Sagan, Carl. *The Demon-Haunted World: Science as Candle in the Dark.* New York: Random House, 1995.

Sodhi, S. S. "University of Toronto Sikh Studies Program." www.sikhspectrum.com, 1993.

Sokal, Alan. "A Plea for Reason, Evidence and Logic." *The Sokal Hoax: The Sham That Shook the Academy.* Edited by the editors of *Lingua Franca.* Lincoln: University of Nebraska Press, 2000: 249–252.

Sommers, Christina Hoff. *Who Stole Feminism? How Women Have Betrayed Women.* New York: Simon and Schuster, 1994.

Sullivan, Denis. Department of Physics, Victoria University of Wellington, New Zealand, private communication, 5 April 2004.

Sullivan, Philip. "An Engineer Dissects Two Case Studies: Hayles on Fluid Mechanics and MacKenzie on Statistics." *A House Built on Sand: Exposing Postmodernist Myths about Science.* Noretta Koertge, editor. New York: Oxford University Press, 1998: 71–98.

Thorne, Kip. *Black Holes and Time Warps: Einstein's Outrageous Legacy.* New York: W. W. Norton, 1994: 124–139.

Tuchman, Barbara W. *The March of Folly: From Troy to Vietnam.* New York: Ballantine Books, 1985: 234–237.

Van Til, Reinder. *Lost Daughters: Recovered Memory Therapy and the People It Hurts.* Grand Rapids, MI: William B. Eerdmans Publishing, 1997: 73–104.

Windschuttle, Keith. *The Killing of History: How Literary Critics and Social Theorists Are Murdering Our Past.* New York: The Free Press, 1997.

Zurcher, Rita. "Farewell to Reason: A Tale of Two Conferences." *Academic Questions* (1996) 9(2): 52–60.

12

The Wedge of Intelligent Design

Retrograde Science, Schooling, and Society

Barbara Forrest and Paul R. Gross

> From the sixth century up to the Enlightenment it is safe to say that the West was thoroughly imbued with Christian ideals and that Western intellectual elites were overwhelmingly Christian. False ideas that undermined the very foundations of the Christian faith (e.g., denying the resurrection or the Trinity) were swiftly challenged and uprooted. Since the Enlightenment, however, we have not so much lacked the means to combat false ideas as the will and clarity.
>
> —William A. Dembski and Jay Wesley Richards,
> *Unapologetic Apologetics*

> Premodernity had one thing going for it that neither modernity nor postmodernity could match, namely, a worldview rich enough to accommodate divine agency.
>
> —William A. Dembski, *Intelligent Design: The Bridge between Science and Theology*

Intelligent design creationists at the Discovery Institute's Center for Science and Culture (CSC), or "the Wedge," as they call themselves, have a paradoxical plan for carrying out their "Wedge Strategy": they will advance toward the future by resurrecting the past.[1] The past for which they yearn, driven by their abhorrence of the modern world, was by every reasonable human standard a failed one. But, as is evident in our epigraphs by two chief Wedge apologists, William Dembski and Jay Richards, they yearn for the premodern age when anti-Christian transgressions such as "denying the Trinity" could be dealt with in summary fashion by the faith's defenders. That it was the brutal excesses of such defense that led to the Enlightenment, which called for reason, science, and secular constitutional government to resist absolute political and religious power, apparently does nothing to recommend the Enlightenment to Dembski, who judges the "ideologies" of "Enlightenment rationalism" and "scientific naturalism" to be "false" and "bankrupt" (Dembski 1999, 14–15). He instead defends "premodernity," because, he asserts, "modernity, with its commitment to rationality and science, is wonderfully adept at discerning the regularities of nature" but "woefully deficient at discerning the hand of God against the backdrop of those regularities" (44). That seems to be his argument against all intellectual life since the dark ages.

More than a decade after the Wedge's coalescence, intelligent design (ID) scientists have produced no science to support their claims that ID is a new, revolutionary scientific paradigm. The ID movement's "scientific" program is encapsulated chiefly in Phillip Johnson's assertion that "evolution is basically a hoax" (Johnson 2003). Although much attention has been given by scientists and philosophers to ID's putatively scientific claims, and also, in our book *Creationism's Trojan Horse: The Wedge of Intelligent Design* (2004), to its religious identity and political strategy, little has been written about the blatantly theocratic ambitions on which the Wedge Strategy depends. In this chapter, we begin to fill this important gap in the scholarly analysis of the ID movement.

As becomes obvious to any objective observer, the Wedge is dedicated to returning our culture to (1) premodern science and science education, based on *their* concept of science (i.e., natural theology, exemplified by William Paley's early-nineteenth-century version of the old argument from design), and (2) a premodern political paradigm, the Christian commonwealth—a republic whose political system incorporates and requires the official sanction of Christianity. This is the system that the American founding fathers designed the U.S. Constitution *expressly to avoid* but that their contemporary religious critics insisted, more than two centuries ago, was the only way to ensure a moral basis for American culture. Like the Wedge today, those critics of the Constitution demanded "cultural renewal" on the basis of sectarian Christian doctrine. And the Wedge, like these early opponents of the Constitution, rejects secular society, the only alternative to which is, of course, theocracy.

Antimodernism

Although the ID movement has had no discernible effect on the way scientists actually do science, the Wedge promotes in the public mind the idea that its premodern paradigm of science and science education is both feasible and desirable. Dembski has argued in the online (relatively mainstream) *Metanexus* forum that ID is *not* natural theology but *is* sound, modern science (Dembski 2001a). Yet in his book *Intelligent Design: The Bridge between Science and Theology* (1999), aimed at ID's Christian audience (its "natural constituency," as stated in "The Wedge Strategy," the movement's tactical document—see note 1), he defends the British natural theology of William Paley and Thomas Reid, as well as that of the American theologian and antievolutionist Charles Hodge. Dembski stresses that ID is linked "both conceptually and historically" to British natural theology and that his purpose in chapter 3 is to refute positivism, "the faulty conception of science" that "effectively did away" with natural theology. He argues that "the blanket dismissal of natural theology in the nineteenth century was not warranted and . . . its core idea of design remains viable" (16, 70–93).

Moreover, while Dembski aims in chapter 3 to "[reopen] the door to divine action" on the "scientific front," he devotes chapter 2 to reopening it on the "theological front" by defending belief in miracles. Displaying his religious motive for promoting

ID as science, he rejects modern science's defining naturalistic methodology, that is, the search for natural explanations for natural phenomena. He rejects it because it "leaves no room for a designing intelligence whose action transcends natural laws" and thereby precludes using miracles to explain the world (Dembski 1999, 68–69). Pointing to the work of Spinoza and Schleiermacher during the rise of modern science and the Enlightenment, Dembski condemns their exclusion of miracles because that makes ID impossible:

> Since miracles had previously constituted the most direct evidence[2] for divine activity in the world, the rejection of miracles became tantamount to the rejection of all evidential support for the Christian faith . . . [T]he idea that God could act identifiably as a designing intelligence was lost. By rendering miracles incoherent Spinoza and Schleiermacher undercut all nonnaturalistic modes of divine activity and thereby rendered design incoherent as well. (Dembski 1999, 50–51)

This means, of course, that ID—which Dembski promotes as a scientific theory— *requires* miraculous interventions in the world's natural order to make it intelligible. Dembski's views are thus not merely premodern—they are archaic and scientifically unworkable. Once miracles are allowed, they explain everything and nothing, which is why modern science abandoned them once and for all in the nineteenth century. However, not only does the Wedge Strategy rest on a *pre*modern framework, but it is markedly *anti*-modern, a rejection of Enlightenment rationalism, secularism, and religious pluralism—the foundations, as it happens, of American democracy.

For Phillip Johnson, the Wedge's founding father, the word "modernism" carries sinister connotations. He uses it as shorthand for "scientific naturalism" and "liberal rationalism," references, respectively, to modern science and to the Enlightenment centrality of reason, the intellectual foundation of modern thought (Johnson 1994a). Taking broad liberties with the rules of causal reasoning and definition, former law professor Johnson transforms the conjunction of science and reason into atheism and the decline of civic virtue: "Modernism is typically defined as the condition that begins when people realize God is truly dead, and we are therefore on our own . . . [T]he death of God makes people free from rules based upon what had been thought to be the word of God, and therefore invites a rethinking of such things as gender roles and sexual morality" (Johnson 1994a, 1994b). Citing increasing illegitimacy as an example of this, he warns that a "constitutional democracy is in serious trouble if its citizenry does not have a certain degree of education and civic virtue" (Johnson 1994b). Since, in Johnson's mind, civic virtue depends upon religion, and civic virtue is the cornerstone of democracy, democracy likewise requires a religious foundation. Q.E.D.

Johnson thus denies that "modernism" is a possible foundation for democracy; rather, he predicts that it will lead to "a growing doubt that there is any such thing as objective truth, with a consequent fragmenting of the body politic into separate groups with no common frame of reference" (Johnson 1994b). His criticism of a constitutional democracy that lacks a religion-based moral code demonstrates his wish not merely for religion as a source of solace and moral strength for individuals who embrace it, but rather for religion as the foundation of American social

structure and public policy. Consequently, consistent with its original nomenclature—
the "Center for the *Renewal* of Science and Culture"—his renamed Center for Science
and Culture seeks to renew American culture and education by returning them to
what he and others claim to be the country's religious foundations.[3]

Thus, the ID movement's desire for a premodern science is interwoven with its
desire for a premodern political system. Yet the premodern, religion-based political
system the ID movement wants is *not* what the founders—with their memories of
bloody European religious wars still fresh—had in mind, and it is *not* what they
encoded in the Constitution of the United States. Isaac Kramnick and R. Laurence
Moore, in *The Godless Constitution* (1997), point out properly that

> the nation's founders, both in writing the Constitution and defending it in the rati-
> fication debates, sought to separate the operations of government from any claim that
> human beings can know and follow divine direction in reaching policy decisions. They
> did this despite their enormous respect for religion, their faith in divinely endowed
> human rights, and their belief that democracy benefited from a moral citizenry who
> believed in God. (12)

An outcry arose from colonial religious critics when they saw that the Constitution
would not codify their sectarian commitments as law. A Pennsylvania pamphleteer
known pseudonymously as "Aristocrotis" penned a condemnation of the "religion of
nature," that is, deism, which was the religious view of many founders—and thun-
dered that they were establishing "a government founded upon nature." This meant,
of course, that the founders had (in his view) shamefully devalued the *created* world.
He decried their exclusion of God and Christianity from the Constitution, concluding
sarcastically with a mock endorsement of its secularism:

> What, [Aristocrotis] asks, "is the world to the federal convention but as the drop of a
> bucket, or the small dust in the balance!..." He argues that the "new Constitution,
> disdains... belief of a deity, the immortality of the soul, or the resurrection of the
> body, a day of judgement, or a future state of rewards and punishments," because its
> authors are committed to a natural religion that is deistic nonreligion. He concludes
> with irony: "If some religion must be had the religion of nature will certainly be
> preferred by a government founded upon the law of nature. One great argument in
> favor of this religion is, that most of the members of the grand convention are great
> admirers of it; and they certainly are the best models to form our religious as well as
> our civil belief on." (Kramnick and Moore 1997, 34–35)

This eighteenth-century railing against the "religion of nature" and "deistic non-
religion" survives intact, without change, in the Wedge's twenty-first-century rejection of naturalism and deism. Dembski (1999) discards both in the same breath:
"Theists know that naturalism is false. Nature is not self-sufficient. God created
nature as well as any laws by which nature operates. Not only has God created the
world, but God upholds the world moment by moment... Theists are not deists"
(104). And Johnson's complaints are virtually identical to those of Aristocrotis.
Johnson regrets the Constitution's establishment of secular rather than religion-based
government; his distaste for the former surfaces in his complaint that "modernist
naturalism" is the "established religious philosophy of America": "Modernism is
established in the sense that the intellectual community, usually invoking the power

of the federal judiciary and the mystique of the Constitution, vigorously and almost always successfully insists that law and public education must be based upon naturalistic assumptions" (Johnson 1994a). His disagreement with judicial decisions favoring church–state separation is therefore clear, since his rejection of the "naturalistic assumptions" upon which he says law and public education are based amounts to his endorsing institutionalized supernatural belief, that is, *an establishment of religion*. But Johnson wrongly equates "secularism" with "naturalism" (see Forrest 2004). His denunciation of "naturalism," aimed at American public institutions and policies, is actually a denunciation of the fact that these institutions are secular, that they are *not* governed by religious authority.

Antisecularism and Religious Exclusionism

The Wedge's antisecularism is of a piece with its antimodernism. It echoes throughout the offerings of leading Wedge members, who display an "us against them" mentality, portraying Christians as the victims of a modernist world:

> For the last 100–150 years, maybe longer, Christians who have held to orthodox Christianity have really been beaten up a lot, . . . And we've not been able to overturn some ideologies that are inimical to the Christian faith—which undercut it and deny it. (William Dembski, as quoted in Hartwig 2001)

> Modernism invades the sanctuary not only in the form of legal regulation, but through television, academic literature, and every form of cultural penetration. As a result, religious colleges, seminaries, and church bureaucracies are saturated with modernist thinking. As this becomes increasingly apparent, Christians are not likely to remain satisfied with a naturalistic culture that will not leave them alone. (Johnson 1994b)

> Christians live in the world with non-Christians. We want to share the Good News with those who have not yet grasped it, and to defend the faith against attacks. Materialism is both a weapon that many antagonists use against Christianity and a stumbling block to some who would otherwise enter the church. To the extent that the credibility of materialism is blunted, the task of showing the reasonableness of the faith is made easier . . . [M]aterialism has a tough time with a universe that reeks of design. (Behe 1998)

Despite denouncing secularism, Wedge leaders deny favoring theocracy. Johnson claims to reject it because of "the Christian teaching about the sinful heart of man" and because "theocrats wielding absolute power will not long remain Christian in any sense that I can recognize" (Johnson 2002a, 169). Publication of our book *Creationism's Trojan Horse* (Forrest and Gross 2004) prompted a similar denial from the Discovery Institute: "One can believe in God and not want to impose theocracy on our culture. One can reject theocracy and still think that religious believers . . . have a right to contend for their views in the public square—whether in science, the humanities, or politics" (Discovery Institute 2004, 5–6). Yet given the strain under which Johnson places his credibility by calling evolution a hoax, the credibility of this solitary denial is negligible, drowned out by his constant drumbeats against secularism. The Discovery Institute's denial is just as hollow.

Given ID's thoroughly religious foundation, ID's Wedge Strategy goal "to see design theory permeate our religious, cultural, moral and political life" translates to enacting ID leaders' religious preferences as public policy. The theological framework from within which they operate is so rigid that they cannot separate their views on either science or public policy from their theology. Indeed, doing so would be sacrilegious. Dembski (1999, 98–99) affirms that science without God is idolatry—a religious offense, a sin. By his own logic, then, the secular government protecting science and education is also a sin. Consequently, just as the only restorative measure for naturalistic science is an infusion of supernaturalism, so the only expiation of the sin of secular government is deseculariation. What the Wedge envisions amounts to theocracy, and Americans need to know this.[4]

In 1996, at the first major Wedge symposium, the "Mere Creation Conference" at Biola University, Johnson named three events as symbols of the secularization of America, a polity that he asserts was founded consciously and deliberately upon divine sanction: the 1959 centennial of Darwin's *The Origin of Species*; the 1960 movie *Inherit the Wind*, based on the Scopes "monkey trial"; and the 1962 Supreme Court decision outlawing state-sponsored prayer in public schools. The latter particularly infuriates Johnson, as it does the Religious Right in general. He yearns for the good old days "before 1962, [when] America was unified by the concept that people of different races and religious traditions all worship their common Creator, the God of the Bible" and before "the 1959 Centennial proclaimed that a blind material process of evolution is our true creator" (Johnson 1996). He mourns the "tremendous change in the ruling philosophy of our country," meaning the *alleged* change from the sovereignty of religious doctrine over American culture and policy to the acceptance of secular ideas: "Science now teaches us that a purposeless material process of evolution created us; . . . and the courts teach us that the very notion of God is divisive, and so must be kept out of public life. The Pledge of Allegiance may say that we are 'one nation, under God,' but we have become instead a nation that has declared its independence from God" (Johnson 1996).

More recently, in 2001, Johnson continued to eulogize bygone days, except that now he portrayed America as an explicitly *Christian* nation—a religious exclusionism disturbingly prevalent in the views of leading Wedge members. Forecasting the demise of twentieth-century "scientific materialism," Johnson looked forward to a revival of America's Christian past: "Now as we enter the 21st century, scientific materialism is creaking and shaking . . . I'm sensing a renewed excitement as we come to realize that maybe we had a better grasp of the truth when we were a Christian country than during those decades when Christian truths were spurned" (Hartwig 2001). Johnson's vision of the past, however, is historically incorrect: the view of American government as founded upon religion is a fabrication of the Christian right. As Kramnick and Moore (1997) note, even the reference to God in the Pledge of Allegiance is not original to the nation's founding, but rather an attempt—which continues today—to bring about the gradual replacement of secular government with a Christian one:

> For fifty years after its founding a strong national consensus existed on the utterly secular nature of the federal government, whatever local and state law and practice may have been . . . It is not true that the founders designed a Christian commonwealth,

which was then eroded by secular humanists and liberals; the reverse is true. The framers erected a godless federal constitutional structure, which was then undermined as God entered first the U.S. currency in 1863, ... *and finally the Pledge of Allegiance in 1954* ...

...In recent years the Christian right, unsuccessful in its attempts to change the godless Constitution, has totally reversed its strategy. In a staggering historical flip-flop, it now celebrates the Constitution by denying its godless foundation ... Its adherents have falsely dressed the founders in godly Christian garb, which, they argue, later godless generations have systematically torn off ... Such is the distortion of American history offered by today's preachers of religious correctness. (143, 148–149; emphasis added)

The inconvenient realities of history, however, like those of evolutionary science, do not deter the Wedge from promoting its cultural agenda. Wedge members see themselves pitted against the modern evil of secularism. They distort the meaning of secularism by equating it with atheism. And since they view atheism as unequivocally evil, they see secularism as an evil to which (their) religion is the only antidote. Should there be doubts of their antisecular intentions for American culture and education, Wedge members themselves have been ready to dispel them. Cited in a July 2001 article by CSC fellow Mark Hartwig in *Boundless* magazine (of the rightist Focus on the Family), Johnson foresees Christianity becoming central to public education and policy:

Secular society, and particularly the educational institutions, have assumed throughout the 20th century that the Christian religion is simply a hangover from superstitious days, ... With the success of intelligent design, however, we're going to understand that, regardless of the details, the Christians have been right all along—at least on the major elements of the story, like divine creation. And that, I think is going to change society's understanding of what constitutes knowledge, of what things are worth knowing. (Hartwig 2001)

Johnson concludes that as a result of ID's (claimed) successes in confirming the Christian account of creation, the argument that "Christian ideas have no legitimate place in public education, in public lawmaking, [and] in public discussion generally" will no longer be credible. In short, ID's confirmation of a religious creation story will have a revolutionary effect: it will return religion to public education and public policy.

Johnson's statements are thus unambiguous: contrary to the Wedge's denials, ID is creationism and is therefore a religious belief.[5] And the expressed religious views of Wedge members reveal not only antisecularism but also a thoroughgoing religious *exclusionism*. Johnson's dream of a country reunified by religious devotion turns out to be less than inclusive, as revealed, for example, in his astonishing reaction to the World Trade Center attack on September 11, 2001:

The strength of America is not in its towers or in its battleships, it's in its faith ... This isn't the same country we were in the previous decades. Now we're seeing how the country is almost cringing in fear of these Muslim terrorists from the Middle East. I see professors afraid to discuss the subject because they're afraid of what the Muslim students will do ... I never thought our country would descend to this level. We are afraid to search the truth and proclaim it. We once knew who the true God was and were able to proclaim it frankly. But since about 1960 we've been hiding from that. We've been trying to pretend that all religions are the same. (Johnson 2002b)

Such exclusionism exists also in the views of Henry "Fritz" Schaefer, a founding Wedge member who maintains an active lecture schedule at universities around the country. In one of his public lectures on his "Leadership University" website, "Questions Intellectuals Ask About Christianity," Schaefer's answers reflect his own brand of exclusionism:

> 12. Will not God accept those of other religions who are sincere?
> [Schaefer] All other religions are diametrically opposed to Christianity on the most crucial question . . . They deny that Jesus is God, . . .
> No one questions the sincerity and intensity of the faith of . . . a Buddhist monk. But sincerity or intensity of faith does not create truth . . .
> . . . Not every religion can be true . . .
> 18. Many non-Christians are offended by the "exclusiveness" of Christianity. Can anything be said in response?
> A) Christianity is "universal" . . . Jesus invites people everywhere to receive the gift of eternal life . . .
> B) Since many basic tenets of different religions are contradictory, someone has to be wrong.
> C) Exclusivity seems unavoidable . . . The exclusion of exclusivity is also exclusive. (Schaefer n.d.)

Despite the twisted logic of Schaefer's last remark, which appears to be the nonsensical assertion that *inclusiveness* is *exclusionary*—that is, religious tolerance excludes religious exclusionists—his position is clear: non-Christians *will be excluded* from heaven.

The most disturbing example of ID proponents' religious exclusionism is in *Unapologetic Apologetics: Meeting the Challenges of Theological Studies* (2001), edited by William Dembski and Jay Wesley Richards and to which they contributed as authors. At first, the book seems unconnected to the ID movement, since it consists largely of essays written in the mid-1990s by students in a Princeton Theological Seminary seminar group. But these students, who organized the seminar to protest Princeton's decreasing emphasis on Christian apologetics, were also organized as the Charles Hodge Society in honor of the nineteenth-century theologian and antievolutionist. And they were led by Dembski and Richards, now leading Wedge figures (Dembski and Richards 2001, 13). Phillip Johnson wrote the foreword, declaring that behind the student movement founded by Dembski and Richards—whom he regards as "Christian revolutionaries"—is "a more general intellectual movement that will bear fruit in the coming century," that is, intelligent design (Johnson 2001a, 9). Johnson's declaration mirrors a goal in the Wedge's strategy document: "Seminaries [will] increasingly recognize & repudiate naturalistic presuppositions" (see note 1). And Dembski's and Richards's essays enunciate the anti-Enlightenment, antinaturalist, and antisecularist viewpoints that underlay the 1996 formation of the Wedge as the Center for the Renewal of Science and Culture.

Dembski and Richards voice an unmistakable desire to return to the days when Christianity was the dominant, not just the majority, religion and when science, education, and society were governed by it. To be sure, Dembski and Richards (2001) recognize that "the inquisitorial method cannot fulfill God's redemptive purposes for the world" (19). But they renounce, too, the idea of secular society, lamenting that "we have permitted the collective thought of the world to be controlled by ideas that prevent Christianity from being regarded as anything but a harmless delusion" (19). They argue that "Christians have a mandate to declare the truth of Christ," which requires "bringing every aspect of life under the influence of this truth." And while acknowledging the "elitism and intrusiveness" of this mandate, they press their point resolutely: "But in fact, unifying every aspect of life under the truth of Christ is the only hope humanity has to find true freedom and fulfillment." Such a holy mission permits no waffling: "Humans must decide their allegiances. There is in the end no straddling of fences. Jesus says that we are either for him or against him. There is no middle ground. This truth is the dark side of the gospel . . . For those who reject it, the gospel signifies sorrow and loss" (18).

Dembski, moreover, takes seriously the notion of heresy; and if the price of defending the faith is civic peace and Christian unity, so be it:

> Within late twentieth-century North American Christianity, *heresy* has become an unpopular word. Can't we all just get along and live together in peace? Unfortunately the answer is no. Peace cannot be purchased at the expense of truth . . . There is an inviolable core to the Christian faith . . . Harsh as it sounds, to violate that core is to place ourselves outside the Christian tradition. This is the essence of heresy, and heresy remains a valid category for today. (Dembski 2001b, 43)

In light of these sentiments, his next comment, "This is not to endorse a McCarthyism that finds heretics under every rock," is hardly reassuring. Though Dembski and Richards may renounce the methods of the medieval faith's defenders, they obviously embrace its aim: theocratic Christian dominion.[6] Such devotion to their salvific duty raises the unavoidable question: are they willing to follow the logic of their own theology regarding the ultimate fate of the few members of their movement who are not only nonevangelicals, but non-Christians? According to Center for Science and Culture fellow Nancy Pearcey, Michael Denton, a long-time member of the Wedge, is an agnostic, and senior CSC fellow David Berlinski is Jewish (Pearcey 2000). Muzzafar Iqbal, who endorsed Dembski's *No Free Lunch* and is a fellow of Dembski's International Society for Complexity, Information, and Design (ISCID), is a Muslim (ISCID, n.d.).

Fortunately, most Christians have moved far beyond the medieval Christianity that expended such terrifying energy in uprooting "false ideas." They have embraced a more tolerant, more humane faith that can accommodate the workings of nature as explained by modern science; they value the secular, constitutional democracy that makes room for people of all faiths and for people of none. The modern world, with its secular government and naturalistic science, does not threaten them but has enabled them to flourish in their faith and to participate in the wonders of scientific discovery. And the modern, secular academy, at every level, must welcome students regardless of religious preference, including the preference for no religion at all.

Nowhere, however, do Dembski and Richards see a greater threat to their aggressive efforts to save Christianity from the modern world than the "secular academy." Consistent with the Wedge's goal of reversing the accommodation of modern seminaries to evolution, Dembski and Richards (2001) stress the need not only to "transform the mainline seminaries in particular" but also "the secular academic world in general" (14). This includes a great deal: public elementary and secondary schools as well as colleges and universities. But more troubling than their evangelical vision of academic revolution is the fact that, while they want to transform the secular academy, Dembski and Richards do not consider themselves bound by its rules (which, thanks to the Enlightenment, are in principle dedicated to rational argument based on evidence and sound reasoning). Rather, they feel free to ignore the rules governing teaching and learning since the seventeenth century: "The secular academy sets ground rules that doom Christianity from the start. For Christian apologists to play by these rules, whether in the name of ecumenism or pluralism, is to capitulate the faith" (15).

But the only rules by which Christian apologists—and ID theorists—are bound in the secular academy are those which properly bind all scholars: the rules of logic and empirical evidence. These rules have always been the bane of supernaturalists who want respect in the intellectual world, because supernatural claims simply have never yet met the burden of evidence required by rules of responsible scholarship. It is therefore no surprise that Dembski and Richards refuse to abide by them, but they have also conveniently adjusted their *attitude*: "Our work as Christian apologists must be of the highest quality and rigor to deserve the respect of the secular academic community ... Our attitude must combine ... the desire to produce work worthy of respect, and a repudiation of any desire for actual acceptance or respectability" (Dembski and Richards 2001, 14).

Although the Wedge seeks acceptance of ID within the secular academic mainstream, its representatives appear to regard the secular academy—indeed, the secular world—with contempt. They seem in their writings not really to consider themselves part of it, but to have positioned themselves as its adversaries: "We are to engage the secular world, reproving, rebuking and exhorting it, pointing to the truth of Christianity and producing strong arguments and valid criticisms that show where secularism has missed the mark" (Dembski and Richards 2001, 15). In Dembski's case, the dichotomy is both literal and attitudinal. With seven academic degrees, Dembski, who has very little teaching experience even in sectarian universities, appears not to have participated fully and professionally in academic-scholarly life since the 1996 completion of his second Ph.D. (he held a 1997–1999 adjunct teaching job at the [Catholic] University of Dallas). In his August 2003 curriculum vitae he listed not a single affiliation with any secular professional organization; the lengthiest organizational affiliation listed was with the Discovery Institute (Dembski 2003). (After the publication of our book [Forrest and Gross 2004], in which we noted his lack of secular affiliations, he added the American Mathematical Society to his list of "Professional Associations" [Dembski 2004b].) His Discovery Institute fellowship, however, now almost a decade long (1996–present), remains his only long-term affiliation. Dembski, who has no formal science credentials but does have an M.Div., has been hired as the first director of the new Center for Science and Theology at the Southern Baptist Theological Seminary, which he admits is "theologically quite conservative" and where he will be "moving within a natural constituency" (Roots 2004). Yet he wants to "transform" the secular academy. (Given ID's inherent religiosity, and Dembski's thinly disguised description of his International Society for Complexity, Information and Design [ISCID] as a science organization without "programmatic constraints like materialism, naturalism, or reductionism"—in short, science via the supernatural—it hardly qualifies as a secular organization.[7])

Johnson likewise positions himself in opposition to secular academia and intellectuals, with comments such as this: "Given this widespread misunderstanding [that the success of Darwinian science is proof of a materialist metaphysics], secular intellectuals generally assume that texts such as John 1:1–14 express a prescientific mythology that modern people cannot take seriously" (Johnson 2001b). (The Wedge substitutes this New Testament reference to creation for Genesis 1 to downplay differences with young-earth creationists: "In the beginning was the Word, and the Word was with God, and the Word was God. / The same was in the beginning with God. / All things were made by him; and without him was not any thing made that was made.") Persistently and falsely conflating secularism with atheism, Johnson indicts the secularism of fellow academics in a 1995 article in *Academe*, the publication of the American Association of University Professors. Using Yale as an example, he disparages valuable intellectual and political ideals while implying that sectarian Christian doctrines should be integral to academic life:

> By [1951, when Yale had abandoned its Christian orientation,] the Christian atmosphere ... represented little more than a religious veneer over the secular [E]nlightenment values of freedom of inquiry, political equality, and public service ... To the extent that Christianity asserts such distinctive doctrines as that a creator brought about our existence for a purpose, or that Jesus really rose from the dead, it is generally regarded in academic and legal circles as inherently bigoted ... Thus a belief system that retains great vitality in the culture at large is ... marginalized and shut out of academic discourse. (Johnson 1995a)

As always, he sees a direct, causal connection between the academic marginalization of Christianity and "evolutionary naturalism": "The contempt with which many evolutionary biologists regard anyone who doubts their theories has to be experienced to be believed. Evolutionary naturalists like to think of themselves as playing the role of Galileo defying an authoritarian church, but to those of us who are skeptical of naturalism, they would be more appropriately cast as the College of Cardinals" (Johnson 1995a).

Decrying modern higher education's secularism, Johnson never acknowledges the obvious conceptual and epistemological malfunctions of theism as an explanatory principle in science, and indeed as the starting point of much serious inquiry outside science—difficulties that many theistic academics acknowledge honestly and deal with personally in various ways. He also ignores the religious and ethnic diversity of modern American campuses as factors in modern academia's increasing secularization. And quite conveniently for his indictment of the academy's supposed religious bigotry, he ignores the widespread presence on campuses of Christian faculty and student groups—organizations, moreover, that host Johnson's lectures at those universities![8]

Antirationalism

As noted above, Dembski (1999) rejects Enlightenment rationalism, insisting that rationalism and naturalistic explanations in science "are on their way out" (14–15). Johnson, too, combines antisecularism with a deeply rooted antirationalism. In 1993, as a law professor at the University of California at Berkeley, he criticized R. Kent Greenawalt, the noted Columbia University legal scholar, for his acceptance of "the crucial modernist assumption that there exists a common secular rationality capable of resolving some important public issues without relying upon controversial and unprovable (i.e., nonrational [religious]) assumptions" (Johnson 1993). This criticism of Greenawalt stems from Johnson's conviction that true "reason" cannot be divorced from religion, betraying Johnson's deep distrust of rationality. Not only, then, does Johnson's antirationalism imply his wish to disenfranchise academics with honest doubts about religion; it also insults those whose intellectual humility (or wisdom) allows them to encompass both reason and religious commitment.

For Johnson, reason is worthless unless built upon a "biblical theistic" foundation: "From a biblical theistic standpoint, human reason possesses a degree of reliability because God created it in His own image. When human reason denies its basis in creation, it becomes unreason. Those who have thought that they were wise in rejecting God end up as fools, carried along by every intellectual fad and approving every kind of hateful nonsense" (Johnson 1993). Consequently, Johnson sees the secular use of reason as dangerous. He justifies this by appealing to ID's all-purpose bogeyman: evolution, and by indicting secular intellectuals as apostates:

> Modernist thinking assumes the validity of Darwinian evolution, which explains the origin of humans and other living systems by an entirely mechanistic process that excludes in principle any role for a creator ... Secularised intellectuals have long been complacent in their apostasy because they were sure they weren't missing anything important in consigning God to the ashcan of history. (Johnson 1993)

And Johnson considers reliance upon reason, when taken as the backbone of higher learning, to be a distinct threat to Christian students:

> The mind has a tendency to believe what it wants to believe ... So you [students] may be going and getting an education not in order to find out some new truth, but in order to rationalize some error that you want to believe in. For academically gifted people, for bright people, for intellectuals, that's the biggest problem of the mind, because the mind that is clever at test-taking and reasoning is also clever at deceiving itself. So you see, you can't rely on your own mind, because it will betray you. It will trick you. You have to be grounded in something more reliable than your own thinking. (Johnson 2000)

For students, that something must be the Bible and religion, which are the only effective inoculation against reason.

Soldiers in the Culture War

The views and words here examined are those of principal Wedge figures. Johnson founded and has been the Wedge's driving force; Dembski has risen rapidly to its intellectual leadership. Their views are broadly representative of the Wedge as a whole (there are at present over forty fellows in the CSC, and numerous, well-placed supporters outside the organization proper). Clearly divergent views are either scarce or absent within the Wedge. Understanding the premodern theological and political framework upon which the ID movement is built illuminates the strategies and tactics they are using to advance their ultimate objectives, which include the wholesale dismissal of political and intellectual (scientific) paradigms that first appeared in the Enlightenment—and that guided the hopes of America's founders.

Robert Pennock (1999) writes accurately that "Phillip Johnson portrays himself as a soldier in the 'culture wars.'" InterVarsity Press's marketing web page for Johnson's 2002 book *The Right Questions* suggests relevant "Resources for Study and Action"; included is Kreeft's *How to Win the Culture War* (2002), in which Kreeft assumes the combative posture of the culture warrior bent on making "our democracy . . . become democratic":

> You *can* turn a clock back, both literally and figuratively. And you'd better, if the clock is keeping bad time . . . This book will offend many people . . . [and] delight many others: because it is not only *about* a war—a "culture war," a spiritual war, a jihad— but it is itself an *act* of war . . . For it is written on a battlefield, in the heat of battle. It is written for soldiers or potential soldiers, enlistees. It is therefore not a carefully researched, . . . politely academic argument. It is not a sweet violin; it is an ugly, blaring trumpet. On a battlefield, a trumpet works better than a violin. (10–12)

This is exactly how Dembski sees the Wedge. In the foreword to a book by one of his CSC fellows, Dembski himself applies a militaristic metaphor, capturing perfectly the essence of the movement he hails as a scientific research program: "The challenge of Intelligent Design to the evolutionary naturalism of Darwin is not the latest flash in the pan of the culture war but in fact constitutes ground zero of the culture war" (Dembski 2002a). And the metaphor extends to education of the young, where CSC fellow John Mark Reynolds invokes it as a guiding principle of Biola University's Torrey Honors Institute, of which he is director and founder, and which is closely allied with the Wedge. (Biola is one of two universities advertised on Access Research Network as "ID Colleges."[9]) Reynolds declares that "Torrey Honors Institute is at war with the modern culture. Torrey does not want to 'get along' with materialism, secularism, naturalism, post-modernism, radical feminism, or spiritualism. We want to win over every facet of the culture, from the arts to the sciences, for the Kingdom of Christ" (Reynolds n.d.).

Another tactic, rejection of the "ground rules of the secular academy," enables Dembski to use false, overblown rhetoric to denounce the modern scientific worldview: "The scientific picture of the world championed since the Enlightenment is not just wrong but massively wrong. Indeed entire fields of inquiry, especially in the human sciences, will need to be rethought from the ground up in terms of intelligent design" (Dembski 1999, 224). It enabled him in July 2002 to say in the preface of an upcoming book that readers should see the work as a "handbook for replacing an outdated scientific paradigm (Darwinism) and as giving a new scientific paradigm (intelligent design) room to develop and prosper" (Dembski 2004a, 21), but to tell attendees at his October 2002 "RAPID Conference" that "because of ID's outstanding success at gaining a cultural hearing, the scientific research part of ID is lagging behind" (Dembski 2002c). Exempting himself from the academy's rules explains the insincerity of his broad-brush attacks on evolutionary science while lacking scientific credentials in any of the research fields needed to give him credibility. Dembski has no formal scientific training in evolutionary biology or elsewhere (Dembski 2003; 2004b).

The Wedge's cynical view of the "secular academy," which includes public schools, fuels their plan to use public education as the vehicle of their advance. They see the secular system as a false system that must be discarded, or if not discarded, then altered sufficiently through pressure on public opinion, through politics, and by favorable judicial rulings, to allow the inclusion of ID creationism *in science classes*. (John Mark Reynolds has gone so far as to sign the "Proclamation for the Separation of School and State": "I proclaim publicly that I favor ending government involvement in education" [Alliance for the Separation of School and State n.d.].) Dembski views public schools as recruiting grounds for future Wedge followers—to whom he hands off the real task of some day producing that convincing science of "design" that he and his contemporaries in the movement promised more than a decade ago and have so far failed to produce:

> Why should ID supporters allow the Darwinian establishment to indoctrinate students at the high school level, only to divert some of the brightest to becoming supporters of . . . evolution, when by presenting ID at the high school level some of these . . . students would go on to careers . . . to develop ID as a positive research program? If ID is going to succeed as a research program, it will need workers, and these are best recruited at a young age. (Dembski 2002b)

This cynicism explains the Wedge's systematic political intrusions into the scheduled processes of reviewing state science standards—for example, in Kansas and Ohio, where they played a major role in attempting to influence the standards.

Finally, the Wedge's portrayal of themselves as victims of discrimination enables them to tap into a scientifically uninformed public's sense of fairness. Notably—and incongruously, given their denial that ID is religion—while condemning the Enlightenment, ID proponents invoke on their behalf the central Enlightenment principle of religious tolerance when they advertise themselves as victims of religious persecution. In light of the regressive religious and political goals underlying the movement, it is both ironic and amusing for the Wedge thus to have co-opted the vocabulary of liberalism and civil liberties: they cry "viewpoint discrimination" and "religious bigotry" whenever their designs upon science education are thwarted. Stephen C. Meyer testified before the U.S. Civil Rights Commission in 1998:

> Biology texts routinely recapitulate Darwinian arguments against intelligent design, yet if these arguments are philosophically neutral and strictly scientific, why are evidential arguments for intelligent design inherently unscientific and religiously charged? The acceptance of this false asymmetry has justified an egregious form of

viewpoint discrimination in American public science instruction. (U.S. Commission on Civil Rights 1999, 217)

Yet Meyer's testimony was given as part of the commission's "Schools and Religion Project"!

What Is to Be Done?

The aspects of the Wedge Strategy discussed above reflect the ID movement's integral place—and its proponents' consciousness of their role—in the larger "culture war" of which serious observers of contemporary American society are aware. The Wedge's place in the war is that of a key expeditionary force within the larger manpower base of the Religious Right. This is not to imply that the entire Religious Right is of one mind as to goals, or that all its members are irredentists, determined to restore the theocracy of some remote yesteryear. But their own words identify the Wedge's leadership as just such irredentists. And as expeditionary forces, they need to be particularly well trained and to keep ultimate purposes as much in mind as immediate tactics. Their most powerful weapon is their ability to turn respect for science and religious pluralism—the "weapons" of the enemy (modern, secular society)—upon that enemy. They must convince the public and the politicians who sooner or later listen to it that intelligent design *is a sound, scientific theory for which sound empirical evidence has already emerged* and is emerging every day, and that ID must therefore have a full hearing and a recognized place in the education of children. That such a public conviction would have disastrous consequences, not only pedagogically but politically and socially, follows from the fact that the claim is false. So what, then, is to be done?

There are two broad categories of responses and possible solutions to the problem posed by the ID movement: long term and short term. Neither the long- nor the short-term initiatives offer a guarantee of success, and this is deeply worrisome. The terrible strains of modern life, in a world already in the grip of rising religious-fundamentalist violence, are much more likely to enhance the appeal of sectarian religious devotion than to foster cool, analytical reasoning. And they are as likely to breed annoyance and impatience with the U.S. Constitution— that wonderful product of the Enlightenment's children—as to enhance support for it.

Long-Term Initiatives

The longest term initiative, and the most difficult to accomplish, is greatly improved science education across the board: in the K–12 public and private schools, in the colleges and universities, and in the media of public communication. Only when the currently low scientific literacy of the American population rises to the level of accurate and sympathetic understanding of science will the appeal of nonscience, pseudoscience, and just plain bad science diminish sufficiently to disable the quackeries that today prey upon people. But let it be noted: at least in America and probably in the United Kingdom as well, no improvement is to be expected until there are major changes in the way schoolteachers are trained to teach science.[10]

Most important is the undergraduate education of future science teachers. They should learn science in content-heavy curricula in which pedagogy courses are secondary to science courses. The science taught in schools is too often filtered through the teacher-education process in the schools of education. That filter not only thins the real material but often distorts it, sometimes with simple errors of understanding, but sometimes with irrelevant politics. It is not uncommon today for schools to declare that they are teaching physical and earth science by having children participate in mock legal proceedings against polluters.

In addition, it is essential for practicing scientists and other professional scholars of science, working through their agencies, to become regularly involved in public education. Such involvement is today insignificant.[11] Every university should have effective scientific outreach programs for local schools. There are already good ones; there must be many more, and the initiative should come from scientists themselves. A model program in this respect is the one established in conjunction with the annual Darwin Day program at the University of Tennessee–Knoxville (UTK). Staffed by UTK's "Tennessee Darwin Coalition," composed of science professors and graduate students, it offers teacher workshops with other Darwin Day events.[12] Coalition members are avid spokesmen for evolution education, but they should be joined by many biological scientists (not, as now, just a few unselfish ones), all of whom are responsible for confronting and refuting false claims about evolution. The same goes for philosophers and historians of science, for example, in respect to such pseudophilosophical arguments as those of Phillip Johnson on "naturalism," "materialism," "theistic science," and the like. There are now a few who do so, and we should be grateful to them, but there need to be many more.

In addition, there should be closer, regular working relationships between professional, disciplinary science organizations and education societies at all levels: local, state, and national. There are such relationships now, of course. The American Association for the Advancement of Science (AAAS), for example, devotes major resources to such outreach. But it is not nearly enough. More organizations must become involved, and all must be more aggressive. Reasonably enough, the national organizations prefer not to make powerful political enemies—such as members of the U.S. Congress. Yet at some point, they must rock the political boat. Working in unison, they would be powerful enough to resist political reprisals. Commendably, AAAS has spoken out forthrightly against ID (AAAS 2002). So has the always-courageous National Center for Science Education (NCSE). Now it is the turn of those powerful scientific organizations that represent the specific disciplines of science, especially the historical sciences: evolution, geology, cosmology. All, not just AAAS and NCSE, should become engaged. A good start would be to emulate the Society for the Study of Evolution, which, at the urging of its 2003 executive vice president, Massimo Pigliucci, established a permanent taskforce devoted exclusively to counteracting creationism.[13]

Finally, there is the perennial issue of individual scientists acting on their own initiative with proscience school board members and legislators during conflicts such as those created by the Wedge. We refer not just to college and university faculty, but to all scientists, including those in industry and government. This is a huge population of substantively trained people, many also parents of school-children, others in positions of community leadership. Far too few of them get involved in arguments over school curricula, or over legislation with scientific content or implications. We know the usual answer: they are too busy, doing what clearly *is* important work. These days, it takes most of one's intellectual and emotional energy just to keep abreast of the advances in one's scientific field, let alone to survive in the intense competition for grants, academic and professional recognition, and—in industry—a share of the profits. But scientists who do not help are letting others, often laypeople and scholars without relevant scientific expertise, fight the battles from which they, with much at stake for the future of their disciplines, are benefiting.

All scientists are indebted to their excellent colleagues who, sometimes to the detriment of their professional work, have engaged in such creationist conflicts as those in, for example, New Mexico, Kansas, Ohio, and Georgia. In 1998, New Mexico physicist Marshall Berman ran for a seat on the New Mexico Board of Education after the board removed evolution and the age of the earth from New Mexico's public school science standards in 1996. Berman won, and he succeeded in getting that decision reversed (Thomas n.d.). In May 2001, biologist Joseph L. Graves, Jr., joined by Louisiana biologist Dave Schultz of Nicholls State University—with final exams approaching!—testified before the Louisiana legislature's House Education Committee. Both opposed a resolution by African-American legislator Sharon Weston-Broome declaring Darwin and evolution to be the source of modern racism. Graves, also African-American, came on his own initiative to help the handful of scientists who were actively involved (Morgan 2001; Schultz 2001).

But there are not nearly enough such scientist-citizens. The creationist opposition doesn't need that sort of input: it has a well-oiled, well-funded public relations machine that echoes the *feelings* (not knowledge) of many, perhaps most, of the well-meaning but scientifically ill-educated public. If you can't fight a public relations machine with one of equal size and weight, then you must fight it with many individuals who obviously know what they're talking about in science, and who *will* talk.

Short-Term Initiatives

Individual scientists (and qualified scholars in other disciplines) can quickly and easily join, or otherwise ally themselves with, organizations already engaged in defense of scientific truth. But even more to this point, such alliances can be made quickly and easily by *groups* or *organizations* of like-minded scientists. The battle to keep religion out of the science classroom is one of the most clearly focused of all church–state separation battles, and there are active organizations working to preserve the principle and the reality of church–state separation. They operate from the national level, such as Americans United for Separation of Church and State, to the state level, such as the Texas Freedom Network. Their work has often included fighting the legal battles against creationism. We are a diverse society, and our diversity is not just racial and ethnic: it is an enormous cultural diversity, and that includes both religious and nonreligious citizens, all of whom have an interest in preserving secular government and education. There is every reason why scientists and their organizations should now stand up to be counted. The coalition of highly qualified scientists and educators with those groups who have fought the lonely fight, decade after decade, against sectarianism in education and in law-making would have a hugely uplifting effect on those groups—and on those joining them, too.

Finally, there are the issues surrounding the principles that are the legacies of the Enlightenment, the scientific revolution, and the rise of parliamentary democracy. Whatever arguments there are about the consequences (intended and unintended) of various features of modernity, among those principles are some that have earned the understanding and acquiescence of most people, at least, but not solely, in the "developed" world. We refer here to full religious and ethnic tolerance, to the requirement for rationality and evidence-based justification in law and other public undertakings, and to the necessary incubator of all the above—secular government. These issues are too infrequently discussed, much less acted upon, in the hard and detailed business, politics, and political correctness (in each era) of scientific and scholarly societies. But surely, if the threat to those principles from the ID movement *is* as indicated by the words of the Wedge's leaders—a threat of cultural revolution to undo those principles—then scientists and their professional organizations ought right now to stop pussyfooting, stop worrying about potential political enemies or the current speech codes of their universities, or for that matter about their fundraising or parking allotments, and give strong voice to what is right.

There is an efficient way to do this promptly. It can and should be done, especially in states whose boards of education and legislatures are beleaguered by creationists and other religious organizations with political muscle (such as Focus on the Family and its state affiliates). The method is the formation of "truth squads," teams of honest, trained, well-credentialed scholars who can communicate forcefully with school boards, politicians, and the media. (The entire Wedge is an *un*truth squad, in effect.) No single individual can be a truth squad. But a group of honest scholars can, if they are qualified in the subject matter and especially if they have the clerical and organizational machinery of their college or university, or their scientific society, or their company, to support them. There are already groups such as the Center for Media and Public Affairs, which monitors, for example, the use of statistical and other social research "studies" in the media.[14] There are also groups like Kansas Citizens for Science and Ohio Citizens for Science, which sprang up in response to ID efforts in their states; they need help.[15] How appropriate it would be, for example, for the state zoological, geological, physical, and science teachers' societies to mount regular watches on the media, on school science standards, on education committees of legislatures now under intense pressure to please a subpopulation who want God (back) in the science class, and to take early, frequent, and proactive measures! The American Geophysical Union (AGU) has an e-mail alert system for developments affecting geophysical science. AGU also offers workshops on counteracting creationism. The American Geological Institute (AGI) provides e-mail alerts and special updates to its members. The American Institute of Biological Sciences (AIBS) has listservs in each state to facilitate communication among concerned activists.[16] State science and education organizations should do likewise, extending their contacts to the local level and linking their efforts with these national ones.

This sort of effort, which can be organized in a matter of a few weeks or months, must exist *before* there is a stealth attack on science education, not *after* one has begun. It doesn't take much time or effort until a skirmish actually starts, but only if the truth squad—ready with a scientifically competent response—is set up and ready to go, is there a chance of putting out the brushfire. Once it starts, the resulting conflagration needs real troops and celebrities to fight it, and that takes more dedication and resources than single scientists or local groups of them can usually manage ad hoc. Scientists are essential in this effort: *they are the only people who know the science needed to fight the pseudoscience.* But they have valuable community allies who can provide assistance: parent–teacher organizations, mainstream clergy, humanist groups, civil liberties organizations—in short, anyone who benefits from the Enlightenment legacies upon which America truly was founded.

Conclusion

Frederick Clarkson, who writes invaluable and underutilized exposés of the Religious Right for *Public Eye* magazine, warns that not only are the culture wars *not* over, but that views once considered extreme are entering the mainstream: "The major institutions of the Christian Right, once bastions of fire and brimstone rhetoric and a transcendent vision of the once and future Christian Nation, have become practitioners of political compromise and coalition building . . . and perhaps most important, the Christian Right is now largely institutionalized throughout society" (Clarkson 2001). We have described a facet of the ID movement that has not received the scrutiny proportionate to its pivotal significance in this larger effort— national in scope—to restructure American institutions and government policy on a sectarian, theistic foundation.

Christian philosopher Robert Audi, in his *Religious Commitment and Secular Reason*, acknowledges forthrightly the difficulties that theists face when they attempt to influence public policy according to their religious loyalties. He also points out the danger of allowing personal religious faith to erupt into politically charged fanaticism. One passage reads as though it might have been crafted especially to describe the Wedge, especially Dembski, whose comments on "heresy" are so chilling:

> There is a danger not only of one religion's dominating others or non-religious people, but also of one person's doing so, or one religiously powerful coterie's doing so . . . , or at least of one or more zealots taking themselves to be important in a way that makes them uncooperative as citizens. This may be in or outside politics. The belief in a supreme God with sovereignty over the world should induce humility, but it need not. Indeed, the better one thinks one represents God—especially when God is being ignored or disobeyed—the more important one may naturally think one is oneself . . . There is a kind of zeal that . . . can erode citizenship and, sometimes, substitute a personal vision for genuine religious inspiration. (Audi 2000, 102)

Audi conveys well the message we have tried to communicate in seeing the Wedge as part of the larger Religious Right network. But if we who value the secular, constitutional democracy constructed by the country's founders, and the understanding of nature made possible by modern science, wish for these legacies to survive for our children and grandchildren, we would do well to heed not only Audi's moving expression of concern, but Kramnick and Moore's more pragmatically phrased one in *The Godless Constitution*:

> Should we be worried? The answer given in this book is yes, . . . [We] are concerned about current pronouncements made by politically charged religious activists, . . . the Religious Right. Their crusade is an old one . . . Whenever religion of any kind casts itself as the one true faith and starts trying to arrange public policy accordingly, people who believe that they have a stake in free institutions, whatever else might divide them politically, had better look out. (1997, 12)

Notes

1. The plan is outlined in "The Wedge Strategy," formulated by the CSC under its original name, Center for the Renewal of Science and Culture. See Discovery Institute, Center for the Renewal of Science and Culture, n.d. Forrest and Gross (2004) discuss the document's authenticity. Discovery Institute now acknowledges ownership of it. Written sometime in the late 1990s as a fund-raising tool, the ten-page document outlined the Wedge's short- and long-term goals, followed by a "Wedge Strategy Process Summary."

2. Please note the implied definition of "direct evidence."

3. The CSC's stated reason for its 2002 name change is that "the former was simply too long and we got tired of saying it." A more likely explanation, ironically, is its desire to pose as a secular entity for strategic purposes, e.g., presenting itself to school boards as a scientific organization. The CSC announced the change in early 2003 in "The Center's Name Change" at www.crsc.org/TopQuestions/nameChange.html. See also the National Center for Science Education's "Evolving Banners at the Discovery Institute" at www.ncseweb.org/resources/articles/4116_evolving_banners_at_the_discov_8_29_2002.asp (Oakland, CA: NCSE). Accessed on December 12, 2004.

4. Theocracy has historically taken different forms and has several meanings. According to Dewey D. Wallace (1987), "Theocracy . . . refers to a type of government in which God or gods are thought to have sovereignty, or to any state so governed" (427). Although the concept of theocracy has no rigorous definition in either social science or the history of religion and does not denote a specific political system (as does "monarchy," e.g.), it "designates a certain kind of placement of the ultimate source of state authority, regardless of the form of government" (427). Four types are designated: "hierocracy, or rule by religious functionaries; royal theocracy, or rule by a sacred king; general theocracy, or rule in a more general sense by a divine will or law; and eschatological theocracy, or future rule by the divine" (427). The meaning we intend with respect to the Wedge's theocratic ambitions is general theocracy, which is "by far the most common, . . . that more general type wherein ultimate authority is considered to be vested in a divine law or revelation, mediated through a variety of structures and polities" (429). This type embodies an ideal shared by the theocracies of John Calvin, Oliver Cromwell, and the Massachusetts Puritans: "a holy community on earth in which the sovereignty was God's and in which the actual law should reflect the divine will and the government seek to promote the divine glory" (429). In Cromwell's England and the Massachusetts Bay Colony, "there was both a hearkening after Old Testament theocratic patterns and a sense of the

importance of government entrusted to truly regenerate persons—or the saints—in an effort to create a holy commonwealth," in which "rule was exercised . . . more through a godly laity than through the clergy" (429). This is the closest description of what the Wedge seems to favor. For example, in "Nihilism and the End of Law" (Johnson 1993), Johnson's disapproval of secular law and longing for a God-based legal system pervades his entire discussion. Johnson, in *Reason in the Balance: The Case against Naturalism in Science, Law, and Education* (1995b), speaks nostalgically of a time when law was biblically based, but disapprovingly of modern, secular law:

> For much of Western history, lawmakers assumed that authoritative moral guidance was available to them in the Bible and in the religious traditions based on the Bible . . . [But] modernist culture retains the prohibition of theft and murder, retains the sabbath merely as a secular day of recreation, discards the admonition to have 'no other gods before me' as meaningless, and regards ambivalently the prohibition of adultery and the command to honor parents. (39)

Johnson's subtitle indicates the "structures and polities" through which he believes divine law should be mediated: science, law, and education.

5. For an example of such denials, see West (2002). For the evidence establishing that ID is merely the most recent form of traditional creationism, see Forrest and Gross (2004, 273–296).

6. For a more detailed discussion of the ID movement's alliances with theocratic individuals and organizations, see Forrest and Gross (2004, 270–273).

7. See the ISCID website at www.iscid.org.

8. See Forrest and Gross (2004, chs. 7, 9), in which we discuss the Wedge's inroads into secular higher education and their alliances with evangelical student and faculty organizations.

9. The other is Oklahoma Baptist University. See "ID Colleges," at www.arn.org/college.htm (Colorado Springs, CO: Access Research Network).

10. For discussion of this and related issues, see Gross (2000).

11. For a good discussion of the need for scientists to become involved in addressing the problem of creationism, see Massimo Pigliucci (2002, ch. 8).

12. The details of this program are available on the Tennessee Darwin Coalition website at http://fp.bio.utk.edu/darwin/bios.html. Accessed on December 10, 2004.

13. See Pigliucci's July 19, 2001, announcement of the establishment of the taskforce as a subcommittee of SSE's Education Committee at www.csicop.org/list/listarchive/msg00248.html. Accessed on December 10, 2004. Barbara Forrest, as president of Citizens for the Advancement of Science Education (CASE), provided a letter of support.

14. See the CMPA's "Science and Health Studies" web page at www.cmpa.com. Accessed on March 1, 2004.

15. See their respective websites at www.kcfs.org and www.OhioScience.org. Accessed on December 10, 2004.

16. For details on AGU, AGI, and AIBS efforts, see www.agu.org/sci_soc/policy/sci_pol.html, www.agiweb.org/gap/email/index.html, and www.aibs.org/mailing-lists/the_aibs-ncse_evolution_list_server.html, respectively. Accessed on December 10, 2004.

References

AAAS. 2002. "AAAS Board Resolution on Intelligent Design Theory" (October 18). Washington, DC: American Association for the Advancement of Science. Accessed on March 1, 2004, at www.aaas.org/news/releases/2002/1106id2.shtml.

Alliance for the Separation of School and State. n.d. "VIP Endorsements of the Separation of School and State." Fresno, CA: Alliance for the Separation of School and State. Accessed on December 10, 2004, at www.HonestEd.com/vips/index.php.

Audi, Robert. 2000. *Religious Commitment and Secular Reason*. New York: Cambridge University Press.

Behe, Michael J. 1998. "Tulips and Dandelions." *Books and Culture* (September/October). Accessed on February 5, 2004, at http://web.archive.org/web/20030622153241/http://www.christianitytoday.com/bc/8b5/8b5034.html.

Clarkson, Frederick. 2001. "The Culture Wars Are Not Over: The Institutionalization of the Christian Right." *Public Eye* (Spring). Accessed on February 6, 2004, at www.publiceye.org/magazine/v15n1/State_of_Christian_Rt.htm#TopOfPage.

Dembski, William A. 1999. *Intelligent Design: The Bridge between Science and Theology*. Downers Grove, IL: InterVarsity Press.

———. 2001a. "Is Intelligent Design a Form of Natural Theology?" Philadelphia, PA: Metanexus Institute (May 11). Accessed on February 5, 2004, at www.metanexus.net/metanexus_online/show_article.asp?3130.

———. 2001b. "The Task of Apologetics." In *Unapologetic Apologetics: Meeting the Challenges of Theological Studies*, edited by William A. Dembski and Jay Wesley Richards. Downers Grove, IL: InterVarsity Press.

———. 2002a. Foreword to *Moral Darwinism: How We Became Hedonists*, by Benjamin Wiker. Downers Grove, IL: InterVarsity Press. Accessed on March 13, 2004, at www.designinference.com/documents/2002.06.foreword_ben_wiker.htm.

———. 2002b. "Then and Only Then: A Response to Mike Gene." "Intelligent Design Forum" (July 26). Colorado Springs, CO: Post to Access Research Network. Accessed on February 6, 2004, at www.arn.org/ubb/ultimatebb.php?ubb=get_topic;f=13;t=000220#000000.

———. 2002c. "Becoming a Disciplined Science: Prospects, Pitfalls, and Reality Check for ID." Address delivered at Research and Progress in Intelligent Design (RAPID) conference (October 25). Accessed on February 6, 2004, at www.designinference.com/documents/2002.10.27.Disciplined_Science.htm.

———. 2003. "Curriculum Vitae" (August). Design Inference Website: William A. Dembski. Accessed on February 6, 2004, at www.designinference.com/documents/CVpdf.aug2003.pdf.

———. 2004a. *The Design Revolution: Answering the Toughest Questions about Intelligent Design*. Downers Grove, IL: InterVarsity Press.

———. 2004b. "Curriculum Vitae" (July). Design Inference Website: William A. Dembski. Accessed on December 11, 2004, at www.designinference.com/documents/PDF_Current_CV_Dembski.pdf.

Dembski, William A., and Jay Wesley Richards. 2001. "Reclaiming Theological Education." In *Unapologetic Apologetics: Meeting the Challenges of Theological Studies*, edited by William A. Dembski and Jay Wesley Richards. Downers Grove, IL: InterVarsity Press.

Discovery Institute. 2004. "The 'Wedge Document'—'So What?'" Seattle, WA: Discovery Institute. Accessed on February 20, 2004, at www.crsc.org/TopQuestions/wedgeresp.pdf.

Discovery Institute, Center for the Renewal of Science and Culture. n.d. "The Wedge Strategy" [Fund-raising proposal]. Seattle, WA: Discovery Institute. Accessed on December 11, 2004, at www.antievolution.org/features/wedge.html.

Forrest, Barbara. 2004. "A Defense of Naturalism as a Defense of Secularism." In *Sidney Hook Reconsidered*, edited by Matthew J. Cotter. Amherst, NY: Prometheus Books.

Forrest, Barbara, and Paul R. Gross. 2004. *Creationism's Trojan Horse: The Wedge of Intelligent Design*. New York: Oxford University Press.

Gross, Paul R. 2000. "Politicizing Science Education." Washington, DC: Thomas B. Fordham Foundation. Accessed on March 1, 2004, at www.edexcellence.net/doc/Gross.pdf.

Hartwig, Mark. 2001. "The Meaning of Intelligent Design." *Boundless* (July 18). Colorado Springs, CO: Focus on the Family. Accessed on February 5, 2004, at www.boundless.org/2000/features/a0000455.html.

ISCID. n.d. "Society Fellows." Princeton, NJ: International Society for Complexity, Information, and Design. Accessed on March 13, 2004, at www.iscid.org/fellows.php.

Johnson, Phillip E. 1993. "Nihilism and the End of Law." *First Things* (March). New York: Institute on Religion and Public Life. Accessed on February 6, 2004, at www.firstthings.com/ftissues/ft9303/articles/pjohnson.html.

————. 1994a. "Is God Unconstitutional? The Established Religion of America," Part 1, *The Real Issue* (September/October). Addison, TX: Christian Leadership Ministries. Accessed on February 5, 2004, at www.leaderu.com/real/ri9403/johnson.html.

————. 1994b. "Is God Unconstitutional? The Established Religion of America," Part 2, *The Real Issue* (November/December). Addison, TX: Christian Leadership Ministries. Accessed on February 5, 2004, at www.leaderu.com/real/ri9404/johnson2.html.

————. 1995a. "What (If Anything) Hath God Wrought?" *Academe* (September/October). Washington, DC: American Association of University Professors. Accessed on February 6, 2004, at www.arn.org/docs/johnson/aaup.htm.

————. 1995b. *Reason in the Balance: The Case against Naturalism in Science, Law and Education*. Downers Grove, IL: InterVarsity Press.

————. 1996. "How to Sink a Battleship: A Call to Separate Materialist Philosophy from Empirical Science." *The Real Issue* (November/December). Addison, TX: Christian Leadership Ministries. Accessed on February 5, 2004, at www.leaderu.com/real/ri9602/johnson.html.

————. 2000. Interview by Hank Hanegraaff. *Bible Answer Man* radio program (December 19). Rancho Santa Margarita, CA: Christian Research Institute.

————. 2001a. Foreword to *Unapologetic Apologetics: Meeting the Challenges of Theological Studies*, edited by William A. Dembski and Jay Wesley Richards. Downers Grove, IL: InterVarsity Press.

————. 2001b. Letter. In "Edward T. Oakes and His Critics: An Exchange." *First Things* (April). New York: Institute on Religion and Public Life. Accessed on February 6, 2004, at www.firstthings.com/ftissues/ft0104/correspondence-oakes.html.

————. 2002a. *The Right Questions: Truth, Meaning and Public Debate*. Downers Grove, IL: InterVarsity Press.

————. 2002b. "The Dick Staub Interview: Phillip Johnson." *Christianity Today* (December 3). Accessed on February 5, 2004, at www.christianitytoday.com/ct/2002/147/22.0.html.

————. 2003. Interview by Hank Hanegraaff. *Bible Answer Man* radio program (February 20). Rancho Santa Margarita, CA: Christian Research Institute.

Kramnick, Isaac, and R. Laurence Moore. 1997. *The Godless Constitution: The Case against Religious Correctness*. New York: W. W. Norton.

Kreeft, Peter. 2002. *How to Win the Culture War*. Downers Grove, IL: InterVarsity Press.

Morgan, Fiona. 2001. "Louisiana Calls Darwin a Racist." *Salon* (May 4). Accessed on February 6, 2004, at http://archive.salon.com/news/feature/2001/05/04/darwin/.

Pearcey, Nancy. 2000. "We're Not in Kansas Anymore." *Christianity Today* (May). Accessed on February 6, 2004, at www.christianitytoday.com/ct/2000/006/1.42.html.

Pennock, Robert T. 1999. "The Science Pages." *Books and Culture* (September/October). Accessed on February 14, 2004, at www.ctlibrary.com/bc/1999/septoct/9b5031.html.

Pigliucci, Massimo. 2002. *Denying Evolution: Creationism, Scientism, and the Nature of Science*. Sunderland, MA: Sinauer Associates.

Reynolds, John Mark. n.d. "Origin of Torrey." La Mirada, CA: Torrey Honors Institute, Biola University. Accessed on February 6, 2004, at www.biola.edu/academics/torrey/about/reynolds.cfm.

Roots, Kimberly. 2004. "Dembski to Head Seminary's Faith and Science Center." *Science and Theology News* (November). Quincy, MA: Science and Theology News. Accessed on December 11, 2004, at www.stnews.org/archives/2004_november/news_dembski_1104.html.

Schaefer, Henry F. n.d. "Questions Intellectuals Ask about Christianity: A Public Lecture by Henry 'Fritz' Schaefer," Leadership University. Addison, TX: Christian Leadership Ministries. Accessed on February 5, 2004, at www.leaderu.com/offices/schaefer/docs/questions.html.

Schultz, Dave. 2001. "Dave Schultz on House Education Committee Resolution 74—Published in the *Houma Courier*." New Orleans, LA: New Orleans Secular Humanist Association. Accessed on February 6, 2004, at http://nosha.secularhumanism.net/essays/schultz1.html.

Thomas, Dave. n.d. "Creationism in New Mexico." Albuquerque, NM: New Mexicans for Science and Reason. Accessed on February 6, 2004, at www.nmsr.org/nmevhist.htm.

U.S. Commission on Civil Rights. 1999. *Schools and Religion: Executive Summary and Transcripts of Proceedings Held in Washington, DC, New York City, and Seattle, WA, Spring/Summer 1998*. Washington, DC: United States Commission on Civil Rights.

Wallace, Dewey D., Jr. 1987. "Theocracy." In *The Encyclopedia of Religion*, edited by Mircea Eliade, 427–430. New York: Macmillan.

West, John G., Jr. 2002. "Intelligent Design and Creationism Just Aren't the Same." *Research News and Opportunities in Science and Theology* (December 1). Accessed on December 10, 2004, at www.arn.org/docs2/news/idandcreationismnotsame011503.htm.

13

When Science Teaching Becomes a Subversive Activity

Pervez Hoodbhoy

I cannot quite decide which is the more dangerous of the two: George Bush and his determination to ensure American military supremacy, or the exploding power of brutal fundamentalist religious forces in countries such as mine (Pakistan). Only the latter concerns me in this chapter.[1] Believing only in their own version of divinely revealed truths, fundamentalists everywhere fiercely oppose women rights, controlling the world's exploding population, or personal liberty in matters of what you may wear, eat, or drink. Claiming divine sanction for their mission to reform society, they derive additional succor from academic postmodernists in the West who have pronounced scientific truths to be mere social and linguistic constructs. Left unopposed, they will surely take us back to the glorious days when the world was without sin.

Incredibly, 400 years after the scientific revolution, we are still here talking about science as a subversive activity, and a moral force for a better world. One might have thought that the battering ram of science and reason, having ceaselessly hammered away for nearly 400 years, by now would have brought down the castles of Christian orthodoxy. You in the West have a wonderful repertoire of heroes—Bruno, Wycliffe, Galileo, and countless others—who stood up against the fanaticism unleashed by the medieval church. Therefore, one wishes that with the Enlightenment they helped bring about, all who profit from human fears of the unknown and spread terror with their terrible threats of eternal hell would have gone with the dinosaurs. But alas, as I visit the United States once again and tune to any of the Christian radio stations, I can see clearly that this has not happened. Today, multiple purveyors of spiritual bliss are in business, preying upon weak minds and spirits, and dwelling upon the fear of death and the unknown. They reject scientifically valid theories such as biological evolution, and battle to limit research and inquiry into nature.

Nevertheless, it is very fortunate that everyone present here lives in the twenty-first century. I, too, share this century with you—part of the time. But about the rest, I'm not so totally sure. A time warp puts me, and the people of my country, somewhere between the seventh and eighth centuries. At other times it seems to be around the fifteenth century or so. Quite definitely, however, it is not the period between the ninth and the fourteenth centuries, when Islamic civilization was in its most intellectually productive and brilliant phase. That was the time when a spirit of relative liberalism and tolerance produced first-rate scientists, philosophers, and scholars such as Al-Kindi, Ibn-Sina, Al-Razi, Ibn-Rushd, Ibn-Khaldun, and many others. They survived persecution by the religious orthodoxy of those times, assisted by their powerful but enlightened patrons, the caliphs and sultans. It was this flowering of the intellect in the lands of Islam that had fueled the European Renaissance.

Tragically, Islam is in a very different phase today. In countries such as Pakistan, where Islam is the state religion and declared to be above the constitution, religion is considered the source of all wisdom and knowledge, including scientific knowledge. This version of Islam—though impossible to follow in its intricate details—is totalistic. It determines what you may eat or drink, how you may dress, and the relation between men and women and is the single-most important determinant of political and social life of the country. No Pakistani airline flight takes off without a prayer relayed over the public address system. A ruling by the highest Islamic court in the country, which the government is finding impossible to implement, has banned interest and decreed that the entire banking structure will have to be revamped. Women by law receive half the inheritance of a man. Furthermore, in a court of law, the testimony of two women is equal to that of one man. But a man may marry up to four women at a time.

To protect this way of life—which may have been quite appropriate in centuries past—the state has at its disposal an enormous amount of power backed by guns, tanks, and now even nuclear weapons. In such a situation, one asks the question, How can there ever be hope for my country, and the many others like it? And how is it possible for us to join the forward march of humanity? To my mind, the answer lies in silent subversion, subversion through the teaching of science.

Subversion comes naturally to science because it is wholly based upon critical inquiry, a fact that automatically makes it unwelcome to all ideologies and faiths. But fortunately, science is also a marvelous Trojan Horse with an enormously attractive exterior. It brings with it all the good things of life—cars, planes, computers, refrigerators, life-saving medicines, soft drinks, and bubble gum. Even members of the Taliban carry cell phones and drive SUVs, although television and the Internet are banned (and chewing gum could also make the list one day). But this great horse also hides within it certain germs, the pathogenic substances that soundlessly attack and weaken cherished beliefs from within.

To understand why science has been so destructive of irrational beliefs, let us go back to the epic trial of Galileo. It was not a question of cosmology or physics that worked the papacy into a hangman's frenzy. Whether the sun goes around the earth, or vice versa, the church couldn't really have cared. Crucially important, however, was that the Word of God stood in danger of being shown up. If, heaven forbid, the earth actually went around the sun then the Bible would be proven wrong, suggesting that its Author would have flunked even freshman physics. This would have placed into jeopardy the entire text of the Bible, including all miracles and all the glorious stories of Joshua, Gideon, and so forth. Science, which nags constantly for empirical proof and obsessively asks for reasons, was just too annoying to be tolerated.

Muslims, who hold that the Bible has suffered distortion in the process of trans-mission, are quite unfazed by the Galileo episode. But there is a deeper level of anxiety among them today than ever before. The cause for this is not unreasonable. For Muslims, the Qu'ran is the literal word of God—unchanged, undistorted, and pure. This is believed to be so because it was orally transmitted over the early decades of Islam, and hence not subject to the accuracy of scribes. Even today, in conservative Islamic societies, when a child grows up, the first thing he learns to read and memorize is the Qur'an. In more liberal societies it comes later. The in-tegrity of the Qur'an cannot be challenged, except upon pain of death.

Given this situation, and confronted with a world that has been created by the extraordinary successes of modern science, those who hold the Qur'an to be the literal word of God have felt compelled to come up with explanations for holy verses pertaining specifically to physical phenomena—the rising and setting of the sun, meteorites streaking across the sky, rain and drought, earthquakes, the hu-man embryo and reproduction, and so forth. Thus, scientific proofs of the Qur'an are anxiously awaited and eagerly seized upon. One indication is the immense popularity across the Muslim world of a book authored by a Frenchman, Maurice Bucaille, entitled *The Bible, the Qur'an, and Science*. It has sold millions of copies and been translated into several languages. The reason for this popularity is not hard to understand—the author has proved, to his full satisfaction, that the Bible is wrong and the Qur'an right in every scientific matter.

While such attempts give some comfort to literalists, it is not enough. Science is still considered dangerous. Indeed, Islamic orthodoxy has indeed come to recognize science as an invasive foreign body and developed a range of distinct immune responses. These fall into three principal categories.

At one level, there is outright rejection of scientific explanations and material causes. Cause and effect must be divorced from each other lest the universe appear to run like a mechanical system. A guide to teaching chemistry in the Islamic way, published in Islamabad, decries the usual way in which the formation of water from hydrogen and oxygen is taught. No, says the book, the teacher must say that when hydrogen and oxygen combine, then, by the Will of Allah, they turn into water.

The same logic applies to calamities. So, for example, something like AIDS occurs because it is divine retribution for immoral behavior, and searching for a cure is both impossible and sinful. Earthquakes too happen because you've been bad. I had a very direct personal experience with this in 1974 when there was a major earthquake in Pakistan that killed nearly 10,000 people. Together with a few of my university colleagues in Islamabad, I had gone for relief work in the distant moun-tains beneath which lay the quake epicenter. Our work was derided as useless and counterproductive by a co-traveling team of proselytizing men with beards be-longing to the Tableeghi Jamaat because, in their opinion, the calamity was purely on account of the affected people's immoral behavior. They had come to preach piety as the sole defense against a heaving, bucking earth.

A second response has been to create a mutated species, but belonging to the same genotype. The new "Islamic science," propagated by the orthodox and lib-erally dosed with postmodernist jargon, is their reply to "Western science." As in the case in the "Creationist science" you are familiar with, causality, logic, and the usual burdensome proofs required by science are happily dispensed with. The practitioners of Islamic science are primarily Ph.D.s who have retired, or are inactive, in the scientific fields they were originally trained in. Hundreds of articles have been published in "scientific journals" and presented in dozens of "Islam and science" conferences. So, for example, the former head of my department combined Einstein's theory of relativity with a verse from the Qur'an, and thereby established that heaven is running away from earth at one centimeter per second less than the speed of light. Others have used Coulombs's law to calculate the degree of hypocrisy (*munafiqat*) in a society, estimated the temperature of Hell, and calculated the chemical composition of *djinnis* (a certain class of fiery spiritual beings).

Perhaps more commonplace than either of the above two kinds of responses is to claim ownership of all scientific discoveries made up to the present—as well as those that will be made in the future. The view that these were anticipated in the Qur'an some 1,400 years ago is widely propagated on state television, and (I suspect) held to be true by many, if not most people, including my students in the university. Provided one learns one's Arabic properly, and does a correct exegesis of the Qur'an, then out will pop the Big Bang theory, black holes, quantum mechanics, DNA, cloning, chaos, and whatever your heart desires. Dozens of conferences have had this message as their basic theme, but perhaps none can rival the grand "First International Conference on Scientific Miracles of the Holy Quran and Sunnah," held by the organization of the same name in Islamabad in 1987, and funded by the Pakistani state to the tune of a couple of million dollars. It brought together 200 Muslim delegates from all over the world. A second conference organized by the same organization is now being scheduled elsewhere.

The problem with such claims to ownership is that they lack an explanation for why quantum mechanics, molecular genetics, and so forth, had to await discovery elsewhere first. Nor is any kind of testable prediction ever made. The same problem lies with technology and inventions: no reason is offered as to why antibiotics, aspirin, steam engines, electricity, aircraft, or computers were not first invented by Muslims. But then, even to ask such questions is considered offensive.

The increasing strength of Islamic movements today, which are largely orthodox and antiscience, has definite material roots. These can be traced to the brutal colonization of Muslim lands from the eighteenth century onward by the imperial powers, their continued domination and humiliation by the West and Israel, and the failure of secular governments in Muslim countries during the latter half of the previous century. Tragically, such reactionary movements can only take Muslims further backward.

In the decades and centuries to come, real science will come into ever sharper confrontation with every kind of pseudoscience, not just in Muslim countries but everywhere. As the pace of scientific discovery accelerates, even college-educated individuals will find it harder to deal with a bewilderingly complex environment. The temptation to opt for simplistic solutions will grow.

Science by itself is not enough to liberate humankind and create a better world. But without science there is little chance of this. For it to be socially progressive, it must not be reduced to a mere functional and utilitarian tool, or to a set of arbitrary rules and an endless number of facts. Science teaching should inspire reflection and enhance our capacity to wonder. I suspect that much of the postmodernist drivel on science, brilliantly exposed by the physicist Alan Sokal, owes to the unfortunate circumstances in which the authors encountered science in their high schools. This is truly sad because there are profound truths that can be discovered only by using the methods of science: how the universe began, why stars shine, whether other planetary civilizations exist, the mysterious world inside an atom, the marvelous molecular arrangements that make DNA and life, and much more. In truth, science is what makes us truly human; without it there would be little but the simple life of the rain forest and the prairie, and no common language shared by different members of the human family.

Note

1. This chapter is based on a talk that was given at the annual meeting of the American Association for the Advancement of Science, held in San Francisco in 2001.

Reference

Bucaille, Maurice. *The Bible, the Qur'an, and Science: The Holy Scriptures Examined in the Light of Modern Knowledge*. Indianapolis, IN: American Trust Publications, 1979.

14

Postmodernism, Hindu Nationalism, and "Vedic Science"

Meera Nanda

In this chapter I first examine how Hindu nationalists construct the myth of "the Vedas as books of science." I claim that the relativist rhetoric of postmodern intellectuals has given philosophical respectability to the eclectic patchwork of science and Hindu metaphysics that goes under the name of "Vedic science." I argue that the mixing up of the mythos of the Vedas with the logos of science must be of great concern not just to the scientific community, but also to religious people, for it is a distortion of both science and spirituality.

I then turn to the philosophical arguments for "alternative sciences" favored by prominent feminists, environmentalists, and postcolonial intellectuals and show how they converge with the right wing's claims of the superiority of "holistic" and "authentic" sciences of Hindus. Although they vehemently disagree about politics, the proponents of religiously based "Vedic science" and culturally based "alternative science" both draw support from postmodernist critiques of science and both threaten the advancement of civil society in India.

The Vedas as Books of Science

In 1996, the British chapter of the World Hindu Council, or Vishwa Hindu Parishad (VHP), produced a slick-looking book, with many well-produced pictures of colorfully dressed men and women performing Hindu ceremonies, accompanied by a warm, fuzzy, and completely sanitized description of the faith. The book, *Explaining Hindu Dharma: A Guide for Teachers* (Prinja 1986), offers "teaching suggestions for introducing Hindu ideas and topics in the classroom" at the middle to high-school level in the British school system. The authors and editors are all card-carrying members of the VHP, the cultural wing of the "family" of parties that make up the right-wing Hindu nationalists in India.[1] The book is now in its second edition and, going by the glowing reviews on the back cover, it seems to have established itself as a much-used educational resource in the British school system.

What "teaching suggestions" does this guide offer? It advises British teachers to introduce Hindu dharma as "just another name" for "eternal laws of nature" first discovered by Vedic seers, and subsequently confirmed by modern physics and biological sciences. After giving a false but incredibly smug account of mathematics, physics, astronomy, medicine, and evolutionary theory contained in the Vedic texts, the guide instructs the teachers to present the Vedic scriptures as "not just old religious books, but as books which contain many true scientific facts...these *ancient scriptures of the Hindus can be treated as scientific texts*" (emphasis added). All that modern science teaches us about the workings of nature can be found in the Vedas, and all that the Vedas teach about the nature of matter, god, and human beings is affirmed by modern science. There is no conflict, there are no contradictions. Modern science and the Vedas are simply "different names for the same truth."

This is the image of Hinduism that the VHP and other Hindutva propagandists want to project around the world. The British case is not an isolated example. Similar initiatives to portray Vedic-Aryan India as the "cradle" of world civilization and science have been launched in Canada and the United States as well.[2] Many of these initiatives are beneficiaries of the generous and politically correct policies of multicultural education in these countries. Under the worthy cause of presenting the "community's" own views about its culture, many Western governments are inadvertently funding Hindutva's propaganda.

But what concerns me in this chapter is not the "Yankee Hindutva" agitators who are importing Hindu chauvinistic politics from India into the West. My concern is with the export of ideas from the West that are providing aid and comfort to the Hindu chauvinists in India. Our concern is with the left-wing postmodern and postcolonial intellectuals in the West, many of them of Indian origin and all sworn enemies of religious fundamentalists, who have given respectability to a set of ideas about science and modernity that are very conducive to a Hindu right-wing project of creating a culturally authentic "Hindu modernity" in India. This "Hindu modernity" is a reactionary modernity,[3] as it aggressively presses modern technology (everything from information technology to nuclear bombs) in the service of an irrational, occult, New Age cosmology derived from upper-caste, Brahminical sacred books. This cosmology has been a source of much social oppression throughout India's history and has staged a comeback, with the full backing of the Indian state, under the just-toppled regime of the Hindu nationalists.[4]

Over the last couple of decades, a set of very fashionable, supposedly "radical" critiques of modern science have dominated Western universities. These critical theories of science go under the label of "postmodernism" or "social constructivism." These theories see modern science as an essentially Western, masculine, and imperialistic way of acquiring knowledge. Intellectuals of Indian origin, many of them living and working in the West, have played a leading role in the development of postmodernist critiques of modern science as a source of colonial "violence" against non-Western ways of knowing.[5]

In this chapter, I examine how this postmodernist left has provided philosophical arguments for Hindutva's claim that Vedas are "just another name" for modern science. As I show here, postmodernist attacks on objective and universal knowledge have played straight into the traditional Hindu view of all perspectives being equally true—within their own context and at their own level. The result is the loud—but false—claims of finding a tradition of empirical science in the spiritual teachings of the Vedas and Vedanta. Such scientization of the Vedas does nothing to actually promote an empirical and rational tradition in India, while it does an incalculable harm to the spiritual message of Hinduism's sacred books.

Before I proceed with this task, I must clarify what I mean by postmodernism.

What Is Postmodernism?

Postmodernism is a mood, a disposition. The chief characteristic of the postmodernist disposition is that it is opposed to the Enlightenment, which is taken to be the core of modernism. Of course, there is no simple characterization of the Enlightenment any more than there is of postmodernism. A rough and ready portrayal might go like this: Enlightenment is a general attitude fostered in the seventeenth and eighteenth centuries on the heels of the Scientific Revolution; it aims to replace superstition and authority of traditions and established religions with critical reason represented, above all, by the growth of modern science. The Enlightenment project was based upon a hope that improvement in secular scientific knowledge would lead to an improvement of the human condition, not just materially but also ethically and culturally. While the Enlightenment spirit flourished primarily in Europe and North America, intellectual movements in India, China, Japan, Latin America, Egypt, and other parts of West Asia were also influenced by it. However, the combined weight of colonialism and cultural nationalism thwarted the Enlightenment spirit in non-Western societies.[6]

Postmodernists are disillusioned with this triumphalist view of science dispelling ignorance and making the world a better place. Their despair leads them to question the possibility of progress toward some universal truth that everyone, everywhere must accept. They argue instead that modern science, which we take to be moving closer to objective truth about nature, is actually just one culture-bound way to look at nature, no better or worse than all other sciences of other cultures. Not just the agenda, but the content of all knowledge is socially constructed. The supposed "facts" of modern science are "Western" constructions, reflecting the interests and cultural biases of the dominant social groups in the Western societies. Postmodernists tend to scoff at the conventional boundaries between science and pseudo-sciences as a mark of elitism and claim to maintain an open mind to a whole range of ways of knowing available around the world.

Following this logic, Indian critics of science, especially those led by the neo-Gandhians such as Ashis Nandy and Vandana Shiva, have argued for developing "local" sciences grounded in the civilizational ethos of India. Other well-known public intellectuals, including such stalwarts as Rajni Kothari, Veena Das, Claude Alvares, and Shiv Vishwanathan, have thrown their considerable weight behind this civilizational view of knowledge. This perspective also has numerous sympathizers among proponents of "patriotic science" and the environmentalist and feminist movements. A defense of local knowledges against rationalization and secularization also underlies the fashionable theories of postcolonialism and subaltern studies, which have found a worldwide following through the writings of Partha Chatterjee, Gayatri Spivak, Homi Bhabha, Dipesh Chakrabarty, and others.[7]

Social constructivist and postmodernist attacks on science have proven to be a blessing for *all* religious zealots, in all major faiths, as they no longer feel compelled to revise their metaphysics in the light of progress in our understanding of nature in relevant fields. But Hinduism displays a special resonance with the relativistic and holistic thought that finds favor among postmodernists. In the rest of this chapter, I examine the general overlap between Hindu apologetics on the right and the postmodernist view of hybridity and alternative sciences on the left.

The Scope of Vedic Sciences in India

In order to understand how postmodern critiques of science converge with Hindutva's celebration of Vedas-as-science, let us follow the logic behind VHP's *Guide for Teachers*. This guide claims that the ancient Hindu scriptures contain "many true scientific facts" and therefore "can be treated as scientific texts." Let us see what these "true scientific facts" are. The prime exhibit is the "scientific affirmation" of the theory of *guna* (Sanskrit for qualities or attributes). Following the essential Vedantic idea that matter and spirit are not separate and distinct entities, but rather a spiritual principle that constitutes the very fabric of the material world, the theory of *guna*s teaches that matter exhibits spiritual/moral qualities. There are three such qualities or *guna*s that are shared by all matter, living or nonliving: the quality or *guna* of purity and calmness seeking higher knowledge (*sattvic*), the quality or *guna* of impurity, darkness, ignorance, and inactivity (*tamsic*), and the quality or *guna* of activity, curiosity, worldly gain (*rajasic*). Modern atomic physics, the VHP's guide claims, has confirmed the presence of these qualities in nature. The evidence? Physics shows that there are three atomic particles bearing positive, negative, and neutral charges, which correspond to the three *guna*s! From this "scientific proof" of the existence of essentially spiritual/moral *guna*s in atoms, the guide goes on to triumphantly deduce the "scientific" confirmation of the truths of all those Vedic sciences that use the concept of *guna*s (e.g., Ayurveda, a popular school of traditional Indian therapies). Having "demonstrated" the scientific credentials of Hinduism, the guide boldly advises British schoolteachers to instruct their students that there is "no conflict" between the eternal laws of *dharma* and the laws discovered by modern science.

If Hindu propagandists can go this far in the United Kingdom, imagine their power in India, where until recently they controlled the central government and its agencies for media, education, and research. This obsession for finding all kinds of modern scientific claims embedded in all kinds of ancient and obscure Hindu doctrines has been dictating the official educational policy of the Bharatiya Janata Party (BJP) ever since it came to power nearly half a decade ago.

Indeed, the Hindu nationalists can teach a thing or two to the creation "scientists" in the United States. Creationists, old and new, are trying to smuggle Christian dogma into secular schools by redefining science in a way that allows God to be brought in as a cause of natural phenomena. This "theistic science" is meant to serve as the thin edge of the wedge that will pry open the secular establishment. Unlike the creationists, who have to contend with the courts and the legislatures in the United States, the Indian government and its agencies, including the courts themselves, wield the wedge of Vedic science intended to dismantle the (admittedly half-hearted) secularist education policies. By teaching Vedic Hinduism as "science," the Indian state and elites can portray India as "secular" and "modern," a model of sobriety and responsibility in contrast with those obscurantist Islamic fundamentalists across the border who insists on keeping science out of their *madrassas*. How useful is this appellation of "science," for it dresses up so much religious indoctrination as "secular education."

Under the kindly patronage of the state, Hindutva's wedge strategy has been a wild success. Vedic astrology is flourishing as an academic subject in public and private colleges and universities and is being put to use in predicting future earthquakes and other natural disasters. Such "sciences" as the *Vastu Shastra* approach to architecture and Vedic mathematics are attracting governmental grants for research and education. While the Ministry of Defense is sponsoring research and development of weapons and devices with magical powers mentioned in the ancient epics, the Health Ministry is investing in research in and development and sale of cow urine, sold as a cure for ailments ranging from acquired immune deficiency syndrome (AIDS) to tuberculosis. Faith healing and priestcraft are other "sciences" receiving public and private funding. In the rest of the culture, miracles and superstitions of all kinds have the blessings of influential public figures, including elected Members of Parliament.[8]

There are two kinds of claims that feed the notion that the traditional natural sciences found in the ancient Vedic texts meet standards of what we mean by science *today*. Both claims are made by the defenders of the Hindu orthodoxy in India.

The first kind declares the entire Vedic corpus as converging with modern science, while the second concentrates on defending such esoteric practices as astrology, *Vastu Shastra*, Ayurveda, and transcendental meditation (TM) as scientific within the Vedic paradigm. The first stream seeks to establish likeness or analogies between cosmologies that are in fact quite unrelated, if not radically opposed. This stream is exemplified by our VHP apologists who insist on finding equivalence between the *guna* theory and the behavior of atomic particles. Other examples include the many analogies and parallels between quantum physics and Vedanta, made famous by such eccentrics as Fritjof Capra and other quantum mystics. This stream does not relativize science: it simply grabs whatever theory of physics or biology may be popular with Western scientists at any given time and claims that Hindu ideas are "like that," or "mean the same," and "therefore" are perfectly modern and rational.

The second stream is far more radical, as it defends this "method" of drawing likenesses and correspondences between unlike entities as perfectly rational and "scientific" within the nondualistic Vedic worldview. The second stream, in other words, relativizes scientific method to dominant religious worldviews: it holds that the Hindu style of thinking using analogies and correspondences "directly revealed to the mind's eye" is as scientific (i.e., empirically testable and logically consistent) within the "holistic" worldview of Vedic Hinduism, as the analytical and experimental methodology of modern science is to the "reductionist" worldview of Semitic religions. The relativist defense of analogical thinking, based upon correspondences and resemblances as a legitimate scientific method not only provides a cover for the first stream, it also provides a generic defense of such emerging "alternative sciences" as "Vedic physics" and "Vedic creationism," as well as defending such pseudosciences as Vedic astrology, palmistry, TM, and New Age Ayurveda (Deepak Chopra style).

Postmodern "Hybridity" and Hindu Eclecticism

Contemporary Hindu propagandists are inheritors of the nineteenth-century neo-Hindu nationalists who started the tradition of dressing up the spirit-centered metaphysics of orthodox Hinduism in modern scientific clothes. The neo-Hindu intellectuals, in turn, were (consciously or unconsciously) displaying the well-known penchant of generations of Sanskrit pundits for drawing resemblances and correspondences between religious rituals, forces of nature, and human destiny. On this view, *any* idea—however new, foreign, and contradictory—can be considered Vedic and therefore Hindu, as long as some kind of resemblance can be found between it and the Vedic corpus. This is the traditional Hindu way of traditionalizing new ideas, denying contradictions, defusing challenges, and thereby perpetuating itself.[9]

Postmodernist theories of knowledge have rehabilitated this "method" of drawing equivalences between different and contradictory worldviews and allowing them to "hybridize" across traditions. The postmodernist consensus is that since truth about the real world-as-it-is cannot be known, all knowledge systems are equivalent to each other in being social constructions. Because they are all equally arbitrary, all expressing the dominant cultural values of their own respective societies, and none any more objective than other, they can be mixed and matched in order to serve the needs of human beings to live well in their own cultural universes. From the postmodern perspective, the VHP justification of the *guna* theory in terms of atomic physics is not anything to worry about—it is merely an example of "hybridity" between two different culturally constructed ways of seeing, a fusion between East and West, tradition and modernity. Indeed, by postmodernist standards, it is not this hybridity that we should worry about, but rather we should oppose the "positivist" and "modernist" hubris that demands that non-Western cultures should give up, or alter, elements of their inherited cosmologies in the light of the growth of knowledge in natural sciences. Let us see how this view of hybridity meshes in with the Hindutva construction of Vedic science.

It is a well-known fact that Hinduism uses its eclectic *mantra*—"Truth is one, the wise call it by different names"—as an instrument for self-aggrandizement. Abrahamic religions go about converting the alien Other through persuasion and through the use of force. Hinduism, in contrast, absorbs the Other by proclaiming its doctrines to be only "different names for the One Truth" contained in Hinduism's own perennial wisdom. The teachings of the outsider, the dissenter, or the innovator are simply declared to be merely nominally different, a minor and inferior variation of the Absolute and Universal Truth known to Vedic Hindus from time immemorial. Christianity and Islam acknowledge the radical otherness and difference of other faiths, even as they attempt to convert them, sometimes at the cost of great violence and mayhem. Hinduism refuses to grant other faiths their distinctiveness and difference, even as it proclaims its great "tolerance." I am not lauding the resort to violence sometimes practiced by Abrahamic religions. Rather, I simply want to point out how Hinduism's intellectual "tolerance" can be a mere disguise for its narcissistic obsession with its own greatness.

Whereas classical Hinduism limited this passive-aggressive form of conquest to matters of religious doctrine, neo-Hindu intellectuals have extended this mode of conquest to the secular knowledge provided by modern science as well. The tradition of claiming modern science to be "just another name" for the spiritual truths of the Vedas started with the Bengal Renaissance. The contemporary Hindutva follows in the footsteps of this tradition.

The Vedic science movement began in 1893 when Swami Vivekananda (1863–1902) addressed the World Parliament of Religions in Chicago. In that famous address, he sought to present Hinduism not just as a fulfillment of all other religions, but also as a fulfillment of all of science. Vivekananda claimed that only the spiritual monism taught by the Advaita Vedanta could fulfill the ultimate goal of natural science, which he saw as the search for the ultimate source of the energy that creates and sustains the world.

Vivekananda was followed by another Bengali nationalist-turned-spiritualist, Sri Aurobindo (1872–1950). Aurobindo proposed a divine theory of evolution that treats biological evolution as the adventures of the World-Spirit finding its own fulfillment through progressively higher levels of consciousness, from matter to man to the yet-to-come harmonious "super-mind" of a socialistic collective. Newer theories of Vedic creationism, which propose to replace Darwinian evolution with "devolution" from the original oneness with Brahman, are now being proposed with utmost seriousness by the Hare Krishnas who, for all their scandals and idiosyncrasies, remain faithful to the essential dogma of the Hindu cosmology that holds that all matter—living and nonliving—is an embodiment of consciousness that can exist apart from matter.[10]

Vivekananda and Aurobindo lit the spark that has continued to fire the nationalist imagination, right to the present time. The Neo-Hindu literature of the nineteenth and early twentieth centuries—especially the writings of Dayanand Saraswati, Servapalli Radhakrishnan (the first president of India after independence), and the many followers of Vivekananda—is replete with celebration of Hinduism as a "scientific" religion. Even secularists such as Jawaharlal Nehru remained captive of this idea that the original teachings of Vedic Hinduism were consonant with modern science, but only corrupted later by the gradual deposits of superstition. Countless gurus and swamis began to teach that the Vedas are simply "another name for science" and that all of science only affirms what the Vedas have taught. This scientistic version of Hinduism has found its way to the West through the numerous *ashram*s and yoga retreats set up, most prominently, by Maharishi Mahesh Yogi and his many clones.

These numerous celebrations of "Vedas as science" all follow a similar intellectual strategy of looking for analogies and equivalences. All invoke extremely speculative theories from modern cosmology, quantum mechanics, vitalistic theories of biology and parapsychology, and other fringe sciences. They then project these sciences back onto Sanskrit texts chosen at will, and their meaning decided by the whim of the interpreter, and claim that the entities and processes mentioned in Sanskrit texts are "like," "the same thing as," or "another word for" the ideas expressed in modern cosmology, quantum physics, or biology.

Thus, there is a bit of a Brahman here and a bit of quantum mechanics there, the two treated as interchangeable; there are references to "energy," a scientific term with a definite mathematical formulation in physics, which gets to mean "consciousness": references to Newton's laws of action and reaction are made to stand for the laws of *karma* and reincarnation; completely discredited "evidence" from parapsychology and the "secret life of plants" is upheld as proof of the presence of different degrees of soul in all matter; "evolution" is taught as the self-manifestation of Brahman, and so on. *The terms are scientific, but the content is religious.* There is no regard for consistency either of scientific concepts or of religious ideas. Both wholes are broken apart, random connections and correspondences are established, and with great smugness, the two modes of knowing are declared to be equivalent and even interchangeable. The driving force, the only idea that gives this whole mishmash any coherence, is the great anxiety to preserve and protect Hinduism from a rational critique and demystification. Vedic science is motivated by cultural chauvinism, pure and simple.

There is no denying that the neo-Hindu "discovery" of modern science in ancient teachings of Vedas and Upanishads did have a limited usefulness. Since they had convinced themselves that their religion was the mother of all sciences, conservative Hindus did not feel threatened by scientific education. As long as science could be treated as "just another name" for Vedic truths, they were even enthusiastic to learn it. The Brahminical traditions of learning and speculative thought served the upper castes well, as they took to modern English education, which included instruction in scientific subjects. Those who would explicitly use scientific learning to challenge the traditional outlook were either lower down on the caste hierarchy or "godless Communists" anyway, and could be safely ignored. The great neo-Hindu "renaissance" succeeded in turning empirical sciences into the handmaiden of the Vedic tradition—the role reason has performed throughout India's history. This is the tradition that the "family" of Hindu nationalist parties have succeeded in institutionalizing in Indian schools, universities, and the public sphere.

What does all this have to do with postmodernism, one may legitimately ask? Neo-Hinduism, after all, has a history dating back at least two centuries, and the analogical logic on which claims of Vedic science are based goes back to times immemorial.

Neo-Hinduism did not start with postmodernism, obviously. And neither does Hindutva share the postmodernist urgency to "overcome" and "go beyond" the modernist fascination with progress and development—far from it. Neo-Hinduism and Hindutva are *reactionary modernist* movements, intent on a mindless and even dangerous technological modernization superimposed on a traditionalist, deeply antisecular and illiberal social agenda. Nevertheless, they do share in a postmodernist approach to science that celebrates the kind of contradictory mish-mash of science, spirituality, mysticism, and pure superstition that that passes as "Vedic science."

Enamored as they are with alternative epistemologies, postmodern theorists favor cultivation of local knowledges. But what happens when traditional cultures *do* need to adopt at least some elements of modern sciences? In such cases, postmodernists recommend exactly the kind of "hybridity" as we have seen in the case of Vedic sciences in which, for example, subatomic particles are interpreted as referring to *gunas*, or where quantum energy is interpreted to be the "same as" *shakti*, the Sanskrit word meaning power, or where *karma* is interpreted to be a determinant of biology in a "similar manner" as the genetic code, and so on. On the postmodern account, there is nothing irrational or unscientific about this "method" of drawing equivalences and correspondences between entirely unlike entities and ideas, even when there may be serious contradictions between the two. On this account, *all* science is based upon metaphors and analogies that reinforce dominant cultures and social power, and all "facts" of nature are really interpretations of nature through the lens of dominant culture. It is perfectly rational, on this account, for Hindu nationalists to want to reinterpret the "facts" of modern science by drawing analogies with the dominant cultural models supplied by Hinduism. Because no system of knowledge can claim to know reality as it really is, because our best confirmed science is ultimately a cultural construct, all cultures are free to pick and choose and mix various "facts," as long as they do not disrupt their own time-honored worldviews.

This view that "Western" science can be reinterpreted to fit into the tradition-sanctioned, local knowledges of "the people" has been advocated by theories of "critical traditionalism" propounded by Ashis Nandy and Bhiku Parekh in India and by the numerous admirers of Homi Bhabha's obscure writings on "hybridity" abroad. In the West, this view has found great favor among feminists, notably Sandra Harding and Donna Haraway, and among anthropologists of science including Bruno Latour, David Hess, and their followers.

The extreme skepticism of postmodern intellectuals toward modern science has landed them in a position where they cannot, if they are to remain true to their beliefs, criticize Hindutva's eclectic takeover of modern science for the glory of the Vedic tradition.

When confronted with the reality of Vedic sciences, Indian critics of modernity, especially Ashis Nandy and his admirers, *have* criticized the right-wing propaganda regarding Vedic sciences, but for reasons that actually open the door to an even more radical defense of Vedic science![11] For these intellectuals, the cardinal sin of Hindu nationalists is not their defense of the high-Hindu tradition—a tradition that has for centuries contributed to the worst kind of ignorance and social inequality. Rather, their cardinal sin is their capitulation to modern scientific thought in the first place, which they have tried to equate with Vedic cosmology. *Authentic* Indian science, on this account, can only come with the rediscovery of India's unique gestalt, which, in the postcolonial narrative, lies in its holism, monism or nondualism, as compared to the tendency of the Western science toward separation of objects from their context. Indian thought is not to be seen either as a copy of modern science, or somehow lacking in empirical sciences, but as encoding a wholly different kind of science altogether, which is the duty of postsecular, postmodern intellectuals to discover and cultivate. Coming from the traditions of the Gandhian and populist left, the postmodernists tend to find these alternative traditions among the nonmodern habits of the heart of the humble, folk traditions of women, peasants, village folk, and assorted subaltern groups. Gandhi is the patron saint of this uniquely Indian, nonmodern way of life. "Real India" equals Gandhi equals "innocent traditions" of nonmodern "communities." Anyone challenging any of the factors in the equation was declared to have a "colonized mind."

I now examine in more detail three distinct arguments that have emerged in the Indian postmodernist literature that converge almost exactly with the Hindutva's defense of the superiority of Vedic sciences. Complete details, along with references to the literature cited here can be found in Nanda (2003).

The Decolonization of Science Argument

Hindutva ideologues see themselves as part and parcel of postcolonial studies. Decolonization of the Hindu mind, the Hindu Right claims, requires understanding science through Hindu categories. Echoing the postcolonial critiques of epistemic violence, Hindutva ideologues such as Murli Manohar Joshi, Konrad Elst, Girilal Jain, David Frawley, N. S. Rajaram, and others see any scientific assessment of the empirical claims made by the Vedic texts as a sign of mental colonialism and Western imperialism.

The Hindu Right combines this demand for authenticity with an essentialist understanding of culture borrowed straight from Oswald Spengler's *Decline of the West*, which holds that each culture has an innate nature, a temper, which must guide all its cultural products from mathematics and physics to painting and poetry. This view of the innate nature of nation—that a nation has a sort of telos (*svabhava* or *chitti*)—is propounded by Deen Dayal Upadhyaya's theory of "integral humanism," which constitutes the official philosophy of the BJP. In fact, it is part of the BJP's official manifesto that it will use India's innate Hinduness as a "touchstone" to decide what sciences will be promoted and how they will be taught. Using this touchstone of an innate, timeless Hindu *svabhava*, Hindutva literature still holds on to the defunct theories of vitalism as valid science. (Vitalism in biology holds that living beings require a special vital force, variously termed *prana* or *shakti* in the Indian literature, over and above "mere" atoms and molecules. In India, Jagdish Chandra Bose first claimed to find evidence of consciousness in plants. Bose's work was falsified and rejected by mainstream biology in his own lifetime but it is still touted as an Indian contribution to world science in Hindutva literature.) Again, it is against the touchstone of "eternal Vedic truths" that Hindu apologists feel justified in interpreting the paradoxes of quantum physics in a mystical manner. There are perfectly realistic interpretations of quantum mechanics, of course, but these are sidelined in Vedic science literature in order to claim that modern physics "proves" the presence of mind in nature, just as claimed by Vedanta.

Reductionist Science versus Holistic Science

The gist of this argument, as it appears in Hindu nationalist writings on Vedic science, is simple—all that is dangerous and false in modern science comes from the Semitic monotheistic habit of dualistic and "reductionist" thinking, which separates the object from the subject, nature from consciousness, the known from the knower. All that is truly universal and true in modern science comes from the Hindu habit of "holistic" thinking, which has always seen the objects in nature and the human subjects not as separate entities but as different manifestations of the same universal consciousness. For the nonlogocentric Hinduism, reality is not objective, but "omnijective," a co-construct of mind and matter together. While Western science treats nature as dead matter, Hindu sciences treat nature as a sacred abode of gods. Thus Hindutva scholars claim that traditions of yoga, TM, and Ayurveda are sciences of the future, for they bring matter in alignment with the "cosmic energy" that permeates all matter. Moreover, Hindu approaches to nature are seen as ecological by definition since they do not treat nature as mere matter to be exploited for private use.

This view of the superiority of Hinduism's "holism" rests upon the strange and totally mistaken assumption that Hindu chauvinists share with left-wing critics of science—that the fundamental methodology of modern science, what is called "reductionism," is not just mistaken but also politically oppressive. Reductionism in science simply means a bottom-up approach to understanding complex natural phenomena by isolating the lower level constituents and studying their interactions under controlled conditions. Reductionism seeks the explanation of the whole by eliminating the need for postulating any extra forces (e.g., consciousness or a vital spirit) over and above the relationships between the building blocks that can be experimentally tested. Far from being simple-minded or sinister, as critics assume, nearly every advance in understanding complex systems—from the replication of DNA at the cellular level to the interactions within ecological systems—owes its success to a reductionist approach to the fundamental building blocks of nature. Whereas its critics see a reductionist methodology as a destructive oversimplification of nature, in actuality the analysis of wholes into their interactive parts leads us to a greater understanding and appreciation of the workings of complex systems.

Owing to a fundamental misunderstanding of how science actually works, coupled with a great deal of cynicism, many left-wing critics among feminist, environmental, and anti-imperialist movements have developed a knee-jerk condemnation of reductionism. Reductionist science is considered bad science with politically oppressive implications. Feminists, including such world-renowned feminist icons as Carolyn Merchant, Sandra Harding, and Donna Haraway, see it as a masculine way of breaking the unity between the object and the subject. Environmentalists, including India's own Vandana Shiva and like-minded ecofeminists, see reductionism as opening the way to ruthless exploitation of nature by divesting it of all sacred meanings. Eco-romantics ignore all counterexamples where sacredness of nature serves as an ideology that serves to keep supposedly sacred groves of trees, rivers, and other natural resources under the control of temples and other powerful institutions. Postcolonial critics, in their turn, see reductionism as a result of Western and capitalist habit of thinking in terms of opposed classes of "us and them."

These kinds of ill-understood and politically motivated challenges to a fundamental methodological norm of modern science have prepared the ground for Hindutva's claims that Hinduism provides a more "holistic," more complete, more ecological and even more feminist way of relating with nature. Most of the claims of superiority of "holism" are unsubstantiated. On closer examination, they end up affirming pseudosciences involving disembodied spirit acting on matter through entirely unspecified mechanisms. Most of the claims of greater ecological and feminist sensitivity in the Hindu practice of treating all nature as a sacred and interconnected whole turn out to be empirically false. In fact, quite often the faith in the divine powers of some rivers and plants serves as an excuse *not* to care for them adequately, precisely because they are considered to share God's miraculous powers to recover and stay pure.[12] Despite all the falsehoods and obscurantisms, the claims of Hindu (or Eastern, more broadly) holism thrive in the academia because of the radical academics' own mistaken and overblown critique of the reductionist methodology of science.

The Symmetry Argument

The symmetry argument claims that all local sciences are equally "scientific" (i.e., rational, coherent, and able to explain observed phenomena) within their own cultural contexts. Modern science, the argument goes, ought to be treated "symmetrically" with all other ways of knowing. As I have shown, this is the crux of the social constructivist and postmodern attacks on modern science.

This argument lies at the heart of the theories of "Vedic physics" and "Vedic creationism." That the verses of the Rig Veda are actually coded formulas of advanced theories of physics has been recently claimed by Subhash Kak, an engineer working in the United States. And a Vedic alternative to Darwinian evolution by natural selection is being pushed by Michael Cremo and his fellow Hare Krishnas in the United States. These newer theories boldly defend Vedic mysticism as a legitimate scientific method and hold Vedic-Hindu metaphysical assumptions to be as rational and empirically adequate as the best of modern science, and as deserving of the status of universal objective knowledge as the conventionally accepted theories of matter and biological evolution.

In a barrage of books and essays, most recently summarized in the publication *In Search of the Cradle of Civilization* (Feuerstein, Kak, and Frawley 1995), Subhash Kak has claimed to find, in a coded form, advanced knowledge of astronomy and computing in the Rig Veda. According to Kak, the design of the fire altars prescribed in the Rig Veda—how many bricks to put where and surrounded by how many pebbles—actually code such findings of modern twentieth-century astronomy as the distance between the sun and the earth, the length of solar and lunar years, and the speed of light. All the Vedic values match exactly with the values we know through modern nineteenth- and twentieth-century physics. The number of bricks and pebbles, moreover, corresponds with the number of syllables in the Vedic verses. The conclusion: "the Vedas are books of physics."

Finding relatively advanced abstract physics in the Rig Veda, the earliest of the four Vedas, is of crucial importance to Hindutva. There is a concerted attempt to show that the Rig Veda was composed at least around three millennia B.C., and not around 1500 B.C. as previously thought. There is also a massive effort afoot in Hindutva circles to promote the idea that the Aryans who wrote the Rig Veda presumably in 3000 B.C. were indigenous to the landmass of India. Under these circumstances, finding advanced physics in Rig Veda will "prove" that India was truly the mother of all civilizations and produced all science known to the Greeks and other ancient cultures.

But anyone making such dramatic claims has to explain how the Vedic ancestors knew all this physics and what their method was.

Kak and colleagues (1995) answer, incredibly, that the Vedic scientists found the laws of physics through deep introspection. Yogic meditation allowed Vedic sages to see in their minds' eyes, the likenesses, homologies, and equivalences between the cosmic, the terrestrial, and the spiritual. This method of seeing analogies and equivalences may be considered magical in the West, they argue, but it is perfectly scientific within India's non-dualist, monist metaphysics that allows no distinctions between matter and spirit, between physical and the psychic, between animate and the inanimate—all are united by the same spiritual energy that is in all. Within these assumptions, yogic introspection is a method of science. Because all science is paradigm bound, Kak and colleagues (1995) insist, citing the authority of Thomas Kuhn and Paul Feyerabend, the much-misunderstood gurus of postmodernists, Vedic science is perfectly scientific within the paradigm of Vedic assumptions.

In fact, Kak and colleagues are not alone in defending the scientificity of yogic meditation as a valid scientific method. Maharishi Mahesh Yogi's "unified science" is based upon this logic. This kind of cultural defense is routinely invoked by those defending such esoteric pseudosciences as Vedic astrology and paranormal beliefs (past-birth memories, out-of-body experiences, and reincarnation).

A similar defense of the method of bhakti yoga as a legitimate source of holistic knowledge lies at the basis of the enormous mass of writings coming out of the Bhakti Vedanta Institute in the United States, the headquarters of the Hare Krishnas. Michael Cremo, a devout Hare Krishna, has boldly proposed a Vedic alternative to Darwinian evolution. Cremo (2003) claims that human beings have not evolved up from lower animals, but rather fallen, or devolved, from their original unity with the pure consciousness of *Brahman*. (He and his associates tried to prove that the fossil record actually supports the Vedic time scale of literally millions of years of life on the earth, including human life.) As evidence, Cremo (2003) cites every possible research into the paranormal ever conducted anywhere to "prove" the truth of holist Vedic cosmology which proposes the presence of a spiritual element in all matter (which takes different forms, thereby explaining the theory of "devolution").

This remarkable compendium of pseudoscience is premised upon the assumption that modern science is a prisoner of Western cultural and religious biases, and as a result, Western scientists have created a "knowledge filter" that keeps out the evidence that supports the Vedic cosmology. Their point is that once you remove the

Western assumptions, the method of yoga can be treated as a legitimate source of scientific hypotheses. These Vedic knowledge claims can be verified by the community of other yogic knowers who have "purified" their sense through meditation to such an extent that they can "directly realize" those signs from the spirit world that are looked down upon by Western-trained scientists as "paranormal."

Utterly incredible though they are, and utterly devoid of any empirical support, Vedic physics and Vedic creationism are being touted as serious scholarship based upon the assumption that different cultural assumptions sanction alternative methods as rational and scientific.

Conclusion

Postmodern intellectuals have transformed their disillusionment with the many shortcomings of the modern world into a radical denunciation of modern science itself. They have denounced the status of modern science as a source of universally valid and objective knowledge as a sign of Western imperialism, patriarchal biases, and Christian dualist thinking. Many prominent public intellectuals in India, sympathetic to populist, indigenist currents in left-inclined social movements, have embraced the postmodernist suspicion of science, and called for "alternative sciences" that reflect the cultural preferences of India's nonmodern masses.

The question before these defenders of "alternative sciences" is this: what do they have to say to the defenders of "Vedic sciences"? For example, what reasons can they give against the supposed scientificity of Vedic astrology? Can they hold on to their relativist view of all sciences as social constructs and yet challenge the scientization of the Vedas that is going on in the theories of Vedic physics or Vedic creationism?

False beliefs about nature have social consequences. It just won't work to say that different peoples have different sciences. Some "sciences" present objectively false ideas about nature, and some of them are deadly. Relativism may sound progressive and tolerant, but it is not harmless.

Any erosion of the dividing line between science and myth, between reasoned, evidence-based public knowledge and the spiritual knowledge accessible to yogic adepts, is bound to lead to a growth of obscurantism dressed up as science. It is time secular and self-proclaimed leftist intellectuals called off their romance with irrationalism and romanticism. It is time to draw clear boundaries between science and myth, and between the Left and the Right.

Notes

1. VHP was established in 1964 in order to "defend, protect and preserve" the Hindu society against the "alien ideologies" of Christianity, Islam, and Communism. VHP is one of the big three that make up the Hindu nationalist "family." The other two are RSS, or Rashtriya Sevak Sangh, which translates into National Volunteers Corp, and the BJP, or Bharatiya Janata Party, which translates into National People's Party. The big three are

supposed to take care of different aspects of Hindutva, or Hindu nationalism: VHP is the religious wing, RSS the cultural "parent" of all nationalists, and BJP the political arm. More information about VHP can be found at their website, www.vhp.org.

2. In the last five years or so, just as Hindu nationalists grew in power in India, many groups of émigré Hindus cropped up in the United States, Canada, and Great Britain that have started to police school textbooks and academic writings for what they see as anti-Hindu biases. They have launched defamation campaigns over the Internet, complete with threats of physical violence, against Western scholars of Hinduism who they see as disrespectful of the Hindu gods and Hindu traditions. Recently, this campaign of intimidation and harassment became the subject of a public debate, fueled by a front-page article in the *Washington Post* titled "Wrath over a Hindu God: U.S. Scholars' Writings Draw Threats from the Faithful" (written by Shnakar Vedantam, April 10, 2004). The writings of the "faithful" that led to this controversy and their responses to the *Washington Post* story can be found on two websites: http://infinityfoundation.com and http://sulekha.com.

3. I have characterized Hindutva as an example of "reactionary modernity" in Nanda (2003). I have borrowed the idea of reactionary modernity from Jeffrey Herf's (1984) well-known work on the Third Reich and the Nazi regime.

4. The Hindu nationalist-led government fell earlier this year. In the 2004 general elections that concluded in May, the BJP-led coalition government was rejected by the Indian voters who favored a left-wing coalition government led by Congress. Undoing the Hin-duization of textbooks and curricula at secondary and university level education is one of the most daunting tasks facing the new government. Irrational and entirely superstitious beliefs in such things as astrology, vitalism, and rebirth have a wide and deep support among the educated middle classes, including even the justices of the Supreme Court, which only recently declared astrology to be a fit subject of education in Indian universities (see "Astrology on a Pedestal," by R. Ramachandran, *Frontline*, June 5–18, 2004, available on www.flonnet.com.). See also my appeal to India's freethinkers to take on the job of de-Hinduization of education and culture by rallying behind "scientific temper" (the Indian term for critical thinking that respects empirical evidence and naturalistic metaphysics). "Calling India's Freethinkers," May 23, 2004, at the website of *The Hindu*, www.hindu.com.

5. Many good, comprehensive anthologies and introductions are available in this burgeoning (and now declining) area of study. For social constructivism, see Jasonoff et al. (1995) and Hess (1997). For a feminist critique of modern science, see Nelson and Nelson (1996) and Harding (1998). For a critical exposition of these theories, see Koertge (1998), Sokal and Bricmont (1998), Brown (2001), and Nola (2003). I offer a critique from a non-Western, secularist point of view (Nanda 2003).

6. See Nanda (2002) for a statement on the Indian Enlightenment.

7. Complete references to these scholars' works relevant to the issue of postcolonial sciences can be found in Nanda (2003). Many of the major postcolonial authors can be found in Chaturvedi (2000). See Young (2003) for an exposition.

8. See Nanda (2003) for complete references.

9. The classic analysis of resemblance as constituting the episteme of Vedic Hinduism is Brian Smith (1989) and, more recently, Axel Michaels (1998).

10. In his latest book, Michael Cremo (2003) has come up with a self-proclaimed "alternative to Darwin's theory."

11. See Nandy (2001).

12. See the work of Kelly Alley (1998) who shows that sacredness of the river Ganges is partly responsible for the lack of environmental action on the part of devout Hindus who believe the river to have the divine, extraordinary power of self-purification.

References

Alley, Kelly. 1998. Idioms of Degeneracy: Assessing Ganga's Purity and Pollution. In Lance Nelson (ed.), *Purifying the Earthly Body of God: Religion and Ecology in Hindu India.* Albany, NY: SUNY Press.

Brown, James R. 2001. *Who Rules in Science: An Opinionated Guide to Science Wars.* Cambridge, MA: Harvard University Press.

Chaturvedi, Vinayak (ed.). 2000. *Mapping Subaltern Studies and the Subaltern.* London: Verso.

Cremo, Michael. 2003. *Human Devolution: A Vedic Alternative to Darwin's Theory.* Badger, CA: Torchlight.

Feuerstein, Georg, Subhash Kak, and David Frawley. 1995. *In Search for the Cradle of Civilization.* Wheaton, IL: Quest Books.

Harding, Sandra. 1998. *Is Science Multicultural?* Bloomington: Indiana University Press.

Herf, Jeffrey. 1984. *Reactionary Modernism: Technology, Culture, and Politics in Weimar and the Third Reich.* Cambridge: Cambridge University Press.

Hess, David. 1997. *Science Studies: An Advanced Introduction.* New York: New York University Press.

Jasanoff, Sheila, Gerald E. Markle, James C. Petersen, and Trevor Pinch (eds.). 1995. *Handbook of Science and Technology Studies.* Thousand Oaks, CA: Sage.

Koertge, Noretta. 1998. Postmodernisms and the Problem of Scientific Literacy. In Noretta Koertge (ed.), *A House Built on Sand.* New York: Oxford University Press.

Michaels, Axel. 1998. *Hinduism: Past and Present.* Princeton, NJ: Princeton University Press.

Nanda, Meera. 2002. *Breaking the Spell of Dharma and Other Essays.* New Delhi: Three Essays Press.

———. 2003. *Prophets Facing Backward: Postmodern Critiques of Science and Hindu Nationalism in India.* New Brunswick, NJ: Rutgers University Press.

Nandy, Ashis. 2001. A Report on the Present State of Health of Gods and Goddesses in South Asia. *Postcolonial Studies* 4(2): 125–141.

Nelson, Lynn Hankinson, and Jack Nelson. 1996. *Feminism, Science and Philosophy of Science.* Dordrecht: Kluwer.

Nola, Robert. 2003. *Rescuing Reason: A Critique of Anti-rationalist Views of Science and Knowledge.* Dordrecht: Kluwer.

Prinja, Nawal K. (ed.). 1996. *Explaining Hindu Dharma: A Guide for Teachers.* Surrey, UK: Vishwa Hindu Parishad.

Smith, Brian, K. 1989. *Reflections on Resemblance, Ritual and Religion.* New York: Oxford University Press.

Sokal, Alan, and Jean Bricmont. 1998. *Fashionable Nonsense: Postmodern Intellectuals' Abuse of Science.* New York: Picador.

Young, Robert. 2003. *Postcolonialism: A Very Short Introduction.* Oxford: Oxford University Press.

Index